Books by Jon Winokur

The War Between the State

Northern
California

vs.

Southern
California

Compiled & Edited by

Jon Winokur

SASQUATCH BOOKS
SEATTLE

··

To Al Rasof

··

Printed in Canada
Published by Sasquatch Books
Distributed by Publishers Group West
10 09 08 07 06 05 04   6 5 4 3 2 1

Cover illustration: Robert Grossman
Book design: Kate Basart
Interior illustrations: Patrick Moriarity

Library of Congress Cataloging-in-Publication Data
Winokur, Jon.
The war between the state : Northern California vs. Southern California / Jon Winokur.
p. cm.
Includes index.
ISBN 1-57061-378-8
1. Los Angeles (Calif.)—Description and travel. 2. Los Angeles (Calif.)—Civilization. 3.
Regionalism—California. 4. San Francisco (Calif.)—Description and travel. 5. San Francisco
(Calif.)—Civilization. I. Title.

F869.L84W56 2004
917.94'940453—dc22
2003066795

Sasquatch Books

119 South Main Street, Suite 400 | Seattle, WA 98104 | 206 / 467-4300
www.sasquatchbooks.com | custserv@sasquatchbooks.com

Contents

Acknowledgments

I'm indebted to everyone who contributed quotations, without whose generosity this book would not exist. I'm also grateful to the U.S. Congress, without whose Fair Use Doctrine I'd be selling oranges on a freeway ramp.

Introduction

The San Andreas Fault extends seven hundred miles through California from northwest to southeast, cleaving the state into two great tectonic plates that move in opposite directions at the rate of an inch a year. California is split culturally as well as geologically: Just as the two plates grind against each other, so do the cultures of California's two great cities, Los Angeles and San Francisco.

What is the source of the rift? Does it lurk in the state's history, perhaps in lingering resentments from the Owens Valley "water wars"? Is it because San Francisco deems itself older and wiser than upstart Los Angeles? Does San Francisco feel inferior to New York and take it out on Los Angeles? Does Los Angeles fail to take San Francisco seriously, dismissing it as merely a nice place to spend a weekend? To quote an infamous Angeleno, "Why can't we all just get along?"

I don't know. We just can't.

California contributes fully 13 percent of America's Gross Domestic Product. If California were a sovereign nation, its economy would be the fifth largest in the world (having surpassed that of France). If California were a nation, Los Angeles and San Francisco would be city-states, like Athens and Sparta, or Rome and Florence, or—yes indeed—Sodom and Gomorrah. And if California were a nation, it would long ago have been torn apart by a bloody civil war.

As it is, of course, the war between Los Angeles and San Francisco is mostly of words. There's a definite failure to communicate here, a basic lack of understanding. It's as if the two regions are fighting each other's stereotypes. (There are also collateral skirmishes: Oakland versus San Francisco, Berkeley versus Hollywood, Los Angeles versus San Diego, the San Fernando Valley versus Civilization, and—California contra mundum—the Golden State versus everybody, especially New York.)

I first became aware of the schism in 1970, when I drove out to California from the East Coast. While filling up after crossing the Rockies, I fell into conversation with a young couple in a dark green Volvo (I swear) at the adjoining pump. They were headed in the opposite direction, to Boston for grad school after attending UC Berkeley. When I mentioned I was moving to California, they asked, in unison, "L.A. or San Francisco?"

"L.A.," I said.

"Too bad," they replied, again in unison, terminating the encounter.

San Franciscans, and Northern Californians in general, look down on Angelenos, and Southern Californians in general ("Northern Californians are to Southern Californians what German Jews are to Russian Jews," according to L.A. resident Howard Ogden). They seem to have a superiority complex, which may be partly justified by their jewel-of-a-city's many delights. But they tend toward condescension, if not outright disdain (Herb Caen: "Isn't it nice that the people who prefer Los Angeles to San Francisco live there?"). San Franciscans may be just a tad smug. But then maybe all northerners, for whatever geographical or sociological or astrological reason, look down on all southerners (Milan/Naples, Dallas/Houston, Gomorrah/Sodom).

Then there are the familiar San Francisco stereotypes: It's a precious, insular little town populated by goofy New Agers and thin-skinned chauvinists—provincial, narcissistic, self-congratulatory. And the whole "Frisco" thing: Oooh, I thought I heard somebody say "Frisco"—let's kill them! On his first visit to San Francisco, Ogden Nash was asked for a rhyme about the city, and he obliged with the couplet:

May I be boiled in oil and fried in Crisco
If I ever call San Francisco Frisco.

Conversely, you never hear anyone from Los Angeles complain about the use of "Ellay." I think it's because there's a certain detachment here. For instance, I've always marveled at the docility of Los Angeles natives in the face of wave upon wave of immigrants (domestic, foreign, and interplanetary). Maybe we southerners, like our insouciant Neapolitan counterparts, simply do not care. Maybe we're too oblivious to know we're being insulted. Or just magnanimous. Or maybe smog makes you apathetic. Whatever, but I think the literary critic David Kipen is right in describing San Francisco's one-way hostility toward Los Angeles as "unrequited hate."

Of course, "Ellay" has much to answer for: We're the Sigalert, armed-response, mansionized, made-for-TV, breast-augmented, audibly tan capital of the universe, and the headquarters of American entertainment imperialism. Southern California is where the pop-culture stone hits the demographic pond, the center of the vaunted ripple effect; irrepressible American fads start here and work their way around the world. "[Southern] Californians invented the concept of life-style. This alone warrants their doom," wrote Don DeLillo, circa 1982. If that was true a quarter century ago, what divine retribution is in store for the land of the drive-in cathedral and the drive-by shooting, the spec screenplay and the personal trainer, the water-bottle holster and the Porsche Bra? What cosmic comeuppance awaits the folks who brought you Vin Diesel?

This brief compilation does not attempt to explain the war between the state, but merely celebrates it. Celebrates, because over the years the feud has produced an abundance of pithy put-downs, sarcastic remarks, and miscellaneous screeds and diatribes. I've tried to assemble the best of them here. I've also mined the wits of my faithful correspondents on both sides of the divide for fresh veins of vitriol. If the result generates more heat than light, well, so be it.

Moving together at an annual rate of one inch, Los Angeles will be a suburb of San Francisco, or vice versa, in about twelve million years. Maybe then we'll make peace. But in the meantime . . .

—*JW, Pacific Palisades*

California

All California is only a sort of theater, where everything goes ahead on the high pressure principle. You can't stand still if you would, and the consequence is that you are whirled around and about, until you are apt to get dizzy.

Joseph B. Crockett (1854)

California is not so much a state of the Union as it is an imagination that seceded from our reality a long time ago. In leading the world in the transition from industrial to post-industrial society, California's culture becomes the first to shift from coal to oil, from steel to plastic, from hardware to software, from materialism to mysticism, from reality to fantasy. California became the first to discover that it was fantasy that led reality, not the other way around.

William Irwin Thompson

People brought up to believe that the phrase "terra firma" has real meaning often find it hard to understand the apparent equanimity with which earthquakes are accommodated in California, and tend to write it off as regional spaciness. It is in fact less equanimity than protective detachment, the useful adjustment commonly made in circumstances so unthinkable that psychic survival precludes preparation.

Joan Didion

There's a theory that almost anything that's fun is going to be ruined sooner or later by people from California. They tend to bring seriousness to subjects that don't deserve it, and they tend to get very good at things that weren't very important in the first place. The example I use is coming across somebody on Venice Beach who had perfected bubble-blowing—knew everything about it, produced these huge bubbles, and spoke at length at the tiniest opportunity about what went into a bubble.

Calvin Trillin

Whatever starts in California unfortunately has a tendency to spread.

Jimmy Carter

California can and does furnish the best bad things that are obtainable in America.

Hinton R. Helper

We can see California coming and we're scared.

James Brady

All good teenagers go to California when they die.

Brian Wilson

Mike Royko's modest proposal for California: Fence in the entire state to protect the rest of the nation.

I've never been out of this country but I've been to California. Does that count?

Bob Bergland

California is like summer or the Christmas holidays. The unhappy children think that they are supposed to be having a good time, and they imagine that everybody else is having a better time. Thus the pervasive mood of envy and the feeling, common especially among celebrities, that somehow they have been excluded from something, that their names have been left off the guest list.

Lewis H. Lapham

Mud slides, brush fires, mass killings, et cetera. We can relax and enjoy these disasters because in our hearts we feel that California deserves whatever it gets.

Don DeLillo

Invited on a lecture tour of California in 1861, the humorist Artemus Ward was asked, "What will you take for 40 nights in California?" "Brandy and water," he replied.

In San Francisco and Los Angeles I encountered a number of sun-baked zealots who insisted upon the ingestion of tasteless grains, gloomy greens and an astonishing variety of obscure vegetables. All of the above were viable only if diligently nurtured in excrement-flavored soil.

Jean-Michel Chapereau

California is a place in which a boom mentality and a sense of Chekhovian loss meet in uneasy suspension.

Joan Didion

Loneliness beside the swimming pool.

Liv Ullman

A semiotic placeholder for a vast and complex network of contemporary phenomena.

Laurence A. Rickels

I wouldn't live in California. All that sun makes you sterile.

Alan Alda

California audiences applaud whenever a musician hesitates long enough to turn a page.

Leonard Michaels

Most people in California come from somewhere else. They moved to California so they could name their kids Rainbow or Mailbox, and purchase tubular Swedish furniture without getting laughed at. It's a tenet also in California that the fiber of your clothing is equivalent to your moral fiber. Your "lifestyle" (as they say) is your ethic. This means that in California you don't really have to do anything, except look healthy, think good thoughts and pat yourself on the back about what a good person you are. And waiters in California want to be called by their first name. I don't know why.

Ian Shoales

California reminds me of the popular American Protestant concept of Heaven: There is always a reasonable flow of new arrivals; one meets many—not all—of one's friends; people spend a good deal of their time congratulating one another about the fact that they are there; discontent would be unthinkable; and the newcomer is slightly disconcerted to realize that now, the devil having been banished and virtue being triumphant, nothing terribly interesting can ever happen again.

George F. Kennan

Eastern snobs who airily condescended to the [California recall] spectacle as merely another example of left-coast madness just didn't get it. As goes California, so goes the nation. It's Disneyland, not Colonial Williamsburg, that prefigures our future, and the action-packed recall ride was nothing if not the apotheosis of the Magic Kingdom. It was fun, it was instructive, it was expensive, it was hawked relentlessly on television, it starred an Audio-Animatronic action figure. And it will set off a chain of unanticipated consequences whose full meaning will become apparent only with time.

Frank Rich

California is to America what America is to the rest of the world.

Howard Ogden

Los Angeles

Los Angeles is, like some incurable disease, a balefully organic phenomenon. Its streets are forever nibbling and probing further into its perimeter hills, twisting like rising water ever higher, ever deeper into their canyons, and sometimes bursting through to the deserts beyond. If the city could be pried out of its setting, one feels, it would be like a dried mat of some bacterial mold, every bump, every corner exactly shaped to its landscape.

Jan Morris

Los Angelization: 1) The process in which rapid population growth, uncontrolled development, increasing congestion, rampant crime and environmental damage combine to make other cities in the Western U.S. resemble Los Angeles. 2) A descent into urban hell.

Jordan Bonfante

How very correct, after all, that here at continent's end we should find only a dumping ground for all that is most exploitedly American: oil pumps pounding like the heartbeat of demons, avenues of used-car lots, supermarkets, motels, the gee dad I never knew a Chevrolet gee dad gee mom gee whiz wham of publicity, the biggest, broadest, best, sprawled and helplessly etherized by immaculate sunshine and sound of sea and unearthly sweetness of flowers blooming in December.

Truman Capote

Essentially, Los Angeles is an extrapolated Indianapolis, with palm trees.

Norman Corwin

This Tahiti in metropolitan form [with its] cheap prettiness [that] depraves everything.

Bertolt Brecht

A large citylike area surrounding the Beverly Hills Hotel.

Fran Lebowitz

One must never overlook the fact that Los Angeles is an entirely manufactured city assembled piece by piece beginning in the 1910s and 1920s—the Henry Ford boom years. Los Angeles without sci-fi caliber infrastructure is not only unimaginable but impossible. Located nowhere, and lacking any inherent sense of "thereness," L.A. is like Xerox paper—it becomes whatever is copied on it.

Douglas Coupland

Community in Los Angeles means homogeneity of race, class and, especially, home values. Community designations—i.e., the street signs across the city identifying areas as "Canoga Park," "Holmby Hills," "Silverlake" and so on—have no legal status. In the last analysis they are merely favors granted by City Council members to well-organized neighborhoods or businessmen's groups seeking to have their areas identified.

Mike Davis

Los Angeles being so big, it should be easy to get a grasp of the city, but it's not. Nobody's ever explained why, with all those people, there's no sense of a city, no feeling for a shared geographic experience.

One answer might be that the people in Los Angeles can't see each other.

This is not a frivolous statement.

The smog divides the city into three-mile chunks—on bad days, people can only see things under three miles away. Perhaps the mind, taught by the eye, gets the idea that all that exists is what it can see. Like the medieval peasant looking up at the mountains surrounding his valley and having only a dim interest in what goes on on the other side, perhaps the mind decides that its three-mile chunk is really the only one that counts, and all those other chunks off in the smog aren't worth worrying about.

This proposition could also explain the success of shopping centers. At the shopping center, they speak the chunk's language.

So does the smog hurt most of the people who live in Los Angeles?

No, but it affects their opinion of Los Angeles.

Marc Norman

A metropolis that exists in a semidesert, imports water three hundred miles, has inveterate flash floods, is at the grinding edges of two tectonic plates, and has a microclimate tenacious of noxious oxides.

John McPhee

I met a woman [in Los Angeles] who subscribes to a longevity cult. She thinks she can live to be 150, at least. That's the trick, in fact, thinking. If she thinks she can, she will. Negative thoughts, she explained, are her main enemy. She's made a few lifestyle changes, too, like living mostly on seeds, for instance. But positive thinking, she said, is the key.

Diane White

In Los Angeles, youth is wasted on the middle-aged.

Berton Averre

Physique, in this bronzed paradise, has taken over from character as the source of identity.

Peter Conrad

[In Los Angeles] the car is the extension of the self and the self is measured by abdominal tautness.

David J. Jefferson

I think there is a lot more plastic surgery in Los Angeles than anywhere else. It's not even a big deal. Most families in Calabasas can afford for their children to have plastic surgery. I mean, they can afford to get them their BMWs and their utility vehicles, so I think they can afford to get their plastic surgery done, too.

I have no idea what costs are for plastic surgery. All I know was that my friend's breast enlargement was less than my nose. My nose was an insane amount of money. I was shocked. I thought that nose jobs were just like a few grand, like $2,000 to $3,000, but I was wrong. Mine was about three times that amount. I think her breast enlargement was like four or five. So my nose was a good $3,000 more than her breasts.

It was definitely worth getting done. It changed the way I feel about myself. It definitely changed my life.

"Lindsey" (AGE 18, QUOTED IN Fast Forward: Growing Up in the Shadow of Hollywood BY LAUREN GREENFIELD)

I don't really trust people who live where there isn't snow, but Los Angeles is good for the spirit. To see people play volleyball on the beach with no net or out-of-bounds—volleyball as pure experience, exploring person-and-ball relationships.

Garrison Keillor

He drove through Glendale to Pasadena, up the hill that led to the San Gabriel Mountains. The air was ugly, and the sunlight was fluorescent, and it made him wonder why anyone would live in this part of the world if they didn't work in the movies. If he didn't work in the movies, he would live in Seattle or San Francisco, or even northern San Diego County, where the ocean was clean and there didn't seem to be a lot of pressure to be famous.

Michael Tolkin

Ancient Alexandria (the city in history Los Angeles most resembles) was obsessed—like Byzantium—with the mystery of Christ's real nature. Was His substance partly human? Wholly divine? The mystery that typically consumes Southern Californians is personal transformation, and what "technologies of the self" should be used to achieve it. As a vale of soul-making, Los Angeles represents a heightened, intensified version of the national cult, for it is a Pelagian city, "Pelagianism" being that most dangerous and seductive doctrine, anathematized by Saint Augustine, that says a man can save his soul by his own exertions. Los Angeles is the voice of Rilke's "Archaic Torso of Apollo" saying, "You must change your life."

David Reid

Cairo by the Mojave

America is exactly like ancient Egypt. In ancient Egypt, individual empowerment was derived through worship of dead Pharaohs. These god-kings lived forever in the afterlife. And for their followers, there was immortality by association. To be buried near a Pharaoh, to work for someone who would be buried near a Pharaoh, to work for someone who worked for someone who would be buried near a Pharaoh—all of these social rankings conferred status in the beyond.

In modern America, a land based on the separation of church and state, a land that promises immortality only if you are famous, the famous are worshiped because they live forever in the media netherworld of the here and now. To work for some-one famous, to work for someone who works for someone famous, to work for someone who works for someone who works for someone famous—there are so many variations on this theme that even the immigrant with the gold tooth who parks his wrecked Datsun near the gates of Bel-Air and peddles "star maps" can earn a few dollars in America's temple. The flip side of this is stalking someone famous, last refuge of the identity-free (read: "hard-core") unemployed. All of which proves that Ronald Reagan was onto something with the trickle-down the-ory; his mistake was applying it to economics, not religion.

It is no accident that Hollywood, mirage-maker to the world and home of the national religion, is in the desert. Just as embalmed kings and queens dwell inside the pyramids of Cairo, so too do the most revered inhabitants of America dwell in the desert civilization of Los Angeles.

Deanne Stillman

When the Ayatollah Khomeini of Iran railed against "The Great Satan," he was not talking solely about the U.S. Department of State or about American science. What really infuriated him was American culture, a vision so powerful it competed with an entire theology—a vision with its spiritual center right here, in Los Angeles.

Ben Stein

This city webbed with boulevards bearing the names of Spanish psychotics and saints. This incomplete city which seems to have no recognizable past, no ground that could be called unassailably sacred. This incomplete city that speaks of an impending terror.

Kate Braverman

It is though God had taken hold of the United States, at the tip of Maine, just as a person might take hold of a handkerchief. He lifted that one corner and began shaking it, and all the unstable elements in the country were shaken loose and deposited in the opposite corner. That is Southern California.

Frank Lloyd Wright (QUOTED BY JACK SMITH)

But not even the soft wash of dusk could help the houses. Only dynamite would be of any use against the Mexican ranch houses, Samoan huts, Mediterranean villas, Egyptian and Japanese temples, Swiss chalets, Tudor cottages, and every possible combination of these styles that lined the slopes of the canyon.

Nathanael West

How can a city go on growing out and out without ever growing up?

Herb Caen

A sad flower in the sand.

John Fante

The terrible thing about L.A. is that you sit down, you're twenty-five, and when you get up you're sixty-two.

Orson Welles (QUOTED BY PETER BOGDANOVICH)

You come out of the hotel, the Vraimont. Over boiling Watts the downtown skyline carries a smear of God's green snot. You walk left, you walk right, you are a bank rat on a busy river. This restaurant serves no drink, this one serves no meat, this one serves no heterosexuals. You can have your chimp shampooed, you can get your dick tattooed, twenty-four hours, but can you get lunch? And should you see a sign on the far side of the street flashing BEEF-BOOZE—NO STRINGS, then you can forget it. The only way to get across the road is to be born there. All the ped-xing signs say DON'T WALK, all of them, all the time. That is the message, the content of Los Angeles: don't walk. Stay inside. Don't walk. Drive. Don't walk. Run!

Martin Amis

Fortunes were made overnight, and along with the speculators, the oil men and the real estate promoters, another group came to the promised land—the old, the sick and the middle-aged, who came not to woo Mammon but to sit out their savings in the sun and die in the shadow of an annuity and an orange tree.

Leo Rosten

Refugees

My father's mentor was Igor Stravinsky. . . . Stravinsky was smart, civilized, educated, worldly—a man who realized that if you were going to be anywhere, it might as well be someplace with no war, no snow, and lots of pretty scenery. He moved to Los Angeles for these reasons, plus there were so many adept musicians—studio musicians able to sight-read practically anything, even him. He loved Los Angeles, loved going to Central Avenue where all the jazz musicians played, loved meeting Jelly Roll Morton, loved the mariachi bands, and loved coming to our house on his birthday, when my mother would make him his favorite dish—enchiladas—and Italian rum cake frosted with toasted almonds for dessert.

Whenever I was at the Stravinskys' home when I was growing up, there were always these wonderful Europeans thrilled to be [in] a place with no war, and flowers, silken nights filled with night-blooming jasmine. If they thought the place was no good they never complained in print. I got the impression that where they came from must be truly sad, but then, these were the kind of people who knew enough to come in out of the cold and be grateful. Not people like Nathanael West who thought nights weren't everything, who took one look at L.A. and decided that the city was a metaphor for apocalyptic chaos. People who had *really* been in apocalyptic chaos took one look at L.A. and decided that they wanted to go on a picnic.

Eve Babitz

Upon arrival to the shores of Los Angeles, asylum seekers, "illegal" recruits, determined actors, fluid nomads, promising directors, and hopeful immigrants find themselves mesmerized by the city's seemingly infinite economic and geographical vastness, the year-round sunshine, the ostentatious wealth seeping out of gated communities, and the sheer possibility that anything can happen. They are simultaneously appalled by the superficiality of the city, the plasticity of the residents, the sprawling mess of traffic jams, and the polluted atmosphere of el pueblo bent on suffocating itself to annihilation.

Deepak Narang Sawhney

A teacher here recently gave a vocabulary test in which she asked her students to provide the antonym of youth. Over half the class answered death.

Truman Capote

In 1993, the cash-strapped Los Angeles Coroner's Office began selling merchandise from a second-floor cupboard. The makeshift store, dubbed "Skeletons in the Closet," has since become a significant revenue source for the underfunded agency, despite objections from a county supervisor who complained that the merchandise reinforces the image of Los Angeles as a dangerous place. Popular items include coroner T-shirts, baseball caps, Post-it pads, and beach towels decorated with a crime-scene body outline. A similar merchandising program was briefly considered by the Houston Coroner, but was rejected as being in bad taste.

When I graduated from college my dad wanted to buy me a new car, knowing that he was never going to get me another car again. Because he has two Mercedes, he has a very good relationship with the Mercedes people. I had wanted a BMW really badly, and I was really uncomfortable about getting a Mercedes, but I didn't have a choice. And if that was going to be my last car, I obviously was going to accept it. I just didn't think it was appropriate for a 21-year-old. It's the stigma attached to a Mercedes.

> *"Wendy"* (AGE 23, QUOTED IN Fast Forward: Growing Up in the Shadow of Hollywood BY LAUREN GREENFIELD)

A good part of any day in Los Angeles is spent driving, alone, through streets devoid of meaning to the driver, which is one reason the place exhilarates some people, and floods others with amorphous unease.

> *Joan Didion*

Before the Santa Monica Freeway was built, you had to drive down Pico, or, more likely, Olympic from the beach to the east. When the freeway opened . . . it was like a miracle. Suddenly the entire town was only 20 minutes from wherever you were. Today, 8.7 million people and numerous squashed rapid-transit bonds later, we're back to taking Olympic or Pico to avoid the 18-hour parking lot that the freeway has become.

> *Rubin Carson*

Quadrangular, reticulated cities (Los Angeles, for instance) are said to produce a profound uneasiness: they offend our synesthetic sentiment of the City, which requires that any urban space have a center to go to, to return from, a complete site to dream of and in relation to which to advance or retreat; in a word, to invent oneself.

Roland Barthes

I was interviewing a woman who had just moved to L.A. from Chicago and was opening a dating service in a downtown office building. As we talked, the subject of her own marital status came up and she told me this story.

She had begun the trip west with her husband. He was dozing in the front passenger seat of the car one night when they ran into a fierce rainstorm just outside of Clinton, Oklahoma. The highway iced over when the rain turned to sleet. Their car skidded on an overpass, went out of control, and slid over an embankment.

The woman, who was driving, was miraculously unhurt, but her husband, horribly injured in the crash, died en route to the hospital.

"That's awful," I said. "What a terrible way to start a new life. Please accept my sincere sympathy."

The woman sighed. "It was just as well," she said, wiping a tear from her eye. "He'd have hated L.A."

Al Martinez

I learned to drive in Illinois. Imagine my surprise when I discovered a stop sign in L.A. is only a suggestion. Once, when I was sitting at one of those stop signs, a panhandler approached and asked if I had any "spare cellphone minutes."

Dick Helton

L.A. Story: One morning a Los Angeles man is watching a live police chase on television but realizes he's late for work, so he slips a blank tape into the VCR to record it. While stopped at a traffic light on the way to his job, the chase catches up with him: The fleeing felon, stuck at the same light, abandons his vehicle, pushes the man out of his car and drives away in it. After being treated for minor injuries, the man is driven home by police, where he sits back, sips a beverage, and watches the video of his own carjacking.

In Southern California the vegetables have no flavor and the flowers have no smell.

H. L. Mencken

[Los Angeles] smells like an overripe cantaloupe.

Neil Simon

L.A. isn't just a city, it's an acts-of-God theme park.

Fritz Coleman

L.A. is like a big cancer cell. You get on the plane and you go away for two weeks and when you come back, another globule of something has been added. It just pops up, and you know it's not going to last more than 20 years, because it's made out of twigs and stucco. Every time I have to leave the house and drive down into Hollywood, which is maybe every two or three weeks, there's incremental growth of ugliness upon ugliness. It never ends.

I used to be the major booster of Southern California, at a time when the world thought San Francisco was the aesthetic center of the universe. I always took great umbrage at that because I thought the whole scene up there was a figment of *Rolling Stone*'s imagination. I used to stick up for L.A., but I don't anymore because there's no longer anything going on here aesthetically that's worth defending.

Frank Zappa

We have two kinds of air [in Los Angeles]: regular and chunky style.

Johnny Carson

There is always something so delightfully real about what is phony here. And something so phony about what is real. A sort of disreputable senility.

Noel Coward

Everything in Los Angeles is too large, too loud and usually banal in concept . . . the plastic asshole of the world.

William Faulkner

The city [from the air] seems dead as putrefying squid with plastic varicose veins stapled into a plastic belly.

Harrison Salisbury

No man could find a better spot on earth, if only he had some intelligent person to talk to. . . . Los Angeles is a waxworks museum. Everything looks real, then you notice it's a fairly good replica which, however, never fools you.

Aldous Huxley

A kind of post-urban process rather than a city.

Herbert Gold

In a thousand years or so, when the first archaeologists from beyond the date-line unload their boat on the sands of Southern California, they will find much the same scene as confronted the Franciscan Missionaries. A dry landscape will extend from the ocean to the mountains. Bel Air and Beverly Hills will lie naked save for scrub and cactus, all their flimsy multitude of architectural styles turned long ago to dust, while the horned toad and the turkey buzzard leave their faint imprint on the dunes that will drift on Sunset Boulevard.

Evelyn Waugh

I wonder what would happen if the Los seceded from the Angeles in Los Angeles?

Kevin Nealon

L.A. is like Vegas—but the losers stay in town.

Jerry Seinfeld

Los Angeles makes the rest of California seem authentic.

Jonathan Culler

Where people carry radios to ball games so they can be told what's happening before their eyes.

Joel Oppenheimer

Take an opium eater's dream to Los Angeles, and they will realize it for you; the more it costs, the more they will believe in it.

George Bernard Shaw

Too many freeways, too much sun, too much abnormality taken normally, too many pink stucco houses and pink stucco consciences.

Clancy Sigal

It's a great place to live, but I wouldn't want to visit there.

Mark Twain

Soon Los Angeles will be in San Diego, swallow San Francisco and pave every acre of earth up to the Gold River. The only historic monuments spared will be the rest rooms in the gasoline stations.

Frank Lloyd Wright

When people in San Diego conjure up a Boschian vision of a solid urban corridor stretching 130 miles from Los Angeles south to the Mexican border, they call their nightmare "Los Diego."

Jordan Bonfante

San Diego has never been sure of what it wanted to be when it grew up. What it did know was that it did not want to become L.A.

Neil Morgan

There are only two modes of transport in Los Angeles: car and ambulance.

Fran Lebowitz

I only go to Los Angeles when I am paid for it.

Robert De Niro

The mighty citadel which had given the world the double feature, the duplex-burger, the motel, the hamfurter, and the shirt worn outside the pants.

S. J. Perelman

L.A.: where there's never weather, and walking is a crime. L.A.: where the streetlights and palm trees go on forever, where darkness never comes, like a deal that never goes down, a meeting that's never taken. The city of angels: where every cockroach has a screenplay and even the winos wear roller skates. It's that kind of town. Creative.

Ian Shoales

There's nothing wrong with Southern California that a rise in the ocean level wouldn't cure.

Ross Macdonald

Southern California, where the American Dream came too true.

Lawrence Ferlinghetti

The San Fernando Valley

One gets the impression that people come to Los Angeles in order to divorce themselves from the past, here to live, or try to live in the rootless pleasure world of an adult child. One knows that if the cities of the world were destroyed by a new war, the architecture of the rebuilding would create a landscape which looked, subject to specification of climate, exactly and entirely like the San Fernando Valley.

Norman Mailer

The San Fernando Valley serves . . . as the nation's favorite symbol of suburbia run rampant. It is the butt of jokes for its profligate sprawl, kooky architecture, unhip telephone area code and homegrown porno industry, as well as for a mythical tribe of nasal-toned, IQ-challenged teenage girls who like to shop. And yet the Valley only became a suburb fairly late in its history, and whether it qualifies for the label anymore is arguable. Its formal identity is as an oversized appendage of the city of Los Angeles.

Kevin Roderick

The Valley consists mostly of unappealing stucco and wood frame homes, mini-malls, car washes, bank buildings, motels that rent their rooms by the hour, taco stands, hair salons, security villages, and drab yellowish apartment buildings occupied by people who speak Spanish and Arabic. With a population of about 1.3 million, it would be the sixth-largest city in the United States if it was one city, but it isn't. Instead it's an unseemly mix of rich and poor crammed together in three hundred square miles of neo-drab. Picture Wilkes-Barre, Pennsylvania, overlayed on Wichita, Kansas, and you've got the Valley.

Al Martinez

The Valley is the New Jersey of Southern California.

Jonathan Roberts

. . . .

In 1959, at the height of the Cold War, Soviet premier Nikita Khrushchev visited Los Angeles. After a luncheon at 20th Century-Fox where he observed filming of Can-Can and pronounced it "decadent," Khrushchev was eager to see Disneyland, but police declared the visit a security risk and, over Khrushchev's objections, took him instead to the San Fernando Valley to inspect a new housing project. Refusing to leave his limousine, the Soviet leader complained, "Putting me in a closed car and stewing me in the sun is not the right way to guarantee my safety. This development causes me bitter regret. I thought I could come here as a free man."

. . . .

The grid of the sweltering Valley, home of a hundred King Bear Auto Centers, a thousand Yoshinoya Beef Bowls, and ten thousand yard sales, some consisting of no more than a couple of "Disco Lady" T-shirts flung out on a scabrous lawn like some kind of SOS.

Sandra Tsing Loh

Detached from Los Angeles, the San Fernando Valley would not become a great city, but a dormitory suburb pretending to have achieved urban status: a community whose signature cultural contribution, at least in terms of gross revenues, would be pornography.

Kevin Starr

Cleveland with palm trees.

Bob Hope

The same people who'll drive from Santa Monica to Pasadena (twenty-five miles) without blinking find lunch in Reseda (sixteen miles) much too far.

Sandra Tsing Loh

Encino: The non-smoking section of the Valley.

Hal Kanter

When we moved to the Valley, I felt like I was being tossed into quicksand.

Robert Redford

It's hot, it's barren, it's vacuous. That may seem a little harsh, but ample parking is about all this vast suburban wasteland has to offer in the way of cultural enlightenment. The Valley's threatened secession from L.A. would be a fiscal drain, but a net gain in other departments.

Danny Feingold

You'll like the Valley. It's cheaper.

Danny Thomas

Hollywood

You can take all the sincerity in Hollywood, place it in the navel of a fruit fly and still have room enough for three caraway seeds and a producer's heart.

Fred Allen

Do you realize that in one session at the Polo Lounge, you change your wife or husband, your job, sell your house and buy a new one, all right there, just moving around from table to table? Unbelievable.

Cleveland Amory

In Hollywood, nothing is black or white. Everything is covered with a layer of gray gauze.

Peter Bart

Hollywood is the kind of town where they stick a knife in your back and then arrest you for carrying a concealed weapon.

Raymond Chandler

Strip away the phony tinsel of Hollywood and you find the real tinsel underneath.

Oscar Levant

["Tinseltown" is derived from] the German verb *tinzelle*—literally, "to book a turkey into 1,200 theaters and make one's money before word of mouth hits."

Charlie Haas

A dreary industrial town controlled by hoodlums of enormous wealth.

S. J. Perelman

People wear resort clothes, but actually Hollywood is an enormous factory.

Marie-France Pisier

Daft but not boring.

J. B. Priestley

Hollywood is a golden suburb for golf addicts, gardeners, men of mediocrity and satisfied stars. I belong to none of those categories.

Orson Welles

All Hollywood corrupts, and absolute Hollywood corrupts absolutely.

Edmund Wilson

You can't find true affection in Hollywood because everyone does fake affection so well.

Carrie Fisher

"Hollywood" is not, of course, a place. Nor is it a synonym for the entertainment business. There are upstanding citizens who make their living in that field. The real Hollywood is the *reductio ad absurdum* of personal liberty. It is ordinary men and women freed by money and social mobility to do anything they want unencumbered by family pressure, community mores, social responsibility, civic duty, or good sense. There's a little streak of it in us all.

P. J. O'Rourke

You get called to L.A. by producers. And by the time you get out there, they sort of forget why they asked you to come.

Michael Herr

A place where you spend more than you make, on things you don't need, to impress people you don't like.

Ken Murray

It's no good explaining to people why one lives in Hollywood. They either understand or they don't.

Christopher Isherwood

Good evening, ladies and gentlemen—and welcome to darkest Hollywood. Night brings a stillness to the jungle. It is so quiet you can hear a name drop. The savage beasts have already begun gathering at the water holes to quench their thirst. Now one should be especially alert. The vicious table-hopper is on the prowl and the spotted backbiter may lurk behind a potted palm.

Alfred Hitchcock

The violet hush of twilight was descending over Los Angeles as my hostess, Violet Hush, and I left its suburbs headed towards Hollywood. In the distance a glow of huge piles of burning motion-picture scripts lit up the sky. The crisp tang of frying writers and directors whetted my appetite. How good it was to be alive, I thought, inhaling deep lungfuls of carbon monoxide.

S. J. Perelman

Hollywood is the only town where everybody at least *thinks* they're cute.

John Waters

While intelligence is the rule in Hollywood, it tends to be a Hollywood intelligence, which is to say untranslatable, suspicious, uneasy, and parochial—pure Hollywood, country-clublike in its distrust of trained intelligence of an outside kind.

Harold Brodkey

There were times, when I drove along the Sunset Strip and looked at those buildings or when I watched the fashionable film colony arriving at some premiere . . . that I fully expected God in his wrath to obliterate the whole shebang.

S. J. Perelman

In 1940, I had my choice between Hitler and Hollywood, and I preferred Hollywood—just a little.

René Clair

Barbra Streisand's erstwhile Malibu estate has been turned into a theme park, the theme being Barbra. Formerly the Barbra Streisand Center for Conservancy Studies, it's been renamed Ramirez Canyon Park, but locals refer to it as "Barbraland."

The property consists of five houses on twenty-two acres that Barbra painstakingly accumulated through the purchase of several adjacent properties, including the house next door, which Barbra bought for twice what the previous owner paid for it. Barbra made extensive improvements, including rerouting a stream and building a barn with hand-singed shingles and an apricot onyx fireplace. Barbra also built the "Art Deco House" solely to display her extensive collection of bric-a-brac.

In 1993, Barbra deeded the property to the Santa Monica Mountains Conservancy in return for a $15 million tax write-off. To defray the operating costs (Barbra made no provision for the $160,000 annual upkeep) the conservancy began renting out the estate for tours, conferences, retreats, weddings, and, yes, bar mitzvahs. When the neighbors sued over the catering trucks and busloads of gawkers, the California Coastal Commission got involved, and a settlement was eventually reached limiting the number of vehicles and tourists and requiring the conservancy to perform "community outreach." Now the only visitors, aside from the occasional group of senior citizens or disadvantaged children, are mostly just fans of Barbra.

Admission: $30. Open: Wednesdays.

San Francisco

Self-reference is one of San Francisco's habits, like the beautiful woman who has a few nagging doubts. A front-page story in the *Chronicle*—on a day when sieges of the British and Libyan embassies in London and Tripoli, mining of Nicaraguan ports, political campaigns, perturbations in the economy, and the unbalanced budget were the big news in other newspapers—concerned the crusade by Warren Hinckle to change the city song from Tony Bennett's "I Left My Heart in San Francisco" to the "San Francisco" made famous by Jeanette MacDonald in a Clark Gable earthquake movie. The first sounds like a ditty about an item forgotten in a hotel room, but the second reminds people of the earthquake past and, more important, to come.

Herbert Gold

Having lived here most of my life, I don't think San Francisco is as sophisticated as it likes to think, but then neither am I. More things are possible here than anywhere else, because of the anything-goes nature of the place, but a lot of second-rate stuff is too easily embraced. (Everyone here should spend at least a year in New York, which I call "urban boot camp," to get some perspective. I put in a ten-year hitch.)

The real problem with San Francisco is that unlike New York and Los Angeles, not enough is at stake here. It's too damn pretty and too damn *liveable,* which accounts for the city's lead-ing export: self-adoration. Even so it's been the hotbed for sev-eral cultural revolutions: the beatnik revolution, the comedy revolution of the fifties, the folksong revolution, the rock revo-lution, the sexual revolution, the gay revolution, even the free speech revolution (if you include Berkeley, the city's crazy brother across the Bridge).

Gerald Nachman

Somebody, maybe it was Herb Caen, once said, "San Francisco is the only city that goes down on itself."

Barnaby Conrad III

San Francisco is a Sagittarian, free spirited and volatile, need-ing—demanding!—freedom to live on the edge. Her Moon is in Scorpio—ready always to rise magnificently from her own ashes. Finally, there's Aquarius rising, assuring us that what San Francisco thinks today is tomorrow's road map for everyone else.

Minerva (San Francisco Chronicle ASTROLOGY COLUMNIST)

There's a curious kind of aristocracy in northern California, unlike anything in L.A. It places a high value on New Age mysticism, naturism, nudity, Oriental thought and massage, and "roughing it" in style at the coastal and mountain retreats within day-tripping reach of San Francisco. The favored spots for those who can afford them are Big Sur, the Esalen Institute, Carmel Valley, and the Tassajara Zen Center.

Ray Mungo

On being told that San Francisco had proclaimed itself "The Paris of the West," the novelist and French minister of culture André Malraux replied, "Ah, the touching arrogance of cities born only yesterday."

San Francisco: A hand-tinted postcard left inside the house too long to molder and fade. Its ink is blurred, the message trivial.

Carolyn See

San Francisco is a toy New York.

Deanne Stillman

San Francisco rock, San Francisco writing, it's always real light-weight, ephemeral stuff. Nothing important has ever come out of San Francisco, Rice-A-Roni aside.

Michael O'Donoghue

San Francisco: a suburb of San Jose without the Rosicrucians or the Pruneyard. (I lived in San Jose from 1961 to 1966 and remember how San Franciscans looked down on upstart San Jose.)

Jess Marlow

In San Francisco a mixed marriage is a man and a woman.

Phyllis Diller

The male-only Bohemian Club was founded in 1872 by a group of San Francisco artists and writers. Its membership, which now includes establishmentarians Henry Kissinger, David Rockefeller, George H. W. Bush, and Walter Cronkite, has changed so drastically over the years that, according to a current joke, "It is rumored that the Bohemian Club intends to expand its membership to include artists and writers."

San Francisco is one of the few cities in the world where a sizeable part of the male population suffers from menstrual envy.

Barnaby Conrad III

At first you're seduced by the sweeping ocean views, cute Victorian houses, picturesque tangerine bridges and storybook bed-and-breakfasts. But on closer inspection, the sheer volume of scented candles, glass-blown swans and seashell ashtrays sends the mind reeling. Banners that boast I LEFT MY HEART IN SAN FRANCISCO should rightly read MY WALLET, since San Francisco's real raison d'être is separating tourists from their money. This too-too-precious chilly, hilly city is determined to stupefy you with caramel corn, sourdough bread, chocolate cable cars and painting-by-numbers that goes by the name of sidewalk art.

Martha Smilgis

Mistaken Identity

I had been employed on the paper [the *San Francisco Examiner*]
for two years when, on a Sunday morning in 1959, I reported
for work to find the editors talking to one another in the
hushed and self-important way that usually means that at least
fifty people have been killed. I assumed that a ship had sunk or
that a building had collapsed. The editors were not in the habit
of taking me into their confidence, and I didn't expect to learn
the terms of the calamity until I had a chance to read the AP
wire. Much to my surprise, the city editor motioned impa-
tiently in my direction, indicating that I should join the circle
of people standing around his desk and turning slowly through
the pages of the pictorial supplement that the paper was
obliged to publish the next day. Aghast at what they saw, unable
to stifle small cries of anguished disbelief, they were examining
twelve pages of text and photographs arranged under the heading
LOS ANGELES—THE ATHENS OF THE WEST. To readers unfamiliar
with the ethos of San Francisco, I'm not sure that I can convey
the full and terrible effect of this headline. Not only was it
wrong, it was monstrous heresy. The residents of San Francisco
dote on a romantic image of the city, and they imagine

themselves living at a height of civilization accessible only to Erasmus or a nineteenth-century British peer. They flatter themselves on their sophistication, their exquisite sensibility, their devotion to the arts. Los Angeles represents the antithesis of these graces; it is the land of the Philistines, lying somewhere to the south in the midst of housing developments that stand as the embodiment of ugliness, vulgarity, and corruptions of the spirit.

Pity, then, the poor editors in San Francisco. In those days there was also a *Los Angeles Examiner,* and the same printing plant supplied supplements to both papers. The text and photographs intended for a Los Angeles audience had been printed in the Sunday pictorial bearing the imprimatur of the *San Francisco Examiner.* It was impossible to correct the mistake, and so the editors in San Francisco had no choice but to publish and give credence to despised anathema.

This so distressed them that they resolved to print a denial.

Lewis H. Lapham

Someone once told me, "San Francisco is a quaint fishing village run by interior decorators." It isn't an intellectual city; it's a life-style city.

Barnaby Conrad III

Where else but in San Francisco would characters such as Sister Boom-Boom, a transvestite who dresses in a miniskirted nun's habit, and a punk rocker named Jello Biafra run for seats on the Board of Supervisors? And where else would 75,000 runners dress like centipedes, gorillas, and six packs of beer to participate in the "moving masquerade ball," otherwise known as the Bay to Breakers Race?

Jo Anne Davidson

There is almost nothing to see in San Francisco that is worth seeing. There is a new park in which you may drive for six or seven miles on a well made road, and which, as a park for the use of a city, will, when completed, have many excellencies. There is also the biggest hotel in the world,—so the people of San Francisco say, which has cost a million sterling,—5 millions of dollars,—and is intended to swallow up all the other hotels.

It was just finished but not opened when I was there. There is an inferior menagerie of wild beasts, and a place called the Cliff House to which strangers are taken to hear seals bark. Everything,—except hotel prices,—is dearer here than at any other large town I know; and the ordinary traveler has no peace left him either in public or private by touters who wish to persuade him to take this or the other railway route to the Eastern States.

There is always a perfectly cloudless sky over head unless when rain is falling in torrents, and perhaps no where in the world is there a more sudden change from heat to cold in the same day. I think I may say that strangers will generally desire to get out of San Francisco as quickly as they can.

Anthony Trollope (1875)

You know how San Francisco has a reputation for having big hills? Well they ain't kidding, folks. I walked all over town . . . and I realized something. When you're on a bike going up a hill, at least you are secure in the knowledge that you'll get to coast down the other side. Walking down a hill, especially a steep hill, sucks almost as much as walking up.

David Grenier

When you get tired of walking around San Francisco, you can always lean against it.

Travel brochure

New Orleans is one of the two most ingrown, self-obsessed little cities in the United States. (The other is San Francisco.)

Nora Ephron

San Francisco is a self-consciously civilized place, pleased by its reasonable scale and unreasonable hills, proud of the slightly loopy beaux arts buildings and the great swaths of pastel houses, altogether seduced by its own fey charms.

Kurt Andersen

San Francisco is a city surrounded on three sides by water, and on all sides by glittering generalities.

Herb Caen

[San Francisco is] nothing but a three-day city—including all the museums.

Leonard Lyons

Whoever laid the town out took the conventional checkerboard pattern of streets and without the slightest regard for the laws of gravity planked it down on an irregular peninsula that was a confusion of steep slopes and sandhills.

John Dos Passos

San Francisco is a mad city—inhabited for the most part by perfectly insane people whose women are of remarkable beauty.

Rudyard Kipling

San Francisco has the meanest politics I've ever seen. . . . This is a combat sport out here. Atlanta seems much more genteel. This is hardball. I pray I don't do anything to piss off ACT UP while I'm out here.

Pat Conroy

An unreasonable city.

William Saroyan

A condition in love with itself.

Jerry Dashkin

Hollywood pretending to be New York.

Jules Siegel

Most things in San Francisco can be bought or taken.

Dashiell Hammett

The first time I got arrested for obscenity was in San Francisco.

Lenny Bruce

San Francisco is the only city I can think of that could survive all the things people are doing to it and still look beautiful.

Frank Lloyd Wright

San Francisco is the center of the known universe. Just ask any of us who live here. It's also home of the pyramid building. What other city would provide ring toss for aliens?

Will Durst

I'd never set foot in San Francisco. Of all the Sodoms and Gomorrahs in our modern world, it is the worst. It needs another quake, another whiff of fire—and—more than all else—a steady trade wind of grapeshot. . . . That moral penal colony of the world.

Ambrose Bierce

Bierce's perverse civic pride was affronted when he learned that a prominent San Franciscan had committed suicide while traveling in the Midwest. "We have an efficient and accommodating coroner and a comfortable though rather badly lighted dead house," he wrote. "Our undertakers have engaging manners, and their hearses easy springs. There is a charming view from every cemetery. In addition to these advantages, San Francisco itself is a very good motive."

The coldest winter I ever spent was a summer in San Francisco.

Mark Twain

When we start getting perfect football weather, you can tell that baseball season is about to begin.

Henry Berman (QUOTED BY HERB CAEN)

A city where tolerance deteriorates into license.

Guy Wright

It's an odd thing, but anybody who disappears is said to be in San Francisco.

Oscar Wilde

In San Francisco there's a sign outside a downtown smut arcade that reads, "Got porn?"

Ian Shoales

Leaving San Francisco ultimately has the feel of leaving the girl or boy you had the most killer hot drunken sex with, but whose irritating idiosyncrasies wound up being too much of a daily drag.

Anonymous

In San Francisco, Halloween is redundant.

Will Durst

The Mysterious East Bay

I always feel I ought to get a passport every time I cross the Bay to Oakland or Berkeley.

Kenneth Rexroth

Oakland

When you get there, there isn't any there there.

Gertrude Stein

The trouble with Oakland is that when you get there, it's there.

Herb Caen

New York was the first major city to utilize the "I Love" campaign and the little red heart. "I ❤ NY" was everybody's bumper sticker for years, after which the Big Apple became a place of peace and love and hardly any crime or violence at all. Thereafter, Americans fell in love with their towns from coast to coast and eventually around the world, flaunting bumper stickers in many languages, like flags of urban passion. Only places like Oakland, to the best of my knowledge, remained unloved, though inhabited. "I Tolerate Oakland" might have worked, but no one suggested it.

Al Martinez

In 2002, Oakland inaugurated a taxicab ad campaign to take business from San Francisco:
"Really want to be taken for a ride? Buy a house in San Francisco."
"Tired of living where the sun don't shine?"
"June 21. The official start of summer in Oakland. And winter in San Francisco."
"Is this cab bigger than your apartment?"
"I left my parka in San Francisco."

It was [Ambrose] Bierce, I believe, who was gazing across the bay the day after the '06 fire and quake when a friend commented, "It looks like nothing happened to Oakland." Bierce nodded. "There are some things," he murmured, "that even the earth can't swallow."

Herb Caen

Richmond

The town of Richmond smells so strongly of gas that I'm afraid to light a match there.

Herb Caen

Berkeley

I last saw Berkeley several years ago, arriving there with a friend early one Saturday afternoon. We made the round of bookstores and then repaired to a sidewalk café, where we were subjected to an endless procession of spaced-out, tie-dyed hippies on the sidewalk and a parade of vintage VW vans on the street. Mildly puzzled by the anachronisms, we finally concluded that Berkeley was stuck in some kind of time warp, because it obviously hadn't changed since the Sixties. Only later did we learn that there was a Grateful Dead concert in Berkeley that night, and that the people we saw on the streets were not locals but rather a traveling band of "Deadheads."

Dubbed "Berserkley" by Herb Caen and the "People's Republic of Berkeley" by others, Berkeley *is* in a time warp politically. The birthplace of the Free Speech Movement and the New Left hasn't changed its counter-cultural ways since the Sixties. It's still a hotbed of political activism, its residents still champion such causes as civil rights, free speech, nuclear disarmament, and animal rights. The difference is that those Sixties radicals are now tenured professors and tech CEOs.

Howard Ogden

A town in which half the people are seeking to overthrow the federal government while the other half are seeking the perfect croissant.

R. Howard Bloch

[Berkeley] seems to me like a sort of graduate-student theme park—of the young, by the young, and for the young.

Stanley Elkin

In 1992, a dedicated cadre of Berkeley bicyclists began "Critical Mass" protests. The group ("not an organization, an unorganized coincidence," according to its "non-website") deliberately blocks traffic around the Bay Area to protest widespread use of the internal combustion engine, handing out leaflets to motorists that read:"We know that you aren't responsible for the organization of our cities around motorized traffic, and if we have contributed to your delay, we're sorry. But maybe you can take this opportunity to reflect on what a world without cars would be like."

According to Critical Mass spokesman David Cohen,"We aren't blocking traffic, we are traffic. They call this a protest, but it's not a protest. It's a celebration. They don't call it a protest when they see a traffic jam on I-80. But I call that fossil fuelishness."

A friend of mine invited me to his birthday party in a bar in the Republic of Berkeley. It was one of those fog-chilled California evenings when the cold knifes you for no good reason and you stand there shivering but certain that it could never get THIS cold in California. And then you comfort yourself with the thought that it doesn't get any *colder*. And then it does.

Andrei Codrescu

I decided to move back to Los Angeles, where I was born, after living in Berkeley for twenty years. The decision was based on my engagement to a famously reclusive writer who uniquely, in my experience, disliked Northern California. I asked him why, and he replied, "You have no privacy there, no anonymity. Everyone pins you down by knowing you. I love the freedom Los Angeles gives me."

The real moment of truth arrived when I told my Berkeley dentist, who had a mandala on the ceiling that swirled above one's nitrous oxide–filled head. I told him I was leaving. He was performing oral surgery at the time.

I said, "I'm really leaffig. I'm in luffgh." (Mouth stuffed with bloody cotton.)

"You CAN'T," he insisted.

"Bugh . . . I yam."

"WHY?!" (expletive deleted).

"I'm ig luff. I'm gegging marred; um, marreed."

"YOU CAN'T REALLY MEAN YOU'LL MOVE TO L.A.!"

He seemed genuinely worried, and possibly about to recommend therapeutic intervention. But congratulations on my upcoming nuptials? Well, no. The shock had been too great. He regarded me with such horror I thought The Alien had burst from my chest. Though after 20 years we were close to being friends, I thought, we never spoke again.

Amy Wallace

....

In 2003, after first denying the incident, newly elected Berkeley mayor Tom Bates was fined $100 after pleading guilty to petty theft for trashing copies of a campus newspaper endorsing his opponent in the November 2002 election. The incident took place in Sproul Plaza, birthplace of the Free Speech Movement, where in 1964 thousands of UC Berkeley students protested a ban on campus political activity.

Amid calls for Bates's resignation, Berkeley city councilman Kriss Worthington argued against removing him: "Getting rid of the mayor because of this would basically be the same as capital punishment." Christopher Hitchens, visiting fellow at the Berkeley Journalism School, called Bates's trashing of the newspapers "a metaphorical moment" and declared: "There's no intolerance like liberal intolerance."

....

Hottubistan

Just across the Golden Gate from San Francisco lies Marin County, a bastion of cultural liberalism and hotbed of social protest where concerned citizens lobby the county board of supervisors for a research center on aging, which would necessarily perform experiments on lab animals, including rats and worms, but before granting the request the board orders a study to measure the effects of animal research on the community's self-esteem. Marin is where county supervisors pass a resolution condemning the Homeland Security Act, and where a bond measure for a new police station is defeated amid charges that the proposed building would have bad feng shui. Marin is the home of In Defense of Animals, an organization for whom dogs and cats are not "pets" to be "owned" by humans like so much disposable property, but rather "companions."

Marin, where aging flower children went to raise families, is stubbornly New Age, still high on organic produce, aromatherapy, channeling, rebirthing. It is the world capital of personal growth, where materialism and environmentalism peacefully coexist: Though it is California's most affluent county, with per capita income of $60,000 and an average home price of a million dollars, much of Marin's 520 square miles is protected from the kind of rampant development typical of most other American suburbs.

In Marin, entrepreneurship is imbued with social consciousness. Take Roxanne's, a Larkspur restaurant with the motto: "Now serving the community at the intersection of sensual flavors, healthy lifestyle and ecological sustainability." Roxanne's opened in 2002, specializing in uncooked vegetables, fruits, and nuts, in other words, all-organic, all-vegan, *raw* food (Roxanne's calls it "living food")—no meat, fish, eggs, or dairy. And no stove in the kitchen: Nothing is heated above 118 degrees, and sunlight is used instead of ovens. House specialties include herbed cashew cheese, sea vegetable salad with kaisou, pineapple yuzu and hijiki vinaigrette, coconut noodles, and almond chile.

Why "living food"? Because humans evolved eating raw foods, and in evolutionary terms, cooking is a relatively recent invention. Cooking denatures the proteins in foods, making them harder to digest and depleting their vitamins and minerals. Why 118 degrees? Heating above that temperature destroys food enzymes, requiring the body to supply its own digestive enzymes. Problem is, our bodies produce only a finite quantity of digestive enzymes during a lifetime, and every cooked meal we eat draws down this enzyme reserve. (Aging, therefore, is really just running out of enzymes.) The good news: Living food is enzyme self-sufficient and thus does not use up our enzymes!

Roxannes's construction and interior design are equally organic: All the wood used in the building is either recycled or certified "sustainably harvested," the walls are painted with a chemical-free, natural pigment from Australia, the tablecloths and napkins are unbleached organic cotton, the banquettes are covered with "organic hemp chenille," the service counters are made from pressed sunflowers, and the lamps from recycled, naturally pigmented crushed glass.

Marin is all about inclusiveness: It's the home of the $3 million Ecology House, the first apartment complex for the "chemically sensitive," people whose compromised immune systems cause them to suffer a raft of debilitating symptoms (dizziness, headaches, memory loss, swollen joints, disorientation) when exposed to certain chemicals. The hypoallergenic building, funded mostly by federal tax dollars, has high-powered ventilators and complex water filtration systems. During construction, "sniff teams" were employed to detect offensive chemicals in raw building materials. Unfortunately, about half the initial occupants said their new apartments made them sick, and to avoid noxious odors, one tenant had to sleep on the patio, another on the bathroom floor.

Marin is a touchy-feely place, emphasis on the "touchy": When former president George H. W. Bush declared "American Taliban" John Walker Lindh a "misguided Marin County hottubber," Marinites seemed more outraged by the stereotype than the fact that one of their own was a traitor. They were almost as upset that the former president pronounced it "MARE-in":

I apologize. I am chastened and will never use "hot tub" and "Marin County'" in the same sentence again.

I won't even try to explain my position except to say I was and remain so offended by John Walker Lindh that I hurt others' feelings.

In the opinion of your outraged letter writers, I condemned all of Marin County with a hot tub reference. Obviously, I struck a nerve.

Now your readers have attacked me on my granddaughters, on my residence, on abortion, on Enron, on my being a Texan and on my pronunciation of Marin. You name it, a lot of angst has surfaced, and it's all my fault. Though I only garnered 23 percent of the vote in Marin in 1992, I was your president and I should have known better. I apologize to those who supported me that were offended, and I also apologize to the unenlightened who did not support me.

I will now soak in my own hot tub and try to be more sensitive to the feelings of others—not John Walker Lindh, though.

George H. W. Bush (LETTER TO Marin Independent Journal)

Marin is a place where all the cliché obsessions of shallow California . . . flourish without irony.

Shelby Steele

The cliché: Marin County is the mellow, back-to-nature, do-your-own-thing capital of American cultural liberalism. The reality: Marin County is the mellow, back-to-nature, do-your-own-thing capital of American cultural liberalism.

Howard Ogden

We are all too eager to define anything we want to do as a right. Some people in Marin have joined a similar trend toward calling whatever bothers them pollution.

Al Martinez

Marinites ought to stop tugging their forelocks and agonizing over how much damage their Birkenstocks are doing to the microbe colonies on the floor of Starbucks.

Michael Ambrosini

Asked for a word for a body of water entirely surrounded by land, a Marin County child answered, "Hot tub?"

Herbert Gold

Los Angeles vs. San Francisco

About ten years ago I met Herb Caen for lunch at Enrico's Coffee House in San Francisco—we used to hang out there. He knew I'd moved to L.A. from the city and the first thing he said was, "I just got back from a weekend in Los Angeles." And then he leaned over and whispered, "I *love* Los Angeles!"

Ronnie Schell

You have to *work* L.A.; San Francisco just lies on its back for you to pet.

Jim Heimann

Expertise is the stock in trade of this metropolis [Los Angeles], and behind the flash and the braggadocio, solid skill and scholarship prosper. There are craftsmen everywhere in L.A., craftsmen in electronics, in film-making, in literature, in social science, in advertising, in fashion. They say that in San Francisco there is less than meets the eye; in Los Angeles there is far more.

Jan Morris

In San Francisco, they look down their pince-nez-pinched noses at L.A. But nobody in L.A. looks disdainfully at Frisco: we're busy, living, learning, driving, and setting the world's standards, for better or worse.

Art Fein

The smug superiority of northerners is simply a case of shabby gentility. These people who came to California first always looked down at the village in the south, which to their dismay has become a booming megalopolis.

Martha Smilgis

I'm fifty. The difference between Los Angeles and San Francisco is Sandy Koufax and Juan Marichal. Similarity? Al Davis.

Phil Mushnick

In Northern California numbers of men are often sighted out with their mothers. Soon one comes to realize these men are actually accompanied by females of a similar age. Women in the northern territories let their hair turn gray! In the South, allowing such a naturally occurring process is punished by social banishment. Upon turning forty, I moved North immediately. I may be old, but I'm no fool.

Louise Rafkin

Local Customs

Having lived in both cities about the same length of time, I have discovered the unique qualities which make them both charming and unbearable:

Weather

In San Francisco, if the sky is the color of steel wool and the wind is whipping your coattails into your face, as long as it is not raining, people will call it "a nice day."

In Los Angeles, it can be a sunny day, not too much smog, 75 degrees but if there's a slight breeze, people actually complain, "It's kind of chilly today."

Transportation

In San Francisco, if you drive, it takes ten minutes to get to your destination and twelve dollars an hour to park.

In Los Angeles, if you drive, it takes two hours to get to your destination and three dollars to park.

Politics

In San Francisco, a politically active person attends meetings, petitions city hall, goes on marches and hands out leaflets for organizations like Gay and Lesbian Metallurgists for Radiation-Free Dolphin-Safe Tuna in Guam.

In Los Angeles, a politically active person writes a big check at a benefit in a private home the size of a dictator's presidential palace, regardless of the cause, because a movie or TV star is going to be there.

Brad Schreiber

I've lived in both metropolitan areas (L.A.: Glendale, West Hollywood, Hollywood, Silverlake; Bay Area: Berkeley, Oakland) and I live in L.A. now. My observation: Methinks S.F. doth protest too much.

Joe Donnelly

The average San Franciscan, if I may presume to identify myself as one, is a notoriously smug character. Visitors, especially from Los Angeles, are quick to point this out, especially after they've received the usual needling remarks about the Colossus of the South. San Franciscans won't deny the charge, either. "Smug, smog, what's the difference?" they'll reply, "Except that you have the smog." *Touché!*

Herb Caen

Our capacity for laughing at our critics, and at ourselves, instead of sulking and rushing to our mirrors for reassurance, like San Franciscans, is one of the reasons I prefer to live here [in Los Angeles].

Jack Smith

A 2002 survey by the USC Center on Philanthropy and Public Policy found that San Francisco County receives $418 in charitable foundation grants per person while Los Angeles County gets only $45 per person. According to the study, the gross disparity exists because funders outside California, especially on the East Coast, identify with San Francisco as a kind of "wannabe Boston," but cannot comprehend the vast, amorphous sprawl of L.A.

Perhaps it is easiest to define Los Angeles by what it is not. Most emphatically it is not eastern. San Francisco is eastern, a creation of the gold rush, colonized by sea, Yankee architecture and Yankee attitudes, boated around the Horn and grafted onto the bay. Any residual ribaldry in San Francisco is the legacy of that lust for yellow riches that attracted those early settlers in the first place. Small wonder Easterners feel comfortable there. They perceive an Atlantic clone; it does not threaten as does the space-age Fort Apache five hundred miles to the south.

John Gregory Dunne

Children in San Francisco are taught two things: to love the Lord and hate Los Angeles.

Will Rogers

San Franciscans like to have fun, and the natives are sexier. And less mummified. Less Botox, collagen, implants and fewer tsunamis of tucks than you find in LA Also, the girls have shapelier legs from walking up and down those hills.

George Christy

I just love San Francisco—such an adorable little boutique city, swaddled in its cotton-wool fog and narcissism. It's as pretty and fragile and fussily precious a place as one of those small spun-glass castles you can buy anywhere from Union Square to Disneyland. Los Angeles, by contrast, is robust, vigorous, realistic, clear-eyed. You get engaged in San Francisco—you draft the pre-nup in Los Angeles.

Patt Morrison

Exercise Etiquette

As a health and fitness professional, I'd say both San Francisco and Los Angeles are interested in health and fitness and both have some of the best instructors in the USA. Both cities offer "cutting edge" classes and instruction. The differences I see:

Workout Attire

SF is much more conservative—loose clothing that doesn't necessarily match—clothes that don't make you stand out—functional but not flashy.

In LA anything goes as long as it shows your body off—tighter, smaller and sexier being key.

Scent

People working out in a group exercise class in the SF area are usually "fragrance free," as they are very aware that people exercising around them may be sensitive to their perfume, cologne or aftershave. In LA you find lots of scent—including unique perfumes, cologne, aftershave etc., blended especially for the person wearing it.

Makeup

In SF women wear little or no makeup when working out. In LA everything from natural to theatrical full face makeup is worn by women, and some men as well.

Tanning

In the SF area very few people in exercise class are tan. In LA everyone is—whether tan from sun, tanning beds or the new methods (spray-on tan—20 seconds for full body, or Instant Tan treatment—lotion applied on total body by a beauty professional who makes sure it's applied evenly, resulting in a "glowing healthy look").

Bottled Water

In SF about half the people exercising carry bottled water with them. In LA water is an accessory—everyone carries water even when not exercising.

Eye Contact

In SF people taking exercise classes rarely make eye contact or get caught "checking out" a fellow exerciser. In LA everyone makes eye contact and there's no such thing as getting "caught" checking out a fellow exerciser, as it's the "norm."

Noise

SF classes are very quiet, not a lot of whooping and yelling. In LA there's a lot of whooping, yelling, screaming, and anything-goes noise.

Hanging Out

In SF people don't hang out in a health club or gym after their workout.

In LA the health club or gym is not just for working out but is also a place to meet friends, new people, people-watch, shop, sign up for ski trips, nature hikes, golf tournaments, etc. If the facility has a restaurant where you can have breakfast, lunch and dinner, all the better. On-site dry cleaners are also appreciated.

Joanie Greggains

. . . .

In 2002, Northern California narrowed the kitsch gap with Southern California when The Village, a "themed housing development" based on the works of Thomas Kinkade, opened near San Francisco. Often cited as America's most popular living painter, Kinkade churns out thousands of "branded" paintings depicting an idealized world of white picket fences and blooming flower beds. The "paintings," not original oils but digitally mass-produced facsimiles made under Kinkade's supervision and retouched by hourly wage workers, are said to hang in one out of every twenty American homes. The self-described "painter of light" (a phrase Kinkade trademarked) also markets calendars, greeting cards, wallpaper, and table-top collectibles.

Designed for buyers seeking a "lifestyle" based on Kinkade's idyllic world, "The Village, a Thomas Kinkade Community," offers four different "cottage-style" models named for Kinkade's daughters (Chandler, Everett, Merritt, and Winsor), ranging in price from $376,000 to $419,000.

Recently it was pointed out to me in a kind of hurtful way, to be honest, that people in Los Angeles are aurally challenged. That is, at social events, we simply do not listen to others. We do not ask them questions about themselves; we do not nod attentively when they speak; really, if we were to examine ourselves, we would realize that we simply have no interest in others at all.

The criticism came from a denizen of San Francisco, which rankles a bit right there. In fact, let me be so bold as to say that after many visits, I've come to feel that San Francisco people listen to one another too much. What with the cappuccinos and the smugness and the flouncing and the book groups, in the end they have little to say and should be punished for it. Come to

L.A., I want to say, where you will be good and ignored like you should be.

Sandra Tsing Loh

Los Angeles is a haven to whose doors people have come from all over the world. It is a fraternity of refugees. . . . Hardly a day goes by without the death of some celebrated European resident, driven here long ago by war, ambition, or persecution, and the British consul general told me that within his area there live more than 50,000 British subjects, some of whom fly Union Jacks from their roofs. San Francisco, up the coast, has an intimacy of a totally different kind, a hereditary or environmental closeness, bound up with the beauty of the place and the allure of its traditions. There is no such grace to the brotherhood of L.A. This is a charmless city really, humorless, often reactionary, a city without a gentry. Its comradeship lies only in a common sense of release or opportunity, tinged with a spice of holiday.

Jan Morris

Everything of any value in Los Angeles was imported. In San Francisco we grow our own.

Stan Burford

L.A. is glitz, glamor and celebrity (think Wolfgang Puck). S.F. is serious foodies and passionate wine aficionados (think Hubert Keller at Fleur de Lys and Silver Oak). While L.A. surely has the edge on "beautiful people," San Francisco is without a doubt the capital of American gastronomy.

Gene Burns

In talk radio, L.A. wants you to have one unbelievably strong opinion and be outraged each hour. San Francisco actually considers both sides. Plus San Francisco doesn't need air conditioning.

Ronn Owens

People down here never, ever criticize other cities in general, and San Francisco in particular. Quite the contrary; everybody gushes about their too-seldom getaways to The City, and wishes L.A. were more walkable and cozy in the way S.F. is.

Mark Miller

Los Angeles is one of the most secret cities I've ever been to. It seems all sunny and open and candid, but it's not. Try to find a friend. Try to find a scene. Try to get comfortable if you're from out of town. Everything happens in living rooms or cars. It's also the only world center I know of built right up against a wilderness, so you can see coyotes loping down Sunset or rattlesnakes in a Pasadena backyard.

San Francisco is tiny. People don't realize that. It's astounding for all us scenery sluts; there's always something new. Like most smallish cities, though, it's controlled by a small group of families. Sometimes a new person gets in, like Willie Brown, but still he knows where the power is—the Catholic/Jewish establishment made up mostly of the descendents of merchant princes who got rich during the Gold Rush.

Jon Carroll

In San Francisco everyone knows a private corner where you can watch the stars from a breathtaking overlook as the moonlight outlines a lover's curves. In Los Angeles, everyone knows Richard Gere's ER nurse's hairdresser.

"Mister San Francisco"(Hank Donat)

In San Francisco when a guy says, "Let's go to a great Italian restaurant," that's what he means. In L.A. when a guy says, "Let's go to a great Italian restaurant," what he means is, "Wait in the car while I shoot you through the head."

Judy Tenuta

One of the San Francisco papers sponsored a "Why I Hate L.A. In A Thousand Words Or Less" contest. The winner, letting success go to his head, moved down to West Hollywood, where he's been pitching screenplays ever since.

Berton Averre

As a San Franciscan, this might be a weird thing to say, but LA has its points. It's a very, very diverse city, much more than SF, it has oodles of cool ethnic-cultural enclaves, and might one day be the capital of a liberated Azatlan. San Francisco is much prettier, but most of the population hides intense self-absorption and politico-economic corruption under a patina of so-called "liberalism" and "progressivism." The local government has assisted the real estate sector in tossing blacks out of the city by the tens of thousands. Poor people cannot afford to live anywhere in SF except eight to a room in the Tenderloin. As of last fall, the city stripped homeless people of their meager VA stipends in a situation where there are virtually no meaningful social services for the homeless, nor the mentally ill. The liberal billionaires in their Pacific Heights mansions rule the politicians by cutting them in on financial deals. In short, SF has fine restaurants, a wonderful population of young and old protestors, poets, writers, nice beaches and parks—but it is more of a dense suburb than a real city (like, say, Mexico City or New York).

Peter Byrne

Deep-imbedded stars and hip-hop mobsters
  versus
Little cable cars and tourist lobsters

Ian Whitcomb

In L.A. we're honest about being phony.

Bill Maher

Los Angeles is mother, San Francisco, stepmother. It is my large and colorful blended family and it is not easy to give them equal love at the same time. When I'm with one it is the place for me. I am comfortable and I'm with the familiar. But I cannot forget the other. It has become fine to have both and I am richer for it. I would like to see them living together, not so far apart. They might really learn to like each other. Or is that too far-fetched?

Adam West

Once my partner died, my move from New York to California was only a matter of time. The only real question was where in California I would live: San Francisco or Los Angeles? I'd lived for periods of three to four months in each city over the past thirty years, and both held considerable attractions to me. For a gay man, especially, San Francisco beckoned, while the out-doors life of L.A. was really intriguing and I suspected I might get more work writing in Los Angeles.

During a book tour to both places, I decided to tell just about everyone I met—old friends, new friends, fans, interviewers, bookstore owners—of my plans to move to "California" very soon, without ever specifying the city.

In San Francisco everyone I spoke to sort of nodded as though what could be more natural and didn't say another word (assuming I guess that I'd be moving there).

In Los Angeles, when I did the same, one person offered me a two-year sublet of a large bright, airy apartment; a second, an actor who worked part-time for a car dealership, offered to get me a good car at a discount, and a third offered me a job at a university teaching writing. The job was part-time, but I had a best-seller out and a contract for a new book and didn't need any job.

What would you have done?

Right.

I lived in the sublet two years then moved to another flat in the same complex before I moved to a little house in the hills.

I still drive the car my friend sold me.

And whenever I appear in San Francisco, which I do often (last year I had a play and a historical exhibit there) people there never fail to ask me what in the world I'm doing living in Los Angeles.

Felice Picano

Old natives of San Francisco thought of their city as Renaissance Florence and Los Angeles as Rome. After September 11th and with Bush's Wars we are all a part of what Pier Paolo Pasolini called the Modern Inferno of Rome—a hell on earth.

Lawrence Ferlinghetti (MARCH 20, 2003, THE DAY THE BOMBING OF IRAQ STARTED)

Berkeley-raised Counting Crows lead singer Adam Duritz was booed loudly when he told a packed house at the Warfield in San Francisco that, "We live in L.A. now."

"Y'know," he said, "that's something y'all are wrong about. It's not a competition, it's just a city."

L.A. is livable but not lovable. San Francisco is just the opposite.

Rod McKuen

San Francisco, the gateway to the Orient, was a city of good food and cheap prices; the first to introduce me to frog's legs à la Provençale, strawberry shortcake and avocado pears. Everything was new and bright, including my small hotel. Los Angeles, on the other hand, was an ugly city, hot and oppressive, and the people looked sallow and anemic. Nature has endowed the north of California with resources that will endure and flourish when Hollywood has disappeared into the prehistoric tar pits of Wilshire Boulevard.

Charlie Chaplin (QUOTED BY HERB CAEN)

San Francisco is a marvelous city, but Los Angeles is a little bit square—not courageous enough.

Rudolph Nureyev

Fog Town versus Smog Town.

Sandow Birk

In Smog and Thunder

Los Angeles artist Sandow Birk's send-up exhibition of history painting, *In Smog and Thunder,* depicts the perennial rivalry between Los Angeles and San Francisco. Birk began the project in 1995, after a visit to San Francisco: "I was astonished by the animosity people [in San Francisco] had toward L.A.," he says. "It was something I didn't know about. It was funny in a way. So I came up with the idea to do a show that would be their worst nightmare—being taken over by L.A."

The satirical paintings are rendered in the classical, heroic style of the Napoleonic era. The first *In Smog and Thunder* show comprised a series of paintings (on loan from the fictitious California War Museum in Tijuana) portraying the destruction of San Francisco by an invading army from Los Angeles. In subsequent works, the "war" includes naval battles and a counterinvasion by San Francisco.

Birk parodies such masters as Goya and Delacroix with panoramic battle scenes full of incongruities and visual puns: saber-brandishing officers exhorting their troops from motorcycles, combatants wielding muskets along with leaf blowers and electric guitars and carrying banners advertising their "sponsors" ("No-Fee Checking"; "Smog Check: Pass or Don't Pay"). In *The Spirit of Los Angeles,* patterned on Delacroix's *Liberty Leading the People (28 July 1830),* the leader wears a Domino's Pizza shirt and carries a Big Gulp cup as he strides through a battlefield of twisted parking meters and abandoned personal computers.

Mock commentary, including sound effects and pseudo-newscasts complete with traffic reports, accompanied the exhibit in the form of an audio tour, which then appeared as a book *(In Smog and Thunder: Historical Works from the Great War of the Californias)* and eventually as a DVD.

Dodgers vs. Giants

The Dodgers were created by Satan. Most baseball fans know that. They are a group of evil men with evil intentions. They wear royal blue and play before fans who do not care anything about baseball.

Jon Carroll (San Francisco Chronicle)

They seem to hate us a lot more than we hate them.

Tommy Lasorda (FORMER DODGERS MANAGER)

The rivalry between the Los Angeles Dodgers and the San Francisco Giants is one of baseball's most bitter feuds. Giants fans despise the Dodgers. During Giants games in San Francisco against other National League teams, fans cheer whenever the scoreboard shows the Dodgers losing a game in another city, and when the Dodgers are in town, they shout "SUCKS" after each and every Dodgers player is introduced by the stadium announcer. San Francisco fans also hate their Los Angeles counterparts. Bleacher brawls with Dodgers rooters foolish enough to show up at Giants home games were a regular occurrence until beer sales were limited. But in Los Angeles, Dodgers fans don't seem to reciprocate the contempt, aside from the occasional, half-hearted, "GIANTS STINK!" chant.

Fledgling Giants fans are taught that no season is a total loss if their team beats the Dodgers in the season series, and that a dismal year can be salvaged if the Giants keep the Dodgers out of the play-offs. (It is not known what young Dodgers fans are taught, other than to bring a radio to the game and avoid traffic by leaving in the seventh inning.)

Scheduling has fueled the rivalry. The two teams traditionally meet at the finale of each season, which has produced a series of last-minute reversals, as when Joe Morgan's home run beat the Dodgers in the last game of the 1982 season, eliminating them from the play-offs, or when the Giants knocked the Dodgers out of the 1991 play-offs by taking two of the season's last three games. Los Angeles got revenge by beating San Francisco 12–1 in the last game of 1993, dashing the Giants' play-off hopes.

The bad blood dates back to the crosstown rivalry of the 1920s, when Dodgers fans would pelt the Giants with debris whenever the New Yorkers crossed the Brooklyn Bridge to play in Ebbets Field. In 1934, Giants manager Bill Terry, asked about the Dodgers' chances to win the pennant, replied: "The Dodgers? Are they still in the league?" In 1951, Bobby Thomson's dramatic home run against the Dodgers ("the shot heard 'round the world") clinched the pennant for the Giants. The wound apparently had not healed by 2001, when the Dodgers front office refused the Giants' request for the Dodgers to wear special jerseys in a game marking the fiftieth anniversary of Thomson's home run.

In 1952, after Giants pitchers twice beaned Dodgers outfielder Carl Furillo, Giants manager Leo Durocher duked it out with Furillo in front of the Giants dugout, sparking a bench-emptying brawl. When Jackie Robinson was traded from the Dodgers to the Giants after the 1957 season, he chose to retire rather than play for the team he had always despised. During the fifties, Sal "the Barber" Maglie, whose nickname derived from his tendency to throw close to batters' chins, routinely knocked down several Dodgers per game, perpetuating the cycle of beanings, knockdowns, and retaliations.

By the end of the 1962 season, the Dodgers and Giants were tied with identical 101–61 records, forcing a three-game play-off for the pennant. According to Dodgers announcer Vin Scully, for the first game, at San Francisco's Candlestick Park, "there wasn't a cloud in the sky, and the infield was drowned." Giants manager Alvin Dark had ordered the groundskeeper to drench the infield in order to slow down the Dodgers' speedy base runner Maury Wills. The Giants won the play-off and went to the World Series.

On August 22, 1965, Giants pitcher Juan Marichal clubbed Dodgers catcher John Roseboro with a bat and a seventeen-minute melee ensued, after which Willie Mays hit a three-run homer off Sandy Koufax to win the game. Marichal was fined and suspended for eight games, and Roseboro sued him for $110,000 but settled out of court for $7,500.

In 1973, Dodgers coach Tommy Lasorda and Giants manager Charlie Fox got into a fistfight while exchanging lineup cards before a game. At Candlestick a few years later, Dodgers outfielder Reggie Smith went into the stands after a fan in response to a racial epithet. During the 2003 season, the rivalry led to the fatal shooting of a Giants fan in the Dodger Stadium parking lot after two families traded insults about their respective teams.

There's been a turnabout since the two National League teams moved west in 1958. The New York Giants won five World Series titles, the Brooklyn Dodgers only one, but the Los Angeles Dodgers have won the World Series five times, while the San Francisco Giants have lost all three times they made it to the World Series, most recently to the Angels, another Southern California team. During home games Giants fans chanted "BEAT L.A.!" even though the Angels are from Anaheim, not Los Angeles.

Dueling Cultures:
Los Angeles vs. San Francisco

Dueling Anthems

"I Love L.A." : "I Left My Heart in San Francisco"

"I Love L.A." (RANDY NEWMAN) *Ironic, bitter; got a lot of airplay during the 1984 Olympics, but is now mostly forgotten—certainly does not have the status of "I Left My Heart in San Francisco."*

"I Left My Heart in San Francisco" (TONY BENNETT) *Adoring, syrupy; has sold millions of copies and won four Grammies. The song, written in Brooklyn Heights, New York, in 1954 by former Bay Area residents George Cory and Douglass Cross, has been "covered" more than two hundred times in a dozen languages and has earned $50,000 a year in royalties for decades.*

Dueling Suicide Venues

Hollywood Sign : Golden Gate Bridge

Fifty-foot-high letters; inaugurated in 1932, when starlet Peg Entwhistle jumped to her death from the "H."

You can throw yourself off one of these letters—most people choose the "D"—and be dead before you hit the coyote shit.

"Ruby Romaine" (Tracey Ullman)

The Golden Gate Bridge Averages one jumper every three weeks; almost a thousand victims since the span opened in 1937.

The Golden Gate Bridge should have a long bungee cord for people who aren't quite ready to commit suicide but want to get in a little practice.

George Carlin

DUELING ELECTIVE SURGERIES
Breast augmentation : Sex change

DUELING HOLY GRAILS
Publicity : Social justice

DUELING ABUSED SUBSTANCES
Cocaine : Amyl nitrate
Collagen : Caffeine
Silicone : Silicon

DUELING CELEBRITY RESTAURATEURS
Wolfgang Puck (pizza) : Alice Waters (salad)

DUELING OSTENSIBLE FOOD FAVORITES
Sushi : Lobster cappuccino

DUELING ACTUAL FOOD FAVORITES
Burritos : Lobster cappuccino

Dueling Forms of Noise Pollution
Leaf blower : Car alarm

Dueling Gay Icons
David Geffen : Harvey Milk

Dueling Eccentrics
Angelyne : Emperor Norton

Dueling Ideologies
*Ars gratia artis** : Political correctness
*(MGM's motto, "Art for art's sake")

Dueling Mixed Marriages
Ramona and Alessandro : Joe DiMaggio and Marilyn Monroe

Dueling Signature Architectural Styles
Faux Tudor manor cum faux French chateau : Victorian

Dueling Forms of Physical Self-Improvement
Bodybuilding : Body-piercing

Dueling Forms of Physical Culture
Bodybuilding : Tantric sex

Dueling Newspapers
Los Angeles Times : *San Francisco Chronicle*

The Los Angeles Times *is read by people who wouldn't mind running the country, if they could spare the time, and if they didn't have to leave L.A. to do it.*

The San Francisco Chronicle *is read by people who aren't sure there is a country, or that anyone is running it; but whoever it is, they oppose all that they stand for. There are occasional exceptions if the leaders are handicapped, minorities, homosexuals, feminists, or atheists . . . who also happen to be illegal aliens from* ANY *country as long as they are Democrats.*

Anonymous

DUELING APPLIANCES
Juicer : Espresso machine

DUELING ENTERTAINERS
Movie stars : City officials

DUELING FRINGE ENTERTAINERS
Starlets : Mimes

DUELING COMPOSERS
John Tesh : Gordon Getty

Dueling Novelists
Jackie Collins : Danielle Steel

Dueling Theaters
Equity Waiver : Street

Dueling Literary Forms
Screenplay : Poem

Dueling Poets
Charles Bukowski : Lawrence Ferlinghetti

Dueling Signature Vehicles
SUV : Cable car

Dueling Obsessions
Anti-aging : Anti-Bush

Dueling Homicidal Maniacs
Charles Manson : Jim Jones

Dueling Social Chroniclers
Army Archerd : Armistead Maupin

Dueling Character Flaws
Presumptuousness : Pretentiousness

Dueling Lawyers-Who-Never-Met-a-Camera-They-Didn't-Like
Gloria Allred : Angela Alioto

Dueling Signature Mayors
Sam Yorty : Willie Brown

Dueling Signature Governors
Ronald Reagan : Jerry Brown

Dueling Victims
Rodney King : Patty Hearst

Dueling Suicide Cults
Heaven's Gate : People's Temple

Dueling Museums
Frederick's of Hollywood Lingerie Museum : Tattoo Art Museum

Dueling Legacies
The movies : Sourdough bread

New York

One of L.A.'s peculiar pleasures is watching New York journalists cruise into town, spend a couple of days trawling for ironies, then grandly spoon out clichés about the city as if they were beluga caviar. In last Sunday's *New York Times,* hotshot reporter Alex Kuczynski did a piece on Hollywood's snooty reaction to the Robert Blake murder trial. Near the end, she was talking to Blake's lawyer Harland Braun and quoted his trenchant insight into L.A.: "This is a town where truth is fantasy, where you'll do anything to get a part, where you'll go to a restaurant where the food is lousy just because everyone else is going there."

Wow, Alex, great stuff. But are you sure he's not talking about New York?

John Powers

Being a newspaperman myself, I think I understand this evidently irresistible urge that Eastern journalists have to throw another cliché at Los Angeles. They are sent out here on expense accounts to write stories that will please their editors, and their editors want to be told that Los Angeles is a dreadful place, so they will feel better about living in New York or Boston or Philadelphia, especially in February.

The reporter settles into the Beverly Hills Hotel in an ambience of cantaloupe and is taken out to Malibu on his first night to a freestyle moonlit party where he is intoxicated by palatable California wines and surprisingly literate and friendly natives, including relays of suntanned beach girls. The next morning he wakes up in his hotel room with his New England conscience and a hangover and feels guilty for having had such a wonderful time. He looks out his window and can't see the Empire State Building and is homesick. He calls room service and orders a Bloody Mary to exorcise his anomie, and while waiting for it . . . he pecks out a few hundred words to reassure the folks back home that Nathanael West was right—that their correspondent is in the capital of kitsch at this very moment, wasting his talent away among Rotarians and retired chiropractors and mindless TV actresses in a plastic wasteland.

Jack Smith

As a native New Yorker, both cities have always been part of an Inscrutable West that fills me with a deep, almost sexual longing. Driving in from LAX, I always laugh with joy. Driving in from SFX, I weep with joy.

Robert Lipsyte

[In Los Angeles] I met screenwriters and script doctors . . . anonymous men and women paid money by the sack, some of them with points on the gross, and realized they might chuck it all for the thrill of seeing their names in print, even on a letter to the editor of the *Los Angeles Times*. We "serious" writers [from New York] on the other hand, were perfectly willing, even eager, to sell out if only they would tell us where to go to do it.

Los Angeles writers and New York writers want to be each other. I liked the idea so much I proposed it as a story to William Shawn, then editor of the *New Yorker*—known to me by his nickname "Sir"—but he shot it down, saying it was "a bit incestuous." Oh well, he probably thought I was losing it in the L.A. sun.

Richard Reeves

Imagine a writer who has grown up in New York or Chicago and has published a couple of novels about life in those cities, to much critical acclaim, working through the winter months in his heated flat, getting up now and then to look out the window at the snow or have a shot of booze or beget a child, but there is nothing to lure him outdoors and away from his typewriter. He has to write at least until spring comes, the sun melts the snow, and the birds begin to sing. . . . What about the writer who has grown up in Los Angeles? Why can't he write a great novel about growing up in Los Angeles? Because you can't write a serious novel about growing up in La La Land, can you? About surfing and starlit rides in an open convertible and orange trees and balmy weather and scads of healthy beach girls? Where's the tension? Where's the conflict? Where's the misery?

Jack Smith

During the years I grew up in the Bay Area, I was continually conscious of the rivalry, not to say war, between San Francisco and Los Angeles—it was a central tenet of the philosophy of my favorite San Francisco columnist, Herb Caen.

And then I moved to Los Angeles and discovered that Angelenos were sublimely unaware of this state of affairs, regarded San Francisco as a nice place to visit for food and sex, and were instead focused on the rivalry between themselves and New York, as exemplified by the title of a book by a Los Angeles columnist, Jack Smith: *The Big Orange*.

And then I moved to New York and discovered that New Yorkers were not only unaware of any cross-continental rivalry, but supremely convinced that they were living in the Absolute Center of the Known Universe.

Meredith Brody

When it's five below in New York, it's 78 in Los Angeles, and when it's 110 in New York, it's 78 in Los Angeles. There are 2 million interesting people in New York—and only 78 in Los Angeles.

Neil Simon

Yes, there are vast areas of the Los Angeles basin which are drab, in common with urban wasteland across the country, but nowhere in L.A. are there to be found the deep, hopeless, barbarous slums, the cold water tenements of rats, roaches and garbage that splotch the complexion of New York.

Norman Corwin

The air [in Los Angeles] is delicious, tangy, and when you return after a stint in a place like New York you can eat it.

John R. Coyne, Jr.

People who say they hate New York City generally avoid New York City, but people who say they hate Los Angeles take up defiant residence in its hardest neighborhoods to chronicle their resistance to its empty and awful culture, and sometimes, for their pains, find themselves honored with grant money.

Judith Lewis

If New York was the melting pot of Europe, Los Angeles was the melting pot of the United States.

John Gregory Dunne

New Yorker *cartoon: Wife to husband as he waters plants next to swimming pool, "You know what I like about L.A.? We don't have to be interesting anymore."*

Hollywood has many, many excesses and a great many not very nice people, but that's true anywhere. The difference between Hollywood and New York is that it's all out in the open.

Hugh Hefner

If you want to be a success in Hollywood, be sure and go to New York.

Bert Lahr

LA is the loneliest and most brutal of American cities; New York gets godawful cold in the winter but there's a feeling of wacky comradeship somewhere in some streets. LA is a jungle.

Jack Kerouac

New York is the city that says, "Fuck you!"; L.A. says, "Fuck me."

Deanne Stillman

I met S. J. Perelman at Gilbert's Books in Hollywood in the '60s—he was back in the literature section. I asked him, "I thought you hated Los Angeles, yet here you are!" Perelman said, "I come back every twenty years just to renew my disgust."

Gary Owens

Los Angeles is where you have to be if you want to be an actor. You have no choice. You go there or New York. I flipped a coin about it. It came up New York, so I flipped again. When you're starting out to be an actor, who wants to go where it's cold and miserable and be poor there?

Harrison Ford

How can you trust a city where the businessmen and the ballplayers all wear pinstripes?

Patt Morrison

Howard Draper had lost his New York survival mechanism. Fifteen years in the laid-back passive-aggressive vacuum of Southern California had stripped him of his protective reflexes. After finishing Wharton he had spent two years with an investment-banking firm on Wall Street. Armed with the noblesse oblige of Andover and Yale, he was able to roll with what punches the city threw at him. But he was twenty-five then, and he had not yet had his nervous system dry-cleaned by the California sun.

Peter Lefcourt

During a cocktail party [in San Francisco] the chatter drifted around to a familiar subject—The Best Place to Live—and a visiting New Yorker remarked typically, "As far as I'm concerned, there's no place as lovely as New York in October." Quietly cut in Edith MacInnis: "It's always October—in San Francisco."

Herb Caen

San Francisco is an inclusive, tolerant, free-spirited place—until you make a joke or say something "incorrect." I'll stay in New York, thank you.

Michael Musto

The following exchange occurred after it was announced that New York and San Francisco were finalists for the 2012 Olympics:

San Francisco is a very nice small town.

NEW YORK MAYOR MICHAEL BLOOMBERG

[He's a] rookie mayor uttering words frankly out of turn.

SAN FRANCISCO MAYOR WILLIE BROWN

A San Franciscan thinks of his city as being on the same level as New York, not as being in the same state as Los Angeles.

Herb Caen

Better to be a critic in San Francisco for the wanna-bes than in New York for the has-beens.

Barbara Bladen

You can relax and listen in San Francisco. You can't in New York.

Ralph Gleason

San Francisco, since the earliest years of the American occupancy, has always been a money town. When John Jacob Astor was clipping dimes in the trade in New York real estate and Commodore Vanderbilt was ferrying passengers to Staten Island for a shilling, the wife of San Francisco's mayor William K. Garrison was pouring tea from a solid gold service, the first such in America, and J. W. Tucker, the town's first jeweler, was advertising silver watches that weighed a full honest pound, since no miner could be found who would carry one that weighed less.

Lucius Beebe

When I got to Los Angeles I didn't know a soul. People in New York said You're mad for going there if you don't know anybody and you can't drive. They said At least go to San Francisco if you want to go West.

David Hockney

America's two great drinking towns are San Francisco and New York. The tradition is studiously observed. "Scotch and water—make that J & B." "Right." You lay your money on the bar. In San Francisco, you pay by the drink. In New York, you can run a check. The difference is you can leave your change on the bar in San Francisco and nobody will steal it.

Herb Caen

The most irritating thing of all is that New Yorkers really don't care what you say about their city.

Russell Baker

It took me little time to discover that belonging to the best society in San Francisco cut no ice in New York.

Gertrude Atherton

A Southern Californian conducts San Francisco's symphony. A Northern Californian edits the *Los Angeles Times Book Review.* The time has come for California to bind up her wounds and unite to face our true foes—to the East.

David Kipen

New York is at once cosmopolitan and parochial, a compendium of sentimental certainties. It is in fact the most sentimental of the world's great cities—in its self-congratulation a kind of San Francisco of the East.

John Gregory Dunne

Sonnet on a Publishing Theme

Sing, muse, or at least contrive a rap
To tell the strife that nearly tore the map.
Two hosts contended long and without cease:
California in the West; against her, the Northeast.

Joan-like, Hester Prynne arrayed her forces,
While Zorro's broke her lines and stole her horses
Till, in this pitched yet literary fray,
It looked as if the West would win the day.

But, just when we stood to teach the East a lesson,
The West collapsed in warfare internecine.
Dissent put us to rout and sealed our fate,
As the Bay turned south an unrequited hate.

Bay readers, mark me, though my song grow venomy:
Forget L.A.—Manhattan is the enemy.

David Kipen

Nomenclature

Southern California place names tend to be slightly zany and vaguely low-rent, like the train stops announced by Mel Blanc on "The Jack Benny Program": "Anaheim, Azusa, and Cucamonga." Then there are Lomita, Artesia, Arcadia, Tarzana (yes, founded by Edgar Rice Burroughs), Panorama City, Cudahy, Chino, Sepulveda, Monrovia, Covina, Gardena ("Freeway City"), Pacoima, Arleta, Rialto, Pomona, Oxnard, Glendora, Reseda, Toluca, Tujunga, Yorba Linda, La Verne, Chula Vista, Studio City, and Canoga Park. Then you have your *Ranchos*: Rancho Cordova, Rancho Cucamonga, Rancho Santa Fe; your *El*s: El Monte, El Toro, El Cajon, El Centro ("Where the sun spends the winter"); your *La*s: La Habra, La Puente, La Crescenta, La Mirada; your *San*s: San Pedro, San Fernando, San Bernardino; your *Los*es: Los Angeles, Los Nietos, Los Serranos, Los Alamitos; your *Del*s: Del Mar, Del Sur, Corona del Mar, Marina del Rey, and your beaches: Hermosa, Redondo, and Laguna.

Many Bay Area place names are also Spanish, of course—San Francisco, San Jose, Contra Costa, San Mateo, San Rafael—but there's a high incidence of the studiously British: Belvedere, Atherton, Sunnyvale, Concord, Richmond, Stanford, Walnut Creek, Brisbane, Millbrae, Belmont, Burlingame, Hillsborough, and Fairfax.

In 1579, Sir Frances Drake claimed San Francisco Bay and its environs for Queen Elizabeth, naming it New Albion. In 1776, Spanish settlers founded San Francisco, calling it Yerba Buena— "good herb." Yerba Buena renamed itself San Francisco in 1847. In 1781, Spanish settlers founded the Pueblo of Los Angeles. Its full name was "El Pueblo de Nuestra Señora la Reina de Los Angeles de Porciuncula"—"The Town of Our Lady the Queen of the Angels of Porciuncula." Both cities have been given a series of nicknames since, but Los Angeles leads in number, if not originality.

Los Angeles Nicknames

Autopia
Double Dubuque (H. Allen Smith)
Moronia (H. L. Mencken)
Cuckooland (Will Rogers)
Smog Town
Smogville
The Land of Fruits and Nuts
Lotus Land
A miner's camp in Lotus Land (F. Scott Fitzgerald)
La La Land
La La Wood

Libido Land

Babylon

Shakeytown

Nowhere City

City of Dreams

City of Broken Dreams

City of Angels

City of Fallen Angels

City of Angles

City of Dreadful Joy (Aldous Huxley)

City of the Living Dead (S. J. Perelman)

Fake Tomato Factory

Kingdom of Sprawl

Lozangeles (Herb Caen)

Plastic Paradise

Queen City of Plastic (Norman Mailer)

Paradise with a Lobotomy (Neil Simon)

Flake Town

Kitsch City

Forty Suburbs in Search of a City

Ellay

El Lay

Tinseltown

Iowa-by-the-Sea

Disneyland Restaged by Dante (Robin Williams)

Hollyweird

Ho Town

Dottyville-on-the-Pacific (W. C. Fields)

Joy's Metropolis (Aldous Huxley)

Off-Ramp Acres . . . Asphalt-by-the-Sea . . . Smogadena . . . Pornadelphia . . . Newer Jersey . . . Unknown Actorville . . . Hellholia. (Jay Leno)

L os Angeles has also been dubbed the Porn, Street Gang, Serial Killer, and Freeway Shooting Capital of the United States.

Herb Caen referred to Angelenos as "Southlandish Characters."

Misnomer: The "Los Angeles River" is actually a concrete culvert devoid of water most of the time. Political prankster Dick Tuck once advised city fathers to "either fill it up or paint it blue."

If there is a river within a thousand miles of Riverside Drive, I never saw it. It's like everything else out here: Endless scorched boulevards, lined with one-story stores, shops, bowling alleys, skating rinks, tacos drive-ins, all of them shaped not like rectangles but like trapezoids. . . .

Tom Wolfe

San Francisco Nicknames

Baghdad-by-the-Bay (Herb Caen)
Frisco
Manhattan Light (Ian Shoales)
The City
The City by the Bay
The City that Knows Chow (Herb Caen)
The Pearl of the Pacific
Heaven on the Half-Shell
Queen City of the West
Fog Town
The City of Miracles (Gelett Burgess)

It was the sailors who first called this port "Frisco," as they called San Diego "Dago," San Pedro "Pedro" and Oakland by several unprintable epithets (that has changed, too). They also thought of this city as the best liberty this side of Port Said, by which they meant they could get screwed and tattooed and maybe even shanghaied but never bored. . . . Frisco was a place for heroic hangovers, prodigious deeds and Herculean lies, all printed immediately by fuzz-cheeked reporters, and only the pompous asses of Nob Hill insisted on "San Francisco, sir, if you please."

Herb Caen

Somebody . . . phoned me a few days ago to ask how I felt about the growing use of "Frisco," I having written a book called *Don't Call It Frisco,* and I said it don't make me no never mind any longer. I don't care what people call us as long as they call us, besides which "Frisco" is a salty nickname, redolent of the days when we had a bustling waterfront.

Herb Caen (1993)

As Herb Caen got close to the end of his life, he rescinded the fatwah on calling San Francisco "Frisco." But he was so powerful that no one was sure he was serious, so the prohibition remains in de facto effect. Like Lenny Bruce's description of the gangster who dies at the bar: It took three days before the waiters got up the nerve to pull the diamond rings off his fingers.

Bruce Bellingham

San Franciscans don't have to worry about their city being called "Frisco" anymore. Everyone except flight attendants (who call it "San Fran") calls San Francisco "Sanfer Sisko." But, please, don't call it "Sisko."

Rob Morse

Remember, always call it Frisco. In Sally Stanford's book about Frisco in the '20s and '30s, she says everyone called it Frisco 'til right after World War II, when GIs who had embarked from San Francisco for the Pacific settled there and then pretentiously insisted, "Don't Call It Frisco." Herb Caen wrote a book called *Don't Call It Frisco,* but he had his tongue firmly in his cheek. Caen wrote for the *San Francisco Chronicle* all his life and was a humanist and a humorist, something that L.A. has always lacked in its newspapers. I love both cities.

Art Fein

A Selective History
of California

COLD WAR

1849

Evening Post begins long tradition of New York condescension toward City by the Bay when it reports that "the people of San Francisco are mad, stark mad."

1876

Investment banker Adolph Sutro is one of many witnesses reporting mysterious, cigar-shaped craft over San Francisco.

1889

Oscar Wilde performs in San Francisco and quips: "When people disappear they always seem to turn up in San Francisco."

1899

Hotel Nymphia opens in San Francisco. Originally "Hotel Nymphomania," owner changes name at request of city fathers.

1906

San Francisco quake leaves 700 dead, 300,000 homeless, and destroys 28,000 buildings, many from fires allowed to burn to collect insurance. Religious fanatics declare quake divine punishment for San Francisco's rampant sin.

1914

San Francisco is last major U.S. city to outlaw prostitution.

1924

Bel Air subdivision opened near Los Angeles by Alphonzo E. Bell, who refuses to sell lots to movie people.

1927

"Exaltation," signal work of "Disumbrationist School" (depicting native woman peeling banana), having been widely hailed by art critics, is exposed as hoax creation of *Los Angeles Times* literary critic Paul Jordan Smith.

1930

Olvera Street market in downtown Los Angeles, billed as authentic remnant of old pueblo, created as tourist attraction.

1937

First proposed in 1869 by town-eccentric Emperor Norton, Golden Gate Bridge opens, linking San Francisco and Marin County. Suicide jumps begin immediately.

1943

"Quiz of Two Cities" radio show pits teams of contestants from San Francisco and Los Angeles, intensifying civic rivalry.

1944

Bing Crosby's "San Fernando Valley" tops U.S. charts, attracting war-weary GIs, though lyrics don't actually say anything nice about Valley.

1948

Newcomer Marilyn Monroe crowned "Artichoke Queen" by Watsonville Kiwanis Club.

Evelyn Waugh's *The Loved One* satirizes Forest Lawn ("Whispering Glades") and Calabasas Pet Cemetery ("Happier Hunting Ground"). Author describes book as "a little nightmare produced by the unaccustomed high-living of a brief visit to Hollywood."

1950

At Shrine Auditorium in Los Angeles, Scientology founder L. Ron Hubbard introduces Sonia Bianca as first "Clear." Bianca proceeds to embarrass Hubbard and disappoint audience by failing to identify color of his tie after he turns away from her.

1954

San Francisco's Joe DiMaggio weds Hollywood's Marilyn Monroe. When they divorce 274 days later he complains, "It's no fun being married to an electric light."

1955

Los Angeles pressure group "Sanity in Art" claims abstract paintings contain maps of secret U.S. military installations.

Ronald Reagan hosts live broadcast at grand opening of Disneyland in Anaheim. Theme park taps into what Kirse Granat May calls "child imagination market" and is indeed biggest step to date toward infantilization of America.

1958

Brooklyn Dodgers and New York Giants move to Los Angeles and San Francisco, respectively. Dodgers owner Walter O'Malley orders new stadium built without drinking fountains to maximize beverage sales.

San Francisco Chronicle columnist Herb Caen, influenced by orbiting Sputnik, coins term "beatnik," variation on Kerouac's "beat generation," to describe poetry-spouting, bongo-playing denizens of San Francisco coffee houses.

1961

Drag queen José Sarria runs for San Francisco Board of Supervisors and gets 5,600 votes.

1965

When El Segundo (Los Angeles County) Rotary Club sponsors contest for city motto, high school student suggests: "El Segundo: Where the Sewer Meets the Sea."

San Francisco Diggers dispense free food and briefly operate "free store" ("just come in and take what you need"). The group also performs street theater and "art happenings" as part of revolutionary "anarcho direct action."

1967

"Summer of Love" in San Francisco's Haight-Ashbury (a.k.a. "Hashbury"). San Francisco police chief Thomas Cahill dubs hippies "The Love Generation" (they are also called "flower children" and "hairy freaks"). Young seekers make pilgrimage to city to join "worldwide spiritual awakening" while hit record "San Francisco" by Scott McKenzie urges youth to "come to San Francisco" and "wear some flowers in your hair." Middle-class tourists flock to scene and poet Rod McKuen issues T-shirt bearing slogan: "Love San Francisco, Haight Ashbury."

San Francisco city cop Bob Geary successfully sues for right to carry ventriloquist's dummy named Brendan O'Smarty on his beat.

Proposal to divide California into two independent states originates in San Francisco.

1970

UC Berkeley awards first "Arts in Magic" bachelor's degree in United States.

1971

Sylmar (San Fernando Valley) earthquake kills eighty and wreaks $500 million in damage. Religious fanatics declare quake divine punishment for L.A.'s rampant sin.

1973

Los Angeles Board of Supervisors declines offer from the "Druids of Los Angeles" to save city's art treasures from future earthquakes by teleporting them to a safer location.

California performance artist Barry Le Va runs back and forth inside small room, bouncing off walls and splattering them with own blood, then presents entire room as "art."

1980

Arson fire destroys Saudi sheikh Muhammad al-Fassi's $7 million, thirty-eight-room, Sunset Boulevard mansion in Beverly Hills. Sickly green structure with anatomically correct statuary (complete with painted-on pubic hair) attracts hordes of tourists and causes traffic jams. After first suspecting disgruntled neighbors, police arrest former chauffeur who set fire to conceal theft of art objects. Remains of house are demolished and lot subdivided.

Grand opening of Robert Schuller's Crystal Cathedral in Garden Grove (Orange County). With construction cost of $16 million, seating for two thousand inside and room for more in parking lot for "drive-in worship," inaugural event is not a religious service but a $1,000-a-plate fund-raiser featuring diva

Beverly Sills, who is paid $15,000 for performance.

1981

Estranged wife of Saudi arms merchant Adnan Khashoggi sues for $2.5 billion divorce settlement, but L.A. court throws out case on ground that Mrs. Khashoggi, a former resident of England, had moved to Van Nuys solely to take advantage of California's community-property laws. Attorney Marvin Mitchelson quips to reporters: "We are happy the case wasn't sent to Saudi Arabia, where we could lose our case and our heads as well!"

1982

L.A.'s "Coroner to the Stars" Thomas Noguchi fired for mismanagement and misuse of office for personal gain.

Moon Unit Zappa's hit record "Valley Girl" adds phrases "gag me with a spoon," "fer sure," "grody to the max," and "barf me out" to national lexicon.

Jane Fonda announces she will produce exercise video. Asked why at Beverly Hills press conference, former anti-capitalist replies: "Money!"

1983

When Irvine Company proposes housing development in Newport Beach designed for families earning $30,000 a year, a resident complains:

"Do we really want this kind of element here? People already get upset when they can't join our yacht clubs. At that level of income we're talking about non-skilled labor, and they can't afford to pick up a credit card at Nieman-Marcus."

Beach Boys drummer Dennis Wilson, only member of group who actually *surfs,* drowns alongside dock in Marina del Rey.

1984

San Francisco hosts Democratic National Convention. Reverend Jerry Falwell, who arrives in what he calls the "Wild Kingdom" a week in advance to discuss "family issues," is greeted by "Sisters of Perpetual Indulgence," group of gay men dressed as nuns on roller skates, who threaten "exorcism" of Falwell.

L.A. Olympics open with David Wolper extravaganza featuring eighty-four pianos playing Gershwin. To surprise of Angelenos and disappointment of San Franciscans, games go off without hitch and L.A. freeways are not crowded all day.

L.A. mayor Tom Bradley dedicates $123 million Tom Bradley International Terminal at LAX, named in Bradley's honor by unanimous vote of Los Angeles airport commissioners, all of whom are Bradley appointees.

1987

Environmental study of Grand Canyon's atmosphere finds traces of methyl chloroform, chemical used by L.A. aerospace and electronics manufacturers, prompting study's author to note: "Even when you've left L.A., you can't escape L.A. air."

When Whittier earthquake shakes KNBC–Los Angeles television studio during live broadcast, newscaster Kent Shocknek dives under anchor desk but keeps talking, so viewers see only gyrating furniture. In response to charge he overreacted, Shocknek replies, "I reported the news. If I disappointed those gore fans who wanted to see a klieg light come crashing down and split my skull open, I'm sorry."

To cash in on Pope John Paul II's visit to Los Angeles, local entrepreneur prints thousands of T-shirts with slogan "Los Angeles Welcomes the Pope" in Spanish, but incorrectly uses the noun *la papa,* so shirts read, "Los Angeles Welcomes the Potato."

1988

Mod singer turned restaurateur Sonny Bono, 53, radicalized after enduring bureaucratic red tape in remodeling restaurant, registers to vote for first time (Republican) and is elected mayor of Palm Springs.

1989

Loma Prieta earthquake devastates San Francisco Bay area during World Series game between San Francisco Giants and Oakland A's, causing sixty-two deaths and $6 billion in damage. Religious fanatics declare quake divine punishment for San Francisco's rampant sin.

San Francisco Port Commission abandons project to plant palm trees along earthquake-ravaged Embarcadero Freeway amid protests that palm trees are "too L.A."

Zsa Zsa Gabor sentenced to three days in jail, 120 hours community service, and psychiatric examination for slapping Beverly Hills policeman.

Actor-activist and recently appointed Malibu honorary mayor Martin Sheen declares Malibu a "nuclear-free zone, a sanctuary for aliens and the homeless, and a protected environment for all life, wild and tame."

Diversity trumps animal rights and health regulation when Berkeley City Council passes ordinance exempting miniature potbelly pigs (favored as pets by Vietnamese voters) from ban on "livestock" within city limits.

1991

When televangelist Jimmy Swaggart is stopped by Indio (Southern California) police with known prostitute in car at same moment multiple earthquakes shake area, scientists name the series of temblors "The Jimmy Swaggart Swarm" in his honor.

Home video showing police assaulting motorist Rodney King recorded by amateur George Holliday, who sells it to Los Angeles TV station for $500. After video airs worldwide, Holliday complains of bad deal and briefly threatens lawsuit for $100 million. He later serves as pitchman for commercial video titled "Shoot News and Make Money with Your Camcorder."

In *L.A. Story,* when Steve Martin tells girlfriend her breasts feel strange she replies, "That's because they're real."

1992

After unsuccessful Senate campaign, Sonny Bono tells reporters: "I can't articulate it. God, if I could I would love it. But you know that's something I guess I'm going to have to learn, is how to throw that articulation out."

Potrero Hill branch of San Francisco Public Library allows North American Man Boy Love Association, pedophile group that openly promotes sex between adult men and minor boys, to hold meetings there until KRON-TV reporter infiltrates group and exposes policy. Instead of excluding NAMBLA, library merely requires it to submit updated application. Explains library official:

"The American Nazi party could probably meet in the main library since we have security there."

Marin County is first U.S. jurisdiction to create "fragrance-free zone" when it bans perfume wearers from certain seats at county park board meetings.

1993

Bob's Big Boy on Riverside Drive (San Fernando Valley) declared State Point of Historical Interest.

For $100 per hour, UC Berkeley psychologist offers role-playing counseling for people who have "issues" with their houses (i.e. clients voice anxieties, house responds).

1994

Northridge quake shakes Los Angeles area, kills fifty-seven and inflicts billions of dollars in property damage. Religious fanatics declare quake divine punishment for L.A.'s rampant sin.

One of five Southern California graffiti vandals arrested in San Francisco over July 4th weekend complains, "We came here to contribute something to this town, and we end up in jail!"

Ruling on whether proposed subway station should be built inside San Francisco International Airport or just outside it, San Francisco judge rejects complaint that ad placed by "inside" advocates is in poor taste. Ad reads: "Taking the train almost to the airport is like not coming."

Berkeley chapter of the "Lesbian Avengers" stages "Bobbit-que," named for Lorena Bobbitt (who cut off husband's penis and threw it from a moving car), to protest state laws allowing a man to rape his wife with impunity. The women serve up "barbequed penis" (actually turkey hot dogs) while chanting, "YES MEANS YES, NO MEANS NO, OR ELSE THAT PENIS HAS TO GO!"

Sonny Bono elected to U.S. Congress. To charges he lacks legislative experience, Representative Bono replies: "People have said to me, 'You can't write songs. You can't play an instrument.' But I've got ten gold records! I can do this job."

1995
City Health Department orders fumigation of San Francisco Opera House for scabies after violinists complain of having to lay down bows during performances in order to scratch.

1996
In *60 Minutes* interview, comedian George Burns takes L.A. custom of dropping names of one's celebrity neighbors to new low when he boasts to Ed Bradley that late wife and comedy partner Gracie Allen is entombed in Forest

Lawn "right next to Eric von Stroheim!"

1997

After death of Princess Diana, Representative Bono introduces legislation making harassment by paparazzi a federal crime.

San Francisco Human Rights Commission rules that The Café, a gay and lesbian bar, illegally discriminated against a straight man and woman who were ejected for necking on the premises. According to witnesses, bartender told couple, "What you're doing is very offensive to people here."

Mill Valley high-school student Ari Hoffman wins first prize at Marin County Science Fair for study on effect of radiation on fruit flies, but is disqualified for cruelty after revelation that thirty-five of two hundred insects died during three-month experiment.

1998

Representative Sonny Bono, 62, killed in skiing accident at Lake Tahoe resort. During nationally televised funeral service, he is eulogized by former wife and performing partner Cher, who stands before flag-draped coffin holding sheaf of notes and declares, "Please excuse my papers, but I've been writing this stupid eulogy for the last forty-eight hours!"

2000

Berkeley celebrates thirty-first anniversary of People's Park with performance by dancing nudists.

Green Party presidential candidate Ralph Nader receives more votes in Berkeley than Republican candidate George W. Bush.

2001

San Francisco extends health-insurance benefits to gender-switching municipal employees. Up to $50,000 will be paid for either male-to-female or female-to-male surgery, plus hormone therapy and other related procedures.

San Francisco D.A.'s office launches "Hairdresser Project," initiative enlisting beauticians as domestic violence monitors to surreptitiously inspect clients' scalps and faces for signs of abuse and report them to police.

Defense attorney Nedra Ruiz cries, shouts, kicks jury box, and gets on all fours during San Francisco dog-mauling trial. Her client, Marjorie Knoller, denies responsibility for death of victim Diane Whipple, suggesting that Whipple's perfume may have brought on attacks from Knoller's two dogs, Bane and Hera. Knoller is convicted of second degree murder, involuntary manslaughter, and "keeping an animal that causes death." After her client is sentenced to four years in prison, attorney Ruiz concedes she may have miscalculated: "I have to think that perhaps my mistakes contributed to this terrible, terrible [sic] unjust verdict."

San Francisco Chronicle executive editor Phil Bronstein attacked by seven-foot-long Komodo dragon while on private tour of Los Angeles Zoo with wife, actress Sharon Stone. "It's L.A. I was just taking a meeting," Bronstein quips from hospital bed after undergoing surgery to reattach severed tendons and rebuild casing of crushed big toe.

2002
Roy Rogers Museum relocates from Victorville, California, to Branson, Missouri, citing drop-off of interest after screen cowboy's death and implying that Southern Californians are unworthy of such cultural nourishment as taxidermied Trigger and tooled-leather portraits of Roy and Dale Evans.

Slogans seen by journalist Josh Harkinson at San Francisco peace rally:

Smoke Iraqi Pot, Not Iraqi People

Tango for Protest

Grannies Against Dead Children

Another Queer Yogic Jew Against War

Future Librarian Against War—Information Not Decimation

Transsexual Lesbian Vegan Epidemiologist Punk for Peace

Beat L.A., Not Iraq! Go Giants!

After security guard at a Santa Monica (Los Angeles County) mall requires woman to cover cleavage while nursing infant, Berkeley sets world record for mass breast-feeding when 1,128 nursing mothers simultaneously suckle their babies at Berkeley Community Theater.

"American Taliban" John Walker Lindh from Marin County confirms prejudices: It is widely believed that "Jihad Johnny" isn't just a resident, but the inevitable product of what Hoover Institution research fellow Shelby Steele calls Marin's "whispy relativism." Salon.com's headline is more direct: "Insta-Traitor: Just add hot-tub water and stir."

Berkeley cab drivers forced to take sensitivity training to better serve such "special-needs" customers as the elderly or those in wheelchairs.

UC Berkeley students taking male sexuality course get "hands-on" experience during "field trip" to gay male strip bar when instructor participates in sex act onstage.

Berkeley toddler peace march protests impending war with Iraq. Most protesters are preschoolers accompanied by older children.

"Why can't George Bush and Saddam Hussein go fight a duel instead of making a whole bunch of others fight," asks one child. "Bush needs a time-out—permanently," says another.

Student organizers of 9/11 memorial at UC Berkeley attempt to exclude American flags, "The Star Spangled Banner," and red, white, and blue ribbons from event as "too patriotic."

O. J. Simpson files lawsuit in Los Angeles seeking reversal of $33 million civil judgment against him for killings of Nicole Brown Simpson and Ron Goldman. Suit claims verdict subjects Simpson to "relentless ridicule."

2003

Confused forty-eight-year-old man pleads no contest to charges he destroyed homosexual-oriented books in San Francisco Public Library. Among mistaken targets were works of Peter Gay and Gay Talese, and book about the Enola Gay, plane that dropped atomic bomb on Hiroshima.

In form of civil disobedience novel even for activist Bay Area, San Francisco protesters calling themselves "Pukers4Peace" stage "vomit-in" outside city hall to demonstrate that war in Iraq makes them sick. The group splatters their "message" at 7 a.m., but by midafternoon there are still pools of vomit everywhere, causing pedestrians to hold noses as they pass. "My puddle is the longest-lasting one," declares one UC Berkeley student proudly.

Santa Monica bans smoking in city parks.

A San Francisco attorney files suit in Marin County Superior Court to outlaw sale of Oreos to children because the cookies contain trans-fatty acids.

Arnold Schwartzenegger elected Governor of California after unprecedented recall of incumbent Gray Davis. Vote reflects ongoing political divide in California: Orange County overwhelmingly backs recall, Los Angeles County is narrowly split, while San Francisco Bay Area is sole region in state where majority votes to keep Davis in office. Field of over one hundred candidates includes porn star Mary Carey, former child actor and security guard Gary Coleman, and *Hustler Magazine* publisher Larry Flynt, who says of his candidacy, "California is the most progressive state in the union. I don't think anyone will have a problem with a smut peddler as governor."

Index

About the Author

Jon Winokur is the author of various books, including *The Traveling Curmudgeon*. Though he lives in Los Angeles, he has somehow managed to stay above the fray.

SASQUATCH BOOKS
SEATTLE

51695

9 781570 613784

Current Clinical Strategies

Handbook of Anesthesiology

2004-2005 Edition

Mark R. Ezekiel, MD, MS

Current Clinical Strategies Publishing

www.ccspublishing.com/ccs

Digital Book and Updates

Purchasers of this book may download the digital book and updates for Palm, Pocket PC, Windows and Macintosh. The digital books can be downloaded at the Current Clinical Strategies Publishing Internet site:

www.ccspublishing.com/ccs/anes.htm

Current Clinical Strategies Publishing
27071 Cabot Road
Laguna Hills, California 92653
Phone: 800-331-8227
Fax: 800-965-9420
Internet: www.ccspublishing.com/ccs
E-mail: info@ccspublishing.com

Printed in USA   ISBN 1-929622-49-X

Table of Contents

Resuscitation Algorithms (ACLS)

Primary and Secondary ABCD Survey

1. **Primary ABCD survey**
   A. **Focus:** basic CPR and defibrillation.
   B. **Airway**: assess and manage the airway with noninvasive devices.
   C. **Breathing**: assess and manage breathing (look, listen, and feel). If the patient is not breathing, give two slow breaths.
   D. **Circulation**: assess and manage the circulation; if no pulse, start CPR.
   E. **Defibrillation**: assess and manage rhythm/defibrillation; shock VF/VT up to 3 times (200 J, 300 J, 360 J, or equivalent biphasic) if necessary.
2. **Secondary ABCD survey**
   A. **Focus:** more advanced assessments and treatments
   B. **Airway**: place airway device as soon as possible.
   C. **Breathing**: assess adequacy of airway device placement and performance; secure airway device; confirm effective oxygenation and ventilation.
   D. **Circulation**: establish IV access; administer drugs appropriate for rhythm and condition.
   E. **Differential Diagnosis**: search for and treat identified reversible causes.
      A. Potentially reversible causes include: hypoxia, hypovolemia, hyperkalemia, hypokalemia and metabolic disorders, hypothermia, tension pneumothorax, tamponade, toxic/therapeutic disturbances, and thromboembolic/mechanical obstruction.

Ventricular Fibrillation and Pulseless Ventricular Tachycardia

1. **Primary ABCD**
2. **Assess rhythm after 3 shocks**; continue CPR for persistent or recurrent VF/VT.
3. **Secondary ABCD**
4. **Epinephrine** 1.0 mg IVP, repeat every 3-5 minutes, or vasopressin 40 units IV, single dose, 1 time only.
5. **Resume attempts to defibrillate,** 360 J within 30-60 seconds.
6. **Consider antiarrhythmics.**
   A. Amiodarone 300 mg IVP or
   B. Lidocaine 1.5 mg/kg IVP, repeat every 3-5 minutes to a total loading dose of 3 mg/kg or
   C. Magnesium sulfate 1-2 grams IV (if Torsades de Pointes or suspected hypomagnesemic state or severe refractory VF) or
   D. Procainamide (if above ineffective) 30 mg/min to max total of 17 mg/kg.
7. **Defibrillate** 360 J, 30-60 sec after each dose of medication.
8. Repeat Amiodarone 150 mg IVP (if recurrent VF/VT), up to max cumulative dose of 2200 mg IV in 24 hours
9. Consider bicarbonate 1 mEq/kg (if known preexisting bicarbonate responsive acidosis, overdose with tricyclic antidepressant, if intubated and continued long arrest interval, hypoxic lactic acidosis, or hypercarbic acidosis).

Asystole

1. **Primary ABCD survey.**
2. **Confirm asystole in two or more leads.** If rhythm is unclear and possible ventricular fibrillation, defibrillate as for VF.
3. **Secondary ABCD survey.**
4. **Consider possible causes:** hypoxia, hyperkalemia, hypokalemia, hypothermia, preexisting acidosis, drug overdose and myocardial infarction.
5. Consider transcutaneous cardiac pacing (if considered, perform immediately)
6. Epinephrine 1.0 mg IVP, repeat every 3-5 minutes.
7. Atropine 1.0 mg IV, repeat every 3-5 minutes up to total dose of 0.04 mg/kg.
8. If asystole persists, consider withholding or ceasing resuscitative efforts.
   A. Before terminating resuscitative efforts consider quality of resuscitation, if atypical clinical features are present, or if support for cease-efforts protocols are in place.

Pulseless Electrical Activity (PEA)

1. **Pulseless electrical activity:** rhythm on monitor, without detectable pulse.
2. **Primary ABCD survey.**
3. **Secondary ABCD survey.**
4. **Consider possible causes:** hypoxia, hypovolemia, hyper-/hypokalemia and metabolic disorders, hypothermia, hydrogen ion acidosis, tension pneumothorax, cardiac tamponade, toxic/therapeutic disturbances (such as tricyclics, digitalis, beta-blockers, calcium channel blockers), pulmonary embolism, and acute myocardial infarction.
5. Epinephrine 1 mg IVP, repeat every 3 to 5 minutes.
6. Atropine 1 mg IVP (if PEA rate less then 60 bpm), repeat every 3 to 5 minutes as needed, to a total does of 0.04 mg/kg.

Bradycardia

1. Slow (absolute bradycardia <60 bpm) or relatively slow (rate less than expected relative to underlying conditions or cause).
2. **Primary ABCD survey.**
3. **Secondary ABCD survey.**
4. **If unstable** (considered unstable if chest pain, shortness of breath, decreased level of consciousness, hypotension, shock, pulmonary congestion, congested heart failure or acute MI are present) interventional sequence:
   A. Atropine 0.5-1.0 mg IVP repeated every 3-5 minutes up to 0.04 mg/kg (denervated transplanted hearts will not respond to atropine, go immediately to TCP, catecholamine infusion or both).
   B. Transcutaneous pacing (TCP) if available: if patient is symptomatic, do not delay TCP while awaiting IV access or atropine to take effect.
   C. Dopamine 5-20 mcg/kg/min.
   D. Epinephrine 2-10 mcg/min.
   E. Isoproterenol 2-10 mcg/min
5. **If stable**
   A. And not in type II or type III AV heart block, observe.
   B. If in type II or type III AV heart block, prepare for transvenous pacer or use

transcutaneous pacemaker until transvenous pacer is placed.

Tachycardia Overview

1. **Assess and evaluate patient.** Is patient stable or unstable? Are there serious signs and symptoms due to tachycardia?
   A. Consider unstable if chest pain, hypotension, CHF, myocardial infarction, ischemia, decreased level of consciousness, shock, dyspnea or pulmonary congestion are present.
2. **If unstable, prepare for immediate cardioversion.**
   A. Establish rapid heart rate as cause of signs and symptoms. If ventricular rate is >150 bpm, prepare for immediate cardioversion.
   B. Rate-related signs and symptoms seldom occur at rates < 150 bpm. May consider brief trial of medications based on specific arrhythmias. Immediate cardioversion is generally not needed if heart rate is <150 bpm.
   C. Have available: oxygen saturation monitor, suction device, IV line, intubation equipment.
   D. Premedicate whenever possible.
   E. **Synchronized cardioversion**
      1. Cardiovert with 100 J, 200 J, 300 J, 360 J. (PSVT and atrial flutter often respond to lower energy levels; start with 50 J).
      2. If delays in synchronization occur and clinical condition is critical, go immediately to unsynchronized shocks.
      3. May need to resynchronize after each cardioversion.
3. **If stable, treat according to arrhythmia.**
   A. Atrial fibrillation/atrial flutter.
   B. Narrow-complex tachycardias.
   C. Stable wide-complex tachycardia: unknown type.
   D. Stable monomorphic VT.
   E. Torsades de Pointes (polymorphic VT).

Tachycardia: Atrial Fibrillation and Atrial Flutter

1. **Evaluation focus: clinical features**
   A. Patient clinically unstable?
   B. Cardiac function impaired?
   C. Wolf-Parkinson-White (WPW) present?
   D. Duration <48 hours or >48 hours?
2. **Treatment focus: clinical evaluation**
   A. Treat unstable patients urgently.
   B. Control heart rate.
   C. Convert the rhythm.
   D. Provide anticoagulation.
3. **Treatment of atrial fibrillation/atrial flutter**
   A. **Rate Control**
      1. **If AF >48 hours** duration, use agents to convert rhythm with extreme caution in patients not receiving adequate anticoagulation because of possible embolic complications.
      2. **Preserved cardiac function**: use only one of the following agents: calcium channel blockers or beta-blockers.

   3. **Impaired heart (EF<40% or CHF)**: use only one of the following agents: digoxin, diltiazem, or amiodarone.
   4. **WPW with preserved heart function**: DC cardioversion or use one of the following primary antiarrhythmic agents: amiodarone, flecainide, procainamide, or sotalol.
   5. **WPW with impaired heart (EF <40% or CHF)**: DC cardioversion or amiodarone.

B. **Convert rhythm**
   1. **Preserved cardiac function with duration <48 hours**: consider cardioversion or any one of the following agents: amiodarone, ibutilide, flecainide, propafenone, or procainamide.
   2. **Preserved cardiac function with duration >48 hours**
      A. **No cardioversion**. Conversion of AF to NSR with drugs or shock may cause embolization of atrial thrombi unless patient has adequate anticoagulation. Use antiarrhythmic agents with extreme caution.
      B. **Delayed cardioversion:** anticoagulation for 3 weeks at proper levels before cardioverting, continue anticoagulation for 4 weeks.
      C. **Early cardioversion:** begin IV heparin at once, TEE to exclude atrial clot, then cardioversion with 24 hours, continue anticoagulation for 4 weeks.
   3. **Impaired heart (EF <40% or CHF) duration <48 hours**: consider DC cardioversion or amiodarone.
   4. **Impaired heart (EF <40% or CHF) duration >48 hours**: anticoagulation (as described above) followed by DC cardioversion.
   5. **WPW with preserved heart function**: DC cardioversion or use one of the following primary antiarrhythmic agents: amiodarone, flecainide, procainamide, or sotalol.
   6. **WPW with impaired heart (EF <40% or CHF)**: DC cardioversion or amiodarone.

Narrow-Complex Supraventricular Tachycardia, Stable

1. **Attempt therapeutic diagnostic maneuver**
   A. Vagal maneuvers (carotid sinus pressure is contraindicated in patients with carotid bruits; avoid ice water immersion in patients with ischemic heart disease).
   B. Adenosine 6 mg rapid IVP (over 1-3 seconds); may repeat with 12 mg rapid IVP in 1-2 minutes for a total of 30 mg.
2. **Junctional tachycardia**
   A. Preserved heart function: no DC cardioversion, amiodarone, beta-blocker, or calcium channel blocker.
   B. Impaired heart (EF <40% or CHF): no DC cardioversion, amiodarone.
3. **Paroxysmal supraventricular tachycardia (PSVT)**
   A. Preserved heart function (priority order): AV nodal blockade (beta-blocker, calcium channel blocker, digoxin), DC cardioversion, antiarrhythmic agents (consider procainamide, amiodarone, or sotalol).
   B. Impaired heart (EF <40% or CHF) (priority order): no DC cardioversion, digoxin, amiodarone, diltiazem.
4. **Ectopic multifocal atrial tachycardia**
   A. Preserved heart function: no DC cardioversion, calcium channel blocker,

beta-blocker, amiodarone.
B. Impaired heart (EF <40% or CHF): no DC cardioversion, amiodarone, diltiazem.

Stable Ventricular Tachycardia

1. Determine if monomorphic or polymorphic. May go directly to cardioversion.
2. **Monomorphic Ventricular Tachycardia**
   A. Preserved cardiac function: procainamide or sotalol; may consider amiodarone or lidocaine.
   B. Impaired heart (EF <40% or CHF): amiodarone (150 mg IV over 10 minutes) or lidocaine (0.5 to 0.75 mg/kg IVP), followed by synchronized cardioversion.
3. **Polymorphic Ventricular Tachycardia**
   A. Normal baseline QT interval (preserved cardiac function): treat ischemia and/or correct electrolytes; consider one of the following medications: beta-blockers, lidocaine, amiodarone, procainamide, or sotalol.
   B. Normal baseline QT interval (Impaired heart): amiodarone (150 mg IV over 10 minutes) or lidocaine (0.5 to 0.75 mg/kg IVP), followed by synchronized cardioversion.
   C. Long baseline QT interval (suggests torsades de pointes): correct abnormal electrolytes; consider one of the following medications: magnesium, overdrive pacing, isoproterenol, phenytoin, or lidocaine.

Pediatric Bradycardia

1. **Assess and support ABCs** as needed, provide oxygen, attach monitor/defibrillator.
2. **If unstable bradycardia** (poor perfusion, hypotension, respiratory difficulty, altered consciousness):
   A. Perform chest compression if despite oxygenation and ventilation heart rate <60 bpm in infant or child and poor systemic perfusion.
   B. Epinephrine: 0.01 mg/kg IV/IO (0.1 mg/kg ET); may repeat every 3-5 minutes at the same dose; consider alternative medications: epinephrine or dopamine infusions.
   C. Atropine: 0.02 mg/kg (min dose 0.1 mg); may repeat once; consider first for bradycardia due to suspected increased vagal tone or primary AV block.
   D. Consider cardiac pacing.
   E. Identify and treat possible causes: hypoxemia, hypothermia, head injury, heart block, heart transplant, toxins/poisons/drugs.
3. **If stable bradycardia**: observe, support ABC's.

Pediatric Pulseless Electrical Activity

1. **Assess rhythm**
   A. Ventricular fibrillation/pulseless ventricular tachycardia
   1. Attempt defibrillation: up to 3 times if needed; initially 2 J/kg, then 2-4 J/kg, then 4 J/kg.
   2. Epinephrine: 0.01 mg/kg IV/IO (0.1 mg/kg ET); may repeat every 3-5

minutes; consider higher doses for second and subsequent doses.
  3. Attempt defibrillation with 4 J/kg within 30-60 seconds after each medication (pattern: CPR-drug-shock).
  4. **Antiarrhythmic**
      A. Amiodarone: 5 mg/kg bolus IV/IO or
      B. Lidocaine: 1 mg/kg bolus IV/IO or
      C. Magnesium: 25 to 50 mg/kg IV/IO for torsades de pointes or hypomagnesemia (maximum 2 gm).
  5. Attempt defibrillation with 4 J/kg within 30-60 seconds after each medication (pattern: CPR-drug-shock).
  B. **Pulseless electrical activity or asystole** (not VF/VT)
    1. Epinephrine: 0.01 mg/kg IV/IO (0.1 mg/kg ET); may repeat every 3-5 minutes; consider higher doses for second and subsequent doses
2. **During CPR**
  A. Attempt/verify tracheal intubation and vascular access; check electrode position and contact.
  B. Identify and treat possible causes: hypoxemia, hypovolemia, hypothermia, hyper/hypokalemia, cardiac tamponade, tension pneumothorax, toxins/poisons/drugs, and thromboembolism.
  C. Consider alternate medications: vasopressors, buffers, antiarrhythmics.

Pediatric Tachycardia with Poor Perfusion

1. **Assess patient**, support ABCs, provide oxygen and ventilation as needed, confirm continuous monitor/pacer attached, evaluate EKG and QRS duration.
2. **QRS normal for age (approximately <0.08 seconds).**
  A. Probable sinus tachycardia: history compatible, P waves present/normal, HR often varies with activity, variable RR with constant PR, infant HR usually <220 bpm, children HR usually <180 bpm.
  B. Probable supraventricular tachycardia: history incompatible, P waves absent/abnormal, HR not variable with activity, abrupt rate changes, infant HR usually >220 bpm, children HR usually >180 bpm.
  C. Consider vagal maneuvers.
  D. Immediate cardioversion with 0.5 -1.0 J/kg (may increase to 2 J/kg) or
  E. Immediate adenosine (if IV access available): 0.1 mg/kg IV/IO, maximum first dose 6 mg, may double and repeat dose once.
  F. Consider alternative medications
    1. Amiodarone: 5 mg/kg IV over 20-60 minutes or
    2. Procainamide: 15 mg/kg IV over 30-60 minutes.
  G. Identify and treat possible causes: hypoxemia, hypovolemia, hypothermia, hyper/hypokalemia, cardiac tamponade, tension pneumothorax, toxins/poisons/drugs, thromboembolism, and pain.
3. **QRS duration wide for age (approximately >0.08 seconds)**
  A. Probable ventricular tachycardia: immediate cardioversion 0.5-1.0 J/kg.
  B. Consider alternative medications
    1. Amiodarone: 5 mg/kg IV over 20-60 minutes or
    2. Procainamide: 15 mg/kg IV over 30-60 minutes or
    3. Lidocaine: 1 mg/kg IV bolus.

Pediatric Tachycardia with Adequate Perfusion

1. **Assess patient,** support ABCs, provide oxygen and ventilation as needed, confirm continuous monitor/pacer attached, evaluate EKG and QRS duration.
2. **QRS normal for age (approximately <0.08 seconds).**
   A. Probable sinus tachycardia: P waves present/normal, HR often varies with activity, variable RR with constant PR, infant HR usually <220 bpm, children HR usually <180 bpm.
   B. Probable supraventricular tachycardia: P waves absent/abnormal, HR does not vary with activity, abrupt rate changes, infant HR usually >220 bpm, children HR usually >180 bpm.
   C. Consider vagal maneuvers.
   D. Establish IV access.
   E. Adenosine: 0.1 mg/kg IV/IO, maximum first dose 6 mg, may double and repeat dose once.
   F. Consult pediatric cardiologist.
   G. Attempt cardioversion: 0.5-1.0 J/kg (may increase to 2 J/kg).
3. **QRS duration wide for age (approximately >0.08 seconds)**
   A. Probable ventricular tachycardia: uncommon in most children; seen in congenital heart disease, cardiomyopathy, myocarditis
   B. Immediate cardioversion with 0.5-1.0 J/kg (may increase to 2 J/kg).
   C. Consider alternative medications
      1. Amiodarone: 5 mg/kg IV over 20-60 minutes or
      2. Procainamide: 15 mg/kg IV over 30-60 minutes or
      3. Lidocaine: 1 mg/kg IV bolus.
4. Identify and treat possible causes: hypoxemia, hypovolemia, hypothermia, hyper/hypokalemia, cardiac tamponade, tension pneumothorax, toxins/poisons/drugs, thromboembolism, and pain.

Newborn Resuscitation

1. **Normal term neonatal vital signs** (first 12 hours of life)
   A. Heart rate (awake): 100-180 bpm; respiratory rate: 30-60/min; systolic blood pressure: 39-59 mmHg; diastolic blood pressure: 16-36 mmHg.
2. **Ventilation management**
   A. Positive-pressure ventilation should be started for apnea, central cyanosis, and heart rates below 100 beats/min. Ventilate at 40-60 breaths/min (when performed without compression) with an initial pressure of 30-40 cm H_2O to overcome surface tension and open the alveoli. Subsequent breaths should have inspiratory pressures of 15-30 cm H_2O and tidal volumes of 6-8 mL/kg.
   B. Assisted ventilation should be continued until spontaneous respirations are present and the heart rate is greater than 100 beats/min.
3. **Chest compression**
   A. Chest compressions should be started (1) if the heart rate is absent or (2) if the heart rate remains <60 bpm after 30 seconds of adequate assisted ventilation.
   B. The sternum is depressed 0.5-0.75 inch at a rate of 120 beats/min. The compression-ventilation ratio in neonates is 3:1 (intubated) and 5:1 (not intubated).

4. Vascular Access
  A. The umbilical vein, the largest and thinnest of the three umbilical vessels, can be cannulated with a 3.5-5.0 F umbilical catheter. The tip of the catheter should be just below skin level and allow free backflow of blood.

5. Apgar Scores
  A. The Apgar scoring system enables rapid evaluation of a newborn's condition at specific intervals after birth (1 and 5 minutes of age).

  B. Apgar score at 1 minute correlates best with intrauterine conditions, the 5- and 10-minute Apgar scores correlate best with neonatal outcome.

  C. A normal Apgar score is 8-10. With scores of 5-7 (mildly asphyxiated) supplemental oxygen and stimulation are normally sufficient. Scores of 3-4 (moderately asphyxiated) typically require temporary assisted positive-pressure ventilation with mask and bag. Scores of 0-2 (severely depressed) mandates the immediate initiation of CPR and intubation.

Apgar Scores			
Score	**0**	**1**	**3**
Heart Rate (BPM)	Absent	<100	>100
Respirations	Absent	Slow, regular	Good, crying
Muscle Tone	Limp	Flexion of extremities	Active motion
Reflex Irritability	No response	Grimace	Cough, sneeze
Color	Blue/pale	Extremities pink	Completely pink

Drugs that may be Given Endotracheally (LANE)

1. Lidocaine, atropine, naloxone, and epinephrine.
2. Drugs administered via the endotracheal route should be diluted to a volume of 3-5 mL of normal saline or followed by a 3-5 mL normal saline flush, followed by several positive-pressure ventilations.

Summary of Basic Life Support Techniques

	Infant (<12 mo)	Child (1-8 yrs)	Adult
Breathing Rate	20 breaths/min	20 breaths/min	10-12 breaths/min
Pulse Check	Brachial or Femoral	Carotid	Carotid
Compression Depth	0.5-1 inches	1-1.5 inches	1.5-2 inches
Compression Rate	>100/min	100/min	100/min
Compression Method	2-3 fingers	Heel of one hand	Hands interlaced
Compression-Ventilation Ratio	5:1 (3:1 for intubated newborn	5:1	15:2 (5:1 with protected airway)
Foreign Body Obstruction	Back blows with chest thrust	Heimlich maneuver	Heimlich maneuver

Pediatric Emergency Drugs and Defibrillation

Drug	Dose	Remarks
Adenosine	0.1-0.2 mg/kg; subsequent doses doubled	Give rapid IV bolus; max single dose 12 mg
Amiodarone	5 mg/kg	Max dose: 15 mg/kg/ per day
Atropine	0.01-0.02 mg/kg Min dose: 0.1 mg	Max single dose: 0.5 mg in child, 1.0 mg in adolescent
Bretylium	5 mg/kg (may be increased to 10 mg/kg)	Give rapid IV Loading dose
Calcium Chloride 10%	0.2-0.25 mL/kg or 20 mg/kg per dose	Infuse slowly
Dopamine	2-20 mcg/kg/min	Titrate to desired effect
Dobutamine	2-20 mcg/kg/min	Titrate to desired effect
Epinephrine	First dose: IV/IO: 0.01 mg/kg; ET: 0.1 mg/kg Subsequent doses: 0.1-0.2 mg/kg IV/IO; ET 0.1 mg/kg	Epinephrine infusion: 0.05-1.0 mcg/kg/min titrate to desired effect Bolus: 1-2 mcg/kg IV
Glucose (D25%)	0.5-1.0 g/kg IV/IO	Max conc of 25% in peripheral vein
Lidocaine	1 mg/kg per dose	Infuse 20-50 mcg/kg/min
Magnesium	25-50 mg/kg	Max dose: 2 gms
Naloxone	0.1 mg/kg up to 5 years or 20 kg	Children over 5 years or 20 kg may be given 2 mg
Procainamide	15 mg/kg over 30-60 min	

Drug	Dose	Remarks
Prostaglandin E₁	0.05-0.1 mcg/kg/min	Titrate to desired effect
Sodium Bicarbonate	1 mEq/kg per dose or 0.3 x kg x base deficit	Infuse slowly; monitor for apnea, hypotension, hypoglycemia
Valium	0.1-0.25 mg/kg	
Defibrillation	2-4 J/kg	
Cardioversion	0.25-1.0 /kg	

Adult Emergency Drugs		
Drug	Dose	Remarks
Adenosine	6 mg over 1-3 sec; 12 mg repeat dose	Give rapid IV bolus; max single dose 12 mg
Amiodarone	150 mg over 10 min, followed by 1 mg/min for 6 hrs, then 0.5 mg/min	For pulseless VT or VF start with 300 mg rapid infusion. Max cum dose: 2.2 gm/24 hours
Atropine	0.5-1.0 mg repeated every 3-5 minutes	Max total dose 3 mg
Amrinone	0.75 mg/kg, over 10-15 min	Infusion 5-15 mcg/kg/min
Calcium Chloride	8-16 mg/kg	Infuse slowly
Dopamine	2-20 mcg/kg/min	Titrate to desired effect
Dobutamine	2-20 mcg/kg/min	Titrate to desired effect
Diltiazem	0.25 mg/kg, followed by 0.35 mg/kg if necessary	Infusion 5-15 mg/hr in AF/flutter
Flecainide	2 mg/kg at 10 mg/min	IV not approved in the US
Ibutilide	Pts >60 kg, 1 mg over 10 min; may repeat in 10 min	Pts <60 kg use initial dose of 0.01 mg/kg
Epinephrine	IV: 1 mg repeat 3-5 min as necessary. ET: 2-2.5 mg	Epinephrine infusion: 1-4 mcg/min titrate to desired effect
Verapamil	2.5-5 mg IV over 2 min; may repeat with 5-10 mg every 15-30 min to max of 20 mg	Do not use in the presence of impaired ventricular function or CHF
Lidocaine	1-1.5 mg/kg; can repeat every 5-10 min to a total dose of 3 mg/kg	Infuse 20-50 mcg/kg/min
Magnesium	1-2 g over 5-60 min	Infusion of 0.5-1 gm/hr

Drug	Dose	Remarks
Procainamide	20 mg/min until arrhythmia suppressed, hypotension develops, QRS complex increases >50% or total dose of 17 mg/kg infused	Urgent situation, 50 mg/min can be used Maintenance infusion: 1-4 mg/min
Sodium Bicarbonate	1 mEq/kg per dose or 0.3 x kg x base deficit	Infuse slowly; monitor for apnea, hypotension, hypoglycemia
Vasopressin	40 U IV, single dose only	Use only one time

Preoperative Evaluation

Anesthesia Preoperative Evaluation

1. The overall goal of the preoperative evaluation is to reduce perioperative morbidity and mortality and alleviate patient anxiety.
2. **Anesthesia preoperative history and physical**
   A. Note the date and time of the interview, the planned procedure, and a description of any extraordinary circumstances regarding the anesthesia.
   B. Current medications and allergies: history of steroids, chemotherapy and herb and dietary supplements (see tables).
   C. Cigarette, alcohol, and illicit drug history, including most recent use.
   D. Anesthetic history, including specific details of any problems.
   E. Prior surgical procedures and hospitalizations.
   F. Family history, especially anesthetic problems. Birth and development history (pediatric cases).
   G. Obstetrical history: last menstrual period (females).
   H. Medical history; evaluation, current treatment, and degree of control.
   I. Review of systems, including general, cardiac, pulmonary, neurologic, liver, renal, gastrointestinal, endocrine, hematologic, psychiatric.
   J. History of airway problems (difficult intubation or airway disease, symptoms of temporomandibular joint disease, loose teeth, etc).
   K. Last oral intake.
   L. Physical exam, including airway evaluation (see below), current vital signs, height and body weight, baseline mental status, evaluation of heart and lungs, vascular access.
   M. Overall impression of the complexity of the patient's medical condition, with assignment of ASA Physical Status Class (see below).
   N. Anesthetic plan (general anesthesia, regional, spinal, MAC). The anesthetic plan is based on the patient's medical status, the planned operation, and the patient's wishes.
   O. Documentation that risks and benefits were explained to the patient.
3. **Preoperative laboratory evaluation**
   A. **Hemoglobin:** menstruating females, children less than 6 months or with suspected sickle cell disease, history of anemia, blood dyscrasia or malignancy, congenital heart disease, chronic disease states, age greater than 50 years (65 years for males), patients likely to experience large blood loss.
   B. **WBC count:** suspected infection or immunosuppression.
   C. **Platelet count:** history of abnormal bleeding or bruising, liver disease, blood dyscrasias, chemotherapy, hypersplenism.
   D. **Coagulation studies:** history of abnormal bleeding, anticoagulant drug therapy, liver disease, malabsorption, poor nutrition, vascular procedure.
   E. **Electrolytes, blood glucose, BUN/creatinine:** renal disease, adrenal or thyroid disorders, diabetes mellitus, diuretic therapy, chemotherapy.
   F. **Liver function tests:** patients with liver disease, history of or exposure to hepatitis, history of alcohol or drug abuse, drug therapy with agents that may affect liver function.
   G. **Pregnancy test:** patients for whom pregnancy might complicate the surgery, patients of uncertain status by history and/or examination.
   H. **Electrocardiogram:** age 50 or older, hypertension, current or past

significant cardiac disease or circulatory disease, diabetes mellitus in a person age 40 or older. An EKG showing normal results that was performed within 6 months of surgery can be used if there has been no intervening clinical event.

I. Chest x-ray: asthma or chronic obstructive pulmonary disease with change of symptoms or acute episode within the past 6 months, cardiothoracic procedures.

J. Urinalysis: genito-urologic procedures; surgeon may request to rule out infection before certain surgical procedures.

K. Cervical spine flexion/extension x-rays: patients with rheumatoid arthritis or Down's syndrome. Routine screening in asymptomatic patients is generally not required.

L. Preoperative pulmonary function tests (PFTs)
  1. There is no evidence to suggest that pulmonary function tests are useful for purposes of risk assessment or modification in patients with cigarette smoking or adequately treated brochospastic disease.
  2. **Candidates for preoperative PFTs**
      A. Patients considered for pneumonectomy.
      B. Patients with moderate to severe pulmonary disease scheduled for major abdominal or thoracic surgery.
      C. Patients with dyspnea at rest.
      D. Patients with chest wall and spinal deformities.
      E. Morbidity obese patients.
      F. Patients with airway obstructive lesions.

4. Pediatric preoperative evaluation: see section on pediatric anesthesia.

Airway Evaluation

1. **Preoperative evaluation:** assessed by historical interview (i.e., history of difficult intubation, sleep apnea) and physical examination and occasionally with radiographs, PFTs, and direct fiber-optic examination. The physical exam is the most important method of detecting and anticipating airway difficulties.
2. **Physical exam**
    A. **Mouth**
      1. **Opening:** note symmetry and extent of opening (3 finger breadths optimal).
      2. **Dentition:** ascertain the presence of loose, cracked, or missing teeth; dental prostheses; and co-existing dental abnormalities.
      3. **Macroglossia:** will increase difficultly of intubation.
    B. **Neck/Chin**
      1. **Anterior mandibular space (thyromental distance):** the distance between the hyoid bone and the inside of the mentum (mental prominence) or between the notch of the thyroid cartilage to the mentum. An inadequate mandibular space is associated with a hyomental distance of <3 cm or a thyromental distance of <6 cm.
      2. **Cervical spine mobility (atlanto-occipital joint extension):** 35 degrees of extension is normal; limited neck extension (<30 degrees associated with increased difficulty of intubation.
      3. Evaluate for presence of a healed or patent tracheostomy stoma;, prior surgeries or pathology of the head and neck (laryngeal cancer); presence of a hoarse voice or stridor.

3. **Airway classification**
   A. **Mallampati classification** (relates tongue size vs pharyngeal size)
      1. **Class 1:** able to visualize the soft palate, fauces, uvula, anterior and posterior tonsillar pillars.
      2. **Class 2:** able to visualize the soft palate, fauces, and uvula. The anterior and posterior tonsillar pillars are hidden by the tongue.
      3. **Class 3:** only the soft palate and base of uvula are visible.
      4. **Class 4:** only the soft palate can be seen (no uvula seen).
   B. **Laryngoscopic view grades**
      1. **Grade 1:** full view of the entire glottic opening.
      2. **Grade 2:** posterior portion of the glottic opening is visible.
      3. **Grade 3:** only the epiglottis is visible.
      4. **Grade 4:** only soft palate is visible.
4. **Predictors of difficult intubation**
   A. **Anatomic variations:** micrognathia, prognathism, large tongue, arched palate, short neck, prominent upper incisors, buckteeth, decreased jaw movement, receding mandible or anterior larynx, short stout neck.
   B. **Medical conditions associated with difficult intubations**
      1. **Arthritis:** patients with arthritis may have a decreased range of neck mobility. Rheumatoid arthritis patients have an increased risk of atlantoaxial subluxation.
      2. **Tumors:** may obstruct the airway or cause extrinsic compression and tracheal deviation.
      3. **Infections:** of any oral structure may obstruct the airway.
      4. **Trauma:** patients are at increased risk for cervical spine injuries, basilar skull fractures, intracranial injuries, and facial bone fractures.
      5. **Down's Syndrome:** patients may have macroglossia, a narrowed cricoid cartilage, and a greater frequency of postoperative airway obstruction/croup; risk of subluxation of the atlanto-occipital joint.
      6. **Scleroderma:** may result in decreased range of motion of the temporomandibular joint and narrowing of the oral aperture.
      7. **Obesity:** massive amount of soft tissue about the head and upper trunk can impair mandibular and cervical mobility, increased incidence of sleep apnea.

ASA Physical Status Classification

1. The ASA (American Society of Anesthesiologists) physical status classification has been shown to generally correlate with the perioperative mortality rate (mortality rates given below).
2. **ASA 1:** a normal healthy patient (0.06-0.08%).
3. **ASA 2:** a patient with a mild systemic disease (mild diabetes, controlled hypertension, obesity [0.27-0.4%]).
4. **ASA 3:** a patient with a severe systemic disease that limits activity (angina, COPD, prior myocardial infarction [1.8-4.3%]).
5. **ASA 4:** a patient with an incapacitating disease that is a constant threat to life (CHF, renal failure [7.8-23%]).
6. **ASA 5:** a moribund patient not expected to survive 24 hours (ruptured aneurysm [9.4-51%]).
7. **ASA 6:** brain-dead patient whose organs are being harvested.
8. **For emergent operations,** add the letter 'E' after the classification.

Preoperative Fasting Guidelines

1. **Recommendations** (applies to all ages)

Ingested Material	Minimum Fasting Period (hrs)
Clear liquids	2
Breast milk	4
Infant formula	6
Non-human milk	6
Light solid foods	6

2. Recommendations apply to healthy patients exclusive of parturients undergoing elective surgery; following these recommendations does not guarantee gastric emptying has occurred.
3. Clear liquids include water, sugar-water, apple juice, non-carbonated soda, pulp-free juices, clear tea, black coffee.
4. Medications can be taken with up to 150 mL of water in the hour preceding induction of anesthesia.

Bacterial Endocarditis Prophylaxis

1. **Antibiotic prophylaxis** is recommended for patients with prosthetic cardiac valves, previous history of endocarditis, most congenital malformations, rheumatic valvular disease, hypertrophic cardiomyopathy, and mitral valve regurgitation.
2. **Prophylactic regimens for dental, oral, respiratory tract, or esophageal procedures**
   A. **Standard regimen**
      1. Adults: amoxicillin 2 g PO 1 hour before procedure.
      2. Children: amoxicillin 50 mg/kg PO 1 hour before procedure.
   B. **Unable to take oral medications**
      1. Adults: ampicillin 2 g IM/IV within 30 min before procedure.
      2. Children: ampicillin 50 mg/kg IM/IV within 30 min before procedure.
   C. **Penicillin allergic**
      1. Adults: clindamycin 600 mg or cephalexin (or cefadroxil) 2 g or azithromycin (or clarithromycin) 500 mg 1 hour before procedure.
      2. Children: clindamycin 20 mg/kg PO or cephalexin (or cefadroxil) 50 mg/kg or azithromycin (or clarithromycin) 15 mg/kg 1 hour before procedure
   D. **Allergic penicillin and unable to take oral medications**
      1. Adults: clindamycin 600 mg IV or cefazolin 1 g within 30 min before procedure.
      2. Children: clindamycin 20 mg/kg IV or cefazolin 25 mg/kg IM/IV within 30 min before procedure.
3. **Prophylactic regimens for genitourinary/gastrointestinal (excluding esophageal) procedures**
   A. **High-risk patients**
      1. Adults: ampicillin 2 g IM/IV plus gentamicin 1.5 mg/kg (not to exceed 120 mg) within 30 min before procedure; 6 hours later ampicillin 1 g IM/IV or amoxicillin 1 g PO.
      2. Children: ampicillin 50 mg/kg IM/IV (not to exceed 2 g) plus gentamicin

        1.5 mg/kg within 30 min before procedure; 6 hours later, ampicillin 25 mg/kg IM/IV or amoxicillin 25 mg/kg PO.

B. High-risk patients allergic to ampicillin/amoxicillin
1. Adults: vancomycin 1 g IV over 1-2 h plus gentamicin 1.5 mg/kg IM/IV (not to exceed 120 mg); complete within 30 min before procedure.
2. Children: vancomycin 20 mg/kg IV over 1-2 h plus gentamicin 1.5 mg/kg IM/IV; complete within 30 min before procedure.

C. Moderate-risk patients
1. Adults: amoxicillin 2 g PO 1 hour before procedure, or ampicillin 2 g IM/IV within 30 min before procedure.
2. Children: amoxicillin 50 mg/kg PO 1 hour before procedure, or ampicillin 50 mg/kg 30 min before procedure.

D. Moderate-risk patients allergic to ampicillin/amoxicillin
1. Adults: vancomycin 1 g IV over 1-2 hours; complete infusion within 30 min before starting procedure.
2. Children: vancomycin 20 mg/kg IV over 1-2 hours; complete 30 min before starting procedure.

4. Miscellaneous notes
A. Total dose for children should not exceed the adult dose.
B. Cephalosporins should not be used in individuals with immediate-type hypersensitivity reaction (urticaria, angioedema, or anaphylaxis) to penicillin.
C. Patients already taking antibiotics for another reason should be given an agent from a different class for endocarditis prophylaxis.
D. Patients at risk for endocarditis who undergo open heart surgery should have prophylaxis directed primarily at staphylococci.
E. Cardiac transplant recipients should probably be considered at moderate risk for endocarditis and receive prophylaxis accordingly.

Premedications

1. The goals of premedications include: anxiety relief, sedation, analgesia, amnesia, antisialagogue effect, increase in gastric fluid pH, decrease in gastric fluid volume, attenuation of sympathetic nervous system reflex responses, decrease in anesthetic requirements, prevent bronchospasm, prophylaxis against allergic reactions, and decrease post-op nausea/vomiting.
2. Sedatives and analgesics should be reduced or withheld in the elderly, newborn/peds (<1 year of age), debilitated, and acutely intoxicated, as well as those with upper airway obstruction or trauma, central apnea, neurologic deterioration, or severe pulmonary or valvular heart disease.

Common Premedications

Agent	Route	Adult (mg)	Peds (mg/kg)	Onset (min)
Pentobarbital	PO		2-4	10-30
Pentobarbital	PR	150-200	3	15-60
Pentobarbital	IM	150-200	2-6	10-15
Methohexital	IM		5-10	5-20
Methohexital	PR		20-35	5-20
Ketamine	IV	0.25-1 mg/kg	0.25-1	1-2
Ketamine	IM	2-3 mg/kg	2-3	5-10
Ketamine	IN		5-6	5-10
Ketamine	PO		6-10	10
Fentanyl	IV	12.5-100	0.01-0.02	1-3
Fentanyl	OFTC		0.015-0.02	5-15
Sufentanil	IN		0.0015-0.003	5
Morphine	IM	5-15	0.05-0.02	
Meperidine	IM	25-100	1-1.5	
Diazepam	PO	2-10	0.1-0.3	
Flurazepam	PO	15-30		20-30
Midazolam	IV	1-5	0.05	
Midazolam	IM	2.5-5	0.1-0.2	2-3
Midazolam	IN		0.1-0.3	5
Midazolam	PO		0.4-1.0	10
Midazolam	PR		0.25-1.0	5-7
Lorazepam	PO	1-4	0.05	20-30
Lorazepam	IV	0.02-0.05	0.02-0.05	3-7
Triazolam	PO	0.125-0.25		15-30
Chloral Hydrate	PO, PR		25-50	20-30
Benadryl	PO	25-75		
Benadryl	IV	10-50		
Phenergan	IM	12.5-50	0.25-1.0	15-20
Vistaril	IM	25-100	0.5-1.0	15-30
Clonidine	PO	0.3-0.4	0.004	30-60
Dexamethasone	IV		0.150	
Droperidol	IV	0.625-1.25	0.05-0.075	3-10
Granisetron	IV	4	0.04	
Ondansetron	IV		0.1	
Atropine	IM, IV	0.3-0.6	0.01-0.02	
Scopolamine	IM, IV	0.3-0.6	0.01-0.02	
Glycopyrrolate	IM, IV	0.2-0.3	0.01	

IM: Intramuscular; IV: Intravascular; PO: Oral; IN: Intranasal; OFTC: Oral Fentanyl Transmucosal Citrate

Aspiration Pneumonia Prophylaxis

Drug	Route	Adult (mg)	Peds (mg/kg)	Onset (min)
Cimetidine (Tagamet)	PO IV	300-800 300	5-10 5-10	60-120 45-60
Ranitidine (Zantac)	PO IV	150-300 50	0.25-1.0	30-60
Famotidine (Pepcid)	PO IV	20-40 20	0.15	60-120
Nizatidine (Axid)	PO	150-300		30-60
Bicitra	PO	15-30	0.4 mL/kg	5-10
Metoclopramide (Reglan)	PO IV	10-15 10	0.15	30-60 1-3
Omeprazole (Prilosec)	PO	20	0.3-0.7	30-60
Lansoprazole (Prevacid)	PO	15-30		

Chemotherapy Agents

Agent	Adverse Effects
5-Fluorouracil/ARA C	Hemorrhage enteritis, diarrhea, myelosuppression
Adriamycin	Cardiac toxicity; risk factors include total cumulative dose over 550 mg/m^2, concomitant cyclophosphamide therapy, prior history of heart disease, age over 65 years
Bleomycin	Pulmonary toxicity; risk factors include total cumulative dose over 200 mg, concomitant thoracic radiation therapy, >65 yrs
Cisplatin	Renal toxicity, neurotoxicity
Cyclophosphamide	Myelosuppression, hemorrhagic cystitis, water retention, pulmonary fibrosis, plasma cholinesterase inhibition
Growth factors	Pulmonary edema, pericardial and pleural effusions
Methotrexate	Renal tubular injury
Mitomycin C	Pulmonary toxicity
Nitrogen Mustard	Myelosuppression, local tissue damage
Nitrosoureas	Myelosuppression, renal pulmonary toxicity
Taxol	Hypersensitivity reaction, myelosuppression, cardiac toxicity, peripheral neuropathy
Vinblastine	Myelosuppression
Vincristine	Neurotoxicity, dilutional hyponatremia

Commonly Used Herbs/Dietary Supplements

Herb	Adverse Effects	Anesthetic Recommendations
Echinacea	Tachyphylaxis; potential hepatotoxicity; interference with immune suppressive therapy	May potentiate barbiturate toxicity; decreased effectiveness of corticosteriods; discontinue as far in advance as possible
Ephedra (Ma Huang)	Hypertension; tachycardia; cardiomyopathy; cerebrovascular accident; cardiac arrhythmias	May interact with volatile anesthetic agents to cause fatal cardiac dysrhythmias; profound intraoperative hypotension; avoid monoamine oxidase inhibitors; discontinue at least 24 hours
Feverfew	Aphthous ulcers; gastrointestinal irritability; headache	Increased risk of intraoperative hemodynamic instability; inhibits platelets
Garlic (ajo)	Halitosis; prolongation of bleeding time; hypotension	Discontinue at least 7 days prior to surgery
Ginger	Prolongation of bleeding time	Inhibits thromboxane synthetase
Ginkgo Biloba	Inhibition of platelet activating factor	Increased intraoperative-postoperative bleeding tendencies; discontinue at least 36 hours prior to surgery
Ginseng	Hypertension; insomnia; headache; vomiting; epistaxis; prolonged bleeding time; hypoglycemia	Increased risk of intraoperative hemodynamic instability; discontinue at least 7 days prior to surgery
Kava Kava	Characteristic ichthyosiform dermopathy	May potentiate sedatives; discontinue 24 hours prior to surgery
St. John's Wort	Dry mouth; dizziness; constipation; nausea; increases drug metabolism by induction of cytochrome P450	Avoid pseudoephedrine, MAOIs, and SSRIs; discontinue at least 5 days prior to surgery
Valerian	GABA-mediated hypnotic effects may decrease MAC	Taper dose weeks before surgery; treat withdrawal with benzodiazepines

Cardiovascular Disease

Cardiac Disease and Anesthesia

1. **Pertinent cardiac history**
   A. **Cardiac reserve:** limited exercise tolerance in the absence of significant pulmonary disease is the most striking evidence of decreased cardiac reserve. If a patient can climb several flights of stairs without symptoms, cardiac reserve is probably adequate.
   B. **Angina pectoris:** an increase in heart rate is more likely than hypertension to produce signs of myocardial ischemia.
   C. **Previous myocardial infarction:** the incidence of myocardial reinfarction in the perioperative period is related to the time elapsed since the previous myocardial infarction and the amount of residual ischemia remaining. The incidence of perioperative myocardial reinfarction generally stabilizes at 5-6% after 6 months from the previous myocardial infarction. Mortality after perioperative MI 20-50%. Infarction rate in the absence of a prior MI 0.13%. Most perioperative myocardial reinfarctions occur in the first 48 to 72 hours postoperatively.
   D. **Dysrhythmias:** ventricular dysrhythmias may indicate underlying cardiac disease. Isolated premature ventricular contractions without evidence of underlying cardiac disease are not associated with increased cardiac risk.
   E. **Prior cardiac surgery or PTCA** does not increase perioperative risk.
2. **Contraindications** to elective noncardiac surgery include a myocardial infarction less than 1 month prior to surgery, uncompensated heart failure, and severe aortic or mitral stenosis.
3. **Evaluation of the cardiac patient for noncardiac surgery**
   A. **Risk factors**
      1. **Major risk factors:** unstable coronary syndromes (recent MI, unstable or severe angina, decompensated CHF, significant arrhythmias, severe valvular disease).
      2. **Intermediate risk factors:** mild angina pectoris, prior MI, compensated or prior CHF, diabetes mellitus.
      3. **Minor risk factors:** advanced age, abnormal EKG, arrhythmias, low functional capacity, history of stroke, uncontrolled systemic hypertension.
      4. **Functional capacity:** perioperative cardiac risk is increased in patients unable to meet a 4-MET (climbing a flight of stairs) demand during most normal daily activities.
      5. **Surgery-specific risk:** high risk surgery includes major emergency surgery, aortic or other major vascular surgery, peripheral vascular surgery, long procedures with large fluid shifts or blood loss; intermediate risk surgery includes CEA, head and neck, intraperitoneal, intrathoracic, orthopedic and prostate surgery; low risk surgery includes endoscopic and superficial procedures, cataract and breast surgery.
   B. **Algorithm for preoperative cardiac evaluation**
      1. **Step 1:** what is the urgency of noncardiac surgery? Certain emergencies do not allow time for preoperative cardiac evaluation.
      2. **Step 2:** has the patient undergone coronary revascularization in the past 5 years? If so, and if clinical status has remained stable without recurrent symptoms/signs of ischemia, further testing is not necessary.

3. **Step 3**: has the patient had a coronary evaluation in the past 2 years? If coronary risk was adequately assessed and the findings were favorable, it is usually not necessary to repeat testing unless the patient has experienced a change or new symptoms of coronary ischemia since the previous evaluation.
4. **Step 4**: does the patient have an unstable coronary syndrome or a major risk factors? Elective surgery should be cancelled or delayed until the problem has been identified, evaluated and treated.
5. **Step 5**: does the patient have intermediate risk factors? If no, consider functional capacity and level of surgery specific risk to identifying patients most likely to benefit from further noninvasive testing.
6. **Step 6**: patients with intermediate predictors of clinical risk and moderate or excellent functional capacity can generally undergo intermediate-risk surgery. Further noninvasive testing should be considered for patients with poor functional capacity or moderate functional capacity undergoing high risk surgery.
7. **Step 7**: patients with minor or no risk factors and moderate or excellent functional capacity are generally safe and don't require further testing. Patients without clinical markers but poor functional capacity who are facing high-risk operations, particularly those with several minor clinical predictors of risk who are to undergo vascular surgery, should be consider for further testing.
8. **Step 8**: the results of noninvasive testing should be used to determine further preoperative management. In some patients corrective cardiac surgery may be consider before the proposed noncardiac surgery.

C. **Cardiac evaluation studies**
   1. **Baseline EKG**: usually normal in 25-50% of patients with coronary artery disease but no prior myocardial infarction. EKG evidence of ischemia often becomes apparent only during chest pain.
   2. **Holter monitoring**: useful in evaluating arrhythmias, antiarrhythmic drug therapy, and the severity and frequency of ischemic episodes.
   3. **Exercise stress testing**: gives estimate of functional capacity along with the ability to detect EKG changes and hemodynamic response. Highly predictive when ST-segment changes are characteristic of ischemia. A normal test does not exclude coronary artery disease but suggests that severe disease is not likely.
   4. **Echocardiography**: evaluates global and regional ventricular function, valvular function, and congenital abnormalities. Detects regional wall motion abnormalities and derives left ventricular ejection fraction.
   5. **Dobutamine stress echo**: reliable predictor of adverse cardiac complications. New or worsening wall motion abnormalities following dobutamine infusion are indicative of significant ischemia.
   6. **Technetium-99m**: extremely sensitive and specific for acute MI and for evaluating cardiac function.
   7. **Thallium imaging (scintigraphy)**: can locate and quantitate areas of ischemia or scarring and differentiate between the two.
   8. **Coronary angiography**: gold standard for evaluating cardiac disease. The location and severity of occlusions can be defined. For fixed stenotic lesions, occlusions greater than 50-75% are generally considered significant. Ventriculography and measurement of intracardiac pressures also provide important information.

4. **Anesthetic management of the cardiac patient for noncardiac surgery**
   A. **The overall goal** is to maintain a favorable balance between myocardial oxygen requirements and myocardial oxygen delivery. Maintenance of this balance (by avoiding tachycardia, systemic hypertension, hypoxemia, diastolic hypotension, acidosis) is more important then the specific technique.
   B. A common recommendation is to **maintain heart rate and systemic blood pressure within 20% of awake values**. However, almost 50% of all new ischemic events are not preceded by or associated with significant changes in HR or BP.
   C. **Perioperative pain management:** effective pain control leads to a reduction in postoperative catecholamine surges and hypercoagulability.
   D. **Intraoperative nitroglycerin:** insufficient data exists to routinely recommend prophylactic IV nitroglycerin in high risk patients.
   E. **Premedications**
      1. Help reduce fear, anxiety and pain, and help prevent sympathetic activation. Continue preoperative cardiac medications up until the time of surgery. Supplemental oxygen should be given to all patients with significant ischemia or who are given sedation.
      2. **Perioperative beta-adrenergic blockade**
         A. Has been shown to reduce the incidence of intraoperative and postoperative ischemic episodes and appears to be superior to prophylaxis with a calcium channel blocker alone.
         B. Eligibility is determined by the presence of any two minor criteria (age greater than 65, hypertension, current smoker, cholesterol greater than 240 mg/dL, or non-insulin dependent diabetes) or any single major criterion (high-risk surgical procedure, history of transient ischemic attack or stroke, insulin dependent diabetes, or chronic renal insufficiency)
   F. **Monitors** (in addition to standard ASA monitors)
      1. **Hemodynamic monitoring:** the most common abnormalities observed during ischemic episodes are hypertension and tachycardia.
      2. **Pulmonary artery catheters:** patients most likely to benefit appear to be those with a recent MI complicated by CHF, those with significant CAD who are undergoing procedures associated with significant hemodynamic stress, and those with systolic or diastolic left ventricular dysfunction, cardiomyopathy, or valvular disease undergoing high-risk operations. Ischemia is frequently associated with an abrupt increase in pulmonary capillary wedge pressure. The sudden appearance of a prominent v wave on the wedge waveform is usually indicative of acute mitral regurgitation from papillary muscle dysfunction or acute left ventricular dilatation.
      3. **ST-segment monitoring:** use of computerized ST-segment analysis in patients at high risk may improve sensitivity for myocardial ischemia detection. Myocardial ischemia occurs by at least a 1-mm downsloping of the ST segment from baseline. Usually, lead II is monitored for inferior wall ischemia and arrhythmias and V_5 for anterior wall ischemia.
      4. **Transesophageal echocardiogram:** ventricular wall motion abnormalities observed by TEE may be the most sensitive indicator of myocardial ischemia but are not practical for routine use and should be reserved for selected high risk patients.
   G. **Postoperative management:** The greatest risk postoperatively is unrecognized ischemia. The majority of perioperative Q-wave myocardial

infarctions occur within the first 3 days following surgery (usually after 24-48 hours). A significant number of non-Q-wave infarctions, however, can present in the first 24 hours. A common presentation is unexplained hypotension (others include CHF and altered mental status).

Perioperative Anticoagulation Management

1. **Patients on chronic anticoagulation therapy**
   A. In general, patients should have their anticoagulation therapy discontinued prior to surgery and restarted postoperatively. Warfarin should be withheld at least 3 days; Clopidogrel should be withheld at least 7 days; Ticlodipine should be withheld at least 10-14 days. Anticoagulation management should be made in consultation with the prescribing physician.
   B. The incidence of thromboembolic complications increases with a prior history of embolism and the presence of a thrombus, atrial fibrillation, , or a prosthetic mechanical valve.
   C. If thromboembolic risk is deemed high, anticoagulation can be stopped the day before surgery and reversed with vitamin K or fresh frozen plasma; intravenous heparin therapy can then be initiated 12-24 hours postoperatively once surgical hemostasis is adequate.
2. **Anticoagulation and neuraxial blockade**: see section in spinal anesthesia.

Anesthesia Following Heart Transplantation

1. **Physiology of cardiac transplantation**
   A. The transplanted heart is totally denervated and direct autonomic influences are absent. Resting heart rate, in the absence of vagal influences, is increased (100-120 beats/min).
   B. Ventricular function is slightly reduced; cardiac output increases owing to increased venous return (preload-dependent). Coronary autoregualtion is preserved.
   C. Increases in heart rate correspond to catecholamine secretion.
   D. Coronary atherosclerosis accelerated; silent ischemia likely.
   E. Drugs that act indirectly via the autonomic system are ineffective.
   F. Beta-adrenergic receptors remain intact.
2. **Preoperative evaluation**
   A. Evaluation should focus on functional status (activity level) and detecting complications of immunosuppression.
   B. Underlying cardiac disease may be asymptomatic (due to denervation).
   C. Baseline EKG may show both donor and native P waves and a right bundle branch block.
   D. Stress doses of corticosteroids are usually needed for major procedures.
3. **Anesthetic considerations**
   A. Maintain preload (a normal or high cardiac preload is desirable)
   B. Sudden vasodilation should be avoided because reflex increases in heart rate are absent. Indirect vasopressors are less effective than direct acting agents because of the absence of catecholamine stores in myocardial neurons.
   C. Increases in heart rate are not seen following anticholinergics, pancuronium, or meperidine. Bradycardia secondary to opioids and cholinesterase

inhibitors is absent.
  D. An anticholinergic must still be given to reverse muscle relaxants in order to block the noncardiac muscarinic effects of acetylcholine.

Hypertension

1. **Preoperative evaluation**
   A. History should assess the severity and duration of the hypertension, drug therapy, and the presence of hypertensive complications.
   B. Surgical procedures on patients with sustained preoperative diastolic blood pressures higher than 110 mmHg or with evidence of end-organ damage should be delayed, if possible, until blood pressure is controlled.
   C. Cardiac and hypertensive medications should be continued up until the time of surgery. Premedication is highly desirable to reduce anxiety.
2. **Anesthetic management**
   A. Blood pressure should be kept within 10-20% of preoperative levels.
   B. Many patients with hypertension display an accentuated hypotensive response to induction (unmasking of decreased intravascular volume) followed by an exaggerated hypertensive response to intubation.
   C. Techniques used to attenuate the hypertensive response to intubation:
      1. Deepening anesthesia with a volatile agent.
      2. Giving a bolus of narcotic: fentanyl, 1-5 mcg/kg; alfentanil, 15-25 mcg/kg; sufentanil, 0.25-0.5 mcg/kg; or remifentanil 0.5-1.0 mcg/kg
      3. Give lidocaine, 1.5 mg/kg IV or intratracheally.
      4. Beta-adrenergic blockade with esmolol, 0.3-1.5 mg/kg; propranolol, 1-3 mg; or labetalol, 5-20 mg.
      5. Pretreatment with an alpha-2 agonist (clonidine, 0.2 mg); has been associated with profound intraop hypotension and bradycardia.
      6. Giving IV nitroprusside or nitroglycerin, 0.5-1 mcg/kg.
      7. Laryngotracheal lidocaine before placement of the ETT.
   D. Intraoperative hypertension not responding to increased anesthesia depth can be treated with various IV agents (see table in pharmacology section).
   E. Postoperative anticipate excessive increases in systemic blood pressure.

Valvular Heart Disease

1. **Mitral stenosis**
   A. **Etiology** is almost always rheumatic.
   B. **Normal mitral valve are is 4-6 cm^2.** Symptoms occur when valve area is reduced to 2.5 cm^2 and become severe with valve area below 1 cm^2. Patients with valve areas between 1.5 cm^2 and 2.0 cm^2 are generally asymptomatic or have only mild symptoms on exertion.
   C. **Features:** dyspnea on exertion; atrial fibrillation (secondary to increased left atrial pressure and distention of the LA); pulmonary edema; pulmonary hypertension; tachycardia; right ventricular hypertrophy; and RV failure.
   D. **Pathophysiology:** stenosis of the mitral valve results in an increased left atrial pressure. This, in turn, results in pulmonary edema and , when chronic, in pulmonary arterial hypertension. Pulmonary congestion results in reduced compliance.

E. **Anesthetic management**
   1. Give prophylactic antibiotics for prevention of endocarditis.
   2. Patients with a history of emboli and those at high risk (older then 40 years; a large atrium with chronic atrial fib) are usually anticoagulated.
   3. Avoid sinus tachycardia or rapid ventricular response rate during AF.
   4. Ventricular filling across the obstructed valve depends on a high atrial pressure; the preload must therefore be maintained.
   5. Avoid large decreases in SVR.
   6. Avoid exacerbate pulmonary hypertension. Hypoxia, hypercarbia, acidosis, atelectasis, and sympathomimetics increase PVR. Oxygen, hypocarbia, alkalosis, nitrates, prostaglandin E_1 and nitric oxide decrease PVR.

2. **Mitral regurgitation**
   A. **Etiologies** include MVP, ischemic heart disease, endocarditis, post-MI papillary muscle rupture, and rheumatic fever.
   B. Characterized by left atrial volume overload and decreased left ventricular forward stroke volume. Produces large 'v' waves.
   C. **Features**: dyspnea, fatigue, and palpitations.
   D. **Signs:** LVH, LV failure, LA dilatation, atrial fib, pulmonary edema.
   E. **Pathophysiology**
      1. There is a reduced left ventricular stroke volume delivered to the aorta with left atrial fluid overload.
      2. Large V waves are seen on PCWP waveforms.
      3. The ventricular overload is volume (not pressure) so ischemia is not a prominent feature (though the LVEDP is high, reducing blood flow)
   F. **Anesthetic management**
      1. Give prophylactic antibiotics for prevention of endocarditis.
      2. The fraction of blood regurgitating depends on: the size of the mitral valve orifice during systole; the heart rate (slow rates are associated with more regurgitation); the pressure gradient across the valve; and the relative resistance of flow to the aorta and atrium (a low SVR favors forward flow to the aorta).
      3. Avoid slow heart rates and acute increases in afterload (SVR)
      4. Excessive volume expansion can worsen the regurgitation by dilating the left ventricle.
      5. The height of the 'v' wave is inversely related to atrial and pulmonary to pulmonary vascular compliance and directly proportional to pulmonary blood flow and the regurgitant volume.

3. **Mitral valve prolapse**
   A. Characterized by a midsystolic click with or without a late apical systolic murmur on auscultation.
   B. **Features:** chest pain, arrhythmias, embolic events, florid mitral regurgitation, infective endocarditis, and rarely, sudden death.
   C. Mitral regurgitation caused by prolapse is exacerbated by decreases in ventricular size (such as occurs with hypovolemia and decreased SVR).
   D. **Anesthetic management**
      1. Give prophylactic antibiotics for prevention of endocarditis.
      2. Hypovolemia and factors that increase ventricular afterload should be avoided.

4. **Aortic stenosis**
   A. **Normal aortic valve area** is 2.5-3.5 cm². Critical AS occurs with areas 0.5-0.7 cm² and transvalvular pressure gradient greater than 50 mmHg.
   B. **Symptoms:** dyspnea, angina, orthostatic or exertional syncope, decreased

exercise tolerance, sudden death.

C. **Pathophysiology:** concentric ventricular hypertrophy enables the left ventricle to maintain SV by generating a significant transvalvular gradient and reduce ventricular wall stress. A decrease in left ventricular compliance as a result of hypertrophy is also seen.

D. **Anesthetic management**
1. Give prophylactic antibiotics for prevention of endocarditis.
2. Maintain normal sinus rhythm and heart rate (rates between 60-90 bpm are optimal). Always have a cardiac defibrillator available.
3. Avoid sudden decrease in SVR and decreases in intravascular volume.
4. Aortic diastolic pressure must be maintained to preserve coronary artery blood flow.
5. Myocardial depression should be avoided.
6. Prominent 'a' waves are often visible on the PCWP waveform.
7. Postoperatively, most patients often require antihypertensive therapy.

5. **Aortic regurgitation**
   A. Acute cases include dissection of the thorax aorta and bacterial endocarditis. Chronic cases include rheumatic heart disease, hypertension, and syphilis.
   B. **Features**: dyspnea, angina pectoris and left ventricular failure.
   C. **Signs**: collapsing pulse, wide pulse pressure, cardiac dilatation.
   D. **Pathophysiology**
   1. Magnitude of regurgitation depends on heart rate (long diastole in bradycardia gives longer for regurgitation to occur), the diastolic aortic pressure, and the size of the orifice during diastole.
   2. The volume overload of the ventricle results in hypertrophy in chronic cases but ischemia is not a prominent finding. However, the aortic diastolic pressure is low and LVEDP is high so myocardial flow maybe Impaired.
   E. **Anesthetic management**
   1. Give prophylactic antibiotics for prevention of endocarditis.
   2. Slight tachycardia is desirable; reduction of SVR can improve forward flow.
   3. Avoid bradycardia, increases in SVR, maintain myocardial contractility, avoid myocardial depressants.

6. **Hypertrophic cardiomyopathy**
   A. Characterized by heterogeneous left ventricular hypertrophied that is without any obvious cause. Affected patients display diastolic dysfunction that is reflected by elevated left ventricular end-diastolic pressures in spite of often hyperdynamic ventricular function.
   B. Symptomatic patients complain of dyspnea on exertion, fatigue, syncope, near-syncope, or angina. Arrhythmias are common.
   C. Preoperative evaluation should focus on the potential for significant dynamic obstruction, malignant arrhythmias, and myocardial ischemia.
   D. **Anesthetic management**
   1. Goals should be to minimize sympathetic activation, expand intravascular volume in order to avoid hypovolemia, and minimize decreases in left ventricular afterload.
   2. Patients with significant obstruction may benefit from some degree of myocardial depression (volatile agents are useful here).

7. **Tricuspid regurgitation**
   A. **Etiology**: most commonly due to dilation of the right ventricle from the pulmonary hypertension that is associated with chronic left ventricle failure.

B. Complications: chronic venous congestion can lead to passive congestion of the liver and hepatic dysfunction; right-to-left shunting through an incomplete closed foramen ovale, which can result in hypoxia.

C. Anesthetic management

1. Avoid hypovolemia and factors that increase right ventricle afterload to help maintain effective right ventricular SV and left ventricular preload.
2. PEEP and high mean airway pressures can reduce venous return and increase right ventricular afterload.
3. Central pressure monitoring: increasing central venous pressure imply worsening right ventricular dysfunction. The x descent is absent and a prominent cv wave is usually present.

8. Pulmonary stenosis

A. Considered severe if pressure gradient is >50 mmHg with a normal CO.

B. Complications: right atrial and right ventricular hypertrophy, RV failure, syncope, angina, and sudden death.

C. Anesthetic management

1. Give prophylactic antibiotics for prevention of endocarditis.
2. Avoid factors which increase right ventricular O_2 requirements such as tachycardia and increased myocardial contractility.
3. Avoid factors decreasing right ventricular O_2 supply (hypotension).

Valvular Heart Disease						
Disease	Heart Rate	Rhythm	Preload	After-load	Contractility	Blood Pressure
Aortic Stenosis	normal, avoid tachy	sinus is essential	increase or main-tain	maintain	maintain	maintain
Aortic Regurg-itation	normal or slight in-crease	sinus	maintain or increase	reduce	maintain or increase	maintain
Mitral Stenosis	normal. avoid tachy	sinus; AF digitalize	maintain or in-crease	maintain avoid increase	maintain	avoid hypo-ten-sion
Mitral Regurg-itation	normal or increase	usually AF, digi-talize	maintain	reduce	maintain or increase	maintain
Ischemic Heart Dz	slow rate	sinus	maintain	reduce	maintain or decrease	normal at rest
IHSS	normal or slight de-crease	sinus, consider pacing	maintain or in-crease	maintain or slight increase	maintain or decrease	maintain

Pulmonary Disease

Pulmonary Risk Factors

1. **Risk factors** include preexisting pulmonary disease, thoracic or upper abdominal surgery, smoking, obesity, age greater than 60 years, and prolonged general anesthesia (>3 hours).
2. **The two strongest predictors of complications are operative site and a history of dyspnea.**
3. **Smoking:** cessation of smoking for 12-24 hours before decreases carboxyhemoglobin levels, shifts the oxyhemoglobin dissociation curve to the right, and increases oxygen available to tissue. Cessation for greater than 8-12 weeks is required to reduce the risk of postoperative pulmonary complications and improve ciliary and small airway function.

Asthma

1. **Preoperative**
   A. Asthma is characterized by airway hyperreactivity and inflammation, manifested by episodic attacks of dyspnea, cough, and wheezing.
   B. Preoperative evaluation should ascertain the severity and control of the asthma, drug therapy, previous steroid use and history of intubation.
   C. PFTs before and after bronchodilation therapy may be indicated in the patient scheduled for thoracic or abdominal surgery.
   D. Patients should be medically optimized prior to surgery. Patients with active bronchospasm presenting for emergency surgery should undergo a period of intensive treatment if possible.
   E. Bronchodilators should be continued up to the time of surgery. Theophylline levels should be checked preoperatively. Bronchodilators, in order of effectiveness, are beta-agonists, inhaled glucocorticoids, leukotriene blockers, chromones, theophyllines, and anticholinergics.
   F. Patients receiving steroids should be given supplemental doses (hydrocortisone 50-100 mg preop and 100mg q8h for 1-3 days postop).
2. **Intraoperative management**
   A. Pain, emotional stress, or stimulation during light general anesthesia can precipitate bronchospasm.
   B. Choice of induction agent is less important then achieving deep anesthesia before intubation and surgical stimulation. The goal during induction and maintenance is to depress airway reflexes so as to avoid bronchoconstriction of hyperreactive airways in response to mechanical stimulation.
   C. Reflex bronchospasm can be blunted prior to intubation by increasing the depth of anesthesia with additional induction agent or volatile agent, or by administering IV or IT lidocaine 1-2 mg/kg.
   D. Intraoperative bronchospasm is usually manifest by wheezing, increasing peak airway pressure, decreased exhaled tidal volumes or a slowly rising wave form on the capnograph. Treatment includes deepening the level of anesthesia, and beta agonists delivered by aerosol or metered dose inhalers. Other causes may mimic bronchospasm include obstruction of the ETT from kinking, secretions, or an overinflated balloon; endobronchial

intubation; active expiratory efforts (straining); pulmonary edema or embolism; and pneumothorax.

- E. In ventilated patients maintain PaO_2 and PCO_2 in normal levels, ventilate at slow rates (6-10 bpm), lower TV (<10 mL/kg), long exhalation times. Airway obstruction during expiration is seen on capnography as a delayed rise of the end-tidal CO2; the severity of obstruction is generally inversely related to the rate of rise in end-tidal CO2.
- F. Patients should be extubated either before airway reflexes return or after the patient is fully awake. Lidocaine may help suppress airway reflexes during emergence.

Chronic Obstructive Pulmonary Disease (COPD)

1. **Preoperative**
   - A. COPD is characterized by expiratory airflow obstruction strongly associated with cigarette smoking. COPD is usually classified as chronic bronchitis or emphysema (see table)
   - B. Evaluation should determine the severity of the disease and elucidate any reversible components such as infection or bronchospasm.
   - C. Patients at greatest risk for complications are those with preoperative pulmonary function measurements less than 50% of predicted.
   - D. A history of frequent exacerbations, steroid dependence, or need for intubation for respiratory support should prompt particular caution in the evaluation and planning for surgery.
2. **Intraoperative management**
   - A. Choice of anesthetic technique is less important then the realization that these patients are susceptible to acute respiratory failure in the postoperative period. Regional anesthesia can decrease lung volumes, restrict the use of accessory respiratory muscles, and produce an ineffective cough, leading to dyspnea and retention of secretions.
   - B. Ventilated patients should be controlled with small to moderate tidal volumes and slow rates to avoid air trapping. Maintain normal arterial pH.
   - C. Patients with an FEV_1 below 50% may require a period of postoperative ventilation, especially following upper abdominal and thoracic operations.

Signs and Symptoms of Chronic Obstructive Pulmonary Disease		
Feature	**Chronic Bronchitis**	**Emphysema**
Cough	Frequent	With exertion
Sputum	Copious	Minimal
Hematocrit	Elevated	Normal
$PaCO_2$ (mmHg)	Usually elevated	Usually normal
Chest X-Ray	Increased lung markings	Hyperinflation
Elastic Recoil	Normal	Decreased
Airway Resistance	Increased	Normal or slight increase
Cor Pulmonale	Early	Late

Restrictive Pulmonary Disease

1. **Characterized by decreased lung compliance.** Lung volumes normally are reduced with preservation of normal expiratory flow rates (normal FEV_1/FVC).
2. **Acute intrinsic pulmonary disorders** (ARDS, pulmonary edema, infection)
   A. Reduced lung compliance is primarily due to an increase in extravascular lung water, from either an increase in pulmonary capillary pressure or an increase in pulmonary capillary permeability.
   B. Elective surgery should be delayed.
   C. Ventilated patients should be controlled with reduced tidal volume, 4-8 mL/kg, with a compensatory increase in the ventilatory rate (14-18 bpm). Airway pressure should generally not exceed 30 cm H_2O.
3. **Chronic Intrinsic Pulmonary Disorders** (interstitial lung disease)
   A. Preoperative evaluation should focus on degree of pulmonary impairment.
   B. Anesthetic drug selection is not critical, however, management of these patients is complicated by a predisposition to hypoxemia and the need to control ventilation.
4. **Extrinsic Restrictive Pulmonary Disorders**
   A. These disorders alter gas exchange by interfering with normal lung expansion and include pleural effusions, mediastinal masses, kyphoscoliosis, pectus excavatum, neuromuscular disorders, and increased intra-abdominal pressure from ascites, pregnancy, or bleeding.

Endocrine Disorders

Diabetes Mellitus

1. **Acute complications:** diabetic ketoacidosis; hyperglycemic, hyperosmolar, nonketotic state; hyperglycemia; hypoglycemia
2. **Chronic complications:** autonomic neuropathy; macrovascular disease (coronary, cerebrovascular, peripheral vascular); microvascular disease (nephropathy, retinopathy); stiff joint syndrome, neuropathy, and increased susceptibility to infection.
3. **Evidence of autonomic neuropathy:** impotence, hypertension, neurogenic bladder, lack of sweating, orthostatic hypotension, resting tachycardia, absent variation in heart rate with deep breathing, painless myocardial ischemia, gastroparesis (vomiting, diarrhea, abdominal distention), asymptomatic hypoglycemia, prolonged QT interval, and sudden death syndrome.
4. **Management of anesthesia**
   ### A. General information
   1. One can estimate the soluble (regular) insulin requirement by taking the daily dose of lente units and multiplying by 1.5. This gives the units of regular insulin required per day.
   2. One unit of insulin (IV) will lower the blood sugar by 25-30 mg/dL in a 70 kg person. Ten grams of dextrose will raise the blood sugar by 30-40 mg/dL in an average 70 kg person.
   3. One in four insulin dependent diabetics may have "stiff joint syndrome" and may be difficult to intubate.
   4. Diabetics may have gastroparesis as a result of autonomic neuropathy. PONV is best treated with metoclopramide 10 mg IV.
   5. In obstetrics, the insulin requirements may drop after delivery.
   6. Lactate is converted to glucose in the liver. Lactated Ringers may cause a blood glucose elevation.
   7. Surgical procedures ideally should be first case.
   8. Because of unreliable subcutaneous absorption, IV insulin is the preferred method of dosing during surgery.
   9. Patients who require NPH or protamine. zinc insulin are at greater risk for allergic reaction to protamine sulfate.
   ### B. Preoperative management
   1. Signs and symptoms of myocardial dysfunction, cerebral ischemia, hypertension, and renal disease should be evaluated preoperatively.
   2. Hyperglycemia, ketoacidosis, and electrolyte disturbances should be corrected before elective surgery.
   3. Glucose/insulin management should maintain glucose between 120-180 mg/dl (see below for additional information).
   4. Metoclopramide and antacid regimens should be considered.
   ### C. Intraoperative management
   1. **Patients taking an oral (hypoglycemia) agent**
      A. Sulfonylurea agents should be withheld within 24 hours of surgery. If taken within 12 hrs, IV glucose supplementation should be started. Other agents can be given until the patient is NPO.
      B. Glucose should be checked before and after the procedure.

2. Insulin-treated type 2 diabetics (NIDDM)

A. Patients with well controlled NIDDM undergoing a brief procedure may not require any adjustment in insulin regimen. For major surgery consider giving half their total normal morning insulin dose as intermediate or long-acting insulin. Regular or rapid-onset insulin should be withheld. Consider starting patient on a glucose-containing infusion preoperatively.

B. Blood glucose should be checked before, during, and after surgery.

3. Insulin-treated type 1 diabetics (IDDM)

A. Patients must receive exogenous insulin to prevent ketoacidosis.

B. Insulin can be given by sliding scale or continuous infusion.

   1. Regular insulin: 50 U/250 cc NS = 0.2 units/cc (flush IV tubing before starting).
   2. Insulin rate in U/hr = blood glucose/150 (use 100 as denominator if patient is on steroids, or is markedly obese, or infected). Alternative dosing. 0.1 units/kg/hr.
   3. An IV of D_5W (1-1.5 ml/kg/hr) should be started prior to insulin.
   4. Adjust insulin infusion as needed to keep glucose levels between 120-180 mg/dL.

4. Postoperative management

A. Monitoring of blood glucose must continue postoperatively.

Oral Hypoglycemia Agents			
Drug	Onset (hrs)	Peak (hrs)	Duration (hrs)
Sulfonylurea			
Tolbutamide	0.5-1	1-3	6-24
Glipizide	0.25-0.5	1-2	12-24
Glipizide XL	1-4	6-12	24-48
Acetoheximide	1-2	8-10	12-24
Tolazamide	4-6	4-6	10-24
Glyburide	0.25-1	1-3	12-24
Chlorpropamide	1-2	3-6	24
Thiazolidinedione			
Pioglitazone	1		24
Biguanide			
Glucophage	1		8-12
Meglitinide			
Repaglinide	0.25		6-7
D-Phenylalanine Derivative			
Netaglinide	0.25		3-4

Insulin Agents			
Drug	Onset (hrs)	Peak (hrs)	Duration (hrs)
Short-Acting			
Lispro	5-15 min	1	4-5
Regular	0.5-1	2-3	5-7
Actrapid	0.25-0.5	1-3	5-7
Velosulin	0.25-0.5	1-3	5-7
Semilente	0.5-1	4-7	18-24
Semitard	0.5-1	4-6	12-16
Intermediate-Acting			
Lente	1-2.5	8-12	18-24
Lentard	1-2.5	8-12	18-24
NPH	1-1.5	4-12	18-24
Long-Acting			
Ultralente	4-8	16-18	36
Ultratard	4-8	12-18	36
PZI	4-8	14-24	36
Glargine	1-2	(none)	24

Pheochromocytoma (catecholamine excess)

1. **Definition:** catechol-secreting tumors usually located in an adrenal gland. Most pheochromocytomas produce both norepinephrine and epinephrine. Endogenous catecholamine levels should return to normal levels within 1-3 days after successful removal of the tumor. Overall mortality: 0-6%.
2. **Clinical manifestations**
   A. **Cardinal manifestations:** hypertension, paroxysmal headaches, palpitations and diaphoresis.
   B. **Other manifestations** include tachycardia, flushing, anxiety, tremor, hyperglycemia, polycythemia, cardiomyopathy, intracerebral hemorrhage, decreased intravascular fluid volume, and weight loss.
   C. Unexpected intraoperative hypertension and tachycardia maybe first indication of undiagnosed pheochromocytoma.
   D. **Diagnosis** is confirmed by abnormally high levels of catecholamines or catechol metabolites in urine. Assay of 24-hour urinary metanephrine is the most reliable indicator of excess catecholamine secretion.
3. **Preoperative evaluations**
   A. **Prazosin or phenoxybenzamine** may be used to produce preoperative alpha-adrenergic blockade. Ten to 14 days are usually required for adequate alpha-receptor blockade. Beta blockade is instituted after the onset of adequate alpha blockade if dysrhythmias or tachycardia persists. A drop in hematocrit is seen with the expansion of intravascular volume.
   B. **Preoperative goals:** blood pressure below 160/95, no ST-T wave changes, restore intravascular fluid volume, and <1 PVC per 5 minutes.
4. **Anesthetic considerations**
   A. **Overall goal** is to avoid sympathetic hyperactivity. Critical times are during tracheal intubation, during manipulation of the tumor, and following ligation of the venous drainage of the tumor.

    B. Hypertension can be treated with phentolamine, nitroprusside, or nicardipine.

    C. Drugs to avoid

       1. **Histamine releasers:** morphine, curare, atracurium.

       2. **Vagolytics and sympathomimetics:** atropine, pancuronium, gallamine, succinylcholine.

       3. **Myocardial sensitizers:** halothane.

       4. **Indirect catechol stimulators:** droperidol, ephedrine, TCAs, chlorpromazine, glucagon, metoclopramide.

    D. Monitors: intraarterial catheter in addition to standard monitors; consider central venous pressure monitoring.

    E. Intraoperative: after tumor ligation, the primary problem is hypotension form hypovolemia, persistent adrenergic blockade, and prior tolerance to the high levels of catecholamines that abruptly ended.

    F. Postoperative: hypertension seen postoperatively may indicate the presence of occult tumors or volume overload.

Hyperthyroidism

1. **Clinical manifestations** may include: weight loss, heat intolerance, muscle weakness, diarrhea, hyperactive reflexes, nervousness, exophthalmos, sinus tachycardia/atrial fibrillation and fine tremors.

2. **Management of anesthesia**

    A. Preoperative: all elective surgery should be postponed until the patient is rendered euthyroid with medical treatment. Preoperative assessment should include normal thyroid function tests, and a resting heart rate <85 beats/min. The combination of beta antagonists and potassium iodide is effective in rendering most patients euthyroid in 10 days. Consider esmolol when surgery cannot be delayed. Antithyroid medications and beta-blockers should be continued through the morning of surgery.

    B. Intraoperative: thiopental is the induction agent of choice, since it possesses some antithyroid activity. Drugs that will stimulate the sympathetic nervous system should be avoided (ketamine, pancuronium, indirect-acting adrenergic agonists, etc.). MAC requirements for inhaled agents or anesthetic requirements are not increased with hyperthyroidism. Cardiovascular function and body temperature should be closely monitored. Patients may have exaggerated response to sympathomimetics.

    C. Postoperative: most serious postoperative problem is thyroid storm, which is characterized by hyperpyrexia, tachycardia, altered consciousness, and hypotension. Most commonly occurs 6-24 hours postoperatively. Treatment includes hydration and cooling, propranolol (0.5 mg increments until heart rate is below 100 beats/min) or esmolol. Consider cortisol (100-200 mg IV every 8 hours), propylthiouracil (250 mg every 6 hours orally) followed by sodium iodide (1 gm IV over 12 hours), and correction of any precipitating cause.

3. **Complications** after total or partial thyroidectomy: recurrent laryngeal nerve palsy, hematoma formation, hypothyroidism, hypoparathyroidism, and pneumothorax.

Hypothyroidism

1. **Clinical manifestations** may include generalized reduction in metabolic activity, lethargy, intolerance to cold, weight gain, constipation, bradycardia, hypoactive reflexes, decreased cardiac function, and depression.
2. **Myxedema coma** results from extreme hypothyroidism and is characterized by impaired mentation, hypoventilation, hypothermia, hyponatremia, and CHF. Treatment is with IV thyroid hormones (300-500 mcg of levothyroxine sodium in patients without heart disease). Cortisol should also be given.
3. **Management of anesthesia**
   A. **Preoperative:** patients with uncorrected severe hypothyroidism or myxedema coma should not undergo elective surgery. Mild to moderate hypothyroidism is not a absolute contraindication to surgery. Patients should be treated with histamine H_2 blockers and metoclopramide because of their slowed gastric emptying times.
   B. **Intraoperative:** ketamine is the induction agent of choice because of the exquisite sensitivity of hypothyroid patients to drug-induced myocardial depression. MAC requirements for inhaled agents are not changed with hypothyroidism. Maintenance usually with nitrous oxide plus supplementation (opioids, ketamine, etc). Monitoring directed toward early recognition of CHF and hypothermia. Other potential problems include hypoglycemia, hyponatremia, anemia, and difficult intubation.
   C. **Postoperative:** recovery from general anesthesia may be delayed by slowed drug biotransformation, hypothermia, and respiratory depression.

Hyperparathyroidism

1. **Clinical manifestations** may include hypertension, ventricular Dysrhythmias, shortened QT interval, impaired renal concentrating ability, dehydration, hyperchloremic metabolic acidosis, nausea/vomiting, muscle weakness, and mental status changes.
2. Management of anesthesia
   A. Preoperative: assessment of volume status; hydration with normal saline and diuresis with furosemide usually decrease serum calcium to acceptable levels (<14 mg/dL, 3.5 mmol/L, or 7 mEq/L).
   B. Intraoperative: avoid hypoventilation (acidosis increases serum calcium); the response to neuromuscular blocking agents may be altered.

Hypoparathyroidism

1. **Clinical manifestations** may include hypotension, congestive heart failure, prolonged QT interval, muscle cramps, neuromuscular irritability (laryngospasm, inspiratory stridor, tetany, etc.), and mental status changes.
2. **General information**
   A. Hypoalbuminemia decreases total serum calcium (a 1 g/dL drop in serum albumin causes a 0.8 mg/dL decrease in total serum calcium); ionized calcium is unaltered.
   B. Signs of neuromuscular irritability include the presence of Chvostek's sign (painful twitching of the facial musculature following tapping over the facial nerve) or Trousseau's sign (carpopedal spasm following inflation of a

tourniquet above systolic blood pressure for 3 minutes).
3. **Management of anesthesia**
   A. **Preoperative:** serum calcium should be normalized in any patient with cardiac manifestations.
   B. **Intraoperative:** avoid hyperventilation or sodium bicarbonate therapy (alkalosis decreases serum calcium); the response to neuromuscular blocking agents may be altered (increased sensitivity); and avoid 5% albumin solutions (may bind and lower ionized calcium)..

Obesity

1. **Definitions**
   A. **Overweight** is defined as up to 20% above predicted ideal body weight.
   B. **Obesity** is defined as more than 20% above ideal body weight.
   C. **Morbid obesity** is defined as more than twice ideal body weight.
2. **Body mass index**
   A. Clinically the most useful index for defining obesity.
   B. **Body mass index (BMI)** = weight (kg)/height^2 (meters squared).
   C. **Overweight** is defined as a BMI greater then 25 kg/m^2.
   D. **Obesity** is defined as a BMI greater than 30 kg/m^2.
   E. **Morbid obesity** is defined as a BMI greater than 35-40 kg/m^2.
3. **Clinical manifestations**
   A. **Cardiovascular:** increased circulating blood volume, increased cardiac output, increased oxygen consumption, systemic hypertension, coronary artery disease, congestive heart failure, and pulmonary hypertension. Cardiac output increases by 0.1 L/min/kg of adipose tissue.
   B. **Pulmonary:** decreased lung volumes and capacities (suggestive of restrictive lung disease secondary to decreased chest wall compliance), arterial hypoxemia (decreased FRC predisposes the obese patient to a rapid decrease in PaO$_2$; if FRC below closing volume may lead to airway closure, ventilation perfusion mismatch, and hypoxemia), obesity-hypoventilation syndrome.
   C. **Liver:** abnormal liver function tests, fatty liver infiltration.
   D. **Metabolic:** insulin resistance (diabetes mellitus), hypercholesterolemia.
   E. **Gastrointestinal:** hiatal hernia, gastroesophageal reflux.
4. **Obesity-hypoventilation syndrome (Pickwickian syndrome)**
   A. Occurs in 8% of obese patients, commonly in the extremely obese.
   B. Hallmarks of this condition are hypoventilation, hypersomnia, and obesity.
   C. Characterized by hypercapnia, cyanosis-induced polycythemia, right-sided heart failure, somnolence, and pulmonary hypertension.
5. **Obstructive sleep apnea syndrome (OSAS)**
   A. Obesity and sleep-induced relaxation of the pharyngeal musculature are thought to cause intermittent upper airway obstruction. Obstruction leads to hypoxemia and hypercarnia, which results in arousal and the return of normal respiration. Repeated awakenings result to daytime somnolence.
   B. OSAS has been associated with increased perioperative complications including hypertension, hypoxia, dysrhythmias, myocardial infarction, pulmonary edema, and stroke. Difficult airway management should also be anticipated.

6. Anesthetic considerations
A. Preoperative
1. Preoperative evaluation of morbidly obese patients for major surgery should include a chest x-ray, EKG, arterial blood gas, and PFTs.
2. The airway should be carefully examined since these patients are often difficult to intubate as a result of limited mobility of the temporomandibular and atlanto-occipital joints, a narrowed upper airway, and a shortened distance between the mandible and increased soft tissue.
3. All obese patients are at an increased risk of aspiration and should be considered to have a full-stomach. Pretreatment with H_2 antagonists, metoclopramide, and sodium citrate should be considered. Avoid sedation in patients with preoperative hypoxia, hypercapnia, or OSAS.

B. Intraoperative
1. The risk of rapid decreases in PaO_2 (due to decreased FRC) is significant; therefore, preoxygenation prior to intubation is essential.
2. Rapid sequence induction/intubation is selected to minimize the risk of pulmonary aspiration. Morbidly obese patients with a difficult airway should be intubated awake.
3. Volatile anesthetics may be metabolized more extensively in obese patients. Obese patients are at an increased risk of halothane hepatitis.
4. Initial drug doses should be based on actual body weight, while maintenance drug doses should be based on idea body weight.
5. Obese patients generally require less local anesthetic (as much as 20-25%) for spinal and epidural anesthesia because of epidural fat and distended epidural veins.

C. Postoperative
1. Respiratory failure is the major postoperative problem of morbidly obese patients. Other problems include deep vein thrombosis, pulmonary embolism, atelectasis and wound infections.
2. The semisitting position will optimize the mechanics of breathing (unload the diaphragm) and will minimize the development of arterial hypoxemia.
3. Patients generally should not be extubated until fully awake.

Corticosteroid Therapy Before Surgery

1. Corticosteroid supplementation should be given to patients being treated for chronic hypoadrenocorticism.
2. Consider supplemental corticosteroids in patients being treated with corticosteroids (unrelated to abnormalities in the anterior pituitary or adrenal cortex) or who have been treated for longer than 1 month in the past 6-12 months.
3. **Empiric regimen for perioperative supplementation**
   A. Patients taking less then 10 mg prednisone/day do not require supplementation.
   B. For patients taking greater then 10 mg prednisone/day consider:
      1. For major surgery: give usual daily dose with premedications, cortisol 25 mg IV on induction, then 100 mg IV by infusion over the next 24 hours. Resume daily dose postoperatively.
      2. For minor surgery: give usual daily dose with premedications and cortisol 25 mg IV on induction. Resume daily dose postoperatively.

Carcinoid Syndrome

1. Carcinoid tumors are the most common GI endocrine tumor.
2. Common manifestations: flushing, bronchospasm, profuse diarrhea, hemodynamic instability, supraventricular dysrhythmias, and hyperglycemia.
3. Anesthetic considerations
    A. In symptomatic patients, preoperative and intraoperative treatment with the somatostatin analogue octreotide (Sandostatin) prevents the release of serotonin, gastrin, vasoactive intestinal peptide, insulin, glucagon, and secretin. The usual dose of octreodtide is 50-300 mcg.
    B. Carcinoid crisis with refractory hypotension and bronchoconstriction should be treated with octreotide (50-100 mcg IV over 30 minutes), fluid resuscitation, and a direct-acting vasopressor.

Liver Disease

Liver Disease and Anesthesia

1. **General considerations**
   A. Anesthetics agents generally reduce hepatic blood flow. Additional factors that reduce hepatic blood flow include hypovolemia, hypocapnia, positive pressure ventilation, surgical traction, excessive sympathetic activation, and patient position.
   B. Elective surgery should be postponed in patients with acute hepatitis. Preoperative LFT's should be stable or decreasing for elective surgery.
2. **Preoperative evaluation**
   A. **History:** evaluation of type of liver disease, previous or present jaundice, history of gastrointestinal bleeding, previous surgical operations, exposure to drugs/alcohol.
   B. **Physical:** degree of ascites, encephalopathy, hepatosplenomegaly, peripheral edema.
   C. **Lab test:** CBC with platelet count, serum bilirubin, albumin, serum electrolytes, creatinine and BUN, PT/PTT, and liver function tests.
   D. **The coagulation system** function should be evaluated and corrected preoperatively (with vitamin K, FFP, or platelets as needed). Adequate hydration and diuresis (1 mL/kg/hr) should be achieved.
   E. **Premedications:** sedatives should be omitted or the dose decreased.
3. **Intraoperative management**
   A. The goal of intraoperative management is to preserve existing hepatic function and avoid factors that may be detrimental to the liver.
   B. Regional anesthesia may be contraindicated because of an increased risk of bleeding and hematoma formation.
   C. A low threshold for rapid sequence induction should exist.
   D. Limit volatile anesthetics (by combining with nitrous oxide and opioids) in order to preserve hepatic blood flow and hepatic oxygenation.
   E. Monitor intraoperative blood gases, pH, coagulation, and urine output.
   F. Avoid or use caution in placing esophageal instrumentation.
4. **Postoperative management**
   A. Postoperative liver dysfunction is likely to be exaggerated presumably owing to nonspecific effects of anesthetic drugs on hepatic blood flow and subsequent hepatocyte oxygenation.

Alcohol Withdrawal Syndrome

1. **Delirium tremens** usually appear 48-72 hours after cessation of drinking. Mortality is about 10%. Alcohol withdrawal during surgery may be associated with a mortality rate as high as 50%.
2. **Manifestations:** tremulousness, hallucinations, disorientation, autonomic hyperactivity (diaphoresis, hyperpyrexia, tachycardia, hypertension), grand mal seizures. Lab findings include hypomagnesemia, hypokalemia, and respiratory alkalosis.
3. **Treatment:** diazepam 5-10 mg IV every 5 minutes until patient becomes sedated) and a beta antagonist (propranolol or esmolol) to suppress

sympathetic nervous system hyperactivity. Consider supplemental thiamine, magnesium and potassium.

Acute and Chronic Alcoholism

1. **The acutely intoxicated patient** requires less anesthetic, are more prone to gastric regurgitation, hypothermia, hypoglycemia, and handle stress and blood loss poorly.
2. **Chronic alcoholic liver disease** progresses in stages: elevated liver transaminases, fatty liver disease, alcoholic hepatitis, and finally cirrhosis and portal hypertension. In chronic alcoholics MAC is increased, plasma cholinesterase synthesis may be decreased.

Postoperative Liver Dysfunction

1. **Surgical interventions** that impair hepatic blood flow or obstruct the biliary system may lead to postoperative liver dysfunction.
2. **Nonsurgical causes:** exacerbation of preexisting hepatic dysfunction.
3. **Halothane-associated hepatitis**
   A. **Predisposing factors** include previous halothane exposure, obesity, advanced age, and female gender. Pediatric patients are less likely to have halothane-related hepatic dysfunction even after repeated exposures at short intervals.
   B. Halothane hepatic dysfunction manifest as post-operative fever and elevated liver function tests. The diagnosis is one of exclusion.
   C. Two entities
      1. **Mild/transient form** related to hypoxia (hepatotoxic lipoperoxidase generated during the metabolism of halothane when hypoxic).
      2. **Fulminant form** possibly secondary to allergic reaction; an oxidative metabolite of halothane, trifluoroacetyl chloride, binds to hepatocytes, creating a neoantigenic structure to which antibodies may be generated. Hepatocellular damage occurs on subsequent exposure.

Renal Disease

Acute and Chronic Renal Failure

1. **Acute renal failure** (ARF)
   A. **Characterized** by a sudden decrease in renal function that results in retention of nitrogenous waste products.
   B. Etiology can be divided into prerenal (acute decrease in renal perfusion), renal (intrinsic renal disease, renal ischemia, or nephrotoxins), and postrenal (urinary tract obstruction or disruption).
   C. **Clinical features** include hypervolemia, hypovolemia, potassium retention, impaired excretion of drugs and toxins, potential progression to CRF.
2. **Chronic renal failure** (CRF)
   A. **Characterized** by a permanent decrease in GFR with a rise in serum creatinine and azotemia.
   B. Most common causes include hypertensive nephrosclerosis, diabetic nephropathy, chronic glomerulonephritis, and polycystic renal disease.
   C. **Clinical features** include hypervolemia, hypertension, accelerated atherosclerosis, uremic pericarditis/effusions, hyperkalemia, hypermagnesemia, hyponatremia, hypocalcemia, hyperphosphatemia, metabolic acidosis, chronic anemia, platelet dysfunction, delayed gastric emptying, increased susceptibility to infection, CNS changes, glucose intolerance, altered pharmacodynamics.
3. **Dialysis** is indicated in ARF and CRF for hyperkalemia, volume overload, uremic complications (encephalopathy, pericarditis, tamponade), acidosis, severe azotemia.

Renal Disease and Anesthesia

1. **Preoperative evaluation**
   A. **General considerations**
      1. Elective surgery should be postponed pending resolution of acute disease processes.
      2. The degree of renal function is the most important factor.
   B. **History**: etiology and degree of renal disease, relevant medications, dialysis status (frequency, date of last dialysis), exercise tolerance, neurologic dysfunction, vitals, location of shunts/fistulas (if present).
   C. **Laboratory**: electrolytes, creatinine, albumin, hemoglobin/hematocrit, PT and PTT, platelet count, and bleeding time should be considered. CXR and EKG should also be reviewed.
2. **Intraoperative management**
   A. **Technique**: either general or regional is acceptable. Current coagulation status and the presence of uremic neuropathy should be determined before proceeding with regional anesthesia.
   B. **Cisatracurium and atracurium** are muscle relaxants of choice.
   C. **Succinylcholine**: can be safely used if serum potassium is not elevated. Dialysis treatment will lower serum cholinesterase levels and thus produce a prolonged response to succinylcholine.

    D. Fluid management: fluids should be administered cautiously and avoid using potassium containing fluids in anuric patients.

3. Postoperative management

    A. Hypertension is common problem aggravated by fluid overload. Patients on dialysis may need postoperative dialysis .

    B. Increased potential for exaggerated CNS depression, electrolyte abnormalities, and tissue oxygenation.

Basics of Anesthesiology

Medical Gas Systems

1. **Oxygen**
   A. Oxygen is stored as a compressed gas at room temperature or refrigerated as a liquid.
   B. The pressure in an oxygen cylinder is directly proportional to the volume of oxygen in the cylinder.
2. **Nitrous oxide**
   A. At room temperature, nitrous oxide is stored as a liquid.
   B. In contrast to oxygen, the cylinder pressure for nitrous oxide does not indicate the amount of gas remaining in the cylinder; 750 psi as long as any liquid nitrous oxide is present (when cylinder pressure begins to fall, only about 400 liters of nitrous oxide remains).
   C. The cylinder must be weight to determine residual volume of nitrous oxide.

Characteristics of Medical Gas E-Cylinders				
	Cylinder Color	Form	Capacity (L)	Pressure (psi)
Oxygen	Green	Gas	660	1900-2200
Nitrous Oxide	Blue	Liquid	1,590	745
Carbon Dioxide	Gray	Liquid	1,590	838
Air	Yellow	Gas	625	1,800
Nitrogen	Black	Gas	650	1800-2200
Helium	Brown	Gas	496	1600-2000

Electrical Safety

1. **Line isolation monitor**
   A. Line isolation monitor measures the potential for current flow from the isolated power supply to ground.
   B. An alarm is activated if an unacceptably high current flow to ground becomes possible (usually 2 mA or 5 mA).
   C. Operating room power supply is isolated from grounds by an isolation transformer. The line source is grounded by the electrical provider while the secondary circuit is intentionally not grounded.
2. **Electrical shock**
   A. **Macroshock**
      1. Refers to the application of electrical current through intact skin.
      2. Currents exceeding 100 mA may result in VF.

B. Microshock
1. Microshock refers to the application of electrical current applied directly to the heart (i.e., guide wires or pacing wires).
2. Currents exceeding 100 μA may induce ventricular fibrillation.
3. The maximum leakage allowed in operating room equipment is 10 μA. Line isolation monitors do not protect a patient from microshock.

Anesthesia Machine

1. **Safety valves and regulators**
   A. **Outlet check value:** prevents gas cylinders from crossfilling.
   B. **Pressure regulator:** reduces cylinder gas pressure to below 50 psi.
   C. **Fail-safe valve:** closes gas lines if oxygen pressure falls below 25 psi to prevent accidental delivery of a hypoxic mixture.
   D. **Diameter index safety system (DISS):** prevents incorrect gas line attachment to the anesthesia machine.
   E. **Pin index safety system (PISS):** interlink between the anesthesia machine and gas cylinder; prevents incorrect cylinder attachment.
   F. **Second stage oxygen pressure regulator:** oxygen flow is constant until pressure drops below 12-16 PSI; whereas other gases shut off if oxygen pressure is less than 30 PSI. This ensures that oxygen is last gas flowing.
2. **Flowmeters** on anesthesia machines are classified as constant-pressure, variable orifice flowmeters.
3. **Vaporizers**
   A. **Classification of modern vaporizers**
      1. **Variable bypass:** part of the total gas flow coming into the vaporizer is bypassed into the vaporizing chamber and then returns to join the rest of the gas at the outlet.
      2. **Flow-over:** the gas channeled to the vaporizing chamber flows over the liquid agent and becomes saturated.
      3. **Temperature-compensated:** automatic temperature compensation device helps maintain a constant vaporizer output over a wide range of temperatures.
      4. **Agent specific.**
      5. **Out of circuit:** not in the breathing circuit.
   B. **Vaporizer output** is not influenced by fresh gas flows until very low flow rates (<250 mL/min) or very high flow rates (>15 L/min).
4. **Anesthesia ventilators**
   A. **Power source:** contemporary ventilators have a pneumatic and electrical power source.
   B. **Drive mechanism:** compressed gas is the driving mechanism.
   C. **Cycling mechanism:** time-cycled, and inspiration is triggered by a timing device.
   D. **Bellows classification:** direction of the bellows during expiration determines the classification. Ascending bellows (bellow ascends during expiration) is safer; a ascending bellow will not fill if a disconnect occurs.
   E. Because the pressure relief valve of the ventilator is closed during inspiration, the circuit's fresh gas flows contribute to the tidal volume delivered to the patient. The amount each tidal volume will increase. (fresh gas flow mL/min) x (% inspiratory time) divided by the respiratory rate.
   F. The use of the oxygen flush valve during the inspiratory cycle of a ventilator

must be avoided because the pressure-relief valve is closed and the surge of circuit pressure will be transferred to the patient's lungs.

Anesthesia Machine Check List

Check list should be conducted before administering anesthesia.
1. **Emergency** ventilation equipment.*
   A. Verify backup ventilation equipment is available and functioning.
2. **High pressure systems.***
   A. Check Oxygen cylinders supply.
      1. Open oxygen cylinder and verify at least half full (about 1000 psi).
      2. Close cylinder.
   B. **Check central pipeline supplies:** check that hoses are connected properly and pipeline gauges read around 50 psi.
3. **Low pressure systems.***
   A. **Check initial status of low-pressure system**.
      1. Close flow control valves and turn vaporizers off.
      2. Check fill level and tighten vaporizers' filler caps.
   B. Perform leak check of machine low-pressure system.
      1. Verify that the machine master switch and flow control valves are 'off'.
      2. Attach suction bulb to common (fresh) gas outlet.
      3. Squeeze bulb repeatedly until fully collapsed.
      4. Verify bulb stays fully collapsed for at least 10 seconds.
      5. Open one vaporizer at a time and repeat 'c' and 'd'.
      6. Remove suction bulb, and reconnect fresh gas hose.
   C. Turn on machine master switch and all other necessary electrical equipment.
   D. Test flowmeters.
      1. Adjust flow of all gases through their full range, checking for smooth operation of floats and undamaged flowtubes.
      2. Attempt to create a hypoxic O_2/N_2O mixture and verify correct changes in flow and/or alarm.
4. **Scavenging system.***
   A. **Adjust and check scavenging system**.
      1. Ensure proper connections between scavenging system and both APL (pop-off valve) and the ventilator relief valve.
      2. Adjust waste-gas vacuum (if possible).
      3. Fully open APL valve and occlude the Y-piece.
      4. With minimum O_2 flow, allow scavenger reservoir bag to collapse completely and verify that absorber pressure reads zero (checks negative pressure valve).
      5. With O_2 flush activated, allow the scavenger reservoir bag to distend fully and then verify that absorber pressure gauge reads less than 10 cm/H_2O (checks positive pressure pop-off valve).
5. **Breathing system**
   A. **Calibrate O_2 monitor***
      1. Ensure monitor reads 21% when exposed to room air.
      2. Verify that low O_2 alarm is enabled and functioning.
      3. Reinstall sensor in circuit and flush breathing system with O_2.
      4. Verify that monitor now reads greater than 90%.

  B. Check initial status of system
   1. Set selector switch to "bag" mode.
   2. Check that breathing circuit is complete, undamaged, and unobstructed.
   3. Verify that CO_2 absorbent is adequate.
   4. Install any breathing-circuit accessory equipment such as humidifier.
  C. Perform leak check of breathing circuit
   1. Set all gas flows to minimum (or zero).
   2. Close APL (pop-off) valve and occlude Y piece.
   3. Pressurize breathing system to 30 cm H_2O with O_2 flush.
   4. Ensure that pressure remains fixed for at least 10 seconds.
   5. Open APL (pop-off) valve and ensure that pressure decreases.
6. Manual and automatic ventilation systems
 A. Test ventilation systems and unidirectional valves
   1. Place a second breathing bag on Y-piece.
   2. Set appropriate ventilator parameters for next patient.
   3. Switch to automatic-ventilation (ventilator) mode.
   4. Turn ventilator on and fill bellows and breathing bag with O_2 flush.
   5. Set O_2 to minimum and other gas flows to zero.
   6. Verify that during inspiration bellows delivers appropriate TV and that bellows fills completely on expiration.
   7. Set fresh gas flow to about 5 liters per minute.
   8. Verify that the ventilator bellows and simulated lungs fill and empty appropriately without sustained pressure at end expiration.
   9. Check for proper action of unidirectional valves.
   10. Test breathing circuit accessories to ensure proper functioning.
   11. Turn ventilator off and switch to manual ventilation mode.
   12. Ventilate manually and assure inflation and deflation of artificial lungs and appropriate feel of system resistance and compliance.
   13. Remove second breathing bag from Y-piece.
7. Monitors
 A. Check, calibrate, and/or set alarm limits of all monitors.
8. Final position
 A. Check final status of machine
   1. Vaporizers off.
   2. APL valve open.
   3. Selector switch should be set to 'bag'.
   4. All flowmeters should be zero (O_2 to minimum flow).
   5. Patient suction level adequate.
   6. Breathing system ready to use.

*These steps need not be repeated if same provider uses the machine in successive cases

Monitoring

1. Capnogram
 A. The normal end-tidal to arterial CO_2 gradient (dCO_2) is 2-5 mmHg. This value reflects alveolar dead space (alveoli ventilated but not perfused).
 B. Causes of increased dCO_2.
   1. Decreased pulmonary arterial pressure.
   2. Upright posture.

    3. Pulmonary embolism. air, fat, thrombus, amniotic fluid.
    4. COPD: causes nonvascular air space at the alveolar level.
    5. Mechanical obstruction of the pulmonary arteries.
    6. Ventilation gas leaving the normal air passages. bronchopleural fistula, tracheal disruption, cuff leak.

C. Factors that increase end-tidal CO_2

    1. Hypoventilation.
    2. Sodium bicarbonate.
    3. Laparoscopy (CO_2 inflation).
    4. Anesthetic breathing circuit error.
        A. Inadequate fresh gas flow.
        B. Rebreathing.
        C. Faulty circle absorber valves.
        D. Exhausted soda lime.
    5. Hyperthermia.
    6. Improved blood flow to lungs after resuscitation or hypotension.
    7. Water in capnograph head.
    8. Tourniquet release.
    9. Venous CO_2 embolism.

D. Causes of decreased end-tidal CO_2.

    1. Hyperventilation.
    2. Apnea, total airway obstruction, or circuit disconnection.
    3. Inadequate sampling volume or sampling tube leak.
    4. Incorrect placement of sampling catheter.
    5. Hypothermia.
    6. Incipient pulmonary edema.
    7. Air embolism.
    8. Decreased blood flow to lungs (reduced cardiac output).

E. Capnography waveforms.

    1. **Increased baseline:** if increased, patient is receiving CO2 during inspiration. Sources include: exhausted CO2 absorber, incompetent unidirectional inspiratory or expiratory valve, deliberate or inadvertent administration of CO2.
    2. **Cleft in alveolar plateau (curare cleft):** occurs when the patient makes spontaneous respiratory efforts or inhales before the next mechanical inspiration.
    3. **Steep plateau:** seen in asthma and COPD.
    4. **Cardiogenic oscillations:** ripple effect, superimposed on the plateau and the descending limb, resulting from small gas movements produced by pulsations of the aorta and heart.

2. Pulse oximetry

A. Technology

    1. Unlike SaO_2, the SpO_2 is a functional saturation defined as the HbO_2 relative to the total of oxyhemoglobin and deoxyhemoglobin.
    2. Oximetry is based on detecting the difference in absorption of particular wavelengths or light by oxygenated and reduced hemoglobin. Oxyhemoglobin absorbs more infrared light (e.g., 940 nm), while deoxyhemoglobin absorbs more red light (e.g., 660 nm).
    3. The change in light absorption during arterial pulsations is the basis of oximetry determination of oxygen saturation.
    4. Pulse oximeters are accurate to within 5% in the range of 70-100%.
    5. Pulse oximeters average pulse data over 5-8 seconds before displaying

a value. Response time to changes in oxygenation also depend to probe location. The farther away from the lungs the longer the response time (ear probes up to 20 s; finger probes up to 35 s).

B. Fetal hemoglobin and bilirubin do not affect pulse oximeter.

C. Sources of error

1. **Dyshemoglobins**

   A. **Carboxyhemoglobin:** because carboxyhemoglobin and oxyhemoglobin absorb light at 660 nm identically, pulse oximeters that only compare two wavelengths of light will register a falsely high reading in patients suffering from carbon monoxide poisoning.

   B. **Methemoglobin:** has the same absorption coefficient at both red and infrared wavelengths, resulting in a 1:1 absorption ratio corresponding to a saturation reading of 85%. Thus, methemoglobinemia causes a falsely low saturation reading when SaO_2 is actually greater then 85% and a falsely high reading if SaO_2 is actually less than 85%.

2. **Intravenous dyes**

   A. Methylene blue, indocyanine green, indigo carmine and IV fluorescein have been shown to interfere to some extent with the pulse oximeter, resulting in reduced saturation measurements.

3. **Excessive ambient light:** fluorescent light, surgical lamps, infrared light, fiberoptic surgical units may result in inaccurate SpO_2 readings..

4. **Motion artifact**: repetitive and persistent motion will tend to cause the SpO_2 to approximate 85%.

5. **Venous pulsations:** pulse oximeter design assumes that the pulsatile component of the light absorbency is due to arterial blood.

6. **Low perfusion or low-amplitude states**: under conditions of low or absent pulse amplitude, the pulse oximeter may not accurately reflect arterial oxygen saturation.

7. **Fingernail polish and synthetic nails:** may result in decreased SpO_2.

8. **Electrocautery**: results in decreased SpO_2 readings from interference caused by wide-spectrum radio frequency emissions at the pulse probe.

9. **Penumbra effect:** pulse oximeters whose sensors are malpositioned may display SaO_2 values in the 90-95% range on normoxemic subjects. This so-called "penumbra effect" can cause underestimation at high saturations, overestimation at low saturations, and a strong dependence of the error on instrument and sensor.

3. Central venous pressure monitoring

A. Indications for central venous pressure monitoring

1. Major surgical procedures involving large fluid shifts or blood losses in patients with good heart function.

2. Intravascular volume assessment when urine output is unreliable or unavailable (e.g., renal failure).

3. Fluid management of hypovolemia or shock.

4. Frequent blood sampling in patients not requiring an arterial line.

5. Venous access for vasoactive, caustic drugs or TPN.

6. Insertion of transcutaneous pacing leads.

7. Inadequate peripheral intravenous access.

8. Aspiration of air emboli.

B. Respiratory influences

1. **End expiration:** CVP measurements should be made at end expiration because pleural and pericardial pressures approach atmospheric pressure under these conditions.

2. **Spontaneous ventilation:** during spontaneous breathing, inspiration causes a decrease in intrapleural pressure and juxtacardiac pressure, which is transmitted in part to the right atrium and produces a decrease in CVP.
3. **Mechanical ventilation:** positive-pressure ventilation causes intrathoracic and juxtacardiac pressure to increase during inspiration, producing a increase in CVP.
4. **PEEP:** as intrathoracic pressure increases from added PEEP, CVP measurements increases. This may be associated with a reduction in transmural filling pressure, preload, and venous return.

C. **Central venous pressure abnormalities**
   1. **Atrial fibrillation:** the a wave disappears, and the c wave becomes more prominent since atrial volume is greater at end-diastole. Fibrillation waves may be noticed in the CVP tracing.
   2. **Isorhythmic A-V dissociation or junctional rhythm:** atrial contraction may occur against a closed tricuspid valve, results in cannon 'a' wave.
   3. **Tricuspid regurgitation:** causes "ventricularization" of the CVP trace, with a broad, tall systolic c-v wave that begins early in systole and obliterates the x descent. Unlike a normal v wave, the c-v wave begins immediately after the QRS, leaving only a y descent.
   4. **Tricuspid stenosis:** prominent a wave as the atrium contracts against a stenotic valve; the y descent following the v wave is obstructed.
   5. **Right ventricular ischemia and infarction**
      A. Diagnosis is suggested by arterial hypotension in combination with disproportionate elevation of the CVP as compared to the PCWP. Mean CVP may approach or exceed the mean PCWP.
      B. Elevated right ventricular filling pressure produces prominent a and v waves and steep x and y descents, giving the waveform an M or W configuration.
   6. **Pericardial constriction:** central venous pressure is usually markedly elevated, and the trace resembles that seen with right ventricular infarction. prominent a and v waves and steep x and y descents, creating a M pattern. Often the steep y descent in early diastole is short lived, and the CVP in mid-diastole rises to a plateau until the a wave is inscribed at end-diastole (similar to the h wave).
   7. **Cardiac tamponade:** venous pressure waveform becomes monophasic with a characteristic obliteration of the diastolic y descent. The y descent is obliterated because early diastolic runoff from atrium to ventricle is impaired by the compressive pericardial fluid collection.

4. **Pulmonary artery catheterization**
   A. Indications for a pulmonary artery catheter
      1. Cardiac disease: coronary artery disease with left ventricular dysfunction or recent infarction; valvular heart disease; heart failure.
      2. Pulmonary disease: acute respiratory failure; severe COPD.
      3. Complex fluid management: shock; acute renal failure; acute burns; hemorrhagic pancreatitis.
      4. Specific surgical procedures: CABG; valve replacement; pericardiectomy; aortic cross-clamping; sitting craniotomies; portal systemic shunts.
      5. High-risk obstetrics: severe toxemia; placental abruption.
   B. **Contraindications**
      1. **Absolute contraindications**
         A. Tricuspid or pulmonic valvular stenosis.
         B. Right atrial or right ventricular masses (e.g., tumor, clot).

       C. Tetralogy of Fallot.
    2. Relative contraindications
       A. Severe dysrhythmias: complete left bundle branch block (because of the risk of complete heart block), Wolff-Parkinson-White syndrome, and Ebstein's malformation (because of possible tachyarrhythmias).
       B. Coagulopathy.
       C. Newly inserted pacemaker wires.
C. Catheter position
    1. Correct position can be confirmed by a lateral chest x-ray. The tip of the catheter should lie in West Zone 3 of the lung (where venous and arterial pressure exceed alveolar pressure 95% of the time).
    2. Indicators of proper tip placement
       A. A decline in pressure as the catheter moves from the pulmonary artery into the "wedged" position.
       B. Ability to aspirate blood from the distal port (eliminating the possibility of overwedging).
       C. A decline in end-tidal CO_2 concentration with inflation of the balloon (produced by a rise in alveolar dead space).
D. Complications
    1. Endobronchial hemorrhage: the incidence of pulmonary artery catheter-induced endobronchial hemorrhage is 0.06%-0.20%. Risk factors include advanced age, female sex, pulmonary hypertension, mitral stenosis, coagulopathy, distal placement of the catheter, and balloon hyperinflation.
    2. Pulmonary infarction.
E. Specific conditions
    1. Cardiac tamponade: tends to be equalization of all cardiac diastolic pressures, RA=RVD=PAD=PCWP.
    2. Myocardial ischemia: elevation in PCWP (>15 mmHg) and 'v' waves (>20 mmHg).
    3. RV infarction: high RA pressures and normal or low PCWP.
F. Factors affecting PCWP and CO measurements
    1. Thermodilution CO may be inaccurate in patients with tricuspid regurgitation, intracardiac shunts, and atrial fibrillation.
    2. PCWP will be greater then LVEDP in mitral stenosis and prolapsing left atrial tumors.
    3. PCWP will be less then LVEDP in decreased ventricular compliance and LVEDP > 25 mmHg.
    4. With large 'a' waves (mitral stenosis, complete heart block, atrial myxoma, early heart failure) use the end-exhalation diastolic PCWP.
    5. With large 'v' waves (mitral regurgitation, left atrial enlargement, VSD) use the end-exhalation diastolic PCWP.
    6. PEEP, by increasing pleural pressure, will artificially elevate the measure PCWP value. To correct for PEEP >10 cmH2O, subtract half the PEEP pressure from the measured PCWP or use the formula: measured PCWP - (PEEP x 0.75)/3.
5. Mixed Venous Oxygen Saturation (SvO_2)
    A. Physiology: SvO_2 is approximately equal to SaO_2 - (VO_2/CO x Hemoglobin). Normal range: 68-77%.
    B. Factors: cardiac output, hemoglobin level, oxygen consumption, and SaO_2.

C. **Causes of increased SvO_2**
1. The most common cause is a permanently wedged catheter.
2. Low VO_2 as seen with cyanide toxicity, carbon monoxide poisoning, increases in methemoglobin, sepsis, and hypothermia.
3. High cardiac output, as seen with sepsis, burns, left to right shunts, atrioventricular fistulas, inotropic excess, hepatitis, and pancreatitis.
4. High SaO_2 and high hemoglobin are not common causes.

D. **Causes of decreased SvO_2**
1. Decreased Hemoglobin.
2. Increased VO_2: fever, exercise, agitation, shivering or thyrotoxicosis.
3. Low SaO_2 with hypoxia, respiratory distress syndrome, or vent changes.
4. Low cardiac output as seen in MI, CHF, or hypovolemia.

E. **Pitfalls in continuous venous oximetry**
1. The most common errors in the continuous measurement of SvO_2 are calibration and catheter malposition. Distal migration of the PA catheter can cause an artifactually high oxygen saturation owing to highly saturated pulmonary capillary blood being analyzed.
2. The light intensity signal may decrease if there is fibrin or deposition over the fiberoptic bundles, or if the catheter tip is lodged against a vessel wall or bifurcation.
3. Large fluctuations in the light intensity may indicate an intravascular volume deficit which allows compression or collapse of the pulmonary vasculature (especially during positive pressure ventilation).
4. Causes of pulse oximetry artifact include, excessive ambient light, motion, methylene blue dye, venous pulsations in a dependent limb, low perfusion, optical shunting.

6. **Neuromuscular monitoring**
A. **Monitoring modalities:** response to electrical stimulation of a peripheral nerve, head lift for 5 seconds, tongue protrusion, tongue depressor, hand grip strength, maximum negative inspiratory pressure.

B. **Peripheral nerve stimulators**
1. Choice of muscle: adductor pollicis (ulnar nerve) and orbicularis oculi are the most common, however, any muscle can be used.
2. Patterns of stimulation: single twitch, tetanic stimulus, TOF, double-burst stimulation, posttetanic count.
3. Factors affecting monitoring: cold hand, nerve damage in the monitored limb (increased inherent resistance to the effects of muscle relaxants).

C. **Patterns of stimulation**
1. Single twitch: supramaximal stimulus (0.2 ms at a frequency of 0.1 Hz); the height of the muscle twitch is determined as a percent of control. Used to monitor the onset of neuromuscular blockade.
2. Tetanic stimulus: frequencies vary from 50 to 200 Hz.
3. Posttetanic single twitch: measured by single-twitch stimulation 6-10 seconds after a tetanic stimulations.
4. Train-of-four: denotes four successive 200 microsecond stimuli in 2 seconds (2 Hz). The ratio of the responses to the first and fourth twitches is a sensitive indicator of nondepolarizing muscle relaxation. Useful in monitoring blockade required for surgical relaxation and in assessing recovery from blockade.
5. Double-burst stimulation: a burst of two or three tetanic stimuli at 50 Hz followed 750 ms later by a second burst. A decrease in the second response indicates residual curaization.

D. **Clinical application:** see table.

7. Chest Radiography

A. Endotracheal tube position: with the head in the neutral position, the tip of the ET tube should rest at the mid-trachea level, 5 cm above the carina. In adults the T5-T7 vertebral level is a good estimate of carinal position.

B. Central venous catheters
   1. Ideal location the mid-superior vena cava, with the tip directed inferiorly.
   2. The tip of the catheter should not be allowed to migrate into the heart.

C. Pulmonary artery catheters
   1. The tip of the catheter should be below the level of the LA (zone 3) to reduce or eliminate transmission of alveolar pressure to the capillaries.
   2. With an uninflated balloon, the tip of the pulmonary artery catheter should overlie the middle third of the well-centered AP chest x-ray (within 5 cm of the midline). Distal migration is common in the first hours after insertion as the catheter softens and loses slack.

D. Intraaortic balloon pump (IABP): diastolic inflation of the balloon produces a distinct, rounded lucence within the aortic shadow, but in systole the deflated balloon is not visible. Ideal positioning places the catheter tip just distal to the left subclavian artery.

Central Pressure Monitoring: Central Venous Pressure Waves			
Component	**EKG**	**Cardiac Cycle**	**Mechanical Event**
a Wave	Follows P wave	End diastole	Atrial Contraction
c Wave	Follows the onset of the QRS	Early systole	Isovolemic ventricular contraction, tricuspid motion toward atrium
v Wave	Follows T wave	Late systole	Systolic filling of atrium
h Wave		Mid diastole	Mid-diastolic pressure plateau (occurs with slow heart rates and prolonged diastole)
x Descent		Midsystole	Atrial relaxation, descent of the base, systolic collapse
y Descent		Early diastole	Early ventricular filling, diastolic collapse

Pulmonary Artery Catheter Distances (cm)			
Vein	Right Atrium	Right Ventricle	Pulmonary Artery

Internal Jugular
   Right
   Left
	20
	25
		30
		35
			40
			50

Subclavian	15	25	40

Antecubital
   Right
   Left
	40
	45
		50
		55
			65
			70

Femoral	30	40	55

Common Diagnostic Patterns			
Condition	PCWP	CO	SVR
Hypovolemic Shock	Low	Low	High
Cardiogenic Shock	High	Low	High
Septic Shock	Low	High	Low

Pulmonary Artery Catheter Measurements and Normal Values			
	Normal Range		Normal Range
CVP	0-10 mmHg	CO	4-8 L/min
Mean RAP	0-10 mmHg	CI	2.5-4 L/min/m^2
RVP	15-30/0-10 mmHg	SV	60-100 mL
PAP	15-30/5-15 mmHg	SVI	35-70 mL/beat/m^2
MPAP	10-20 mmHg	SVR	900-1500 dynes/s/cm^5
PCWP	5-15 mmHg	PVR	50-150 dynes/s/cm^5
Mean LAP	4-12 mmHg		

Comparison of Tests of Neuromuscular Function	
Test	**Estimated Receptors Occupied (%)**
Tidal volume	80
Twitch height	75-80
Tetanic stimulation (30 Hz)	75-80
Vital capacity	75-80
Train-of-four	75-80
Tetanic stimulation (100 Hz)	50
Inspiratory force	50
Head lift (5 seconds)	33

Pharmacology

Basic Pharmacology

1. Stages of general anesthesia

A. **Stage 1** (amnesia) begins with induction of anesthesia and ends with the loss of consciousness (loss of eyelid reflex). Pain perception threshold during this stage is not lowered.

B. **Stage 2** (delirium/excitement) is characterized by uninhibited excitation. Agitation, delirium, irregular respiration and breath holding. Pupils are dilated and eyes are divergent. Responses to noxious stimuli can occur during this stage may include vomiting, laryngospasm, hypertension, tachycardia, and uncontrolled movement.

C. **Stage 3** (surgical anesthesia) is characterized by central gaze, constricted pupils, and regular respirations. Target depth of anesthesia is sufficient when painful stimulation does not elicit somatic reflexes or deleterious autonomic responses.

D. **Stage 4** (impending death/overdose) is characterized by onset of apnea, dilated and nonreactive pupils, and hypotension may progress to circulatory failure.

2. Pharmacokinetics of inhaled anesthetics

A. **Anesthetic concentration:** The fraction of a gas in a mixture is equal to the volume of that gas divided by the total volume of the mixture.

B. **Partial pressure:** The partial pressure of a component gas in a mixture is equal to the fraction it contributes toward total pressure.

C. **Minimum alveolar concentration (MAC)**

1. The minimum alveolar concentration of an inhalation agent is the minimum concentration necessary to prevent movement in 50% of patients in response to a surgical skin incision.

2. The minimum alveolar concentrations required to prevent eye opening on verbal command, to prevent movement and coughing in response to endotracheal intubation, and to prevent adrenergic response to skin incision have been defined. These are called MAC Awake, MAC Endotracheal Intubation, and MAC BAR (for blockade of autonomic response). In general, MAC Awake is 50% MAC, MAC Endotracheal Intubation is 130% MAC, and MAC BAR is 150% MAC. MAC Amnesia, 25% MAC, has defined as the concentration that blocks anterograde memory in 50% of awake patients.

3. MAC values for different volatile agents are additive. The lower the MAC the more potent the agent.

4. The highest MACs are found in infants at term to 6 months of age. The MAC decreases with both increasing age and prematurity.

5. Factors that increase MAC include hyperthermia, drugs that increase CNS catecholamines, infants, hypernatremia, and chronic ethanol abuse.

6. Factors that decrease MAC include hypothermia (for every Celsius degree drop in body temperature, MAC decreases 2-5%), preoperative medications, IV anesthetics, neonates, elderly, pregnancy, alpha-2 agonists, acute ethanol ingestion, lithium, cardiopulmonary bypass, opioids, and PaO_2 less than 38 mmHg.

7. Factors that have no effect on MAC include duration of anesthesia,

gender, thyroid gland dysfunction, hyperkalemia, and hypokalemia.

D. **Alveolar uptake:** The rate of alveolar uptake is determined by:

1. **Inspired concentration:** A high inspired anesthetic partial pressure (PI) accelerates induction of anesthesia. This effect of the high PI is known as the concentration effect.

2. **Alveolar ventilation:** Increased ventilation increases the rate of alveolar uptake of anesthetic. The net effect is a more rapid rate of rise in the alveolar partial pressure of an inhaled anesthetic and induction of anesthesia.

3. **Anesthetic breathing system:** The rate of rise of the alveolar partial pressure of an inhaled anesthetic is influenced by (1) the volume of the system, (2) solubility of the inhaled anesthetics into the components of the system, and (3) gas inflow from the anesthetic machine.

4. **Uptake of the inhaled anesthetic**

   A. **Solubility:** The solubility of inhaled anesthetics is defined as the amount of anesthetic agent required to saturate a unit volume of blood at a given temperature and can be expressed as the blood:gas partition coefficient. The more soluble the agent, the greater the uptake into the pulmonary capillaries. The solubility of the inhalation agent in blood is the most important single factor in determining the speed of induction and recovery in individual patients.

   B. **Cardiac output:** A high cardiac output results in more rapid uptake such that the rate of rise in the alveolar partial pressure and the speed of induction are slowed.

   C. **Alveolar to venous partial pressure difference**: A large alveolar to venous gradient enhances the uptake of anesthetic by pulmonary blood and tends to slow the rise in the alveolar partial pressure.

E. **Second gas effect:** The ability of the large volume uptake of one gas (first gas) to accelerate the rate of rise of the alveolar partial pressure of a concurrently administered companion gas (second gas) is known as the second gas effect.

F. **Elimination:** Most of the inhaled agents are exhaled unchanged by the lungs. Hyperventilation, a small FRC (function residual capacity), a low solubility, a low cardiac output, or a large mixed venous-alveolar tension gradient increases the rate of decay.

G. **Diffusion hypoxia** results from dilution of alveolar oxygen concentration by the large amount of nitrous oxide leaving the pulmonary capillary blood at the conclusion of nitrous oxide administration. This can be prevented by filling the patient's lungs with oxygen at the conclusion of nitrous oxide administration.

3. **Pharmacokinetics of intravenous anesthetics**

A. **Volume of distribution:** The apparent volume into which a drug has been distributed; dose of drug administered IV divided by the plasma concentration; binding to plasma protein, high degree of ionization, and low lipid solubility limit passage of drugs to tissue and result in small volume of distribution.

B. **Plasma concentration curve.**

1. **Distribution (alpha) phase:** The alpha phase corresponds to the initial distribution of drug from the circulation to tissues.

2. **Elimination (beta) phase:** The second phase is characterized by a gradual decline in the plasma concentration of drug and reflects its elimination from the central vascular compartment by renal and hepatic mechanisms.

C. **Elimination half-time** is the time necessary for the plasma concentration of drug to decline 50 percent during the elimination phase.

D. **Redistribution:** Following systemic absorption of drugs, the highly perfused tissues (brain, heart, kidneys, liver) receive a proportionally larger amount of the total dose; the transfer of drugs to inactive tissue sites (i.e., skeletal muscle) is known as redistribution.

E. **Physical characteristics of the drug**
1. Highly lipid-soluble drugs (most intravenous anesthetics) are taken up rapidly by tissues.
2. With water-soluble agents, molecular size is an important determinant of diffusibility across plasma membranes.
3. Degree of ionization: The degree of ionization is determined by the pH of the biophase and the pKa of the drug. Only nonionized (basic) molecules diffuse across the biological membranes.

Local Anesthetics

1. **Mechanism of action of local anesthetics**
   A. Local anesthetics prevent increases in neural membrane permeability to sodium ions, slowing the rate of depolarization so that threshold potential is never reached and no action potential is propagated.
   B. Most local anesthetics bind to sodium channels in the inactivated state, preventing subsequent channel activation and the large transient sodium influx associated with membrane depolarization. Rapidly firing nerves are more sensitive and, therefore, are blocked first.

2. **Metabolism**
   A. **Esters**
      1. Ester local anesthetics are predominantly metabolized by pseudocholinesterase (plasma cholinesterase). Cerebrospinal fluid lacks esterase enzymes, so the termination of action of intrathecally injected ester local anesthetics depends upon their absorption into the bloodstream.
      2. P-aminobenzoic acid, a metabolite of ester local anesthetics, has been associated with allergic reactions.
   B. **Amides**
      1. Metabolized by microsomal enzymes in the liver; the amide linkage is cleaved through initial N-dealkylation followed by hydrolysis.
      2. Metabolites of prilocaine (o-toluidine derivatives), which accumulate after large doses (greater than 10 mg/kg), convert hemoglobin to methemoglobin. Benzocaine can also cause methemoglobinemia.

3. **Physiochemical factors**
   A. **Lipid solubility:** increased lipid solubility increases potency.
   B. **Protein binding:** the greater the protein binding (alpha$_1$-acid glycoprotein), the longer the duration of action.
   C. **pKa:** determines the onset time. pKa is the pH at which 50% of the local anesthetic is in the charged form and 50% uncharged. Local anesthetics with a pKa closer to physiologic pH will have a higher concentration of nonionized base and a more rapid onset.
   D. **Ion trapping:** refers to the accumulation of the ionized form of a local anesthetic in acidic environments due to a pH gradient between the ionized and non-ionized forms. This can occur between a mother and an acidotic fetus (i.e., fetal distress), resulting in the accumulation of local anesthetic

in fetal blood.

E. pH of the drug solution: increasing the pH of the drug solution will increase the fraction of the non-ionized form, resulting in a faster onset. Most local anesthetic solutions are prepared commercially as a water-soluble HCL salt (pH 6-7). Agents with epinephrine added are made more acidic (pH 4-5) because epinephrine is unstable in alkaline environments.

F. Minimum concentration of local anesthetic (Cm) is the minimum concentration of local anesthetic that will block nerve impulse conduction and is analogous to the minimum alveolar concentration (MAC).

4. Rate of systemic absorption of local anesthetics (from high to low): intravenous > tracheal > intercostal > caudal > paracervical > epidural > brachial plexus > sciatic/femoral > subcutaneous.

5. Spread of anesthesia and blockade

A. Differential blockade of nerve fibers: myelinated fibers are more readily blocked then unmyelinated ones.

B. Local anesthetics deposited around a peripheral nerve diffuse along a concentration gradient to block nerve fibers on the outer surface before more centrally located fibers.

C. Sequence of clinical block (progresses in order): sympathetic block with peripheral vasodilation and skin temperature elevation, loss of pain and temperature sensation, loss of proprioception, loss of touch and pressure sensation, motor paralysis.

6. Preparations

A. Hydrochloride salts: this preparation increases the solubility in water and is usually acidic to enhance the formation of the water-soluble ionized form. Plain solutions usually have an adjusted pH of 6, while solutions containing a vasoconstrictor have an adjusted pH of 4 because of the lability of catecholamine molecules at alkaline pH.

B. Antimicrobial preservatives (paraben derivatives): usually added to multidose vials. Only preservative-free solutions should be used in spinal, epidural, or caudal anesthesia to prevent neurotoxic effects.

C. Antioxidant: added to slow the breakdown of local anesthetics.

7. Adjuvants

A. Epinephrine

1. May be added to local anesthetics to produce local vasoconstriction, to limit systemic absorption, to prolong the duration of effect, tp decrease surgical bleeding, to increase the intensity of the block by direct alpha agonist effect on antinociceptive receptors in the spinal cord, and to assist in the evaluation of a test dose.

2. The maximum dose of epinephrine should not exceed 10 mcg/kg in pediatric patients and 200-250 mcg in adults.

3. Epinephrine should not be used in peripheral nerve blocks in areas with poor collateral blood flow or in intravenous regional techniques.

B. Phenylephrine has been used like epinephrine, but with no advantage.

C. Sodium bicarbonate

1. Raises the pH and increases the concentration of nonionized free base.

2. The addition of sodium bicarbonate (e.g., 1 mL 8.4% sodium bicarbonate is added to each 10 mL of 1% lidocaine) speeds onset, improves quality of block, prolongs blockade by increasing the amount of free base available and decreases pain during subcutaneous infiltration.

8. Toxicity and effects

A. Allergic reactions

1. **Ester-type local anesthetics:** may cause allergic reactions form the

metabolite para-aminobenzoic acid and persons sensitive to sulfa drugs (e.g., sulfonamides or thiazide diuretics).

2. Ester local anesthetics may produce allergic reactions in persons sensitive to sulfa drugs.

3. Allergic reactions to amides are extremely rare and are probably related to the preservative and not the amide itself. Multidose preparations of amides often contain methylparaben, which has a chemical structure similar to that of p-aminobenzoic acid.

4. Local hypersensitivity reactions: may produce local erythema, urticaria, edema, or dermatitis.

B. Local toxicity

1. **Transient radicular irritation (TRI) or transient neurologic symptoms (TNS)**

   A. Characterized by dysesthesia, burning pain, low back pain, and aching in the lower extremities and buttocks. The etiology of these symptoms attributed to radicular irritation. The symptoms usually appear within 24 hours after complete recovery from spinal anesthesia and resolve within 7 days.

   B. Can occur after unintentional subarachnoid injection of large volumes or high concentrations of local anesthetics. Increased incidence when the lithotomy position is used during surgery.

   C. An increase incidence of neurotoxicity associated with the subarachnoid administration of 5% lidocaine has been reported.

2. **Cauda equina syndrome**

   A. Occurs when diffuse injury to the lumbosacral plexus produces varying degrees of sensory anesthesia, bowel and bladder sphincter dysfunction, and paraplegia.

   B. Initially reported due to 5% lidocaine and 0.5% tetracaine given via a microcatheter. There may be increased risk when large doses of local anesthetic are placed in the subarachnoid space as may occur during and following a continuous spinal anesthetic, accidental subarachnoid injection of the intended epidural dose or repeated spinal doses.

3. Chloroprocaine has been associated with neurotoxicity. The cause of this neural toxicity may be the low pH of chloroprocaine (pH 3.0).

C. System toxicity

1. **Cardiovascular toxicity**

   A. Local anesthetics depress myocardial automaticity (spontaneous phase IV depolarization) and reduce the duration of the refractory period (manifesting as prolonged PR interval and widening QRS.

   B. Myocardial contractility and conduction velocity are depressed at higher concentrations. Smooth muscle relaxation causes some degree of vasodilation (with the exception of cocaine).

   C. Cardiac dysrhythmia or circulatory collapse is often a presenting sign of local anesthetic overdose during general anesthesia.

   D. Intravascular injection of bupivacaine has produced severe cardiotoxic reactions, including hypotension, atrioventricular heart block, and dysrhythmias such as ventricular fibrillation. Pregnancy, hypoxemia, and respiratory acidosis are predisposing risk factors. Ropivacaine lacks significant cardiac toxicity because it dissociates more rapidly from sodium channels. Levobupivacaine has less cardiotoxic effects then bupivacaine.

   E. Cocaine: only local anesthetic that causes vasoconstriction at all

doses.
2. **Respiratory effects**
    A. Lidocaine depresses the hypoxic drive (response to low PaO_2).
    B. Apnea can result from phrenic and intercostal nerve paralysis or depression of the medullary respiratory center following direct exposure to local anesthetic agents (e.g., postretrobulbar apnea syndrome).
3. **Central nervous system toxicity**
    A. Early symptoms of overdose include circumoral numbness, tongue paresthesia, and dizziness. Sensory complaints may include tinnitus and burred vision. Excitatory signs (e.g., restlessness, agitation, nervousness, paranoia) often precede central nervous system depression (slurred speech, drowsiness, unconsciousness).
    B. Tonic-clonic seizures may result from selective blockade of inhibitory pathways. Respiratory arrest often follows seizure activity.
    C. CNS toxicity is exacerbated by hypercarbia, hypoxia, and acidosis.
4. **Musculoskeletal effects**: local anesthetics are myotoxic when injected directly into skeletal muscle.
5. **Other adverse effects**
    A. **Horner syndrome:** can result from blockade of B fibers in the T1-T4 nerve roots. Clinical signs include ptosis, miosis, anhydrosis, nasal congestion, vasodilation, and increased skin temperature.
    B. Methemoglobinemia: can be formed after large doses of prilocaine, benzocaine and EMLA cream.
    C. Decreased coagulation: lidocaine has been demonstrated to prevent thrombosis, decrease platelet aggregation and enhance fibrinolysis of whole blood.

Local Anesthetics: Dosages for Infiltration Anesthesia

Drug	Plain Solution		Epinephrine Solution	
	Max Dose (mg)	Duration (min)	Max Dose (mg)	Duration (min)
Procaine	400	30-60	600	30-90
Chloroprocaine	800	30-45	1000	30-90
Lidocaine	300	30-120	500	120-360
Mepivacaine	300	45-90	500	120-360
Prilocaine	500	30-90	600	120-360
Bupivacaine	175	120-240	225	180-420
Etidocaine	300	120-180	400	180-420
Ropivacaine	200	120-360		

Local Anesthetics: Dosages for Spinal Anesthesia

Drug	Preparation	T10 Level (mg)	T6 Level (mg)	T4 Level (mg)	Duration Plain (min)	Duration w/epi (min)
Procaine	10%	75	125	200	30-45	60-75
Lidocaine	5.0% in 7.5% glucose	25-50	50-75	75-100	45-60	60-90
Tetracaine*	1% in 10% glucose	6-8	8-14	12-20	60-90	120-180
Bupivacaine	0.75% in 8.25% dextrose	6-10	8-14	12-20	90-120	120-150
Ropivacaine	0.2-1%	8-12	12-16	16-18	90	140

*For hypobaric spinal: tetracaine diluted with sterile water to 0.3% solution
**Preparation concentration of tetracaine is 1%; tetracaine is diluted with 5.0% glucose for hyperbaric solution and normal saline for isobaric solution

Local Anesthetics: Dosages for Epidural Anesthesia

Drug	Usual Conc %	Usual Vol (mL)	Total Dose (mg)	Onset (min)	Duration (min)
Chloroprocaine	2-3	15-30	300-900	5-15	30-90
Lidocaine	1-2	15-30	150-500	5-15	60-120
Mepivacaine	1-2	15-30	150-300	5-15	60-180
Prilocaine	2-3	15-30	150-600	5-15	60-180
Bupivacaine	0.25-0.75	15-30	37.5-225	5-15	120-240
Etidocaine	1.0-1.5	15-30	150-300	5-15	120-240
Ropivacaine	0.2-1.0	15-30	75-200	10-20	120-240

Local Anesthetics: Maximum Dose

Drug	Plain (mg)	Epi (mg)	Plain (mg/kg)	Epi (mg/kg)
Amides				
Bupivacaine	175	225	2.5	3
Dibucaine			1	
Etidocaine	300	400	4	5
Lidocaine	300	500	4.5	7
Mepivacaine	300	500	4.5	7
Prilocaine	500	600	6	9
Ropivacaine	200		2.5	2.5
Esters				
Chloroprocaine	800	1000	12	15
Cocaine			3	
Procaine	500	600	7	8
Tetracaine	100	200	1.5	2.5

Neuromuscular Blocking Agents

1. **Depolarizing neuromuscular blocking agents**
   A. **Succinylcholine** is the only depolarizing muscle relaxant and is made up of two joined acetylcholine molecules. Succinylcholine mimics the action of acetylcholine by depolarizing the postsynaptic membrane at the neuromuscular junction.
   B. **Depolarizing blockade** is characterized by: muscle fasciculation followed by relaxation, absence of fade after tetanic or train-of-four stimulation, absence of posttetanic potentiation, potentiation of the block by anticholinesterases, and antagonism by nondepolarizing relaxants.
   C. **Metabolism**
      1. Succinylcholine has a rapid onset of action (30-60 seconds) with a short duration of action (5-10 minutes). Succinylcholine is rapidly metabolized by pseudocholinesterase into succinylmonocholine (later broken down to choline and succinic acid) as it enters the circulation such that only a fraction (approximately 10%) of the injected does ever reaches the neuromuscular junction.
      2. As serum levels fall, succinylcholine molecules diffuse away from the neuromuscular junction and is broken down to choline and succinic acid in the plasma.
   D. **Adverse side effects of succinylcholine**
      1. **Cardiac**
         A. Ganglionic stimulation may increase heart rate and blood pressure in adults; may produce bradycardia, junctional rhythm and sinus arrest in children after first dose and after second dose in adults (with short dose interval).
      2. **Hyperkalemia**
         A. Normal muscle releases enough potassium during succinylcholine-induced depolarization to raise serum potassium by 0.5-1.0 mEq/L.
         B. Massive release of intracellular potassium can result from situations where there is a proliferation of extrajunctional receptors. Associated conditions include: patients with thermal injuries, massive trauma, severe intra-abdominal infection, neurologic disorders (spinal cord injury, encephalitis, stroke, Guillain-Barre syndrome, severe Parkinson's disease), ruptured cerebral aneurysm, polyneuropathy, myopathies (e.g., Duchenne's dystrophy) and tetanus. This potassium release, due to up-regulation of extrajunctional acetylcholine receptors, is not reliably prevented by pretreatment with a nondepolarizer muscle relaxant.
         C. Patients with renal failure may safely receive succinylcholine if they are not already hyperkalemic or acidemic.
      3. **Increased intracranial pressure, increased cerebral blood flow, and increased intraocular pressure.**
      4. **Increased intragastric pressure:** results from fasciculation of abdominal muscles; increased pressure averages 15-20 mmHg (adult); the increase in intragastric pressure is offset by an increase in lower esophageal sphincter tone.
      5. **Myalgia and myoglobinuria:** incidence reduced by pretreating with a small dose of nondepolarizing relaxant.
      6. **Fasciculations:** can be prevented by pretreatment with a small dose of nondepolarizing relaxant.
      7. **Trismus:** patients afflicted with myotonia may develop myoclonus after

succinylcholine administration.
8. **Malignant hyperthermia:** maybe triggered in susceptible patients.
9. **Phase II block** may occur with repeated or continuous infusions and is characterized by tetanic or TOF fade, tachyphylaxis, partial or complete reversal with anticholinesterases.
10. **Prolonged blockade**
   A. Decreased plasma cholinesterase in last trimester of pregnancy, liver disease, starvation, carcinomas, hypothyroidism, burn patients, cardiac failure, uremia, and after therapeutic radiation.
   B. Inhibition of plasma cholinesterase: occurs with use of organophosphate compounds, drugs that inhibit acetylcholinesterase, and other drugs (MAO inhibitors, phenelzine).
   C. Plasma cholinesterase deficiency (see below).

E. **Pseudocholinesterase abnormalities**
   1. **Heterozygous atypical enzyme:** 1 in 50 patients has one normal and one abnormal gene, resulting in a prolonged block (20-30 minutes).
   2. **Homozygous atypical enzyme:** 1 in 3000 patients has two abnormal genes, which produce an enzyme with 1/100 the normal affinity for succinylcholine. Blockade may last 6-8 hours or longer.
   3. **Dibucaine,** a local anesthetic, inhibits normal pseudocholinesterase activity by 80%, but inhibits the homozygous atypical enzyme by only 20% and the heterozygous enzyme by 40-60%. The percentage of inhibition of pseudocholinesterase activity is termed the dibucaine number. The dibucaine number is proportional to pseudocholinesterase function and independent enzyme amount.
   4. Other abnormalities: individuals sensitive to succinylcholine may have a fluoride-resistant enzyme (normal dibucaine number but low fluoride number) or a silent gene with complete absence of plasma cholinesterase (dibucaine number 0) and no esterase activity.

F. **Hemodialysis:** plasma cholinesterase levels are not usually altered.

G. **Drug interactions with succinylcholine**
   1. Cholinesterase inhibitors (echothiophate eye drops and organophosphate pesticides) enhance the action of succinylcholine.
   2. Nondepolarizing muscle relaxants antagonize depolarizing phase I blocks. An exception to this interaction is pancuronium, which augments succinylcholine blockade by inhibiting pseudocholinesterase.
   3. Other drugs (that potentiate the neuromuscular block) include antibiotics (streptomycins, colistin, polymyxin, tetracycline, lincomycin, clindamycin), antidysrhythmics (quinidine, lidocaine, calcium channel blockers), antihypertensives (trimethaphan), cholinesterase inhibitors, furosemide, inhalational gas, local anesthetics, lithium, MAO inhibitors, and magnesium.

2. **Non-depolarizing neuromuscular agents**
   A. **Mechanisms:** reversible competitive antagonism of Ach.
   B. **Nondepolarizing blockade** is characterized by: absence of fasciculations, fade during tetanic and TOF stimulation, PTP, antagonism of block by depolarizing agents and anticholinesterases.
   C. **Pharmacologic characteristics** (see table)
      1. **Temperature:** hypothermia prolongs blockade by decreasing metabolism and delaying excretion.
      2. **Acid-base balance:** respiratory acidosis potentiates the blockade of most nondepolarizing relaxants and antagonizes the reversal.
      3. **Electrolyte abnormalities:** hypokalemia and hypocalcemia augment

a nondepolarizing block. Hypermagnesemia potentiates blockade.
4. **Age:** neonates have an increased sensitivity to nondepolarizing agents.
5. **Drug interactions:** drugs that potentiate nondepolarizing relaxants include volatile agents, local anesthetics, calcium channel blockers, aminoglycosides, polymyxins, lincosamines, hexamethonium, trimethaphan, immunosuppressants, high-dose benzodiazepines, dantrolene, and magnesium.
6. **Synergistic blockade:** may result when steroidal NMBD (vecuronium, rocuronium) are combined with benzylisoquinolines (atracurium).

3. **Sensitivity to neuromuscular blockade:** muscles have different sensitivities to muscle relaxants. The most resistant to most sensitive muscles are: vocal cord, diaphragm, orbicularis oculi, abdominal rectus, adductor pollicis, masseter, pharyngeal, extraocular.
4. Diseases that alter the response to muscle relaxants (see table).
5. **Monitoring neuromuscular blockade:** see monitoring section.

Dosages of Muscle Relaxants

Drug	Dose (mg/kg)					Infusion
	Intubation	N₂O/Opioid	Inhalation	Maintenance		mcg/kg/min
Atracurium	0.4-0.6	0.3-0.4	0.2-0.3	0.1-0.15		4-12
Cisatracurium	0.15-0.2	0.05	0.03-0.04	0.01-0.02		1-2
d-Tubocurarine	0.5-0.6	0.3-0.5	0.2-0.3	0.1-0.15		
Doxacurium	0.05-0.08	0.02-0.03	0.015-0.02	0.005-0.01		
Metocurine	0.3-0.4	0.15-0.2	0.1-0.15	0.05-0.1		
Mivacurium	0.15-0.25*	0.1	0.08	0.05-0.1		3-15
Pancuronium	0.08-0.12	0.05-0.06	0.03	0.01-0.015		
Pipecuronium	0.07-0.09	0.04-0.06	0.03	0.005-0.01		
Rapacuronium	1.5-2.5	1.0-1.5	0.6-1.0	0.2-0.5		9-12
Rocuronium	0.6-1.2	0.3-0.4	0.2-0.3	0.1-0.15		8-12
Succinylcholine	1.0-1.5			0.04-0.07		10-100
Vecuronium	0.1-0.2	0.05	0.03-0.04	0.01-0.02		0.8-2.0

*Given in divided doses (0.15 mg/kg followed in 30 seconds by 0.10 mg/kg). For children 2 to 12 years, the recommended dose of is 0.20 mg/kg, administered over 5 to 15 seconds

Muscle Relaxants					
Drug	ED 95 (mg/kg)	Onset (min)	Duration (min)	Histamine Release	Elimination and Misc
Atracurium	0.25	3-5	20-35	+	Hofmann elimination and ester hydrolysis, laudanosine
Cisatracurium	0.05	1-2	60	None	Hofmann elimination
d-Tubo-curarine	0.51	3-5	60-90	+++	70% renal; 20% biliary; autonomic ganglia block
Doxacurium	0.03	4-6	60-90	None	35% renal
Gallamine	3	4-5	70-80	None	80-100% renal; muscarinic block
Metocurine	0.28	3-5	60-90	+	80-100% renal; autonomic ganglia block-ade
Mivacurium	0.09	2-3	12-20	+	plasma cholinesterase
Pancuronium	0.07	3-5	60-90	None	70% renal; 15-20% liver; muscarinic block (10-15% HR increase)
Pipecuronium	0.06	3-5	60-90	None	90% renal; 10% liver
Rapacuronium	0.75-1.0	1-2	15-20	+	50% hepatic; 25% renal
Rocuronium	0.3	1-2	20-35	None	10-25% renal; 50-70% biliary; 10-20% hepatic
Succinyl-choline	0.25	1	5-10	Rare	Plasma cholinesterase muscarinic and nicotinic stim
Vecuronium	0.06	3-5	20-35	None	10-20% renal; 40-60% biliary; 20% hepatic

Diseases with Altered Responses to Muscle Relaxants		
Disease	Response to depolarizers	Response to Nondepolarizers
Amyotrophic lat sclerosis	Contracture	Hypersensitivity
Burn injury	Hyperkalemia	Resistance
Cerebral palsy	Slight hypersensitivity	Resistance
Familial periodic paralysis	Myotonic and hyperkalemia	Hypersensitivity
Guillain-Barre syndrome	Hyperkalemia	Hypersensitivity
Hemiplegia	Hyperkalemia	Resistance on affected side

Disease	Response to depolarizers	Response to Nondepolarizers
Muscular denervation	Hyperkalemia and contracture	Normal response or resistance
Muscular dystrophy (Duchenne type)	Hyperkalemia and malignant hyperthermia	Hypersensitivity
Myasthenia gravis	resistance and proneness to phase II block	Hypersensitivity
Myasthenic syndrome	Hypersensitivity	Hypersensitivity
Myotonia	Generalized muscular contractions	Normal or hypersensitivity
Severe chronic infection	Hyperkalemia	Resistance

Anticholinesterases

1. **Mechanism of action:** cholinesterase inhibitors inactivate acetylcholinesterase by reversibly binding to the enzyme increasing the amount of acetylcholine available to compete with the nondepolarizing agent.
2. In **excessive doses**, acetylcholinesterase inhibitors can paradoxically potentiate a nondepolarizing neuromuscular blockade and prolong the depolarization blockade of succinylcholine.
3. Anticholinesterases increases acetylcholine at both nicotinic and muscarinic receptors. Muscarinic side effects can be blocked by administration of atropine or glycopyrrolate. See table for muscarinic side effects.
4. **Cholinergic receptors**
   A. Nicotinic receptors (2 subtypes)
   1. NM: found at the neuromuscular junction in skeletal muscle.
   2. NN: found in autonomic ganglia (sympathetic and parasympathetic), the adrenal medulla, and the CNS.
   B. Muscarinic receptors (5 subtypes; all found within the CNS)
   1. M1: located in autonomic ganglia and various secretory glands.
   2. M2: found mainly in the heart and brainstem.
   3. M3: found in smooth muscle, exocrine glands, and cerebral cortex.
   4. M4: found in the neostriatum.
   5. M5: found in the substantia nigra.

Anticholinesterases				
	Edrophonium	Neostigmine	Pyridostigmine	Physostigmine
Dose (mg/kg)	0.5-1.0	0.035-0.07 (up to 5 mg)	0.15-0.35	0.01-0.03 (per dose)
Onset (min)	1-3	7-10	10-13	5
Duration (min)	40-70	65-80	80-130	30-300
Renal Excretion (%)	70	50	75	metabolized by plasma esterases

	Edro-phonium	Neostigmine	Pyrido-stigmine	Physostigmine
Atropine (mcg/kg)	7-10	15-30	15-20	
Glycopyrrolate	do not use	7 mcg/kg	7 mcg/kg	
Misc				anticholinergic overdose treatment

Muscarinic Side Effects of Cholinesterase Inhibitors	
Organ System	Muscarinic Side Effect
Cardiovascular	Decreased heart rate, dysrhythmias
Pulmonary	Bronchospasm, increased bronchial secretions
Cerebral	Diffuse excitation (physostigmine only)
Gastrointestinal	Intestinal spasm, increased salivation
Genitourinary	Increased bladder tone
Ophthalmologic	Pupillary constriction

Anticholinergics

1. **Mechanism of action:** competitively inhibits the action of acetylcholine at muscarinic receptors with little or no effect at nicotinic receptors.
2. **Central anticholinergic syndrome**
   A. Scopolamine and atropine can enter the central nervous system and produce symptoms of restlessness and confusion that may progress to somnolence and unconsciousness. Other systemic manifestations include dry mouth, tachycardia, atropine flush, atropine fever, and impaired vision.
   B. Physostigmine, a tertiary amine anticholinesterase, is lipid-soluble and reverses central anticholinergic toxicity. An initial dose of .01-0.03 mg/kg is recommended and may need to be repeat after 15-30 minutes.
   C. Glycopyrrolate does not easily cross the blood-brain barrier, and thus does not cause a central anticholinergic syndrome.

Pharmacological Characteristics of Anticholinergic Drugs			
	Atropine	Scopolamine	Glycopyrrolate
Tachycardia	+++	+	++
Bronchodilation	++	+	++
Sedation	+	+++	0
Antisialagogue	++	+++	+++
Amnesia	+	+++	0

	Atropine	Scopolamine	Glycopyrrolate
Duration of action	IV: 15-30 min IM: 2-4 hr	IV: 30-60 min IM: 4-6 hr	IV: 2-4 hr IM: 6-8 hr
Dose-Adult	Premed: 0.2-0.4 mg IV Brady: 0.4-1.0 mg IV	0.3-0.6 mg IV/IM	0.1-0.2 mg IV/IM
Dose-Pediatric	Premed: 10 mcg/kg Brady: 20 mcg/kg	6 mcg/kg IV/IM	4-8 mcg/kg IV/IM
O = No effect; + = Minimal effect; ++ = Moderate effect; +++ = Marked effect			

Benzodiazepines

1. **Mechanism of action**
    A. Benzodiazepines selectively attach to alpha subunits to enhance the chloride channel gating function of the inhibitory neurotransmitter GABA.
    B. Benzodiazepine receptors mostly occur on postsynaptic nerve endings in the central nervous system.
    C. Benzodiazepines undergo hepatic metabolism via oxidation and glucuronide conjugation.
2. **Systemic effects**
    A. **Central nervous system effects**
        1. Amnestic, anticonvulsant, hypnotic, muscle-relaxant, and sedative effects in a dose-dependent manner.
        2. Reduced cerebral oxygen consumption, cerebral blood flow and ICP.
    B. **Cardiovascular effects**
        1. Mild systemic vasodilation and reduction in cardiac output; heart rate usually unchanged.
        2. Pronounced effect in hypovolemic patients, those with poor cardiac reserve, or if administered with an opioids.
        3. Midazolam reduces blood pressure and SVR more than diazepam.
    C. **Respiratory effects**
        1. Mild dose-dependent decrease in respiratory rate and tidal volume.
        2. Increased respiratory depression with opioids and pulmonary disease.
    D. **Miscellaneous effects**
        1. Reduces MAC by up to 30%.
        2. Pain during IV/IM injection and thrombophlebitis occurs with diazepam (secondary to its organic solvent propylene glycol).
        3. Crosses the placenta and may lead to neonatal depression.
        4. Erythromycin inhibits midazolam metabolism; cimetidine reduces metabolism of diazepam.
        5. Heparin displaces diazepam from protein-binding sites and increases the free drug concentration.
        6. Benzodiazepine administered to patient receiving valproate may precipitate a psychotic episode.
3. **Reversal**
    A. Flumazenil (Mazicon, Romazicon), an imidazobenzodiazepine, is a competitive antagonist of benzodiazepines.
    B. **Dosage**
        1. **Reversal of conscious sedation:** 0.2 mg IV over 15 seconds; give

additional 0.1 mg IV bolus every 60 seconds to achieve desired effect, to a total of 1 mg.

2. **Reversal of overdose:** 0.2 mg IV over 30 seconds; if necessary, give 0.3 mg IV 60 seconds later, if no effect, give 0.5 mg boluses every 60 seconds to a total of 3 mg.

3. **Reversal of resedation:** 0.2 mg IV (to 1 mg/hr), or infusion 0.5 mg/hr.

4. **Diagnosis in coma:** 0.5 mg IV repeated up to 1.0 mg IV.

C. Duration of antagonism is brief (45-90 minutes) and may require repeated doses. Peak effect occurs in approximately 10 minutes.

D. Flumazenil may induce seizures, acute withdrawal, nausea, dizziness, agitation, or arrhythmias.

E. Flumazenil is contraindicated in patients with tricyclic antidepressant overdose and patients receiving benzodiazepines for control of seizures or elevated intracranial pressure. Use caution in patients who have received long-term treatment with benzodiazepines.

Benzodiazepines			
	Midazolam (Versed)	Diazepam (Valium)	Lorazepam (Ativan)
Relative Potency	3	1	5
Induction	0.2-0.6 mg/kg	0.3-0.6 mg/kg	
Maintenance	0.05 mg/kg prn or 0.25-1.5 mcg/kg/min		
Sedation (mg/kg)	IM: 0.07-0.2 IN: 0.2-0.5 IV: 0.025-0.1 PO: 0.5-0.75 PR: 0.3-0.5	IV: 0.05-0.2 PO: 0.2-0.5 PR: 0.2-0.5	IV/IM: 0.02-0.08 PO: 0.05
Duration	IM: 2 hrs IV: 20-30 min	IV: 20-30 min	IM/IV/PO: 6-8 hrs
Elimination Half-Time	1-7.5 hrs	22-50 hrs	10-20 hr

Oral Benzodiazepines	
Drug	Dose
Alprazolam (Xanax)	0.25-0.5 mg TID/QID (up to 4 mg/day)
Chlordiazepoxide (Librium)	5-25 mg TID/QID
Clonazepam (Clonopin)	Initial: 0.5 mg TID Maintenance: 0.05-0.2 mg/kg
Clorazepate (Tranxene)	7.5-15 mg BID-QID or 11.25-22.5 qHS
Diazepam (Valium)	2-10 mg BID-QID
Estazolam (Prosom)	0.5-2 mg qHS

Drug	Dose
Flurazepam (Dalmane)	15-30 mg qHS
Lorazepam (Ativan)	1-10 mg BID/TID
Oxazepam (Serax)	10-30 mg TID/QID
Quazepam (Doral)	7.5-15 mg qHS
Temazepam (Restoril)	15-30 mg qHS
Triazolam (Halcion)	0.125-0.25 qHS

Opioids

1. **Classification of opioids receptors**
   A. **Mu receptor:** morphine is the prototype exogenous ligand.
      1. **Mu-1:** the main action at this receptor is analgesia, but also responsible for miosis, nausea/vomiting, urinary retention, and pruritus. The endogenous ligands are enkephalins.
      2. **Mu-2:** respiratory depression, euphoria, sedation, bradycardia, ileus and physical dependence are elicited by binding at this receptor.
   B. **Delta:** modulation of mu receptor, physical dependence. High selective for the endogenous enkephalins, but opioids drugs still bind (leu-enkephalin and beta-endorphin).
   C. **Kappa:** ketocyclazocine and dynorphin are the prototype exogenous and endogenous ligands, respectively. Analgesia, sedation, dysphoria, and psychomimetic effects are produced by this receptor. Binding to the kappa receptor inhibits release of vasopressin and thus promotes diuresis. Pure kappa agonists do not produce respiratory depression.
   D. **Sigma:** N-allylnormetazocine is the prototype exogenous ligand. While this receptor binds many types of compounds, only levorotatory opioids isomers have opioids activity. The sigma receptor binds primarily dextrorotatory compounds. Dysphoria, hypertonia, tachycardia, tachypnea, and mydriasis are the principal effects of this receptor.
2. **Systemic effects**
   A. **Central nervous system effects**
      1. **Sedation and analgesia** dose-dependent; euphoria.
      2. **Amnesia** with large doses (not reliable).
      3. **Reduces MAC.**
      4. **Decreases cerebral blood flow and metabolic rate.**
      5. **Toxicity**
         A. **Dysphoria and agitation** may occur (higher with meperidine).
         B. **Seizures** may be produced by meperidine (normeperidine, major metabolite, is potent convulsant).
         C. **ICP may increase** if ventilation and $PaCO_2$ are not controlled.
   B. **Cardiovascular effects**
      1. **Minimal contractility effects** except meperidine (direct myocardial depressant); may enhance depressant effects of other agents.
      2. **Bradycardia,** dose-dependent, by stimulating the central nuclei on the vagus nerves increasing vagal tone; meperidine, may increase heart rate because of its atropine-like structure.

C. **Respiratory effects**
   1. **Respiratory depression:** dose-related depression on the ventilatory response to CO_2 by direct effect on respiratory centers resulting in increased arterial carbon dioxide tension, decreased breathing rate, increased tidal volume, decreased minute ventilation and decreased ventilatory response to carbon dioxide
   2. **Cough suppression:** dose-dependent decrease in cough reflex.
D. **Pupillary constriction:** opioids stimulate the Edinger-Westphal nucleus of the oculomotor nerve to produce miosis.
E. **Muscle rigidity**
   1. Large IV doses may produce generalized hypertonus of skeletal muscle, which, in its most severe form, can prevent ventilation.
   2. Benzodiazepine pretreatment may help in preventing rigidity.
F. **Gastrointestinal effects**
   1. **Nausea/vomiting:** direct stimulation of the chemoreceptor trigger zone.
   2. Decrease gastric motility; increase tone and secretions of GI tract.
   3. **Biliary colic:** spasm of sphincter of Oddi (less with meperidine).
G. **Urinary retention:** increases tone of ureter and vesicle sphincter, making voiding difficult (can be reversed with atropine).
H. **Endocrine:** may block stress response to surgery at high doses.
I. **Placenta:** can cross the placenta causing neonatal depression.
J. **Histamine release**
   1. May produce local itching, redness or hives near the site of injection and may cause a decrease in SVR, hypotension, and tachycardia.
   2. Morphine and meperidine release histamine, but fentanyl, sufentanil, alfentanil, and remifentanil do not.
K. **Tolerance:** both acute and chronic tolerance may occur.
L. **Drug interactions:** administration of meperidine in a patient taking a monoamine oxidase inhibitor may result in delirium or hyperthermia.

Pharmacokinetics of Intravenous Opioids

	Meperidine	Morphine	Fentanyl	Sufenta	Alfentanil	Remifentanil
Comparative Potency	0.1	1	75-125	500-1000	10-25	250
Peak Effect (min)	5-7	20-30	3-5	3-5	1.5-2	1.5-2
Duration (hr)	2-3	3-4	0.5-1	0.5-1	0.2-0.3	0.1-0.2
Half-Life (hr)	3-4	2-4	1.5-6	2.5-3	1-2	0.15-0.3
Clearance (mL/min/kg)	10-17	14.7	11.6	12.7	6.4	40
Vol of Distribution (L/kg)	2.8-4.2	3.2	4.1	2.86	0.86	0.3-0.4
Partition Coefficient (lipid solubility)	38.8	1.4	860	1,778	130	17.9
Protein Binding (%)	60	26-36	84	92	92	80

Meperidine Dosing

Indication	Adult	Pediatric
Sedation	50-150 mg IV, IM	1-2 mg/kg IV, IM
Incremental Dosing	50-150 mg IV, IM q3-4 hr	0.5-2 mg/kg IV, IM, SC q3-4 hrs
Epidural	Bolus: 20-50 mg Cont Infusion: 10-50 mg/hr	
Postop Shivering	12.5 mg IV	
Continuous Infusion		0.3-1.5 mg/kg/hr

Morphine Dosing

Indication	Adult	Pediatric
Sedation	2-10 mg IV	0.05-0.1 mg/kg IV
Incremental Dosing	2-20 mg q2-4 hr IV, IM, SC	0.05-0.2 mg/kg q2-4 hr IV, IM, SC
PCA	Bolus: 1-3 mg Lockout: 6-20 min Basal rate: 0-1 mg/hr	Bolus: 0.01-0.03 mg/kg Lockout: 6-20 min Basal rate: 0-0.03 mg/kg/hr
Epidural	Bolus: 2-6 mg q8-24 hr Cont Inf: 0.2-1 mg/hr	0.03-0.05 mg/kg (max: 0.1 mg/kg or 5 mg/24 hr)
Intrathecal	0.1-0.5 mg	0.01 mg/kg
Continuous Infusion	0.8-10 mg/hr IV (up to 80 mg/hr)	Sickle Cell/Cancer Pain: 0.025-2 mg/kg/hr Postop Pain: 0.01-0.04 mg/kg/hr

Remifentanil Dosing

Indication	Initial Bolus	Bolus	Continuous Infusion
General Anesthesia	1 mcg/kg (over 1 minute)	0.5-1	0.05-2 mcg/kg/min
Sedation	0.5-1 mcg/kg		0.025-2 mcg/kg/min

Alfentanil Dosing

Indication	Anesthesia Duration (min)	Initial Dose (mcg/kg)	Maintenance (Increment or Infusion)
Incremental Dosing	<30	8-20	3-5 mcg/kg or 0.5-1 mcg/kg/min
	30-60	20-50	5-15 mcg/kg
Continuous Infusion	>45	50-75	0.5-3 mcg/kg/min
Anesthetic Induction	>45	150-300	0.5-3 mcg/kg/min
Blunt Hypertensive Response to Intubation		15-40	

Fentanyl Dosing

Indication	Initial Dose	Supplemental Dose	Continuous Infusion
Premedication	25-100 mcg		
Sedation (minor procedure)	0.5-2 mcg/kg		
Adjunct to GA	2-50 mcg/kg	25-50	
General Anesthesia	50-150 mcg/kg	25-100	0.5-5 mcg/kg/hr
Postoperative Analgesia	0.5-1.5 mcg/kg		

Sufentanil Dosing

Indication	Dose	Maintenance	Infusion
GA: Minor Procedures	1-2 mcg/kg	10-25 mcg	
GA: Moderate Procedures	2-8 mcg/kg	10-50	0.3-1.5 mcg/kg/hr
GA: Major Procedures	8-30 mcg/kg	10-50	0.5-1.5 mcg/kg/hr

Common Parenteral Opioids

Drug	Equianalgesic Dose (mg)	Adult Dose
Meperidine	75	50-150 mg q2-4 hr
Morphine	10	2-20 mg q2-6 hr
Hydromorphone	1.5	1-4 mg/dose q4-6 hr
Fentanyl	0.1	1-2 mcg/kg q30-60 min

Opioids Agonist-Antagonist		
Drug	Adult Dosing	Pediatric Dosing
Buprenorphine (Buprenex)	0.4 mg IV q 4-6 hr	0.004 mg/kg IV q 6-8 hr
Butorphanol (Stadol)	0.5-2 mg IV q 3-4 hr	Not recommended
Dezocine (Dalgan)	2.5-10 mg IV q 2-4 hr	
Nalbuphine (Nubain)	10 mg IV q 3-4 hr	0.1 mg/kg IV q 3-4 hr
Pentazocine (Talwin)	50 mg PO q 4-6 hr	Not recommended

Common Oral Opiates	
Drug	Dose

Codeine/Aspirin
  Empirin #3 (30 mg/325 mg)
  Empirin #4 (60 mg/325 mg)
	Adult: 1-2 tabs q4-6 hr

Codeine/Aspirin/Bultabital/Caffeine Fiorinal (30 mg/325 mg/50 mg/40 mg)	Adult: 1-2 tabs q4-6 hr

Codeine/Tylenol
  Tylenol #2 (15 mg/300 mg)
  Tylenol #3 (30 mg/300 mg)
  Tylenol #4 (60 mg/300 mg)
	Adult: 1-2 tabs q4-6 hr

Codeine/Tylenol/Bultabital/Caffeine Fioricet (30 mg/325 mg/50 mg/40 mg)	Adult: 1-2 tabs q4-6 hr
Hydrocodone/Aspirin Lortab ASA (5mg/500 mg)	Adult: 1-2 tabs q4-6 hr
Hydrocodone/Ibuprofen Vicoprofen (7.5 mg/200 mg)	Adult: 1-2 tabs q4-6 hr

Hydrocodone/Tylenol
  Lorcet-HD (5 mg/500 mg)
  Lorcet Plus (7.5 mg/750 mg)
  Lorcet (10 mg/650 mg)
  Lortab (2.5 mg/500 mg)
  Lortab (5 mg/500 mg)
  Lortab (7.5 mg/500 mg)
  Lortab (10 mg/500 mg)
  Norco (5 mg/325 mg)
  Norco (7.5 mg/325 mg)
  Norco (10 mg/325 mg)
  Vicodin (5 mg/500 mg)
  Vicodin ES (7.5 mg/750 mg)
  Vicodin HP (10 mg/660 mg)
	Adult (5 mg): 1-2 tab q4-6 hr
	Adult (7.5 mg): 1 tab q4-6 hr
	Adult (10 mg): 1 tab q4-6 hr

Hydromorphone Dilaudid (1, 2, 3, 4 mg)	Adult: 1-4 mg PO q4-6 hr Ped: 0.03-0.08 mg/kg q4-6 hr
Levorphanol Levo-Dromoran (2 mg)	Adult: 1 tab PO q6-8 hr

Drug	Dose
Meperidine 　Demerol (50, 100 mg)	Adult: 1-2 tabs PO Q4-6 hr
Methadone 　Dolophine (5, 10 mg)	Adult: 2.5-10 mg PO q3-4 hr
Morphine (Immediate Release) 　Tabs: 10, 15, 30 mg 　Caps: 15, 30 mg	Adult: 1-2 tabs PO q3-4 hr
Morphine CR (Controlled Release) 　MS Contin (15, 30, 60, 100, 200 mg)	Adult: q12 hr dosing
Morphine ER (Extended Release) 　Avinza (30, 60, 90, 120 mg)	Adult: q12-24 hr dosing
Morphine SR (Sustained Release) 　Oramorph SR (15, 20, 60, 100 mg)	Adult: q12 hr dosing
Oxycodone/Oxycodone terephthalte/Aspirin 　Percodan (4.5 mg/0.38 mg/325 mg)	Adult: 1-2 tabs q4-6 hr
Oxycodone/Tylenol 　Percocet (2.5 mg/325 mg) 　Percocet (5 mg/325 mg) 　Percocet (7.5 mg/325 or500 mg) 　Percocet (10 mg/325 or 650 mg)	Adult: 1-2 tabs q4-6 hr
Oxycodone Controlled Release 　OxyContin (10, 20, 40, 80, 160 mg)	Adult: q12 dosing
Pentazocine/Aspirin 　Talwin Compound (12.5 mg/325 mg)	Adult: 1-2 tabs q4-6 hr
Pentazocine/Naloxone 　Talwin Nx (50 mg/5 mg)	Adult: 1-2 tabs q3-4 hr
Pentazocine/Tylenol 　Talacen (25 mg/650 mg)	Adult: 1 tab q4-6 hr
Propoxyphene 　Darvon (65 mg)	Adult 1-2 tabs q4-6 hr
Propoxyphene/Aspirin/Caffeine 　Darvon C-65 (65 mg/389 mg/32.4 mg)	Adult: 1-2 tabs q4-6 hr
Propoxyphene Napyslate 　Darvon-N (100mg)	Adult: 1-2 tabs q4-6 hr
Propoxyphene Napyslate/Tylenol 　Darvocet N50 (50 mg/325 mg) 　Darvocet N100 (100 mg/325 mg)	Adult: 1-2 tabs q4-6 hr
Tramadol 　Ultram (50 mg)	Adult: 1-2 tabs q4-6 hr
Tramadol/Tylenol 　Ultracet (37.5 mg/325 mg)	Adult 1-2 tabs q4-6 hr

Opioid Antagonist

1. **Naloxone (Narcan)**
   A. **Pure opioids antagonists:** administration results in displacement of opioids agonists from opioids receptors.
   B. Peak effects seen in 1-2 minutes; duration approximately 30 minutes.
   C. **Side effects**
      1. Pain: may lead to abrupt onset of pain.
      2. Sudden antagonism can activate the sympathetic nervous system, resulting in cardiovascular stimulation.
   D. **Dosage**
      1. Bolus: adult: 0.04 mg IV in titrated bolus every 2-3 minutes until the desired effect; ped: 1-4 mcg/kg titrated.
      2. Continuous infusion: 5 mcg/kg/hr IV, will prevent respiratory depression without altering the analgesia produced by neuraxial opioids.

Nonsteroidal Anti-Inflammatory Drugs (NSAIDs)

1. **Mechanism of action:** anti-inflammatory effects are due to the inhibition of cyclooxygenase, which prevents the formation of inflammatory mediators such as prostaglandins and thromboxanes.
2. **Adverse effects**
   A. **Common:** GI effects (gastritis, peptic ulcer, GI bleeding, abdominal pain, nausea, vomiting, diarrhea), decreased hemostasis (platelet dysfunction), surgical bleeding, renal dysfunction and failure, drug interactions.
   B. **Other effects:** hepatic necrosis, asthma, vasomotor rhinitis, antioneurotic edema, urticaria, laryngeal edema, hypotension, impede cartilage repair.
3. **Contraindications to NSAID use:** history of peptic ulcer disease or intolerance to NSAIDs; bleeding, bleeding diatheses, or anticoagulant therapy; renal failure, renal dysfunction, or risk factors for renal dysfunction; old age (particularly with risk factors); prophylactic use in major surgery.

Nonsteroidal Anti-Inflammatory Drugs (NSAIDs)	
Generic Name	**Dosage**
Acetaminophen (Tylenol)	Adult: 500-1000 mg PO q4 h Ped: 10-15 mg/kg PO q4 h; 15-20 mg/kg PR q4 h
Acetylsalicylic Acid	Adult: 325-650 mg PO q4 h Ped: 10-15 mg/kg PO q4 h; 15-20 mg/kg PR q4
Celecoxib (Celebrex)	Adult:100 mg BID or 200 mg qd; 200 mg BID
Choline Mg Trisalicylate (Trilisate)	Adult: 500-1000 mg PO q8-12 hr Ped: 7.5-15 mg/kg PO q6-8 h
Choline Salicylate (Arthropan)	Adult: 870 mg q3-4 h
Diclofenal Sodium (Voltaren)	Adult: 25-75 mg q8-12 hr
Diflunisal (Dolobid)	Adult: 250-500 mg q8-12 hr
Etodolic Acid (Lodine)	Adult: 200-400 mg q6-8 hr

Generic Name	Dosage
Fenoprofen Calcium (Nalfon)	Adult: 300-600 mg PO q6 hr
Flurbiprofen (Anasid)	Adult: 50-100 mg BID/TID
Ibuprofen (Motrin)	Adult: 200-800 mg PO q6-8 hr Ped: 5-10 mg/kg PO q6-8 hr
Indomethacin (Indocin)	Adult: 25-50 mg q8-12 hr
Ketoprofen (Orudis)	Adult: 25-75 mg PO q6-8 hr
Ketorolac (Toradol)	Adult: 10 mg PO q6-8 hr; 30-60 mg IV q6 h Ped: 0.5 mg/kg PO q6-8 hr
Meclofenamate Sodium (Meclomen)	Adult: 50-100 mg q4-6 hr
Meloxicam (Mobic)	Adult: 7.5-15 mg qd
Naproxen (Naprosyn)	Adult: 250-500 mg PO q8-12 h Ped: 5-10 mg/kg PO q8-12 hr
Naproxen Sodium (Anaprox)	Adult: 275-550 mg PO q6-8 hr
Piroxicam (Feldene)	Adult: 10-20 mg qd Ped: 0.2-0.3 mg/kg/day qd
Rofecoxib (Vioxx)	Adult: 12.5-50 mg PO qd
Salsalate (Disalcid)	Adult: 1-1.5 gm q8-12 hr
Sulindac (Clinoril)	Adult: 150 -200 mg q12 hr
Tolmetin (Tolectin)	Adult: 200-600 mg q8 hr Ped: 15-30 mg q6-8 hr
Valdecoxib (Bextra)	Adult: 10 mg qd (arthritis) or 20 mg BID

Intravenous Induction Agents

1. **Sodium thiopental (Pentothal)** and other barbiturates
   A. **Preparation:** thiopental is prepared as a 2.5% solution, water-soluble, pH of 10.5, and stable for up to 1-2 weeks if refrigerated.
   B. **Mechanism of action:** depresses the reticular activating system, reflecting the ability of barbiturates to decrease the rate of dissociation of the inhibitory neurotransmitter GABA from its receptors.
   C. **Pharmacokinetics**
      1. **Short duration of action** (5-10 minutes) following IV bolus reflects high lipid solubility and redistribution from the brain to inactive tissues.
      2. Protein binding parallels lipid solubility, decreased protein binding increases drug sensitivity.
      3. Protein binding of thiopental in neonates is about half that in adults, suggesting a possible increased sensitivity to this drug in neonates.
      4. Fat is the only compartment in which thiopental continues to accumulate 30 minutes after injection.
   D. **Effects on organ systems**
      1. **Cardiovascular:** induction doses cause a decrease in blood pressure (peripheral vasodilation) and tachycardia (a central vagolytic effect).
      2. **Respiratory:** barbiturate depression on the medullary ventilatory center

decreases the ventilatory response to hypercapnia and hypoxia. Laryngospasm and hiccuping are more common after methohexital than after thiopental.

3. **Cerebral:** barbiturates constrict cerebral vasculature, decreasing cerebral blood flow and intracranial pressure. Barbiturates cause a decline in cerebral oxygen consumption (up to 50% of normal) and slowing of the EEG (an exception is methohexital which activates epileptic foci). This effect may provide some brain protection from transient episodes of focal ischemia (e.g., cerebral embolism), but probably not from global ischemia (e.g., cardiac arrest).

4. **Renal:** barbiturates decrease renal blood flow and glomerular filtration rate in proportion to the fall in blood pressure.

5. **Hepatic:** hepatic blood flow is decreased.

E. **Adverse effects**
   1. Barbiturates are contraindicated in patients with acute intermittent porphyria, variegate porphyria, and hereditary coprophyria.
   2. Venous irritation and tissue damage (reflects possible barbiturate crystal formation); intraarterial injection results in severe pain and possible gangrene.
   3. Myoclonus and hiccuping.

2. **Etomidate**
   A. **Mechanisms of action:** etomidate depresses the reticular activating system and mimics the inhibitory effects of GABA. The disinhibitory effects of etomidate on the parts of the nervous system that control extrapyramidal motor activity contribute to a high incidence of myoclonus.

   B. **Pharmacokinetics:** like other barbiturates, redistribution is responsible for decreasing the plasma concentration to awakening levels. Biotransformation is five times greater for etomidate than for thiopental.

   C. **Effects on organ systems**
      1. **Cardiovascular:** minimal depressant cardiovascular changes.
      2. **Respiratory:** less affected with etomidate than thiopental.
      3. **Cerebral:** decreases the cerebral metabolic rate, cerebral blood flow, and intracranial pressure (may activate seizure foci).
      4. **Endocrine:** induction doses of etomidate transiently inhibit enzymes involved in cortisol and aldosterone synthesis. Long term infusions lead to adrenocortical suppression.

   D. **Drug interactions:** fentanyl increases the plasma level and prolongs the elimination half-life of etomidate.

   E. **Adverse effects**
      1. Myoclonic movements on induction, opioids levels are decreased.
      2. High incidence of nausea and vomiting.
      3. Venous irritation due to propylene glycol additive.
      4. Adrenal suppression.

3. **Propofol**
   A. **Mechanisms of action:** propofol increases the inhibitory neurotransmission mediated by gamma-aminobutyric acid.

   B. **Pharmacokinetics:** highly lipid solubility. Short duration of action results from a very short initial distribution half-life (2-8 minutes). Elimination occurs primarily through hepatic metabolism to inactive metabolites. Recovery from propofol is more rapid and accompanied by less hangover than other induction agents.

   C. **Effects on organ systems**
      1. **Cardiovascular:** decrease in arterial blood pressure secondary to a

drop in systemic vascular resistance, contractility, and preload. Hypotension is more pronounced than with thiopental. Propofol markedly impairs the normal arterial baroreflex response to hypotension.

2. **Respiratory:** propofol causes profound respiratory depression. Propofol induced depression of upper airway reflexes exceeds that of thiopental.

3. **Cerebral:** decreases cerebral blood flow and intracranial pressure. Propofol has antiemetic, antipruritic, and anticonvulsant properties.

D. Other effects
1. **Venous irritation:** pain may be reduced by prior administration of opioids or lidocaine.
2. Propofol is an emulsion and should be used with caution if lipid disorder present. Propofol is preservative free.
3. Very low incidence of anaphylaxis.
4. Allergic reactions may reflect patient sensitivity to the solvent, isopropylphenol structure of propofol, or sulfite preservative.
5. Occasional myoclonic movement.
6. Subhypnotic doses (10-15 mg) can help treat nausea/vomiting.

4. Ketamine
A. Mechanism of action:
ketamine blocks polysynaptic reflexes in the spinal cord, inhibiting excitatory neurotransmitter effects. Ketamine functionally dissociates the thalamus from the limbic cortex, producing a state of dissociative anesthesia.

B. Structure:
ketamine is a structural analogue of phencyclidine (PCP).

C. Pharmacokinetics:
metabolized in the liver to multiple metabolites.

D. Effects on organ systems
1. **Cardiovascular:** ketamine increases arterial blood pressure, heart rate, and cardiac output. The direct myocardial depressant effects of ketamine (large doses) are unmasked by sympathetic blockade or patients who are catecholamine depleted.
2. **Respiratory:** ventilation is minimally affected with normal doses of ketamine. Ketamine is a potent bronchodilator.
3. **Cerebral:** ketamine increases cerebral oxygen consumption, cerebral blood flow, and intracranial pressure.

E. Drug interactions:
nondepolarizing muscle relaxants are potentiated by ketamine. The combination of ketamine and theophylline may predispose patients to seizures.

F. Adverse effects
1. **Increased salivation** (can be attenuated by pretreatment with an anticholinergic).
2. **Emergence delirium:** characterized by visual, auditory, proprioceptive and confusional illusions; reduced by benzodiazepine (midazolam) premedication.
3. **Myoclonic movements.**
4. **Increased ICP.**
5. **Eyes:** nystagmus, diplopia, blepharospasm, and increased intraocular pressure.

Comparative Pharmacologic Effects and Doses of IV Agents

	Propofol	Thiopental	Etomidate	Ketamine
Induction Dose (mg/kg IV)	1.5-2.5	3-5	0.2-0.6	1-2 (4-8 mg IM)
Anesthesia Maintenance	50-300 mcg/kg/min	30-200 mcg/kg/min	10-20 mcg/kg/min	0.5-1 mg/kg IV prn 15-90 mcg/kg/min IV
Sedation	25-100 mcg/kg/min	0.5-1.5 mg/kg	5-8 mcg/kg/min	0.2-0.8 mg/kg IV 2-4 mg/kg IM
Systemic BP	Decreased	Decreased	NC or Dec	Increased
Heart Rate	NC or Dec	Increased	NC or Dec	Increased
SVR	Decreased	Decreased	NC or Dec	Increased
CBF	Decreased	Decreased	Decreased	Increased
ICP	Decreased	Decreased	Decreased	Increased
Respiratory Depression	Yes	Yes	Yes	No
Analgesia	No	No	No	Yes
Emergence Delirium	No	No	No	Yes
Nausea/Vomiting	Decreased	NC	Increased	NC
Adrenocortical Suppression	No	No	Yes	No

NC = no change; Dec = decreased

Inhaled Anesthetics

1. **Sevoflurane**
   A. **Advantages**
      1. Well tolerated (non-irritant, sweet odor), even at high concentrations, making this the agent of choice for inhalational induction.
      2. Rapid induction and recovery (low blood:gas coefficient)
      3. Does not sensitize the myocardium to catecholamines as much as halothane.
      4. Does not result in carbon monoxide production with dry soda lime.
   B. **Disadvantages**
      1. Less potent than similar halogenated agents.
      2. Interacts with CO_2 absorbers. In the presence of soda lime (and more with barium lime) compound A (a vinyl ether) is produced which is toxic to the brain, liver, and kidneys. Thus it is recommended that, in the presence of soda lime, fresh gas flow rates should not be less than 2 L/min, and use of barium lime is contraindicated.
      3. About 5% is metabolized and elevation of serum fluoride levels has led to concerns about the risk of renal toxicity. In theory, sevoflurane should be avoided in the presence of renal failure.

    4. Postoperative agitation may be more common in children then seen with halothane.

2. Desflurane

A. Advantages

1. Rapid onset and offset of effects due to low blood:gas solubility. Has the lowest blood:gas solubility of the potent inhalational agents.
2. Stable in the presence of CO_2 absorbers.
3. Pharmacodynamic effects are similar to those of isoflurane.
4. No increase in CBF and ICP if IPPV started at induction.

B. Disadvantages

1. Requires a special vaporizer which is electrically heated and thermostatically controlled. Output from the vaporizer is determined by an electronically controlled pressure regulating valve.
2. Low potency.
3. Pungency makes it unsuitable for inhalational induction. Irritation of the airways may be of concern in patients with brochospastic disease.
4. Rapidly increasing the inhaled concentration or exceeding 1.25 MAC can result in significant sympathetic nervous system stimulation with tachycardia and hypertension.

3. Isoflurane

A. Advantages

1. Suitable for virtually all types o surgery.

B. Disadvantages

1. May have coronary steal effect.
2. Pungent odor makes unsuitable for inhalational induction.

4. Enflurane

A. Advantages

1. Non-pungent odor (sweet etheral odor) and non-irritant; however, rarely used for inhalational induction.

B. Disadvantages

1. Can cause tonic clonic muscle activity and an epileptiform EEG trace and should not be used in seizure patients.
2. Increases in cerebral blood flow and ICP more than isoflurane.
3. Causes some sensitization of the myocardium to catecholamines and tends to decrease arterial blood pressure by decreasing systemic vascular resistance and having a negative inotropic effect.
4. Causes more respiratory depression than isoflurane or halothane.
5. 2.4% metabolized, resulting in increased blood fluoride levels. Should not be used for longer than 9.6 MAC hours to avoid fluoride-induced renal toxicity.
6. May cause hepatic necrosis (vary rare).

5. Halothane

A. Advantages

1. Potent inhalational agent.
2. Sweet, nonirritating odor suitable for inhalational induction.
3. Bronchodilator.

B. Disadvantages

1. Requires preservative, 0.01% thymol, the accumulation of which can interfere with vaporizer function.
2. Risk of halothane hepatitis (dysfunction).
3. Sensitizes myocardium to catecholamines more than other agents.
4. Causes vagal stimulation which can result in marked bradycardia.

 5. Potent trigger for malignant hyperthermia.
 6. Relaxes uterine muscle.
 C. Recommendations
 1. Avoid repeat exposure within 6 months.
 2. History of unexplained jaundice or pyrexia after a previous halothane anesthetic is a contraindication to repeat exposure.
 3. Use caution with epinephrine. Avoid concentrations >1:100,000.
6. Nitrous oxide
 A. Advantages
 1. Powerful analgesic properties.
 2. Decreases the MAC and accelerates the uptake of these agents.
 3. Appears to be safe in patients with MH susceptibility.
 4. Rapid induction and recovery (low blood:gas solubility).
 5. No effect on smooth muscle.
 B. Disadvantages
 1. Decreases myocardial contractility (offset by stimulating effect on the SNS, increasing SVR). Also increases PVR in patients with preexisting pulmonary hypertension.
 2. 35 times more soluble than nitrogen in blood, thus causing a rapid increase in the size of air-filled spaces. Also leads to diffusion hypoxia when N_2O is stopped.
 3. Supports combustion and can contribute to fires.
 4. Increases risk of postoperative nausea and vomiting.
 5. May increase intracranial pressure by increasing cerebral blood flow.
 6. Inhibits methionine synthetase (prolonged exposure may lead to megaloblastic bone marrow changes).
 7. Long-term use can lead to peripheral neuropathy.
 8. Possible teratogenic effect.

Inhaled Anesthetics: General Properties

Agent	MAC[1]	Blood:gas coefficient[2]	Vapor pressure[3]	Metabolism (%)[4]
Isoflurane	1.15	1.4	239	0.2
Enflurane	1.68	1.8	175	2-5
Halothane	0.75	2.3	243	15-20
Desflurane	6.0	0.42	664	<0.1
Sevoflurane	2.05	0.69	157	2%
Nitrous Oxide	105	0.47	39,000	0.0004

1=Minimum alveolar concentration (MAC) at one atmosphere at which 50% of patients do not move in response to a surgical skin incision.
2=Blood:gas partition coefficient is inversely related to the rate of induction.
3=Vapor pressure is reported as mmHg at 20°C.
4=Percentage of absorbed anesthetic undergoing metabolism.

Effects of Inhaled Anesthetics on Organ Systems					
	Sevo-flurane	Isoflurane/ Desflurane	Halothane	Enflurane	Nitrous Oxide
CO	0	0	-*	--*	0
HR	0	+	0	++*	0
BP	--	--*	-*	--*	0
SV	--	-*	-*	--*	-
Contractility	--	--*	---*	--*	-*
SVR	-	--	0	-	0
PVR	0	0	0	0	+
ICP	+	+	++	++	+
CBF	+	+	++	+	+
Seizures	-	-	-	+	-
Hepatic BF	-	-	--	--	-
RR	+	+	++	++	+
TV	-	-	-	-	-
PaCO$_2$	+	+	+	++	0
*=Dose Dependent; 0=No Change; -=Decrease; +=Increase; ?=Uncertain					

Adrenergic Agonists

1. **Adrenergic receptors** (locations)
   A. **Alpha receptors**
      1. **Alpha-1:** vascular smooth muscle (vasoconstriction), genitourinary (contraction), intestinal (relaxation), liver (glycogenolysis, gluconeogenesis), and heart (increased contractile force, arrhythmias).
      2. **Alpha-2:** pancreatic beta cells (decreased insulin secretion), platelets (aggregation), nerve terminals (decreased NE release), and vascular smooth muscle (vasoconstriction).
   B. **Beta receptors**
      1. **Beta-1:** heart (increased contractile force, rate, and atrioventricular node conduction), and juxtaglomerular cells (increased renin secretion).
      2. **Beta-2:** vascular smooth muscle (relaxation), bronchial (relaxation), GI (relaxation), genitourinary (relaxation), and skeletal muscle (glycogenolysis, uptake of K$^+$), liver (glycogenolysis, gluconeogenesis).
      3. **Beta-3:** adipose tissue (lipolysis)
   C. **Dopamine receptors** (at least 5 know subtypes)
      1. **Dopamine-1:** vascular smooth muscle (renal, mesentery, coronary causing vasodilation), renal tubules (natriuresis, diuresis), juxtaglomerular cells (increased renin release).
      2. **Dopamine-2:** postganglionic sympathetic nerves (inhibits NE release), smooth muscle (renal, mesenteric causing possible constriction).

Adrenergic Agonists: Receptor Selectivity

Drug	Alpha1	Alpha2	Beta1	Beta2	Dop1	Dop2
Clonidine	+	+++	0	0	0	0
Dobutamine	0/+	0	+++	+	0	0
Dopamine	++	++	++	+	+++	+++
Dopexamine	0	0	+	+++	++	+++
Ephedrine	++	?	++	+	0	0
Epinephrine	++	++	+++	++	0	0
Fenoldopam	0	0	0	0	+++	0
Isoproterenol	+		++++	++++		
Methyldopa	+	+++	0	0	0	0
Norepinephrine	++	++	++	0	0	0
Phenylephrine	+++	+	+	0	0	0
Terbutaline	0	0	+	+++	0	0
Key: + =Increased; - =Decreased; 0 =No Change						

System Effects of Adrenergic Agonist

Drug	HR	MAP	CO	PVR	Broncho-dilation	Renal BF
Dobutamine	+	+	+++	-	0	+
Dopamine	+/++	+	+++	+	0	+++
Ephedrine	++	++	++	+	++	--
Epinephrine	++	+	++	-/+	++	--
Isoproterenol	+++	-	+++	--	+++	-/+
Methyldopa	-	--	-	--	0	+
Norepinephrine	-	+++	-/+	+++	0	---
Phenylephrine	-	+++	-	+++	0	---
HR = heart rate; MAP = mean arterial pressure; CO = cardiac output; PVR = pulmonary vascular resistance; BF = blood flow						

Adrenergic Agonists		
Drug	Bolus	Continuous Infusion
Dobutamine		2-20 mcg/kg/min
Dopamine		1-20 mcg/kg/min
Dopexamine		0.5-6 mcg/kg/min
Ephedrine	2.5-50 mg or 0.1 mg/kg	
Epinephrine	0.01-1.0 mg	2-20 mcg/min or 0.05-0.2 mcg/kg/min
Fenoldopam		0.1-0.8 mcg/kg/min
Isoproterenol		0.01-0.2 mcg/kg/min
Norepinephrine	0.1 mcg/kg	2-20 mcg/min or 0.05-0.3 mcg/kg/min
Phenylephrine	50-100 mcg	0.25-1 mcg/kg/min

Pharmacology of Parenteral Antihypertensive Agents			
Drug	Site of Vasodilation	Advantages	Side Effects/Problems
Hydralazine	Direct dilator arterial >> venous	No CNS effects	Reflex tachycardia, lupus, local thrombophlebitis
Labetalol	Alpha and beta blockers	No overshoot hypotension Maintained CO, HR	Exacerbation of CHF, asthma, AV block, bronchospasm
Nitroglycerin	Direct dilator (venous > arterial)	Coronary dilator	Headache, Absorbed into IV tubing, ETOH vehicle
Nitroprusside	Direct dilator (balanced)	Immediate action Easy to titrate No CNS effects	Hypotension Reflex tachycardia Cyanide toxicity Methemoglobin
Phentolamine	Alpha blocker direct vasodilator	Pheochromo-cytoma MAO crisis	Reflex tachycardia Tachyphylaxis
Trimethaphan	Ganglionic blocker	Aortic aneurysm Subarachnoid bleed	Anticholinergic effects Decreased cardiac output

Parenteral Treatment of Acute Hypertension

Agent	Dosage Range*	Onset	Duration
Diazoxide	1-3 mg/kg slowly	2-10 min	4-6 hr
Enalaprilat	0.625-1 mg	5-15 min	4-6 hr
Esmolol	0.5 mg/kg over 1 min 50-300 mcg/kg/min	1 min	12-20 min
Fenoldopam	0.1-1.6 mcg/kg/min	4-5 min	<10 min
Hydralazine	5-20 mg	5-20 min	4-8 hr
Labetalol	5-20 mg	1-2 min	4-8 hr
Methyldopa	250-1000 mg	2-3 hr	6-12 hr
Nicardipine	5-15 mg/hr	1-5 min	3-6 hr
Nifedipine (SL)	10 mg	5-10 min	4 hr
Nitroglycerin	5-200 mcg/min	1 min	3-5 min
Nitroprusside	0.25-10 mcg/kg/min	30-60 sec	1-5 min
Phentolamine	1-5 mg	1-10 min	20-40 min
Propranolol	1-3 mg	1-2 min	4-6 hr
Trimethaphan	1-6 mg/min	1-3 min	10-30 min

Comparison of Calcium Channel Blockers

Drug	Route	Dose (mg)	Half-Life (hours)
Amlodipine	PO	2.5-10	30-50
Bepridil	PO	200-400	24
Diltiazem	PO IV	30-60 0.25-0.35 mg/kg	4 4
Felodipine	PO	5-20	9
Isradipine	PO	2.5-5.0	8
Nicardipine	PO IV	60-120 0.25-0.5 mg/kg	2-4 2-4
Nifedipine	PO SL	30-180 mg 10	2 2
Nimodipine	PO	240	2
Verapamil	PO IV	40-240 5-15	5 5

*=Total oral dose per day divided into three doses unless otherwise stated

Corticosteroids

Corticosteroids: Systemic Comparison Chart			
	Equivalent Dose (mg)	Glucocorticoid Potency*	Mineralocorticoid Potency
Short-Acting			
Cortisone	25	0.8	2
Hydrocortisone	20	1	2
Intermediate-Acting			
Prednisone	5	4	1
Prednisolone	5	4	1
Triamcinolone	4	5	0
Methylprednisolone	4	5	0
Fludrocortisone		10	4
Long-Acting			
Dexamethasone	0.75	25-30	0
Betamethasone	0.6-0.75	25	0
*=Glucocorticoid potency compared to hydrocortisone mg for mg basis			

Adjunct Pharmacotherapy in Pain Management

1. Antidepressants
   A. Cyclic antidepressants
      1. **Mechanisms:** all tricyclics inhibit serotonergic and/or noradrenergic reuptake; clinical benefits often begin after 2-3 weeks of treatment.
      2. **Adverse effects:** anticholinergic reactions (dry mouth, constipation, blurred vision, prolonged gastric emptying, urinary retention); cardiac effects (tachycardia, T-wave flattening or inversion, prolongation of the PR, QRS, QT intervals); other effects (orthostasis, sedation, extrapyramidal syndromes, weight gain, sexual dysfunction, jaundice, leukopenia, rashes).
      3. **Withdrawal:** may manifest as anxiety, fever, sweating, myalgia, nausea, headache, vomiting, dizziness, dyskinesia, akathisia.
      4. **Anesthetic considerations:** may increase anesthetic requirements (secondary to increased brain catecholamine activity); potentiation of centrally acting anticholinergic agents may increase postoperative confusion; may see exaggerated response to both indirect-acting vasopressors and sympathetic stimulation.
   B. Monoamine oxidase inhibitors
      1. **Mechanisms:** blocks the enzyme monoamine oxidase, thus inhibiting the breakdown of monoamines; results in increased neurotransmitters epinephrine, norepinephrine, and dopamine; requires 2 weeks to achieve inhibition and 2-4 weeks for clinical effects.
      2. **Adverse effects:** orthostatic hypotension, agitation, tremor, seizures, muscle spasms, urinary retention, paresthesias, jaundice, tyramine-

induced hypertensive crisis (e.g., some cheeses, chianti wine, chocolate, liver, fava beans, avocados); exaggerated response to indirect-acting sympathomimetics; interaction with opioids (may cause excitatory or depressive reactions; excitatory reaction thought to be central serotonergic overactivity manifesting as hypertension, hypotension, tachycardia, diaphoresis, hyperthermia, muscle rigidity, seizures, coma; meperidine has been associated with fetal excitatory reactions); inhibition of hepatic enzymes

3. **Anesthesia considerations:** discontinuation of MAO inhibitors preop is controversial and should be guided by the patient's dependence on these drugs; avoid opioids if possible (morphine is the preferred narcotic); avoid ketamine and pancuronium.

C. **Selective serotonin reuptake inhibitors (SSRIs)**

1. **Mechanisms:** blockade of the presynaptic serotonin reuptake pump.
2. **Adverse effects:** may cause headaches, stimulation or sedation, fine tremor, tinnitus, rare extrapyramidal symptoms (dystonia, akathisia, dyskinesia, tardive dyskinesia), nausea, vomiting, diarrhea, sexual dysfunction; overall fewer side effects then other antidepressants.

Tricyclic Antidepressants (TCAs)

Drug	Antichol Activity	Central Action	Sedation	Adult Dosage (mg)	
				Initial	Range
Tertiary Amines					
Amitriptyline (Elavil)	Strong	S/(N)	Strong	10-25 qhs	10-100
Clomipramine (Anafranil)	Moderate	S/(N)	Strong	25 qhs	25-300
Doxepin (Sinequan)	Moderate	S	Strong	10-25 qhs	10-150
Imipramine (Tofranil)	Moderate	N/S	Moderate	10-25 qhs	10-100
Secondary Amines					
Desipramine (Norpramin)	Minimal	N	Mild	10-25 qhs	25-150
Nortriptyline (Pramelor)	Mild	N/S	Moderate	10-25 qhs	10-100
Protriptyline (Vivactil)	Moderate	N	Minimal	15 qhs	15-40
Amoxapine (Asendin)	Minimal	N	Mild	100 qhs	100-200

Antichol = anticholinergic; S = serotonergic; N = norepinephrinergic; (N) = weekly norepinephrinergic

Monoamine Oxidase Inhibitors (MAO Inhibitors)

Drug	Initial Adult Dose (mg)	Dose Range (mg)
Isocarboxacid (Marplan)	30	30-50
Phenelzine (Nardil)	45	45-90
Tranylcypromine (Parnate)	20	20-60

Selective Serotonin Reuptake Inhibitors (SSRIs)

Drug	Initial Adult Dose (mg)	Dose Range (mg)
Fluoxetine (Prozac)	10	10-80
Fluvoxamine (Luvox)	50	50-300
Paroxetine (Paxil)	10	10-50
Sertraline (Zoloft)	50	50-200
Venlafaxine (Effexor)	75	75-300

Atypical Antidepressants

Drug	Initial Adult Dose (mg)	Dose Range (mg)
Bupropion (Wellbutrin)	75-100	75-450
Maprotiline (Ludiomil)	75	50-300
Nefazodone (Serzone)	50	50-600
Trazodone (Desyrel)	25-50	25-150

Neuroleptics (Antipsychotics)

Drug	Initial Adult Dose	Dose Range
Typical Neuroleptics		
Chlorpromazine (Thorazine)	10-50 mg 2-4/day	30-800 mg/day
Fluphenazine (Prolixin)	0.5-10 mg/day 3-4/day	2-40 mg/day
Haloperidol (Haldol)	0.5-2 mg 2-3/day	1-100 mg/day
Perphenazine (Trilafon)	4-16 mg 2-4/day	8-64 mg/day
Trifluoperazine (Stelazine)	1-2 mg BID	2-6 mg/day
Atypical Neuroleptics		
Clozapine (Clozaril)	25 mg 1-2/day	25-450 mg/day
Olanzapine (Zyprexa)	5 mg qd	20 mg/day
Risperidone (Risperdol)	1 mg BID	2-8 mg/day

Antispasmodics/Muscle Relaxants		
Drug	**Initial Adult Dose**	**Dose Range**
Baclofen (Lioresal)	5 mg TID	15-80 mg/day
Carisoprodol (Soma)	350 mg TID and qHS	
Chlorzoxazone (Paraflex)	500 TID/QID	250-750 mg TID/QID
Cyclobenzaprine (Flexeril)	10 mg TID	20-60 mg/day
Diazepam (Valium)	2-5 mg 2-4/day	2-10 mg 2-4/day
Metaxalone (Skelaxin)	2 tabs (400 mg/ea) TID/QID	
Methocarbamol (Robaxin)	1.5 gm QID	up to 4.5 gm in 3-6 divided doses
Orphenadrine (Norflex)	1 tab (100 mg) BID	
Tizanidine (Zanaflex)	4-8 mg qHS	12-36 mg/day

Anticonvulsants		
Drug	**Initial Adult Dose**	**Dose Range**
Carbamazepine (Tegretol)	100 mg BID	200-1200 mg/day BID-TID
Clonazepam (Clonopin)	0.5 mg qHS	0.5-4 mg/day qd-BID
Gabapentin (Neurontin)	300 mg TID	900-3600 mg/day
Lamotrigine (Lamietal)	25 mg qHS	200 mg BID
Oxcarbazepine (Trileptal)	75-150 mg qd or BID	300-1200 mg BID
Phenytoin (Dilantin)	100 mg TID	10-15 mg/kg
Topiramate (Topamax)	25-50 mg qd	100-200 mg BID
Valproic Acid (Depakene)	15 mg/kg/day BID/TID	60 mg/kg/day TID
Zonisamide (Zonegran)	100 mg/day	100-600 mg/day

Misc Pharmacotherapy Adjuncts		
Drug	**Initial Adult Dose**	**Dose Range**
Mexilentine (Mexitil)	150 mg qHS	up to 900 mg/day TID
Fentanyl Transdermal (Duragesic)	1 patch 48-72 hr	25, 50,75, 100 mcg/hr
Lidocaine 5% Patch (Lidoderm)	1-3 patches/24 hr	

Drugs for Migraine Prophylaxis		
Drug	Initial Dose	Max Daily Dose
Amitriptyline (Elavil)	10-25 mg qd	300 mg
Atenolol	50 mg qd	200 mg
Diltiazem	60 mg BID	360 mg
Divalproex (Depakote)	500 mg qd	1000 mg
Fluoxetine (Prozac)	20 mg qd	80 mg
Gabapentin (Neurontin)	300 mg BID	1800 mg
Metoprolol	50 mg BID	450 mg
Nadolol	40 mg qd	320 mg
Naproxen	250 mg TID	1500 mg
Propranolol	20 mg TID	240 mg
Timolol	10 mg BID	30 mg
Topiramate (Topamax)	25 mg BID	400 mg
Verapamil	80 mg TID	480 mg

Antibiotics

Commonly Used Antibiotics		
Drug	Adult IV Dose	Ped IV Dose
Amikacin	300 mg q8 hrs	7.5-22.5 mg/kg/day divided q8 hrs
Ampicillin	0.5-3 gm q6 hrs	50-100 mg/kg divided q6-12 hrs
Ampicillin-Sulbactam (Unasyn)	1-2 gm q6-8 hrs	100-200 mg/kg/day divided q6 hrs
Aztreonam	1 gm q8 hrs	30 mg/kg/dose q6-12 hr
Cefazolin (Ancef)	1.0 gm q6-8 hrs	20-40 mg/kg q8-12 hr
Cefotetan	1-2 gm q12 hrs	20-40 mg/kg q12 hrs
Cefoxitin	1-3 gm q6-8 hrs	20-40 mg/kg q4-8 hrs
Ceftazidime	1 gm q8-12 hrs	75-150 mg/kg q8-12 hrs
Ceftriaxone	1 gm q12-24 hr	50-75 mg/kg q12-24 hrs
Cefuroxime	750-1500 mg q8 hrs	20-50 mg/kg q8 hrs
Chloramphenicol	0.25-1 gm q6 hrs	20 mg/kg q6 hrs
Ciprofloxaxin	400 mg q12 hrs	5-10 mg/kg q12 hrs
Clindamycin	600 mg q8 hrs	5-10 mg/kg q 8 hrs
Co-Trimoxazole (Bactrim)	160 mg q12 hrs	4-5 mg/kg q 12 hrs
Doxycycline	100 mg q12 hrs	2.5 mg/kg q12 hrs

Drug	Adult IV Dose	Ped IV Dose
Erythromycin	0.5-1.0 gm q6-8 hrs	2.5-5 mg/kg 6 hrs
Fluconazole	200-400 mg	10 mg/kg
Gentamicin	60-120 mg q8-12 hrs	2.0 mg/kg q8-12 hrs
Imipenem-Cilastatin	500 mg q6 hrs	25 mg/kg q6-12 hrs
Levofloxacin	500 mg qd	5-10 mg qd
Metronidazole (Flagyl)	30 mg/kg/day q6 hrs	30 mg/kg/day divided q6 hrs
Nafcillin	1-2 gm q4 hrs	50-100 mg/kg/day divided q6 hrs
Penicillin G	0.5-2 million U q4-6 hrs	30,000-50,000 IU/kg q4-6 hrs
Piperacillin	4 gm q6 hrs	200-300 mg/kg/day divided q4-6 hrs
Pipercillin-Tazobactam (Zosyn)	3 gm q6 hrs	300-400 mg/kg/d divided q6-8 hrs
Ticarcillin-Clavulanate (Timentin)	3.1 q4-6 hrs	
Tobramycin	3-6 mg/kg/day divided q8 hrs	6-7.5 mg/kg/day divided q8 hrs
Trimethoprim-Sulfamethoxazole (Bactrim)	160 mg q12 hrs	4-5 mg/kg q 12 hrs
Vancomycin	0.5-1.0 gm q6-12 hrs	10 mg/kg q6-12 hrs

Drugs and Drips

Acetaminophen (Tylenol)
   Actions: inhibits the synthesis of prostaglandins in the CNS and peripherally blocks pain impulse generation; produces antipyresis from inhibition of hypothalamic heat-regulating center (no anti-inflammatory effects).
   Indications: treatment of mild-moderate pain and fever.
   Dose (adult): 325-650 mg PO/PR every 4 hours (max 4 gm/24 hrs).
   Dose (ped < 12 years): 10-15 mg/kg PO/PR every 4-6 hours as needed (do not exceed 2.6 gm in 24 hours).
   Dose (neonate): 10-15 mg/kg PO/PR every 6-8 hours.
   Clearance: metabolized in the liver to sulfate and glucuronide metabolites, while a small amount is metabolized by microsomal mixed function oxidase to an intermediate which is conjugated with glutathione and inactivated.
   Adverse effects: anemia, blood dyscrasias, nausea, rash, vomiting.
   Comments: severe hepatic toxicity on overdose or when combined with alcohol; adjust dose in renal failure; for rectal dosing some advocate higher dosing (30-45 mg/kg/dose).

Acetazolamide (Diamox)
   Actions: inhibits carbonic anhydrase, increasing the excretion of bicarbonate.
   Indications: respiratory acidosis with metabolic alkalosis; increased intraocular and intracranial pressure.
   Dose (diuretic): adult: 250-375 mg PO/IV; ped: 5 mg/kg/dose qd-qod PO/IV.

Dose (altitude sickness): adult: 250 mg PO q8-12 hours.
Dose (urine alkalinization): 5 mg/kg/dose PO repeated 2-3 times.
Dose (secondary metabolic alkalosis): 3-5 mg/kg/dose q6 hrs for 4 doses.
Dose (hydrocephalus): 20 mg/kg/24 hrs in divided doses every 8 hours, may increase to 100 mg/kg/24 hrs up to max dose of 2 gm/24 hrs
Clearance: 70-100% excreted unchanged in the urine within 24 hours.
Contraindications: hepatic failure, severe renal failure.
Adverse effects: may increase insulin requirements in diabetic patients; may cause renal calculi in patients with past history of calcium stones; may cause hypokalemia, thrombocytopenia, aplastic, anemia, increased urinary excretion of uric acid, and hyperglycemia.
Comments: tolerance to desired effects occurs in 2-3 days; rare hypersensitivity reaction in patients with sulfa allergies.

Adenosine (Adenocard)
Actions: adenosine slows conduction through the A-V node, interrupting the re-entry pathways through the A-V node.
Indications: PSVT, Wolf-Parkinson-White syndrome.
Dose (adult): 6 mg rapid IV bolus; may be repeated within 1-2 minutes with 12 mg (up to two doses).
Dose (ped): 0.1-0.2 mg/kg rapid IV/IO; may increase dose by 0.05 mg/kg increments every 2 min to max of 0.25 mg/kg (up to 12 mg), or until termination of SVT (max single dose: 12 mg).
Dose(neonate): 50 mcg/kg rapid IV; may increase dose by 50 mcg/kg every 2 minutes to a maximum dose of 250 mcg./kg.
Clearance: RBC and endothelial cell metabolism.
Contraindications: second and third degree AV heart blocks; sick sinus syndrome (unless paced).
Adverse effects: chest pain, facial flushing, hypotension, palpitations, dyspnea, headache, lightheadedness; may precipitate bronchoconstriction.
Comments: large doses may cause hypotension; not effective in atrial flutter/fibrillation or ventricular tachycardia; effects antagonized by methylxanthines and potentiated with dipyridamole; asystole for 3-6 seconds after administration is common.

Albumin
Actions: increases intravascular oncotic pressure and mobilizes fluid from interstitial into intravascular space.
Indications: hypovolemia; symptomatic relief for hypoproteinemia.
Dose (adult): 25 gm/dose IV, may repeat prn.
Dose (ped): 0.5-1 mg/dose IV, may repeat prn.
Dose (neonate): 0.25-0.5 mg/kg IV, may repeat prn.
Contraindications: CHF, severe anemia; 25% concentration contraindicated in preterm infants (risk of IVH).
Adverse effects: rapid infusion may cause fluid overload; may cause rapid increase in serum sodium levels.
Comments: use 5 micron filter or larger; max dose: 6 gm/kg/day; both 5% and 25% albumin have sodium concentration of 130-160 mEq/L.

Albuterol (Proventil, Ventolin)

Actions: beta$_2$-receptor agonist.

Indications: bronchospasm.

Dose (aerosol-MDI): 1-2 puffs (90 mcg/spray) every 4-6 hrs prn.

Dose (nebulization): **Adult and ped >12 yrs:** 2.5-5 mg/dose every 6 hrs.
Ped (5-12 yrs): 2.5 mg/dose every 4-6 hrs.
Ped (1-5 yrs): 1.25-2.5 mg/dose every 4-6 hrs.
Ped (<1 yr): 0.05-0.15 mg/kg/dose every 4-6 hrs.

Dose (PO): adult (and ped > 12yrs): 2-4 mg/dose 3-4 times/day; ped (6-12 yrs): 2 mg/dose 3-4 times/day; ped (<6 yrs): 0.1-0.2 mg/kg/dose 3 times/day.

Clearance: metabolized by the liver to an inactive sulfate.

Adverse effects: possible beta-adrenergic overload, tachyarrhythmias, palpitations, hypertension, chest pain, CNS stimulation, headache, insomnia, increase blood glucose; systemic effects are dose related.

Comments: for acute exacerbations, more frequent dosing may be used; use caution in patients with hyperthyroidism, diabetes, cardiovascular disorders.

Aminocaproic Acid (Amicar)

Actions: stabilizes clot formation by inhibiting plasminogen activators (fibrinolysis inhibitor) and plasmin.

Indications: excessive acute bleeding from hyperfibrinolysis, chronic bleeding tendency; antidote for excessive thrombolysis.

Dose: loading dose of 100-150 mg/kg IV over the first 30-60 minutes followed by constant infusion of 33.3 mg/kg/hour for about 8 hours or until bleeding controlled. Most common regimen for adult: 5 gram loading (started prior to skin incision) followed by constant infusion of 1 gm/hour.

Clearance: primarily renal elimination.

Contraindications: DIC, hematuria.

Adverse effects: hypotension, bradycardia, dysrhythmias, elevated LFT's, thrombosis, nausea, diarrhea, weakness, headache, decreased platelet function, false increase in urine amino acids.

Comments: reduce dose by 75% in patients with oliguria or ESRD; use caution in cardiac, renal or hepatic disease.

Aminophylline (Theophylline)

Actions: inhibits of phosphodiesterase, resulting in bronchodilation with positive inotropic and chronotropic effects.

Indications: bronchospasm, infantile apneic spells.

Dose (loading): 5-7 mg/kg IVPB over 15-30 min (6 mg/kg PO).

Maintenance (IV): 1) Neonates: 0.2 mg/kg/hr
2) Infants 6 wk - 6 months: 0.5 mg/kg/hr.
3) Infants 6 months - 1 year: 0.6-0.7 mg/kg/hr.
4) Children 1 - 9 years: 1 mg/kg/hr.
5) Children 9-12 years: 0.9 mg/kg/hr.
6) Children 12-16: 0.7 mg/kg/hr
7) Adult smokers: 0.8 mg/kg/hr.
8) Adult non-smokers: 0.5 mg/kg/hr.
9) Adults w/CHF/liver disease: 0.25 mg/kg/hr.

Dose (neonatal apnea): load with 5-6 mg/kg IV/PO, followed by maintenance dose: 1-2 mg/kg/dose every 6-8 hrs IV/PO.

Therapeutic level (theophylline): bronchospasm:10-20 mg/L; neonatal apnea 6-13 mg/L.

Clearance: hepatic metabolism; renal elimination (10% unchanged).

Adverse effects: nausea, vomiting, anorexia, dizziness, headaches, agitation, tachyarrhythmias, ventricular arrhythmias, palpitations, overdosage hyperreflexia, convulsions, hypotension, tachypnea.

Comments: aminophylline contains about 80% theophylline by weight.

Amiodarone (Cordarone)

Actions: inhibits adrenergic stimulation, decreases A-V conduction and the sinus node function, prolongs the PR, QRS, and QT intervals, and produces alpha- and beta-adrenergic blockade.

Indications: refractory or recurrent ventricular tachycardia or VF, SVT, PSVT.

Dose (cardiac arrest): adult: 300 mg IVP; consider repeating 150 mg IVP in 3-5 minutes, max dose: 2.2 gm IV/24 hours; ped: 5 mg/kg IV/IO.

Dose (tachyarrhythmias-adult): load with 150 mg IV over first 10 minutes (may repeat 150 mg every 10 minutes for breakthrough VF/VT); then infuse 360 mg IV over 6 hours (1 mg/min) followed by a maintenance infusion of 540 mg IV over 18 hours (0.5 mg/min).

Dose (tachyarrhythmias-ped): load with 5 mg/kg IV over 20-60 minutes followed by a maintenance infusion of 5-10 mcg/kg/min; supplemental doses may be given for breakthrough episodes of VT/VF up to a max of 15 mg/kg/d.

Clearance: biliary elimination.

Contraindications: severe sinus node dysfunction, marked sinus bradycardia, second and third degree AV block, bradycardia induced syncope (except if pacemaker is placed), cardiogenic shock, thyroid disease.

Adverse effects: may cause severe sinus bradycardia, ventricular arrhythmias, AV block, liver and thyroid function test abnormalities, hepatitis, cirrhosis; pulmonary fibrosis may follow long-term use; increases serum levels of digoxin, oral anticoagulants, diltiazem, quinidine, procainamide, and phenytoin.

Comments: avoid during pregnancy and while breast feeding; use with caution in renal failure.

Amrinone (Inocor)

Actions: phosphodiesterase inhibitor (rapid inotropic agent) causing increase in cardiac output while pulmonary vascular resistance and preload decrease (positive inotropic and vasodilator properties), slightly increases atrioventricular conduction.

Indications: treatment of low cardiac output states, adjunctive therapy for pulmonary hypertension, intractable heart failure.

Dose (adult/ped): load with 0.75 mg/kg IV over 2-3 minutes followed by a maintenance infusion of 5-15 mcg/kg/min; infusion mixtures (typically 100 mg in 250 cc) must not contain dextrose; dose should not exceed 10 mg/kg/24 hours.

Dose (neonate): load with 0.75 mg/kg IV over 2-3 minutes followed by maintenance infusion of 3-5 mcg/kg/min.

Clearance: variable hepatic metabolism; renal/fecal excretion.

Adverse effects: worsening myocardial ischemia, thrombocytopenia, hypotension, tachyarrhythmias hepatic function abnormalities, nausea/vomiting; contraindicated if allergic to bisulfites.

Comments: do not administer furosemide (Lasix) in same IV line; use reduced dose (50-75% of dose) in renal failure.

Aprotinin (Trasylol)

Actions: inhibitor of several proteases (including trypsin, kallikrein, and plasmin) and inhibits factor XIIa activation of complement; protects glycoprotein Ib receptor on platelets during cardiopulmonary bypass.

Indications: prophylactic use to reduce bleeding and transfusion requirements in high-risk cardiac surgery patients.

Test dose: 0.1 mg/kg or 1 mL (1.4 mg) administer IV via a central line; wait at least 10 minutes for possible adverse reaction (i.e., rash, bronchospasm, hypotension).

High dose (adult): 200 mL (280 mg) IV over 20-30 minutes; 200 mL (280 mg) into pump prime volume; followed by 50 mL/hr (70 mg/hr) maintenance.

Low dose (adult): 100 mL (140 mg) IV over 20-30 minutes; 100 mL (140 mg) into pump prime volume; followed by 25 mL/hr (35 mg/hr) maintenance.

Dose (ped): 171.5 mL/m^2 or 240 mL/m^2 over 20-30 minutes; 171.5 mL/m^2 into pump prime volume; followed by 40 mL/m^2/hour maintenance.

Clearance: renal elimination.

Adverse effects: allergic reactions and anaphylaxis; hypotension may occur with rapid administration.

Comments: aprotinin prolongs whole blood clotting time of heparinized blood (prolonged PTT); patients may require additional heparin even in the presence of adequate anticoagulation by activated clotting time (ACT); all doses of aprotinin should be administered through a central line; no other drugs should be administer in the same line.

Aspirin (Acetylsalicylic Acid)

Actions: irreversibly inhibits platelet cyclo-oxygenase, inhibits the formation of platelet-aggregating substance thromboxane A$_2$ platelet aggregation, acts on hypothalamus heat-regulating center to reduce fever.

Indications: treatment of mild to moderate pain, inflammation, and fever; adjunctive treatment of Kawasaki disease; used for prophylaxis of myocardial infarction and transient ischemic episodes.

Dose (adult): analgesic and antipyretic: 325-650 mg every 4-6 hours PO or rectal; anti-inflammatory: 2.4-5.4 g/day PO in divided doses; myocardial infarction prophylaxis: 75-325 mg/day PO.

Dose (ped): analgesic and antipyretic: 10-15 mg/kg PO/PR every 4-6 hours (up to 60-80 mg/kg/24 hr); anti-inflammatory: 60-100 mg/kg/day PO divided every 6-8 hours; Kawasaki disease: 80-100 mg/kg/24 hrs PO in 4 divided doses during febrile phase until defervesces, then decrease to 3-5 mg/kg/24 hrs PO every am (continue for at least 8 weeks).

Clearance: primarily by hepatic microsomal enzymes.

Adverse effects: may cause GI upset, allergic reactions, liver toxicity, decreased platelet aggregation.

Comments: active peptic ulcer disease (use rectal suppository); use caution if history of hypersensitivity or allergy, bleeding disorders, severe hepatic disease, renal dysfunction, gastritis, gout; associated with Reye's syndrome (do not use in patients <16 years of age for treatment of chicken pox or flu-like symptoms).

Atenolol (Tenormin)

Actions: beta$_1$-selective adrenergic receptor blockade.

Indications: hypertension, angina, postmyocardial infarction.

Dose (adult): PO: 50-100 mg/day; IV: 5 mg prn.

Dose (ped): 1-1.2 mg/kg/dose PO qd; max dose: 2 mg/kg/24 hrs.

Dose (post MI): adult: 5 mg IV over 5 minutes, then repeat in 10 minutes if initial dose tolerated; maintenance: start 50 mg/dose PO every 12 hrs x 2 dose 10 min after last IV dose followed by 100 mg/24 hrs in 1-2 doses for 6-9 days (discontinue if bradycardia or hypotension require treatment).

Clearance: renal, intestinal elimination.

Contraindications: pulmonary edema, cardiogenic shock.

Adverse effects: may cause bradycardia, hypotension, second or third degree AV block, dizziness, fatigue, lethargy, headache,.

Comments: high doses block B_2-adrenergic receptors; caution in patients on calcium-channel blockers, diabetes, asthma; adjust dose in renal impairment; avoid abrupt withdrawal; IV administration rate max: 1 mg/min.

Atropine Sulfate

Actions: competitive blockade of acetylcholine at muscarinic receptors; increases cardiac output, dries secretions, antagonizes histamine and serotonin.

Indications: bradycardia; antisialagogue; exercise-induced asthma, antidote for organophosphate pesticide poisoning, mydriasis and cycloplegia.

Dose (antisialagogue): adult 0.2-0.4 mg IV; ped 0.01 mg/kg/dose IV/IM.

Dose (bronchospasm): 0.025-0.05 mg/kg/dose in 2.5 ml NS q6-8 hours via nebulizer (min dose 0.25 mg; max dose: 1 mg).

Dose (bradycardia): adult 0.5-1.0 mg IV may repeat every 3-5 minutes; ped: 0.02 mg/kg IV may repeat every 3-5 minutes.

Dose (PEA/asystole): adult: 0.5-1 mg IV may repeat every 3-5 minutes; ped: 0.02 mg/kg every 3-5 minutes (max single dose: 0.5 mg in children, 1 mg in adolescents).

Minimum dose: 0.1 mg IV.

Clearance: 50-70% hepatic metabolism; renal elimination.

Contraindications: patients sensitive to sulfites.

Adverse effects: may cause tachydysrhythmias, AV dissociation, premature ventricular contractions, dry mouth, urinary retention, CNS effects (dizziness, hallucinations, restlessness, fatigue, headache).

Comments: not effective in second degree AV block type II; avoid in new third degree block with wide QRS complexes, and hypothermic bradycardia.

Bicarbonate (Sodium Bicarbonate)

Actions: hydrogen ion neutralization.

Indications: metabolic acidosis, gastric hyperacidity, alkalinization agent for urine, treatment of hyperkalemia.

Dose (metabolic acidosis): IV dosage should be based formula:

Adult: $NaHCO_3$ (mEq) = 0.2 x weight (kg) x base deficit (mEq/L).

Ped: $NaHCO_3$ (mEq) = 0.3 x weight (kg) x base deficit (mEq/L).

Dose (cardiac arrest): adult: 1 mEq/kg/dose; pediatric: 0.5-1.0 mEq/kg/dose; neonates should receive 4.2% solution.

Contraindications: respiratory alkalosis, unknown abdominal pain, inadequate ventilation during CPR, excessive chloride loss.

Adverse effects: may cause metabolic alkalosis, hypercarbia, hyperosmolality, hypernatremia, hypokalemia, hypomagnesemia, hypocalcemia, hyperreflexia, edema, tissue necrosis (extravasation); may decrease cardiac output, systemic vascular resistance, and myocardial contractility.

Comments: use with caution in patients in CHF, renal impairment, cirrhosis, hypocalcemia, hypertension, concurrent corticosteroids; crosses placenta;

8.4% solution is approximately 1.0 mEq/mL; 4.2% solution is approximately 0.5 mEq/mL.

Bretylium Tosylate (Bretylol)

Actions: initially, release of norepinephrine into circulation, followed by prevention of synaptic release of norepinephrine; suppression of ventricular fibrillation and ventricular arrhythmias; increase in myocardial contractility (direct effect).

Indications: treatment of VF/VF and other serious ventricular arrhythmias.

Dose: 5 mg/kg IV push initially, followed by 5-10 mg/kg every 15-30 min to total of 30-35 mg/kg.

Continuous infusion: 1-2 mg/min (2 gm/250 cc D_5W).

Clearance: excreted unchanged in urine.

Contraindications: digitalis-induced ventricular tachycardia.

Adverse effects: hypotension (potentiated by quinidine or procainamide), nausea/vomiting following rapid injection; may cause PVCs and increased sensitivity to digitalis and catecholamines.

Comments: reduce dose in renal impairment.

Bumetanide (Bumex)

Actions: loop diuretic with principal effect on the ascending limb of the loop of Henle. Increased excretion of Na, K, Cl, Ca, Mg, phosphate, and H_2O.

Indications: edema, hypertension, intracranial hypertension.

Dose (adult): 0.5-1.0 mg IV over 2-3 minutes; may repeat q2-3 hours prn; maximum dose of 10 mg/day. Continuous infusion of 0.9-1 mg/hour may be more effective then bolus.

Dose (ped >6 months): 0.015-0.1 mg/kg/dose; max dose

Clearance: hepatic metabolism; 81% renal excretion (45% unchanged).

Adverse effects: electrolyte losses, dehydration, deafness (rapid infusion ototoxic), hypotension, encephalopathy, dizziness, metabolic alkalosis.

Comments: cross-allergenicity may occur in patients allergic to sulfonamides; use caution in hepatic dysfunction.

Caffeine

Indications: diuretic; relief of post-dural puncture headache; treatment of idiopathic apnea of prematurity.

Preparations: available as caffeine (anhydrous), caffeine citrate, and caffeine and sodium benzoate; 1 mg caffeine base is equivalent to 2 mg of caffeine citrate or caffeine and sodium benzoate.

Dose (postdural puncture headache): adult: 500 mg caffeine benzoate IV (500 mg caffeine benzoate in 500 mL NS given over 2 hours) or 300 mg caffeine PO, may repeat at 8 hour intervals; ped (>12 yrs): 8 mg/kg caffeine benzoate IV every 4 hrs as needed.

Dose (neonatal apnea): load with 10-20 mg/kg IV/PO as caffeine citrate; maintenance dose: 5-10 mg/kg once daily starting 24 hrs after load.

Contraindications: symptomatic cardiac dysrhythmias, peptic ulcer.

Adverse effects: tachycardia, palpitations, headache, insomnia, nervousness, restlessness, gastric irritation, nausea, vomiting, anxiety.

Comments: caffeine benzoate not recommended for neonates (associated with kernicterus in neonates); IV caffeine should be given as a slow infusion.

Calcium Chloride

Actions: essential for maintenance of cell membrane integrity, muscular excitation-contraction coupling, glandular stimulation-secretion coupling, and enzyme function; increases blood pressure.

Indications: hypocalcemia, hyperkalemia, hypomagnesemia, CPR.

Dose (hypocalcemia): adult: 500-1000 mg/dose (8-16 mg/kg IV), repeat q6 hrs as needed; ped: 10-20 mg/kg/dose, repeat q4-6 hrs as needed.

Dose (hypocalcemia secondary to citrated blood transfusion): 33 mg/100 mL of citrated blood exchanged.

Dose (cardiac arrest): adult: 250-500 mg/dose (or 2-4 mg/kg/dose), may repeat q10 minutes if necessary; ped: 20 mg/kg/dose, may repeat q10 min.

Dose (calcium antagonist toxicity; mag intoxication): adults: 500-1000 mg/dose over 5-10 minutes, may repeat or start infusion; ped: 10-20 mg/kg/dose, may repeat as necessary.

Adverse effects: may cause bradycardia or arrhythmia (especially with digitalis), hypertension, increased risk of ventricular fibrillation, can be irritating to veins, extravasation may lead to necrosis.

Comments: do not mix with sodium bicarbonate; not used routinely in ACLS; avoid rapid IV administration; central-line administration is preferred IV route; 10% $CaCl_2$= 100 mg/mL = 1.36 mEq Ca^{2+}/mL.

Calcium Gluconate

Actions: essential for maintenance of cell membrane integrity, muscular excitation-contraction coupling, glandular stimulation-secretion coupling, and enzyme function; increases blood pressure.

Indications: hypocalcemia, hyperkalemia, hypomagnesemia.

Dose (hypocalcemia): adult: 2-15 g/24 hours as a continuous infusion or divided doses; ped: 200-800 mg/kg/day as a infusion or 4 divided doses.

Dose (hypocalcemia secondary to citrated blood transfusion): 100 mg/100 mL of citrated blood exchanged.

Dose (calcium antagonist toxicity; mag intoxication): adults: 1-2 grams; ped: 100 mg/kg/dose.

Dose: adult: 15-30 mg/kg IV; pediatric: 60-100 mg/kg slow IV.

Adverse effects: may cause bradycardia or arrhythmia (especially with digitalis), hypertension, increased risk of ventricular fibrillation, and can be irritating to veins.

Comments: do not mix with sodium bicarbonate; not used routinely in ACLS; avoid rapid IV administration; central-line administration is preferred IV route; 10% Calcium gluconate = 0.45 mEq Ca^{2+}/mL (calcium less available with calcium gluconate than with calcium chloride due to binding of gluconate).

Captopril (Capoten)

Actions: competitive inhibitor of angiotensin-converting enzyme (ACE); prevents conversion of angiotensin I to angiotensin II, a potent vasoconstrictor; results in lower levels of angiotensin II which causes an increase in plasma renin activity and a reduction in aldosterone secretion (decreases preload and afterload).

Indications: hypertension, congestive heart failure, left ventricular dysfunction after myocardial infarction, diabetic nephropathy.

Dose (adult): initially 12.5-25 mg/dose PO bid-tid; increase weekly if necessary by 25 mg/dose to max dose of 450 mg/24 hours.

Dose (ped): initially 0.3-0.5 mg/kg/dose q8 hours; titrate upward if needed to max dose of 6 mg/kg/24 hours.

Dose (infant): initially 0.15-0.3 mg/kg/dose; titrate upward if needed to max dose of 6 mg/kg/24 hours (qd-qid).

Dose (neonate): 0.1-0.4 mg/kg/24 hours PO (q6-8 hours).

Clearance: hepatic metabolism; 95% renal excreted.

Adverse effects: may cause rash, proteinuria, neutropenis, cough, angioedema, hyperkalemia, hypotension, diminution of taste, bronchospasm.

Comments: use caution in collagen vascular disease; avoid in pregnant patients; exaggerated response in renal artery stenosis and with diuretics.

Chloral Hydrate (Noctec)

Actions: central nervous system depressant effects are due to its active metabolite trichloroethanol, mechanism unknown.

Indications: sedative/hypnotic.

Dose (adult): sedative: 250 mg PO 3 times daily; hypnotic: 500-1000 mg PO/PR at bedtime or 30 minutes prior to procedure (max 2 gm/24 hr).

Dose (ped): sedation/anxiety: 5-15 mg/kg/dose PO/PR q8 hr (max 500 mg); sedation (non-painful procedure): 50-75 mg/kg dose 30-60 minutes prior to procedure, may repeat 30 minutes after initial dose if needed; hypnotic: 20-40 mg/kg/dose PO up to a max of 50 mg/kg/24.

Dose (neonate): 25 mg/kg/dose PO for sedation prior to a procedure or 50 mg/kg as hypnotic.

Duration: 4-8 hours (peak effect in 30-60 minutes).

Adverse effects: may cause GI irritation, paradoxical excitement, hypotension, myocardial/respiratory depression.

Comments: contraindicated in patients with hepatic or renal disease; not analgesic; do not exceed 2 weeks of chronic use.

Chlorothiazide (Diuril)

Action: inhibits sodium reabsorption in the distal tubules causing increased excretion of sodium and water as well as potassium, hydrogen ions, magnesium, phosphate, calcium.

Indications: management of mild-moderate hypertension, or edema associated with congestive heart failure, pregnancy, or nephrotic syndrome in patients unable to take oral hydrochlorothiazide.

Dose (adult): 500 mg to 2 gm/day PO (100-500 mg/day IV at 50-100 mg/min) divided in 1-2 doses;(max dose 2 gm/day)

Dose (ped): 20 mg/kg/day PO (4 mg/kg/day IV) in 2 divided doses.

Dose (infant <6 months): 20-40 mg/kg/day PO (2-8 mg/kg/day IV) in 2 divided doses.

Clearance: renal elimination.

Adverse effects: may increase serum calcium, bilirubin, glucose, uric acid; may cause alkalosis, pancreatitis, dizziness, hypokalemia, and hypomagnesemia.

Comments: use with caution in liver and severe renal disease.

Chlorpromazine (Thorazine)

Actions: blocks postsynaptic mesolimbic dopaminergic receptors in the brain; exhibits a strong alpha-adrenergic blocking effect and depresses the release of hypothalamic and hypophyseal hormones; depress the reticular-activating system.

Indications: treatment of nausea/vomiting, psychoses, Tourette's syndrome, mania, intractable hiccups (adults), behavioral problems (children).

Dose (adult): nausea/vomiting: 10-25 mg PO, 25-50 mg IV/IM, 50 mg PR;

intractable hiccups: 25-50 mg PO/IM (25-50 mg slow IV) 3-4 times daily; psychosis: initial 25 mg IV/IM, may repeat (25-50 mg) in 1-4 hours.

Dose (ped >6 months): nausea/vomiting and psychosis: 0.5-1 mg/kg/dose IV/IM q6-8 hours (max dose for <5 yrs: 40 mg/kg/day; max for 5-12 yrs: 75 mg/kg/day), 0.5-1 mg/kg/dose PO q4-6 hrs, 1 mg/kg/dose PR q6-8 hours.

Adverse effects: drowsiness, jaundice, lowered seizure threshold, extrapyramidal/anticholinergic symptoms, hypotension, arrhythmias, agranulocytosis, neuroleptic malignant syndrome.

Comments: EKG changes include prolonged PR interval, flattened T waves, and ST depression.

Cimetidine (Tagamet)

Actions: competitive inhibition of histamine at H_2 receptors of the gastric parietal cells resulting in reduced gastric acid secretion, gastric volume, and hydrogen ion concentration.

Indications: pulmonary aspiration prophylaxis, gastroesophageal reflux, gastric acid hypersecretion, anaphylaxis prophylaxis.

Dose (adult): 300 mg qid or 400 mg BID or 400-800 mg qhs IV/IM/PO.

Dose (ped): 20-40 mg/kg/day IV/IM/PO divided q6 hours.

Dose (infant): 10-20 mg/kg/day IV/IM/PO divided q6-12 hours

Dose (neonate): 5-20 mg/kg/day IV/IM/PO divided q6-12 hours.

Clearance: hepatic metabolism, 75% renal elimination.

Adverse effects: diarrhea, rash, myalgia, confusion, neutropenia, gynecomastia, elevated liver function tests, or dizziness may occur.

Comments: inhibits cytochrome P-450 oxidase system, therefore increase levels of hepatically metabolized drugs may occur; adjust dose in renal failure.

Citrate (Bicitra)

Actions: absorbed and metabolized to sodium bicarbonate.

Indications: gastric acid neutralization, aspiration pneumonia prophylaxis.

Dose (adult): 15-30 mL PO 15-30 minutes prior to induction.

Dose (ped): 5-15 mL PO 15-30 minutes prior to induction.

Adverse effects: may have laxative effect, hypocalcemia, metabolic acidosis.

Comments: contraindicated in patients with sodium restriction or severe renal impairment. Do not use with aluminum based antacids. 1 mL of Bicitra contains 1 mEq of sodium and the equivalent of 1 mEq of bicarbonate. 5 mL of Bicitra contains 500 mg sodium citrate and 334 mg citric acid.

Clonidine (Catapres)

Actions: central alpha2-adrenergic agonist, decreases systemic vascular resistance and heart rate.

Indications: hypertension; autonomic hyperactivity secondary to drug withdrawal.

Dose (adult): initial: 0.1 mg bid PO, increase in 0.1 mg/24 hr increments at weekly intervals until desired response (max dose: 2.4 mg/24 hr)

Dose (ped): 5-10 mcg/kg/day in divided doses every 6-12 hours, increase at 5-7 day intervals to 5-25 mcg/kg/24 hr (max dose: 0.9 mg/24 hr).

Dose (epidural): ped: 0.5-2.0 mcg/kg/hr; adult: 30-40 mcg/hr.

Clearance: 50% hepatic metabolism; elimination 20% biliary, 80% renal.

Adverse effects: hypotension, dry mouth, dizziness, drowsiness, fatigue, constipation, anorexia, arrhythmias, local skin reactions with patch.

Comments: abrupt withdrawal may cause rebound hypertension or arrhythmias; signs of sympathetic overactivity may occur.

Dantrolene (Dantrium)

Actions: reduction of calcium release from sarcoplasmic reticulum, prevents or reduces increase in myoplasmic calcium ion concentration.

Indications: malignant hyperthermia, skeletal muscle spasticity, neuroleptic malignant syndrome.

Preparation: dantrolene is packaged as 20 mg of lyophilized powder to be dissolved in 60 mL of sterile water; dissolves slowly into solution.

Dose (MH): 2.5 mg/kg IV, repeat dose every 5 minutes until symptoms are controlled up to a cumulative dose of 10 mg/kg; after the acute reaction has been terminated: 1 mg/kg every 6 hours for 24-48 hours then gradually taper or switch to oral therapy.

Adverse effects: muscle weakness, GI upset, drowsiness, sedation, abnormal liver function, tissue irritant; additive effect with neuromuscular blockers.

Comments: prophylactic IV treatment is not recommended.

Desmopressin Acetate (DDAVP)

Actions: synthetic analog of human ADH used to treat neurogenic diabetes insipidus; enhances reabsorption of water in kidneys by increasing cellular permeability of the collecting ducts; promotes release of coagulation factors (procoagulant factor VII, von Willebrand factor) from vascular endothelium.

Indications: diabetes insipidus; controlling bleeding in patients with hemophilia A, von Willebrand's disease and thrombocytopenia (uremia); primary nocturnal enuresis.

Preparation: dilute IV to 0.5 mcg/mL in NS; administer slow IV.

Dose (hemophilia): 0.3 mcg/kg slow IV over 30 minutes preop.

Dose (diabetes insipidus): adult: 2-4 mcg/day in 2 divided doses IV.

Adverse effects: may cause headache, nasal congestion, abdominal cramps, hypertension.

Comments: use with caution in hypertension, coronary artery disease, patients with predisposition to thrombus; chlorpropamide, carbamazepine, and clofibrate potentiate the antidiuretic effect.

Dexamethasone (Decadron)

Actions: decreases inflammation by suppression of migration of polymorphonuclear leukocytes and reversal of increased capillary permeability; suppresses normal immune response; 25 times the glucocorticoid potency of hydrocortisone.

Indications: chronic inflammation; cerebral edema, septic shock, airway edema, antiemetic.

Dose (antiemetic): ped: 0.15 mg/kg IV.

Dose (anti-inflammatory): adult: 0.75-9 mg/day IV/IM/PO in divided doses q6-12 hours; ped: 0.08-0.3 mg/kg/day IV/IM/PO in divided doses q6-12 hours.

Dose (airway edema): adult: 4-6 mg IV/IM; ped: 0.25 mg/kg/dose IV/IM.

Dose (cerebral edema): adult: load with 10 mg IV followed by 4 mg IV/IM q6 hours; ped: load with 1-2 mg/kg/dose IV followed by 1-1.5 mg/kg/day (16 mg/day max) in divided doses q4-6 hours.

Dose (croup): ped: 0.6 mg/kg/dose IV/IM.

Dose (unresponsive shock): adult: 1-6 mg/kg IV (up to 40 mg), may repeat q2-6 hours while shock persists.

Adverse effects: delayed wound healing, seizures, osteoporosis, hyperglycemia, diarrhea, nausea, GI bleeding, cushingoid effects.

Comments: use with caution in patients with hypothyroidism, cirrhosis, hypertension, CHF, ulcerative colitis, thromboembolic disorders ; may cause adrenocortical insufficiency (Addison's crisis) with abrupt withdrawal.

Dextran 40 (Rheomacrodex)
Actions: immediate, short-lived plasma volume expansion (secondary to its highly colloidal osmotic effect); prevents RBC aggregation, decreasing blood viscosity and platelet adhesiveness.

Indications: inhibition of platelet aggregation; improvement of blood flow in low-flow states (e.g., vascular surgery); intravascular volume expander.

Dose (shock-adult): load 500 mL IV over 15-30 minutes; maximum daily doses: first 24 hrs: 20 mL/kg and then 10 mL/kg/day thereafter; therapy should not exceed beyond 5 days.

Dose (shock-ped): maximum dose: 20 mL/kg during first 24 hrs and not >10 mL/kg/day thereafter, do not treat beyond 5 days.

Dose (thrombosis/embolism prophylaxis): adult: begin during surgical procedure and give 500-1000 mL on day of surgery and continue for 2-3 days in a dose of 500 mL daily; thereafter 500 mL may be given every 2-3 days during period of risk.

Clearance: 75% excreted in the urine.

Adverse effects: may cause volume overload, anaphylaxis, bleeding tendency, interference with blood cross matching, or false elevation of blood glucose level. Can cause renal failure.

Digoxin (Lanoxin)
Actions: positive inotropic effects (inhibition of the sodium/potassium ATPase pump which acts to increase the intracellular sodium-calcium exchange to increase intracellular calcium leading to increased contractility); negative chronotropic effects (direct suppression of the AV node conduction to increase effective refractory period and decrease conduction velocity).

Indications: CHF, ventricular heart rate control in atrial fib/flutter, PSVT.

Dose: see chart.

Pharmacokinetics: onset of action is about 30 min following IV.

Clearance: renal elimination (50-75% unchanged).

Therapeutic level: 0.8-2.0 ng/mL. Maintenance dose affected by body size and renal function.

Adverse effects: symptoms of digoxin toxicity include mental depression, confusion, headaches, drowsiness, anorexia, nausea, vomiting, weakness, visual disturbances, delirium, EKG abnormalities (arrhythmias) and seizures.

Comments: toxicity potentiated by hypokalemia, hypomagnesemia, hypercalcemia; use cautiously in Wolff-Parkinson-White syndrome and with defibrillation; heart block potentiated by beta blockers or calcium channel blockers.

Dosage Recommendations for Digoxin				
	Total Digitalizing Dose[1] (mcg/kg)*		**Daily Maintenance Dose[2] (mcg/kg)***	
Age*	**PO**	**IV/IM**	**PO**	**IV/IM**
Preterm Infant	20-30	15-25	5-7.5	4-6
Full-Term Infant	25-35	20-30	6-10	5-8
1 mo - 2 yr	35-60	30-50	10-15	7.5-12
2 - 5 yr	30-40	25-35	7.5-10	6-9
5 - 10 yr	20-35	15-30	5-10	4-8
>10 yr	10-15	8-12	2.5-5	2-3
Adult	0.75-1.5 mg	0.5-1 mg	0.125-0.5 mg	0.1-0.4 mg

*=based on lean body weight and normal renal function for age; decrease dose in patients with decreased renal function; digitalizing dose often not recommended in infants and children.
1=give one-half of the total digitalizing dose (TDD) in the initial dose, then give one-quarter of the TDD in each of two subsequent doses at 8 to 12 hour intervals; obtain EKG 6 hours after each dose to assess potential toxicity.
2=divided every 12 hours in infants and children <10 years of age; given once daily to children >10 years of age and adults.

Diltiazem (Cardizem)

Actions: calcium channel antagonist that slows conduction through SA and AV nodes, dilates coronary and peripheral arterioles, and reduces myocardial contractility.

Indications: angina pectoris, temporary control of rapid ventricular rate during atrial fibrillation/flutter; conversion of paroxysmal supraventricular tachycardia to normal sinus rhythm, hypertension.

Dose (oral tablet): adult: 30-120 mg PO 3-4 times/day; dosage should be increased gradually, at 1- to 2- day intervals until optimum response is obtained; usual maintenance dose 240-360 mg/day.

Dose (sustained release capsules): adult: 60-120 mg PO twice daily.

Dose (IV): adult: initial dose: 0.25 mg/kg bolus over 2 minutes; second bolus of 0.35 mg/kg may be administered after 15 minutes if no response; may follow with continuous infusion of 5-15 mg/hour for up to 24 hours (mix 125 mg in 100 cc in D_5W and titrate to heart rate).

Dose (hypertension): ped: 1.5-2 mg/kg/day PO in 3-4 divided doses up to a maximum of 3.5 mg/kg/day.

Contraindications: atrial fib/flutter patients with WPW or short PR syndrome, sick sinus syndrome or second- or third-degree AV block except with a pacemaker, wide-QRS tachycardias of uncertain origin, poison/drug-induced tachycardia; active metabolite has 1/4 to1/2 of the coronary dilation effect.

Adverse effects: hypotension, bradycardia, heart block, impaired contractility, transient increase in LFTs, injection site reaction, flushing, and arrhythmia.

Comments: safety and efficacy have not been established for children.

Diphenhydramine (Benadryl)

Actions: H₁ receptor antagonist; has sedative, antiemetic, and anticholinergic properties.

Indications: allergenic reactions, extrapyramidal reactions, sedation, prevention of motion sickness and as an antitussive.

Dose (adult): 25-50 mg PO every 4-6 hours; 10-50 mg/dose IV every 4 hours, not to exceed 400 mg/day or 100 mg/dose.

Dose (ped >10 kg): antihistamine: 5 mg/kg/day PO/IV/IM in divided doses every 6-8 hours, not to exceed 300 mg/day or 75 mg/dose; pruritus: 0.5-1 mg/kg/dose PO/IV/IM every 4-6 hours; antiemetic: 1 mg/kg/dose PO/IV/IM every 4-6 hours; sleep-aid: 1 mg/kg/dose.

Clearance: primarily hepatic metabolism and renal excretion.

Adverse effects: may cause hypotension, tachycardia, dizziness, urinary retention, seizures.

Dobutamine (Dobutrex)

Action: stimulates $beta_1$-adrenergic receptors, causing increased contractility and heart rate, with minimal effect on $beta_2$ and alpha adrenergic receptors.

Indications: cardiogenic shock, severe CHF; low cardiac output.

Preparation (adult): 250 mg/250 D5W (1 mg/cc).

Preparation (ped): weight (kg) x 30 = mg of drug in 100 mL; 1 mL/hr = 5 mcg/kg/min.

Dose: 2-20 mcg/kg/min, titrate to desired effect (max dose 40 mcg/kg/min).

Clearance: hepatic metabolism and renal excretion.

Contraindications: avoid in patients with idiopathic hypertrophic subaortic stenosis.

Adverse effects: tachyarrhythmias (less than dopamine), hypertension, myocardial ischemia, headache, nausea, can increase ventricular rate in atrial fibrillation.

Comments: Do not mix with sodium bicarbonate; lowers CVP and wedge pressure but has little effect on pulmonary vascular resistance.

Dolasetron mesylate (Anzemet)

Actions: selective serotonin receptor antagonist, blocking serotonin both peripherally on vagal nerve terminals and centrally in the chemoreceptor trigger zone.

Indications: prevention/treatment of postoperative nausea and vomiting.

Dose (adult): PONV prophylaxis: 100 mg PO 2 hrs before surgery or 12.5 mg IV 15 minutes before surgery; PONV treatment: 12.5 mg IV 15 before the end of surgery.

Dose (ped >2 yrs): PONV prophylaxis: 1.2 mg/kg (100 mg max) PO 2 hrs before surgery or 0.35 mg/kg (max 12.5 mg) IV 15 minutes before surgery; PONV treatment: 0.35 mg/kg (max 12.5 mg) IV 15 minutes before the end of surgery.

Clearance: hepatic metabolism.

Adverse effects: may cause headaches, dizziness EKG interval changes, hypertension, transient increases in liver enzymes.

Comments: use with caution in patients who have or may develop prolongation of cardiac conduction intervals, particularly Qtc intervals.

Dopamine (Intropin)

Actions: dopaminergic, alpha and beta adrenergic agonist.

Indications: shock, poor perfusion, decreased splanchnic perfusion, low cardiac output, oliguria.

Preparation (adult): 400 mg/250 cc D5W = 1600 mcg/cc.

Preparation (ped): weight (kg) x 30 = mg of drug in 100 mL; 1 mL/hr = 5 mcg/kg/min.

Dose: range 2-20 mcg/kg/min (max dose 50 mcg/kg/min) titrate to effect.

2-5 mcg/kg/min: stimulates dopamine receptors, redistribute blood flow to kidneys, inhibits aldosterone.

5-10 mcg/kg/min: beta, > alpha receptor stimulation, increases heart rate, cardiac contractility, cardiac output, and to a lesser extent renal blood flow.

10-15 mcg/kg/min: alpha and beta$_1$ stimulation.

>15 mcg/kg/min: alpha effects predominate, decreased renal perfusion.

Clearance: MAO/COMT metabolism.

Contraindications: pheochromocytoma or ventricular fibrillation.

Adverse effects: tachycardia, arrhythmias, nausea/vomiting; superficial tissue necrosis and sloughing may occur with extravasation (treat with phentolamine).

Comments: do not mix with sodium bicarbonate.; effects are prolonged and intensified by MAO inhibitors.

Dopexamine (Dopacard)

Actions: synthetic analogue of dopamine, beta-2 and dopamine agonist (little beta-1 or alpha activity); increases cardiac output, heart rate, and renal blood flow; decreases SVR with little change in blood pressure.

Indications: shock, poor perfusion, decreased splanchnic perfusion, low cardiac output, oliguria.

Dose: 0.5-6 mcg/kg/min titrated to desired effect.

Contraindications: patients taking MAO inhibitors, pheochromocytoma.

Adverse effects: hypotension, tachycardia, nausea/vomiting, anginal pain, tremor, headache

Comments: severe hypertension may occur in patients taking MAO inhibitors; do mix with sodium bicarbonate.

Doxapram (Dopram)

Actions: stimulates respiration through action on respiratory center in medulla or indirectly on peripheral carotid chemoreceptors.

Indications: respiratory and CNS stimulant for respiratory depression secondary to anesthesia, drug-induced CNS depression; acute hypercapnia secondary to COPD.

Dose (adult): initial 0.5-1.0 mg/kg may repeat at 5 minute intervals (max 2 mg/kg); infusion: 5 mg/minute until adequate response or adverse effects seen, decrease to 1-3 mg/minute (usual total dose: 0.5-4 mg/kg).

Dose (neonatal apnea/apnea of prematurity): initial: 1-1.5 mg/kg/hr; maintenance: 0.5-2.5 mg/kg/hr, titrated to the lowest rate at which apnea is controlled.

Clearance: hepatic metabolism.

Adverse effects: angina, ectopic beats, hypotension, tachycardia, headache, nausea/vomiting, dyspnea.

Comments: not for use in newborns since doxapram contains a significant amount of benzyl alcohol.

Doxazosin (Cardura)

Actions: long-acting selective inhibitor of postjunctional alpha$_1$-adrenoreceptors; does not alter renal blood flow.

Indications: hypertension.

Dose (adult): start at 1 mg PO daily (may increase to 16 mg/d).

Clearance: hepatic metabolism.
Adverse effects: significant first-dose effect with marked postural hypotension and dizziness; max reduction in blood pressure 2-6 hrs after dose.

Doxepin (Adapin)

Actions: increases the synaptic concentration of serotonin and/or norepinephrine in the CNS by inhibition of their reuptake by the presynaptic neuronal membrane; analgesic action: modulation of neurotransmitter function or may potentially affect endogenous opioid substances.
Indications: treatment of depression, anxiety disorders; analgesic for certain chronic and neuropathic pain.
Dose (adult): initial 30-150 mg/day PO at bedtime or in 2-3 divided doses (may increase up to 300 mg/day).
Dose (adolescent): initial 25-50 mg PO in single or divided doses (may increase to 100 mg/day).
Clearance: hepatic metabolism and renal elimination.
Contraindications: narrow-angle glaucoma.
Adverse effects: dizziness, headache, sedation, constipation, nausea, weakness, somnolence, unpleasant taste.
Comments: avoid use during lactation, use caution in pregnancy, do not discontinue abruptly.

Droperidol (Inapsine)

Actions: dopamine (D_2) receptor antagonist, antiemetic effect (blocks dopamine stimulation of the chemotrigger zone), sedation (alters the action of dopamine in the CNS, at subcortical levels).
Indications: nausea/vomiting, agitation, sedation.
Dose (adult): PONV:0.625-2.5 mg IV/IM; sedation: 2.5-10 mg IV prn; premed: 2.5-10 mg IM,
Dose (ped): PONV prophylaxis: 0.05-0.06 mg/kg IV; PONV treatment: 0.01-0.03 mg/kg/dose q8 hrs up to 24 hrs; premed: 0.1-0.15 mg/kg IM.
Adverse effects: evokes extrapyramidal reactions in 1%; possible dysphoric reactions; cerebral vasoconstrictor; can decrease blood pressure by alpha blockade and dopaminergic antagonism; laryngospasm; bronchospasm; may lower seizure threshold; associated with QT interval prolongation.
Comments: used in neuroleptanalgesia, potentiates other CNS depressants.

Enalapril/Enalaprilat (Vasotec)

Actions: competitive inhibitor or angiotensin-converting enzyme (ACE); results in lower levels of angiotensin II which causes an increase in plasma renin activity and a reduction in aldosterone secretion.
Indications: hypertension, congestive heart failure, left ventricular dysfunction after myocardial infarction.
Preparation: enalapril is PO; enalaprilat is IV.
Dose (hypertension): adult: 2.5-5 mg/day PO (enalapril) then increase as required (usual dose: 10-40 mg/day in 1-2 divided doses); 0.625-5 mg/dose IV (enalaprilat) over 5 minutes every 6 hours
Dose (heart failure): adult: initiate with 2.5 mg PO (enalapril) 1-2 times daily (usual dose: 5-20 mg/day).
Dose (ped): enalapril (PO): 0.1 mg/kg/day increasing as needed over 2 weeks to 0.5 mg/kg./day; enalaprilat (IV): 5-10 mcg/kg/dose administered q8-24 hrs.
Clearance: hepatic metabolism of enalapril to active metabolite (enalaprilat); renal and fecal elimination.

Contraindications: idiopathic or hereditary angioedema, bilateral renal artery stenosis, primary hyperaldosteronism, pregnancy.

Adverse effects: causes increased serum potassium, increased renal blood flow volume-responsive hypotension; can cause angioedema, blood dyscrasia, cough, lithium toxicity, worsening of renal impairment; subsequent doses are additive.

Comments: dosing needs to be adjusted in renal and hepatic impairment.

Enoxaparin (Lovenox)

Actions: inhibits thrombosis by inactivating both factor Xa and factor IIa without significantly affecting bleeding time, platelet function, PT, or APTT.

Indications: prophylaxis and treatment of thromboembolic disorders, prevention of ischemic complications of unstable angina and non-Q -wave myocardial infarction (when administered with aspirin).

Dose (DVT prophylaxis-adult)

Knee replacement surgery: 30 mg SC q12 hrs, give first dose within 12-24 hours after surgery, average duration of therapy: 7-10 days.

Hip replacement surgery: 30 mg SC q12 hrs with first dose 12-24 hrs after surgery or 40 mg SC once daily with first dose 9-15 hrs after surgery; average duration of therapy: 7-10 days.

Abdominal surgery in high-risk patients: 40 mg SC once daily with first dose 2 hrs prior to surgery; average duration of therapy: 7-10 days.

Dose (DVT treatment-adult): 1 mg/kg SC q12 hrs or 1.5 mg/kg SC qd (start warfarin within 72 hrs and continue enoxaparin until INR is between 2-3).

Dose (acute coronary syndromes-adult): 1 mg/kg SC twice daily in conjunction with aspirin therapy (100-325 mg PO).

Dose (ped <2 months): DVT prophylaxis: 0.75 mg/kg/dose SC q12 hrs; DVT treatment: 1.5 mg/kg/dose SC q12 hrs.

Dose (ped >2 months): DVT prophylaxis: 0.5 mg/kg/dose SC q12 hrs; DVT treatment: 1 mg/kg/dose SC q12 hrs.

Clearance: hepatic metabolism with renal excretion.

Adverse effects: may cause fever, confusion, thrombocytopenia, hypochromic anemia, pain/erythema at injection site.

Comments: more predictable dose-response characteristics than unfractionated heparin; the risk of epidural hematoma formation is increased in patients who have indwelling epidural catheters or are also receiving other drugs that may adversely affect hemostasis; safety and efficacy in pediatric patients not established.

Ephedrine

Actions: alpha- and beta-adrenergic stimulation, norepinephrine release at sympathetic nerve endings (indirect).

Indications: hypotension, nasal congestion, bronchospasm.

Dose (adult): 5-50 mg/dose IV or 25-50 mg/dose IM/SC.

Dose (ped): 0.2-0.3 mg/kg/dose.

Clearance: mostly renal elimination.

Adverse effects: may cause hypertension, dysrhythmias, myocardial ischemia, CNS stimulation, decrease in uterine activity.

Comments: minimal effect on uterine blood flow; avoid in patients taking monoamine oxidase inhibitors; tachyphylaxis with repeated dosing.

Epinephrine (Adrenalin)

Actions: direct alpha and beta adrenergic receptor stimulation, resulting in bronchial smooth muscle relaxation and cardiac stimulation (positive inotrope, chronotrope), dilation of skeletal muscle vasculature (low dose), decreased renal blood flow, dilates the pupil.

Indications: heart failure, hypotension, cardiac arrest, bronchospasm, anaphylaxis, severe bradycardia; added to local anesthetics to decrease systemic absorption, increase duration of action, and decrease toxicity.

Preparation (adult).: 2 mg/250 cc (15 cc/hr = 2 mcg/min).

Preparation (ped): weight (kg) x 0.6 = mg of drug in 100 mL; 1 mL/hr = 0.1 mcg/kg/min.

Dose (cardiac arrest):

    Adult: 1 mg IV every 3-5 minutes during resuscitation; alternating regimens include: intermediate: 2-5 mg IV q3-5 minutes; escalating: 1 mg, 3 mg, 5 mg, IV at 3 minute intervals; high: 0.1 mg/kg IV q3-5 minutes; intratracheal: 2-2.5 times the IV dose.

    Ped: first dose: 0.01 mg/kg IV/IO, subsequent doses: 0.1-0.2 mg/kg) IV/IO q3-5 minutes; intratracheal: 0.1 mg/kg.

    Neonates: 0.01-0.03 mg/kg IV/IO q3-5 minutes.

Dose (bradycardia):

    Adult: 2-10 mcg/min infusion; bolus 10-20 mcg.

    Ped: 0.01 mg/kg IV/IO or 0.1 mg/kg ET

Dose (refractory hypotension):

    Adult: 0.1-1 mcg/kg/min IV (max 1.5 mcg/kg/min).

    Ped: 0.1-1 mcg/kg/min IV (max 1.5 mcg/kg/min).

Dose (bronchospasm):

    Adult: 0.1-0.5 mg IM/SC (aqueous 1:1000) q10-15 minutes to 4 hrs; 0.1-0.3 ml/dose SC (susphrine suspension 1:200); 0.1-0.25 mg IV.

    Ped: 0.01 mcg/kg SC (aqueous 1:1000) q15 minutes to 4 hrs; 0.005 ml/kg/dose SC (susphrine suspension 1:200).

Dose (hypersensitivity reaction):

    Adult: 0.2-0.5 mg IM/SC q20 min to 4 hrs or 0.1-0.25 mg IV.

    Ped: 0.01 mg/kg SC q15 minutes for 2 doses then q4 hrs as needed.

Clearance: MAO/COMT metabolism.

Adverse effects: may cause hypertension, dysrhythmias, headache, nervousness, nausea/vomiting, myocardial ischemia; dysrhythmias potentiated by halothane; metabolic effects: increases adipose tissue lipolysis, liver glycogenolysis, inhibits release of insulin.

Comments: crosses placenta; necrosis may occur at site of repeated local injection; ETT doses should be diluted with NS to a volume of 3-5 ml.

Epinephrine, Racemic (Vaponefrin)

    Actions: mucosal vasoconstriction (see epinephrine).

    Indications: airway edema, bronchospasm.

    Dose (adult): inhaled via nebulizer: 0.5 mL of 2.25% solution in 2.5-3.5 mL of NS q1-4 hr prn.

    Dose (ped >2 yrs): inhaled via nebulizer: 0.25-0.5 mL of 2.25% solution in 2.5-3.5 mL NS.

    Dose (ped <2 yrs): inhaled via nebulizer:0.25 mL of 2.25% solution in 2.5-3.5 mL NS.

    Clearance: MAO/COMT metabolism.

    Adverse effects: see epinephrine.

    Comments: rebound airway edema may occur.

Ergonovine (Ergotrate)

Actions: constriction of uterine and vascular smooth muscle.

Indications: postpartum uterine atony and bleeding, uterine involution.

Dose: 0.2 mg IV in 5 mL NS given over 1 minute (IV route is used only in emergencies). 0.2 mg IM q2-4 hours for less than 5 doses; then PO: O.2-0.4 mg q6-12 hours for 2 days or prn.

Clearance: hepatic metabolism and renal elimination.

Adverse effects: may cause hypertension from system vasoconstriction, arrhythmias, coronary spasm, cerebrovascular accidents, uterine tetany, or gastrointestinal upset; overdose may cause convulsions or stroke.

Esmolol (Brevibloc)

Actions: selective $beta_1$-adrenergic blockade; short half-life (2-9 minutes).

Indications: SVT, myocardial ischemia, hypertension.

Standard adult conc.: 10 mg/mL (infusion mix 2.5 gm ampul in 250 cc).

Dose (bolus): 5-100 mg IV prn.

Dose (infusion): adult: load 500 mcg/kg IV bolus over 1 minute followed by maintenance starting at 50 mcg/kg/min titrated to response (max 500 mcg/kg/min); ped: load 100-500 mcg/kg IV over 1 minute followed by maintenance infusion stating at 50 mcg/kg/min (max 500 mcg/kg/min)

Clearance: degraded by RBC esterases; renal elimination.

Adverse effects: bradycardia, AV conduction delay, hypotension, congestive heart failure, myocardial depression, $beta_2$ activity at high doses.

Comments: may increase digoxin level by 10%-20%; morphine may increase esmolol levels.

Ethacrynic Acid (Edecrin)

Actions: inhibits reabsorption of sodium and chloride in the ascending loop of Henle and distal renal tubule, interfering with the chloride-binding cotransport system, cause increased excretion of water, sodium, chloride, magnesium and calcium.

Indications: CHF, hepatic and renal disease, ascites, edema.

Dose (adult): 50-100 mg/day PO in 1-2 divided doses, may increase to max of 400 mg/day; 0.5-1 mg/kg/dose (max 100 mg/day).

Dose (ped): 1 mg/kg/dose once daily, may increase to max of 3 mg/kg/day; 1 mg/kg/dose IV (max 3 mg/kg/day).

Clearance: hepatic metabolized to active cysteine conjugate (35%-40%); 30%-60% excreted unchanged in bile and urine.

Adverse effects: may potentiate the activity of antihypertensives, neuromuscular blocking agents, digoxin, and increase insulin requirements in diabetic patients; risk of ototoxicity.

Etomidate (Amidate)

Actions: augments the inhibitory tone of GABA in the CNS (produces unconsciousness in approximately 30 seconds).

Indications: induction and maintenance of general anesthesia.

Dose (induction of anesthesia): 0.2-0.3 mg/kg IV.

Dose (maintenance): 10 mcg/kg/min IV with N 20 and opiate.

Dose (sedation): 5-8 mcg/kg/min; used only for short periods of time due to inhibition of corticosteroid synthesis.

Clearance: hepatic.

Adverse effects: direct cerebral vasoconstrictor, minimal cardiovascular effects, pain on injection, myoclonus may occur in about 1/3 of patients during induction, adrenocortical suppression, nausea/vomiting.

Famotidine (Pepcid)

Actions: competitive inhibition of histamine at H_2 receptors of the gastric parietal cells, which inhibits gastric acid secretion.

Indications: pulmonary aspiration prophylaxis, peptic ulcer disease.

Dose (adult): duodenal ulcer: 40 mg/day PO at bedtime for 4-8 wks; hypersecretory conditions: initial 20 mg PO q6 hrs, may increase to 160 mg PO q6 hrs; GERD: 20 mg PO twice daily for 6 wks; Esophagitis: 20-40 mg twice daily for up to 12 wks; IV dosing: 20 mg q12 hrs.

Dose (ped): PUD: 0.5 mg/kg/day at bedtime or divided doses (max 40mg/day); IV dosing: 0.6-0.8 mg/kg/day in 2-3 doses (max 40 mg/day).

Clearance: 30%-35% hepatic metabolism, 65%-70% renal elimination.

Adverse effects: may cause confusion, dizziness, headache, diarrhea.

Comments: rapid IV administration may increase risk of cardiac arrhythmias and hypotension; administer slow IV.

Flumazenil (Mazicon)

Actions: competitive inhibition of GABA; antagonizes the effect of benzodiazepines on the GABA/benzodiazepine receptor complex.

Indications: reversal of benzodiazepine sedation or overdose.

Dose (adult): benzodiazepine overdose: first dose 0.2 mg IV over 15 seconds, second dose 0.3 mg IV over 30 seconds, if no adequate response give third dose 0.5 mg IV over 30 seconds, may repeat at 1 minute intervals up to a total dose of 3 mg; reversal of conscious sedation: 0.2 mg IV over 15 seconds, may repeat at 1 minute intervals to a total dose of 1 mg.

Dose (ped): 0.01 mg/kg IV (max 0.2 mg/kg), then 0.005-0.01 mg/kg/dose given at 1 minute intervals up to a max total dose of 1 mg.

Clearance: 100% hepatic metabolism; 90%-95% renal elimination of metabolite.

Adverse effects: seizures, acute withdrawal, nausea, dizziness, agitation, arrhythmias, hypertension.

Drug interactions: do not use in suspected tricyclic drug overdose, seizure-prone patients, unknown drug overdoses.

Comments: does not reverse narcotics or nonbenzodiazepine induced CNS depression.

Furosemide (Lasix)

Actions: increase in excretion of sodium, chloride, phosphate, calcium, potassium and water by inhibiting reabsorption in the loop of Henle.; decrease CSF production.

Indications: edema, hypertension, intracranial hypertension, renal failure, hypercalcemia, congestive heart failure.

Dose (adult): 2-100 mg IV q6-12 hrs (max 1000 mg/day); continuous infusion: initial 0.1 mg/kg followed by infusion dose of 0.1 mg/kg/hr doubled every 2 hours to a max of 0.4 mg/kg/hr.

Dose (ped): 0.5-2 mg/kg/dose q6-12 hrs (max dose: 6 mg/kg/dose).

Dose (neonate): 0.5-1 mg/kg/dose IV/PO q8-12 hrs (max PO dose: 6 mg/kg/dose; max IV dose: 2 mg/kg/dose).

Clearance: hepatic metabolism; renal elimination.

Adverse effects: may cause electrolyte imbalance, dehydration, transient hypotension, deafness, hyperglycemia, or hyperuricemia.

Comments: Sulfa-allergic patients may exhibit hypersensitivity.

Gabapentin (Neurontin)

Actions: unknown.

Indications: postherpetic neuralgia, treatment of partial and secondary generalized seizures, treatment of neuropathic pain.

Preparation: tablets.

Dose (antiseizure):

Adult: initial 300 mg on day 1, 300 mg twice daily on day 2, and 300 mg 3 times/day on day 3; doses can be increased over a week to an initial total dose of 1200 mg/day divided 3 times/day.

Adult (effective anticonvulsant): 900-1800 mg/day in 3 divided doses; the dose can be increased up to 1.8-2.4 gms/day depending on the therapeutic response; maximum dose: 3.6 gms/day.

Ped (3-12 yrs): initial 10 mg/kg/dose one time on day 1, 20 mg/kg/day twice daily on day 2, and 30 mg/kg/day divided 3 times/day on day 3; maintenance: 30-45 mg/kg/day divided 3 times/day (some patients may require up to 90 mg/day).

Dose (postherpetic neuralgia):

Adult: initial: 300 mg on day 1, 600 mg/day divided 2 times/day on day 2, then 900 mg/day divided 3 times/day; dose can be titrated up as needed for pain relief to a daily dose of 1800 mg/day divided 3 times/day.

Clearance: renal excretion.

Adverse effects: somnolence, dizziness, ataxia, fatigue, nystagmus.

Comments: adjust dose in renal impairment; do not withdrawal abruptly.

Glucagon

Actions: stimulates adenylate cyclase to produce increased cyclic AMP which promotes hepatic glycogenolysis and gluconeogenesis, increasing blood glucose; produces relaxation of smooth muscle of stomach, duodenum, small intestine, and colon; positive inotropic and chronotropic effect.

Indications: hypoglycemia, duodenal or choledochal relaxation, refractory beta-adrenergic blocker toxicity.

Dose (hypoglycemia): neonates: 0.025-0.3 mg/kg/dose (maximum: 1 mg/dose); children: 0.025-0.1 mg/kg/dose (not to exceed 1 mg/dose, repeated in 20 minutes as needed); adults: 0.5-1.0 mg, may repeat in 20 minutes.

Dose (GI relaxation): 0.25-2 mg IV 10 minutes prior to procedure.

Clearance: renal and hepatic proteolysis.

Adverse effects: may cause anaphylaxis, nausea, vomiting, hyperglycemia, positive inotropic and chronotropic effects; high doses potentiate oral anticoagulants.

Comments: do not mix in normal saline (use sterile water); do not use in presence of insulinoma or pheochromocytoma.

Glycopyrrolate (Robinul)

Actions: blocks the action of acetylcholine at parasympathetic sites in smooth muscle, secretory glands, and the CNS.

Indications: decreased gastrointestinal motility, antisialagogue, bradycardia, control of upper airway secretions, adjunct treatment of peptic ulcer disease, reversal of neuromuscular blockade.

Dose (antisialagogue):

Adult: 2.5-10 mcg/kg/dose IV/IM every 3-4 hrs.

Ped (children): 4-10 mcg/kg/dose IV/IV every 3-4 hrs, maximum: 0.2 mg/dose or 0.8 mg/24 hours; 40-100 mcg/kg/dose PO 3-4 times/day.

Ped (neonate/infant): 4-10 mcg/kg/dose IV/IM every 4-8 hrs; 40-100 mcg/kg/dose PO every 8-12 hrs.

Dose (preoperative):

Adult: 4.4 mcg/kg IM 30-60 minutes before procedure.

Ped (<2 yrs): 4.4-8.8 mcg/kg/dose IM 30-60 minutes before procedure.

Ped (>2 yrs): 4.4 mcg/kg IM 30-60 minutes before procedure.

Dose (intraoperative):

Adult: 0.1 mg IV repeated as needed at 2-3 minute intervals.

Ped: 4.4 mcg/kg IV (max: 0.1 mg), repeat at 2-3 minute intervals as needed.

Dose (reverse neuromuscular blockade): 0.2 mg IV for each 1 mg of neostigmine or 5 mg of pyridostigmine administered or 5-10 mcg/kg/dose (maximum dose: 200 mcg/dose).

Dose (peptic ulcer): adult: 0.1-0.2 mg IV/IM TID-QID or 1-2 mg PO BID-TID.

Clearance: renal elimination.

Adverse effects: tachycardia, nausea, constipation, confusion, bronchospasm, blurred vision, and dry mouth.

Comments: better antisialagogue with less chronotropy than atropine; does not cross blood-brain barrier or placenta; use with caution in hepatic and renal disease, ulcerative colitis, asthma, glaucoma, ileus, or urinary retention.

Granisetron (Kytril)

Actions: selective 5-HT3-receptor antagonist, blocking serotonin, both peripherally on vagal nerve terminals and centrally in the chemoreceptor trigger zone.

Indications: prevention and treatment of postoperative nausea and vomiting, prophylaxis and treatment of chemotherapy-related nausea and vomiting.

Dose (chemo-induced nausea/vomiting): adult: 10-20 mcg/kg/dose IV 30 minutes prior to chemotherapy; ped (>2 yrs): 10 mcg/kg/dose IV 30 minutes prior to chemotherapy; only give on days of chemotherapy; max dose: 40 mcg/kg/day divided every 12 hrs.

Dose (postoperative nausea/vomiting): adult: 1 mg IV given over 30 sec.

Clearance: hepatic metabolism.

Adverse effects: constipation, anemia, headache, fever, abdominal pain, elevated liver enzymes.

Comments: safety/effectiveness in pediatric patients for the prevention and treatment of postoperative nausea/vomiting has not been established.

Haloperidol (Haldol)

Actions: blocks postsynaptic mesolimbic dopaminergic D1 and D2 receptors in the brain; depresses the reticular activating system.

Indications: treatment of psychosis, Tourette's disorder, sedation for severely agitated or delirious patients, postoperative antiemetic.

Dose (adult): 0.5-5 mg PO 2-3 times/day (usual max 30 mg/day); 2-5 mg (as lactate) IM every 4-8 hrs as needed.

Dose (ped 3-12 yrs; 15-40 kg):

Initial: 0.05 mg/kg/day PO or 0.25-0.5 mg/day PO given in 2-3 divided doses; increase by 0.25-0.5 mg every 5-7 days (max: 0.15 mg/kg/day).

Maintenance: agitation or hyperkinesia: 0.01-0.03 mg/kg/day PO once daily; nonpsychotic disorders: 0.05-0.075 mg/kg/day PO in 2-3 divided doses; psychotic disorders: 0.05-0.15 mg/kg/day PO in 2-3 divided doses. IM dosing (as lactate): 0.025-0.07 mg/kg/day in 3 divided doses to a max of 0.15 mg/kg/day.

Antiemetic: 0.01 mg/kg/dose IV every 8-12 hrs.

Dose (ICU sedation): mild agitation: 0.5-2 mg IV/IM; moderate agitation: 2-5 mg IV/IM; severe agitation: 10-20 mg IV/IM; continuous infusion: 1-40 mg/hr (100 mg/100 mL D5W).

Clearance: hepatic metabolism; renal/biliary elimination.

Adverse effects: may cause extrapyramidal reactions or mild alpha-adrenergic antagonism; can prolong QT interval and produce ventricular arrhythmias, notably torsade de pointes; can lower seizure threshold; may precipitate neuroleptic syndrome.

Comments: use caution in patients with cardiac disease.

Heparin

Actions: potentiates the action of antithrombin III; blocks conversion of prothrombin and activation of other coagulation factors (factors IX, X, XI, XII, and plasmin); prevents conversion of fibrinogen to fibrin; stimulates release of lipoprotein lipase; affects platelet aggregation.

Indications: prophylaxis and treatment of thromboembolic disorders, anticoagulation for cardiopulmonary bypass, DIC.

Preparation: 1 mg = 100 units.

Dose (adult):

Thromboembolic prophylaxis: 5000 units SC every 8-12 hrs.

Thromboembolic treatment:

Intermittent IV: 10,000 units to start, then 5000-10,000 units (50-70 units/kg) every 4-6 hrs.

IV infusion: 5000 units (or 35-100 units/kg) to start, then approximately 1000 units/hr (or 15-25 units/kg/hr) with dose adjusted according to PTT or APTT results (usual dose range: 10-30 units/kg/hr).

Dose (ped):

Infant (<1 yr): initial loading dose: 50-75 units/kg IV over 10 minutes; then initial maintenance dose: 28 units/kg/hr (range: 15-35 units/kg); adjust dose by 2-4 units/kg/hr every 4-8 hrs as required.

Children (>1 yr):

Intermittent IV: load 50-100 units/kg, then 50-100 units/kg every 4 hrs.

IV infusion: initial loading dose: 75 units/kg over 10 minutes, then 20 units/kg/hr (range: 15-25 units/kg/hr), adjust dose by 2-5 units/kg/hr every 4-8 hrs as required according to PTT results.

Dose (line flushing): 10 units/mL is used for infants <10 kg while 100 units/mL is used for older infants, children, and adults.

Dose (arterial lines): adult: 1 unit/mL; neonates: 0.5-2 units/ml.

Dose (CPB): load with 300 units/kg IV; maintenance: 100 units/kg/hr IV, titrate to coagulation tests (ACT).

Clearance: primarily by reticuloendothelial uptake, hepatic biotransformation.

Reversal: reverse with protamine sulfate.

Adverse effects: hemorrhage, allergic reactions, thrombocytopenia, allergic reaction, diurese, altered protein binding, decreased MAP, decreased antithrombin III concentration, altered cell morphology,

Comments: does not cross placenta.

Hydralazine (Apresoline)

Actions: direct vasodilation (relaxation) of arterioles (with little effect on veins); associated with reflex tachycardia, increased cardiac output, and plasma volume.

Indications: hypertension, hypertension secondary to pregnancy induced hypertension, primary pulmonary hypertension.

Dose (adult): oral: 10-100 mg 3-4 times/day (max dose: 300 mg/day); IV/IM: initial: 5-20 mg/dose every 4-6 hrs, may increase to 40 mg/dose.

Dose (PIH): 5 mg/dose then 5-10 mg every 20-30 minutes as needed.

Dose (ped): 0.75-3 mg/kg/day divided every 6-12 hrs (max dose 5 mg/kg/day in infants and 7.5 mg/kg/day in children divided every 6-12 hrs or 200 mg/day): IV/IM: 0.1-0.2 mg/kg/dose every 4-6 hrs, may increase to 40 mg/kg/dose.

Clearance: extensive hepatic metabolism; renal elimination.

Adverse effects: hypotension, reflex tachycardia, systemic lupus erythematosus syndrome, Coombs' test positive hemolytic anemia; increases coronary, splanchnic, cerebral, and renal blood flows.

Hydrocortisone (Solu-Cortef)

Actions: anti-inflammatory, antiallergic, mineralocorticoid effect; stimulation of gluconeogenesis; inhibition of peripheral protein synthesis; membrane stabilizing effect.

Indications: adrenocortical insufficiency, inflammation and allergy, cerebral edema from CNS tumors, asthma.

Dose (acute adrenal insufficiency): adult: 100 mg bolus IV, then 300 mg/day IV 3 divided doses or as a continuous infusion; older children: 1-2 mg/kg/dose IV, then 150-250 mg/day IV in 3-4 divided doses; infants/young children: 1-2 mg/kg/dose IV, then 25-150 mg/day IV in 3-4 divided doses.

Dose (anti-inflammatory/immunosuppressive): adult: 15-240 mg (sodium phosphate) IV/IM every 12 hrs or 100-500 mg (succinate) IV/IM every 2-10 hrs.; ped: 1-5 mg/kg/day IV divided every 6-8 hrs.

Dose (congenital adrenal hyperplasia): 30-36 mg/m^2/day PO with 1/3 of dose every morning and 2/3 every evening; maintenance: 15-25 mg/m^2/day PO in 3 divided doses.

Dose (physiologic replacement): ped: 0.5-0.75 mg/kg/day PO divided every 8 hrs or 0.25-0.35 mg/kg/day IM once daily.

Dose (shock): adult: 500 mg to 2 gm IV/IM every 2-6 hrs; ped: 50 mg/kg IV/IM, may repeat in 4 hrs.

Dose (stress coverage for surgery): 1.5-4 mg/kg/day IV as a continuous infusion beginning at the time of surgery and continuing for 24 hrs or 40-100 mg/m^2/day divided every 6-8 hrs.

Dose (status asthmaticus): 1-2 mg/day/dose IV every 6 hrs for 24 hrs, then maintenance of 0.5-1 mg/kg IV every 6 hrs.

Clearance: hepatic metabolism; renal elimination.

Adverse effects: may cause adrenocortical insufficiency (Addison's crisis) with abrupt withdrawal, delayed wound healing, CNS disturbances, osteoporosis, or electrolyte disturbances.

Hydroxyzine (Vistaril)

Actions: antagonizes action of histamine on H$_1$ receptors; CNS depression; antiemetic.

Indications: anxiety, nausea and vomiting, allergies, sedation.

Dose (ped): 2-4 mg/kg/day PO divided every 6-8 hrs; 0.5-1 mg/kg/dose IM every 4-6 hrs as needed.

Dose (adult): antiemetic: 25-100 mg/dose IM every 4-6 hrs as needed; anxiety: 25-100 mg PO 4 times/day (max: 600 mg/day); preop sedation: 50-100 mg PO or 25-100 mg IM; pruritus: 25 mg PO 3-4 times/day.

Clearance: hepatic (P-450) metabolism; renal elimination.

Adverse effects: may cause dry mouth, drowsiness, tremor, convulsions, blurred vision, hypotension; may cause pain at injection site.

Comments: IV administration not recommended.

Ibuprofen (Motrin; Advil)
Actions: inhibits prostaglandin synthesis by decreasing the activity of the enzyme, cyclo-oxygenase, which results in decreased formation of prostaglandin precursors.
Indications: mild to moderate pain, fever, dysmenorrhea, inflammatory disease and rheumatoid disorders.
Dose (ped):
Antipyretic (6 months to12 yrs): temp <102.5°F (39°C): 5 mg/kg/dose PO; temp >102.5°F PO: 10 mg/kg/dose every 6-8 hrs; max 40 mg/kg/day.
Juvenile rheumatoid arthritis: 30-50 mg/kg/day divided every 6-8 hrs.
Analgesic: 5-10 mg/kg/dose PO every 6-8 hrs.
Dose (adult):
Inflammatory disease: 400-800 mg/dose 3-4 times/day; max 3.2 gm/day
Analgesia/pain/fever/dysmenorrhea: 200-400 mg/dose every 4-6 hrs.
Clearance: hepatic metabolism.
Contraindications: active GI bleeding and ulcer disease.
Adverse effects: GI distress, rashes, ocular problems, granulocytopenia, anemia, platelet aggregation inhibition.
Comments: use caution with aspirin hypersensitivity, hepatic/renal insufficiency, dehydration, and patients receiving anticoagulants; may increase serum levels of digoxin, methotrexate, lithium; may decrease the effects of antihypertensives, furosemide, thiazide diuretics.

Indigo Carmine (Indigotindisulfonate sodium)
Actions: rapid glomerular filtration causing blue urine.
Indications: evaluation of urine output; localizing of ureteral orifices.
Dose: 40 mg IV slowly (5 mL of 0.8% solution).
Clearance: renal elimination.
Adverse effects: hypertension from alpha adrenergic stim, lasts 15-30 min.

Indocyanine Green (Cardio-Green)
Actions: binds to plasma proteins, with distribution within plasma volume.
Indications: cardiac output measurement by indicator dye dilution.
Dose: 5 mg IV (diluted in 1 mL of NS) rapidly injected into central circulation.
Clearance: hepatic elimination.
Adverse effects: may cause allergic reactions or transient increases in bilirubin levels.
Comments: use caution in patients with iodine allergy.

Indomethacin (Indocin)
Actions: inhibits prostaglandin synthesis by decreasing the activity of cyclo-oxygenase, resulting in decreased prostaglandin precursor formation.
Indications: management of inflammatory diseases; closure of ductus arteriosus; intraventricular hemorrhage prophylaxis.
Dose (inflammation): adult: 25-50 mg PO every 6-12 hrs or 1-3 mg/kg/24 hr in divided doses every 6-8 hrs, max dose: 200 mg/24 hr; ped: 1-2 mg/kg/24 hr PO in 2-4 divided doses, max: 4 mg/kg/24 hrs.
Dose (ductus arteriosus closure): initial dose 0.2 mg/kg/dose IV over 20-30 minutes followed with 0.1-0.25 mg/kg for 2 doses at 12-24 hrs intervals.
Dose (intraventricular hemorrhage prophylaxis): 0.1 mg/kg/dose IV every

24 hrs for 3 doses.

Clearance: hepatic metabolism.

Contraindications: acting bleeding, coagulation defects, necrotizing enterocolitis, renal insufficiency.

Adverse effects: may cause decreased urine output, platelet dysfunction, decreased GI blood flow, reduce the antihypertensive effects of beta-blockers (hydralazine and ACE inhibitors), fetal hepatitis reported in JRA.

Comments: reduction in cerebral blood flow associated with rapid IV infusion.

Insulin

Indications: hyperglycemia, diabetes mellitus, hyperkalemia.

Actions: facilitation of glucose transport into cells; inhibition of glycolysis, gluconeogenesis, lipolysis, glycogenolysis, and ketogenesis; facilitation of K^+ and Mg^{2+} transport into cells; enhancement of glycogen synthesis; increased conversion of glucose to fatty acid.

Infusion (adult): 50 U reg insulin in 250 cc D_5W (0.2 U/cc; 5 cc/hr = 1 U/hr).

Dose (diabetes mellitus): children/adults: 0.5-1 units/kg/day in divided doses; adolescents (growth spurts): 0.8-1.2 units/kg/day in divided doses.

Dose (hyperkalemia): administer 1 unit of insulin for every 3-4 gms dextrose given, or 0.05-0.1 units/kg/hr infused with glucose.

Dose (diabetic ketoacidosis): children/adults: IV loading dose: 0.1 unit/kg, then maintenance continuous infusion: 0.1 unit/kg/hr (range 0.05-0.2 units/kg/hr); optimum rate of decrease for glucose is 80-100 mg/dL/hr.

Dose (glucose intolerance in low birth weight infants <1000 gm): IV infusion: 0.04-0.05 units/kg/hr, titrate to desired blood glucose concentration.

Clearance: hepatic and renal metabolism; 30%-80% renal elimination; unchanged insulin is reabsorbed.

Adverse effects: hypoglycemia, allergic reactions, synthesis of insulin antibodies.

Comments: absorbed by plastic in IV tubing.

Isoproterenol (Isuprel)

Actions: synthetic sympathomimetic amine that acts on $beta_1$- and $beta_2$-adrenergic receptors; positive chronotrope and inotrope; decreases systemic and pulmonary vascular resistance; increases coronary and renal blood flow.

Indications: bradycardia, shock where increasing HR will increase CO, shock with severe aortic regurgitation, heart failure, pulmonary hypertension, refractory asthma or COPD, carotid sinus hypersensitivity, bradycardia in heart transplant patients, refractory torsades de pointes, beta blocker overdose, temporary use in third degree AV block until pacemaker insertion, vasoconstrictive shock states.

Dose (adult): AV nodal block: IV infusion: 5 mcg/minute initially, titrate to response (dose range: 2-20 mcg/minute); Shock: 0.5-5 mcg/minute IV; adjust according to response.

Dose (ped): cardiac arrhythmias: IV infusion: initial: 0.02-0.1 mcg/kg/minute; maintenance: 0.05-2 mcg/kg/min.

Clearance: hepatic and pulmonary metabolism; 40%-50% renal excretion.

Standard conc. (adult): 1 mg/250 cc; 15 cc = 1 mcg.

Adverse effects: arrhythmogenic, may increase myocardial ischemia, hypertension, CNS excitation, nausea/vomiting, pulmonary edema, paradoxical precipitation of Adams-Strokes attacks.

Isordil (Isosorbide Dinitrate)

Actions: stimulation of intracellular cyclic-GMP results in vascular smooth muscle relaxation of both arterial and venous vasculature; decrease preload and afterload; coronary vasodilation; esophageal relaxation.

Indications: prevention and treatment of angina pectoris, congestive heart failure, hypertension, myocardial infarction, dysphagia, esophageal spasm.

Dose (adult): angina: 5-40 mg PO 4 times/day or 40-80 mg PO every 8-12 hours in sustained released dosage form; congestive heart failure: initial dose: 10 mg PO TID, target dose: 40 mg PO TID, max dose: 80 mg 3 TID.

Clearance: hepatic metabolism.

Contraindications: severe anemia, increased intracranial pressure, shock.

Adverse effects: flushing, postural hypotension, dizziness, headache, lightheadedness, weakness.

Comments: tolerance may develop with chronic exposure.

Ketamine (Ketalar)

Actions: produces a cataleptic-like state in which the patient is dissociated fro the surrounding environment by direct action on the cortex and limbic system; releases endogenous catecholamines which causes increased HR, CO, cardiac work, and myocardial oxygen requirements; direct stimulation of the CNS leads to increased sympathetic nervous system outflow; reduces polysynaptic spinal reflexes.

Indications: induction and maintenance of general anesthesia; sedation, pain.

Dose (induction of anesthesia): 0.5-2 mg/kg IV; 6-10 mg/kg IM

Dose (maintenance): 10-100 mcg/kg/min IV or 30-50% of initial dose.

Dose (sedation and analgesia): 0.2-0.8 mg/kg IV; 2-6 mg/kg IM; 3 mg/kg intranasally; 6-10 mg/kg PO.

Clearance: hepatic metabolism.

Contraindications: seizures, psychosis, hypertension, conditions in which hypertension may be harmful, thyrotoxicosis, angina.

Adverse effects: direct myocardial depressant; potentiates action of sedatives, hypnotics opioids; dysphoric reactions; increases cerebral blood flow, intraocular pressure; increases upper airway secretions, heightens laryngeal reflexes.

Comments: commonly combined with anticholinergic agents to decrease hypersalivation.

Ketorolac (Toradol)

Actions: inhibits prostaglandin synthesis through cyclo-oxygenase inhibition, which results in decreased formation of prostaglandin precursors.

Indications: short-term management (<5 days) of moderate to severe pain.

Dose (adult):

<50 kg IV/IM: initial: 30 mg, then 15 mg every 6 hrs thereafter; max daily dose: 60 mg/24 hrs.

>50 kg IV/IM: initial: 30-60 mg, then 15-30 mg every 6 hrs thereafter; max dose: 120 mg/24 hrs for patients <65 yrs of age and 60 mg/24 hrs for patients >65 yrs of age or renally impaired.

>50 kg PO: 10 mg prn every 6 hrs; max dose: 40 mg/24 hrs.

Dose (ped): initial: 0.4-1 mg/kg/dose IV followed by a maintenance dose of 0.2-0.5 mg/kg/dose every 6 hrs.

Clearance: hepatic and renal metabolism; renal elimination.

Contraindications: prophylaxis before surgery and intraoperatively when hemostasis is critical; patients who have developed nasal polyps, angioedema, or bronchospastic reactions to other NSAIDs; active peptic ulcer disease, recent GI bleed or perforation; advanced renal disease; hepatic failure; labor and delivery and nursing mothers; cerebrovascular bleeding; hemorrhagic diathesis; spinal or epidural anesthesia.

Adverse effects: adverse effects are similar to those of other nonsteroidal anti-inflammatory drugs and include peptic ulceration, GI bleeding, nausea, dyspepsia, drowsiness, decreased platelet function, interstitial nephritis.

Comments: duration of therapy should not exceed 5 days; pediatric dosing has not been established by manufacturer.

Labetalol (Normodyne, Trandate)

Actions: selective alpha$_1$-adrenergic blockade with non-selective beta-adrenergic blockade; ratio of alpha/beta blockade = 1.7 (IV).

Indications: hypertension, controlled hypotension.

Dose (adult): IV: 5-20mg or 1-2 mg/kg increments up to 40-80 mg/dose at 10 minute intervals; hypertensive emergencies: 20-80 mg/dose q10 min prn with max total dose of 300 mg; continuous infusion: 0.05 mcg/kg/min or 2-150 mg/hr, titrate to response.

Dose (ped): IV: 0.2-1 mg/kg/dose prn every 10 minutes (max bolus: 20 mg); continuous infusion: 0.4-1 mg/kg/hour (max 3 mg/kg/hr).

Adverse effects: may cause bradycardia, AV conduction delay, bronchospasm in asthmatics, and postural hypotension.

Clearance: hepatic metabolism, renal elimination.

Contraindications: asthma, CHF, cardiogenic shock, heart block.

Adverse effects: may cause orthostatic hypotension, edema, CHF, bradycardia, AV conduction disturbances, bronchospasm, urinary retention, and skin tingling.

Comments: crosses the placenta; cimetidine increases bioavailability.

Levothyroxine (Synthroid, T$_4$)

Actions: exogenous thyroxine.

Indications: hypothyroidism.

Dose (adult):

Oral: 12.5-50 mcg/day to start, then increase by 25-50 mcg/day at intervals of 2-4 weeks; average adult dose: 100-200 mcg/day.

IV/IM: 50% of oral dose.

Thyroid suppression: 2.6 mcg/kg/day for 7-10 days.

Myxedema coma or stupor: 200-500 mcg IV one time, then 100-300 mcg the next day if necessary.

Dose (ped):

Oral (0-6 months): 8-10 mcg/kg/day or 25-50 mcg/day.

Oral (6-12 months): 6-8 mcg/kg/day or 50-75 mcg/day.

Oral (1-5 yrs): 5-6 mcg/kg/day or 75-100 mcg/day.

Oral (6-12 yrs): 4-5 mcg/kg/day or 100-150 mcg/day.

Oral (>12 yrs): 2-3 mcg/kg/day or >150 mcg/day.

IV/IM: 50%-75% or the oral dose.

Clearance: metabolized in the liver to triiodothyronine (active); eliminated in feces and urine.

Contraindications: recent myocardial infarction, thyrotoxicosis, uncorrected adrenal insufficiency.

Adverse effects: hyperthyroidism, rash, growth disturbances, hypertension, arrhythmias, diarrhea, weight loss.

Comments: increases effects of warfarin; phenytoin, carbamazepine may decrease levothyroxine levels; tricyclic antidepressants may increase toxic potential of both drugs; 100 mcg levothyroxine = 65 mg thyroid USP.

Lidocaine (Xylocaine)

Actions: blocks both the initiation and conduction of nerve impulses by decreasing the permeability of the neuronal membrane to sodium ions, which results in inhibition of depolarization with resultant blockade of conduction; suppresses automaticity of conduction tissue.

Indications: local anesthesia, peripheral nerve blocks, epidural/spinal anesthesia, ventricular dysrhythmias.

Dose: see section on 'Local Anesthetics' for local infiltration, spinal/epidural anesthesia, peripheral nerve block, topical dosing; see section on 'Resuscitation Algorithms' for additional arrhythmia dosing.

Dose (antiarrhythmic): adult: 1-1.5 mg/kg IV over 2-3 minutes, may repeat doses of 0.5-0.75 mg/kg in 5-10 minutes up to a total of 3 mg/kg; continuous infusion: 1-4 mg/minutes; ped: 1 mg/kg IV, may repeat x 2 doses; continuous infusion: 20-50 mcg/kg/min.

Standard adult concentration: 2 gm/250 cc; (7 cc/hr = 1 mg/min).

Clearance: hepatic metabolism to active/toxic metabolites; renal elimination (10% unchanged).

Contraindications: Stokes-Adams attacks, WPW syndrome, SA, AV or intraventricular heart blocks with a pacemaker.

Adverse effects: CNS depression, hypotension, asystole, seizures, respiratory arrest, tinnitus, drowsiness, disorientation, heart block, taste disorder, vomiting.

Comments: endotracheal dose 2-2.5 times the IV dose; endotracheal doses should be diluted to 1-2 mL with NS prior to administration; decrease dose in patients with CHF, shock, or hepatic disease; crosses the placenta.

Lorazepam (Ativan)

Actions: depresses CNS activity by binding to the benzodiazepine site on the GABA receptor complex, modulating GABA activity.

Indications: preoperative sedation/anxiolysis, amnesia, antiemetic adjunct, sedation, alcohol withdrawal, seizures.

Dose (preoperative sedation): 0.05 mg/kg IM (max 2 mg); 0.04-0.05 mg/kg IV (max 2 mg); 4 mg PO (adult).

Dose (induction agent): 0.1-0.25 mg/kg IV bolus.

Dose (conscious sedation): 0.02-0.05 mg/kg IV (max 4 mg).

Dose (antiemetic adjunct): adult: 0.5-2 mg PO every 4-6 hrs or 0.5-2 mg IV every 4-6 hrs; ped (2-15 yrs): 0.05 mg/kg IV up to 2 mg.

Dose (ICU sedation ventilated patients): 0.25-2 mg every 4 hrs prn.

Dose (antianxiety): adult: 1-10 mg/day PO in 2-3 divided doses (usual dose 2-6 mg/day); ped: 0.05 mg/kg PO or 0.05 mg/kg IV.

Dose (status epilepticus): adult: 4 mg/dose IV over 2-5 minutes, may repeat in 10-15 minutes; ped: 0.05-0.1 mg/kg/dose IV over 2-5 minutes, may repeat in 10-15 minutes.

Clearance: conjugated with glucuronide acid.

Contraindications: narrow-angle glaucoma, severe hypotension.

Adverse effects: may cause respiratory depression, sedation, dizziness, mild ataxia, mood changes, rash, and GI symptoms.

Comments: flumazenil is the antidote.

Magnesium Sulfate

Actions: central nervous system depressant and anticonvulsant, inhibits release of acetylcholine at the neuromuscular junction, decreases sensitivity of motor end-plate to acetylcholine, decreases muscle excitability, decreases uterine hyperactivity (increasing uterine blood flow), acts on myocardium by slowing rate of SA node impulse formation and prolonging conduction times.

Indications: pregnancy induced hypertension, tocolytic therapy, hypomagnesemia, torsades de pointes, ventricular arrhythmias due to digitalis toxicity.

Dose (hypomagnesemia): adult: 1-2 gms IV every 6-8 hrs or 250 mg/kg over a 4 hr period prn or 3 gms PO every 6 hrs prn; ped: 25-50 mcg/kg/dose IV (0.2-0.4 mEq/kg) every 4-6 hrs for 3-4 doses; neonates: 25-50 mcg/kg/dose (0.2-0.4 mEq/kg) every 8-12 hrs prn.

Dose (seizures and hypertension): adult: 1 gm IV every 6 hrs for 4 doses or 3 gm PO every 6 hrs for 4 doses; ped: 20-100 mg/kg/dose IV every 4-6 hrs prn.

Dose (PIH/tocolysis): load with 4 gm over 20 minutes followed by maintenance infusion of 1-3 gms/hr.

Dose (Torsades de pointes): 1-2 gm in 10 mL over 1-2 minutes; infusion with 0.5-1 gm/hr; 5-10 gms may be administered for refractory arrhythmias.

Dose (cathartic): adult: 10-30 gm PO; ped: 0.25 gm/kg/dose PO.

Dose (maintenance requirements): 0.2-0.5 mEq/kg/24 hrs.

Clearance: renal elimination.

Levels: normal plasma level is 1.5 to 2.2 mEq/L; treatment of pregnancy induced hypertension the therapeutic level is 4-5 mEq/L; tocolysis: 3.3-6.6 mEq/L; seizure threshold: 4-7 mEq/L; loss of patellar reflex: 5-10 mEq/L; respiratory depression and prolonged PR and QT intervals and widened QRS complex: >10 mEq/L; SA and AV nodal blocks: >15 mEq/L; cardiac arrest: >25 mEq/L.

Contraindications: heart block, serious renal impairment, hepatitis, Addison's disease.

Adverse effects: hypotension, respiratory depression, complete heart block, hypermagnesemia.

Comments: potentiates neuromuscular blockade; potentiates CNS effects of anesthetics, hypnotics, opioids; calcium gluconate should be available as antidote.

Mannitol (Osmitrol)

Actions: increases the osmotic pressure of glomerular filtrate, which inhibits tubular reabsorption of water and electrolytes and increased urinary output.

Indications: intracranial hypertension, glaucoma, diuresis, promotion of diuresis in the prevention and/or treatment of oliguria or anuria due to acute renal failure.

Dose (oliguria-adult): test dose: 12.5 gms over 3-5 minutes to produce a urine flow of at least 30-50 mL/hr for 1-3 hrs, then load with 0.5-1 mg/kg (50-100 gms) followed by maintenance infusion 0.25-0.5 gm/kg every 4-6 hrs.

Dose (oliguria-ped): test dose: 200 mg/kg over 3-5 minutes to produce a urine flow of at least 1 mL/kg for 1-3 hrs, then load with 0.5-1 gm/kg followed by maintenance infusion 0.25-0.5 gm/kg given every 4-6 hrs.

Dose (cerebral edema): 0.25-1 gm/kg IV over 30 minutes, not to exceed 1-2 gm/kg in 2-6 hrs, (in acute situation, can bolus 1.25-25 gm over 5-10 min).

Dose (preop for neurosurgery): 1-2 gm/kg over 30-60 minutes.

Contraindications: severe renal disease, active intracranial bleed, dehydration, and pulmonary edema.

Adverse effects: rapid administration may cause vasodilation and hypotension; may worsen or cause pulmonary edema, intracranial hemorrhage, systemic hypertension.

Metaproterenol (Alupent)

Actions: beta$_1$- and beta$_2$-adrenergic stimulation; relaxes bronchial smooth muscle by action on beta$_2$ receptors with little effect on heart rate.

Indications: bronchodilator in reversible airway obstruction due to asthma or COPD.

Dose (oral): adults and ped >9 yrs: 20 mg 3-4 times/day; ped 6-9 yrs or <27 kg: 10 mg 3-4 times/day; ped 2-6 yrs: 1-2.6 mg/kg/day divided every 6 hrs; ped <2 yrs: 0.4 mg/kg/dose given 3-4 times/day (in infants the dose can be given every 8-12 hrs).

Dose (single dose solutions): children: 2.5 mL of 0.6% solution every 4-6 hrs; infants: 2.5 mL of 0.4% solution.

Dose (inhalation): adults and ped >12 yrs: 2-3 inhalations every 3-4 hrs, max 12 inhalations in 24 hrs; children <12 yrs: 1-2 inhalations every 4-6 yrs, max 12 inhalations in 24 hrs.

Dose (nebulizer): adults:0.2-0.3 mL of 5% solution in 2.5-3 mL NS every 4-6 hrs; ped: 0.01-0.02 mL of 5% solution (min dose 0.1 mL; max dose 0.3 mL) in 2-3 mL NS every 4-6 hrs.

Contraindications: cardiac arrhythmias, narrow angle glaucoma.

Adverse effects: cardiac arrhythmias, tachycardia, increased myocardial oxygen consumption, hypertension, nervousness, headaches, nausea, palpitations, tremor.

Comments: nebulizers may be given more frequently in the acute setting; use caution inpatients with hypertension, CHF, hyperthyroidism, CAD, diabetes, or sensitivity to sympathomimetics.

Methohexital (Brevital)

Actions: ultra short-acting barbiturate; binds to site on GABA receptor complex increasing chloride ion channel openings and exerting increased GABA effect; depresses reticular activating system.

Indications: induction, maintenance of general anesthesia; electroconvulsive therapy; cardioversion.

Dose (adult): induction: 1-1.5 mg/kg IV; maintenance: 20-40 mg IV every 4-7 minutes or infusion: 6 mg/min; sedation: 0.2-0.4 mg/kg IV.

Dose (ped): IM: 5-10 mg/kg/dose; IV 1-2 mg/kg/dose; rectal: 20-35 mg/kg/dose (max dose is 500 mg).

Clearance: hepatic metabolism; renal elimination.

Contraindications: porphyria.

Adverse effects: hypotension, hiccups, coughing, muscle twitching, myoclonic activity, nausea, vomiting, respiratory depression, sedation, seizures, tachycardia, thrombophlebitis, pain on injection.

Comments: earlier recovery time and less cumulative effect than thiopental; higher incidence of excitatory phenomena (cough, hiccups, involuntary movements); activates epileptic foci (unlike other barbiturates).

Methylene Blue (Urolene Blue)

Actions: low dose promotes conversion of methemoglobin to hemoglobin; high dose promotes conversion of hemoglobin to methemoglobin; less useful than sodium nitrate and amyl nitrite.

Indications: antidote for cyanide poisoning and drug induced methemoglobinemia; an indicator dye for genitourinary surgery.
Dose (marker): 100 mg (10 mL of 1% solution) IV.
Dose (methemoglobinemia): 1-2 mg/kg IV of 1% solution over 10 minutes; repeat q1 hr prn.
Clearance: tissue reduction, urinary and biliary elimination.
Adverse effects: may cause RBC destruction (with prolonged use); hypertension; bladder irritation; nausea; diaphoresis; may inhibit nitrate induced coronary artery relaxation; may cause hemolysis in patients with glucose-6-phosphate-dehydrogenase deficiency
Comments: interferes with pulse oximetry for 1-2 minutes..

Methylergonovine (Methergine)
Actions: constriction of uterine and vascular smooth muscle.
Indications: prevention and treatment of postpartum and postabortion hemorrhage caused by uterine atony or subinvolution.
Dose: 0.2 mg IV in 5 mL NS given over 1 minute (IV only in emergencies, after delivery of placenta). 0.2 mg IM q2-4 hours for less than 5 doses; 0.2-0.4 mg PO q6-12 hours for 2 days (PO given after IV/IM dose)..
Clearance: hepatic metabolism; renal elimination.
Adverse effects: may cause hypertension from systemic vasoconstriction, arrhythmias, coronary spasm, uterine tetany, or gastrointestinal upset.

Methylprednisolone (Solu-Medrol)
Actions: decreases inflammation by suppression of migration of polymorphonuclear leukocytes and reversal of increased capillary permeability; has 5 times the glucocorticoid potency of hydrocortisone.
Preparations: only methylprednisolone sodium succinate salt may be given IV; methylprednisolone acetate has sustained IM effect.
Indications: anti-inflammatory or immunosuppressant agent, treatment of low back pain.
Dose (adult):
　Epidural: 50-100 mg for 3 treatments separated by a min of 1 week.
　Intra-articular/intralesional: 4-40 mg, up to 80 mg for large joints every 1-5 weeks.
　Anti-inflammatory/immunosuppressant: 2-60 mg/day PO in 1-4 divided doses to start, followed by gradual reduction in dosage to the lowest possible level consistent with maintaining an adequate response.
　PO: 2-60 mg in 1-4 divided doses.
　IM (sodium succinate): 10-80 mg/day once daily.
　IM (acetate): 40-120 mg every 1-2 weeks.
　IV (sodium succinate): 10-250 mg over several minutes repeated as needed every 4-6 hrs.
　Status asthmaticus: load 2 mg/kg/dose IV (sodium succinate), then 0.5-1 mg/kg/dose every 6 hrs for up to 5 days.
　Lupus nephritis: 1 gm/day IV (sodium succinate) for 3 days.
Dose (ped):
　Anti-inflammatory/immunosuppressant: 0.12-1.7 mg/kg/day IV/IM/PO in divided doses every 6-12 hrs; pulse therapy: 15-30 mg/kg/day once daily for 3 days.
　Status asthmaticus: load 2 mg/kg IV, then 1 mg/kg/dose every 6 hrs.
　Lupus nephritis: 30 mg/kg/IV every other day for 6 doses.
　Acute spinal cord injury: 30 mg/kg IV over 15 minutes, followed in 45

minutes by a continuous infusion of 5.4 mg/kg/hr for 23 hrs.
Clearance: hepatic metabolism; renal elimination.
Contraindications: serious infections except septic shock or tuberculous meningitis.
Adverse effects: may cause hypertension, pseudotumor cerebri, acne, Cushing's syndrome, adrenal axis suppression, GI bleeding, hyperglycemia, and osteoporosis.
Comments: use caution in hyperthyroidism, cirrhosis, nonspecific ulcerative colitis, hypertension, osteoporosis, thromboembolic tendencies, CHF, convulsive disorders, myasthenia gravis, thrombophlebitis, peptic ulcer, diabetes.

Metoclopramide (Reglan)

Actions: blocks dopamine receptors in chemoreceptor trigger zone of the CNS; enhances the response to acetylcholine of tissue in upper GI tract causing enhanced motility and accelerated gastric emptying without stimulating gastric, biliary, or pancreatic secretions.
Indications: symptomatic treatment of diabetic gastric stasis, GERD, pulmonary aspiration prophylaxis, antiemetic.
Dose (adult):
   GERD: 10-15 mg/dose PO up to 4 times/day 30 minutes before meals.
   Gastroparesis: 10 mg PO 30 minutes before each meal and at bedtime; 10 mg IV/IM 4 times daily.
   Antiemetic (chemotherapy induced): 1-2 mg/kg IV 30 minutes before chemotherapy, repeat every 2 hrs for 2 doses, then q3 hrs for 3 doses.
   Postoperative nausea/vomiting: 10 mg IV.
Dose (ped):
   GERD: 0.4-0.8 mg/kg/day IV/IM/PO in 4 divided doses.
   Gastroparesis: 0.1 mg/kg/dose IV/IM/PO up to 4 times/day.
   Antiemetic (chemotherapy induced): 1-2 mg/kg IV/IM/PO 30 minutes before chemotherapy and every 2-4 hrs (pretreatment with diphenhydramine will decrease risk of extrapyramidal reactions).
   Postoperative nausea/vomiting: 0.1-0.2 mg/kg IV repeat q6-8 hrs prn.
Clearance: hepatic metabolism; renal elimination.
Contraindications: GI obstruction, pheochromocytoma, seizure disorder, Parkinson's disease.
Adverse effects: may exacerbate depression, extrapyramidal reactions may occur, restlessness, somnolence, diarrhea, weakness, headache, anxiety, leukopenia.
Comments: for elderly patients reduce adult dose in half.

Metoprolol (Lopressor)

Actions: beta$_1$-adrenergic blockade (beta$_2$-antagonism at high doses).
Indications: hypertension, angina pectoris, arrhythmias, symptomatic treatment of hypertrophic subaortic stenosis, myocardial infarction, pheochromocytoma.
Dose (adult): 100-450 mg PO in 2-3 divided doses, begin with 50 mg twice daily and increase at weekly intervals (for elderly patients start with 25 mg/day PO); 5 mg IV every 2 minutes for 3 doses in early treatment of MI, thereafter give 50 mg PO every 6 hrs.
Dose (ped): 1-5 mg/kg/day PO twice daily, increase in 3 day intervals.
Clearance: hepatic metabolism.
Contraindications: uncompensated CHF, cardiogenic shock, severe

bradycardia or heart block greater then first degree, sinus node dysfunction, AV conduction abnormalities, hypotension.

Adverse effects: may cause bradycardia or heart block, clinically significant bronchoconstriction, dizziness, fatigue, insomnia.

Mexilentine (Mexitil)

Actions: sodium channel blocker, antiarrhythmic, antineuralgia adjunct; structurally similar to lidocaine.

Indications: neuropathic pain, ventricular arrhythmias, PVC suppression.

Dose (adult): initial: 150 mg PO qHS, gradually titrated as tolerated up to 900 mg/day in three divided doses.

Adverse effects: nausea, vomiting, heartburn, dizziness, tremor, changes in vision, nervousness, confusion, headache, fatigue, depression, rapid heartbeat, general weakness.

Comments: caution in patients with cardiac disease, hypotension, liver disease, a history of seizures or allergies.

Milrinone (Primacor)

Actions: phosphodiesterase inhibitor, increases cAMP potentiating delivery of calcium to myocardial contractile systems resulting in a positive inotropic effect, inhibition of phosphodiesterase in vascular tissue results in vasodilation.

Indications: low output heart failure, congestive heart failure

Dose (adult): load 50 mcg/kg IV over 10 minutes, followed by a continuous infusion of 0.375-0.75 mcg/kg/min and titrate to effect.

Dose (ped): load 50 mcg/kg IV over 10 minutes, followed by a continuous infusion of 0.5-1.0 mcg/kg/min and titrate to effect.

Clearance: renal elimination.

Adverse effects: increased ventricular ectopy, nonsustained ventricular tachycardia, supraventricular tachycardia; may aggravate outflow tract obstruction in IHSS; hypotension; headaches.

Comments: the presence of renal impairment may significantly increase the terminal elimination half-life; do not inject furosemide into IV lines containing milrinone (precipitate-forming chemical reaction may occur).

Morphine Sulfate

Actions: binds to opiate receptors in the CNS and exerts effect via potassium channel opening and inhibition of calcium channels, causing inhibition of ascending pain pathways, altering the perception of and response to pain; produces generalized CNS depression.

Indications: pain management, treatment of ischemic pain not relieved by nitroglycerin, acute cardiogenic pulmonary edema, premedication.

Dose (adult):

Oral: prompt release: 10-30 mg every 4 hrs prn; controlled release: 15-30 mg every 8-12 hrs.

Bolus IV/IM/SC: 2-10 mg (up to 20 mg) every 2-6 hrs prn (for acute pain relief every 5-35 minutes).

Continuous IV infusion: 0.8-10 mg/hr (may increase up to 80 mg/hr).

Epidural: bolus: 2-6 mg in lumbar region; if inadequate pain relief within 1 hr may give 1-2 mg (max: 10 mg/24 hrs); cont. infusion: 0.2-1 mg/hr.

Intrathecal: 0.1-0.5 mg (max 1 mg), repeat doses not recommended.

PCA: load: 5-10 mg (give 2 mg every 5-10 minutes as needed until desired response); bolus: 1-2 mg; lockout 5-10 min

Dose (ped):
    Oral: prompt release: 0.2-0.5 mg/kg/dose every 4-6 hrs prn; controlled release: 0.3-0.6 mg/kg/dose every 12 hrs.
    Bolus IV/IM/SC: 0.1-0.2 mg/kg/dose every 2-4 hrs.
    Continuous infusion: postoperative pain: 0.01-0.04 mg/kg/hr; sickle cell and cancer pain: 0.04-0.07 mg/kg/hr.
    Epidural: 0.03-0.05 mg/kg up to a max of 0.1 mg/kg or 5 mg/24 hrs.
Dose (neonate):
    Neonate: 0.05-0.2 mg/kg/dose IV/IM/SC every 4 hrs prn; continuous infusion: 0.01 mg/kg/hr (do not exceed rates of 0.015-0.02 mg/kg/hr due to decreased elimination and increased CNS sensitivity).
    Neonatal opiate withdrawal: 0.08-0.2 mg/kg/every 3-4 hrs prn.
Adverse effects: dependence, CNS and respiratory depression, nausea, vomiting, urinary retention, constipation, hypotension, bradycardia, increased ICP, miosis, biliary spasm, allergy may occur, histamine release (may cause itching and bronchospasm).
Comments: naloxone may be used to reverse effects; neonates may require higher doses due to decreased amounts of active metabolites; adjust dosing in renal failure.

Nadolol (Corgard)
Actions: competitively blocks response to beta$_1$- and beta$_2$-adrenergic stimulation; does not exhibit any membrane stabilizing or intrinsic sympathomimetic activity.
Indications: treatment of hypertension and angina pectoris; prevention of myocardial infarction; prophylaxis of migraine headaches.
Dose (adult): initially 40-80 mg/day, increase gradually by 40-80 mg increments at 3-7 day intervals until optimum response is obtained with prolong slowing of heart rate; doses up to 160-240 mg/day in angina and 240-320 mg/day in hypertension may be necessary; max: 640 mg/day.
Dose (elderly): 20 mg/day; increase doses by 20 mg increments at 3-7 day intervals; usual dosage range: 20-40 mg/day.
Clearance: renal elimination.
Contraindications: uncompensated CHF, cardiogenic shock, heart block.
Adverse effects: may cause drowsiness, insomnia, bronchospasm, bradycardia, congestive heart failure, AV dissociation, hypoglycemia.

Naloxone (Narcan)
Actions: opioid antagonist; competes and displaces opioid agonist at the receptor site.
Indications: reverses CNS and respiratory depression in suspected narcotic overdose; neonatal opiate depression; opiate induced puritus.
Dose (adult):
    Postanesthesia narcotic reversal: 0.04-0.4 mg IV every 2-3 minutes prn.
    Narcotic overdose: 0.4-2 mg IV every 2-3 minutes as needed.
    Continuous infusion: 0.005 mg/kg loading dose followed by infusion of 0.0025 mg/kg/hr (range 0.0025-0.16 mg/kg/hr).
Dose (ped):
    Postanesthesia narcotic reversal: 0.01 mg/kg IV: repeat every 2-3 min.
    Opiate intoxication: birth to 5yrs or <20 kg: 0.1 mg/kg IV: repeat every 2-3 minutes if needed; >5 yrs or >20 kg: 2 mg/dose, if no response, repeat every 2-3 minutes if needed.
    Continuous infusion: 0.005 mg/kg loading dose followed by infusion of

0.0025 mg/kg/hr (range 0.0025-0.16 mg/kg/hr).

Dose (neonate): narcotic-induced asphyxia: 0.01 mg/kg every 2-3 minutes as needed; may need to repeat every 1-2 hrs.

Clearance: hepatic metabolism; primary renal elimination.

Adverse effects: may cause reversal of analgesia, hypertension, arrhythmias, pulmonary edema, , tremulousness, delirium or withdrawal syndrome.

Comments: renarcotization may occur because antagonist has short duration; caution in hepatic failure and chronic cardiac disease.

Nicardipine (Cardene)

Actions: dihydropyridine calcium channel blocker, producing a relaxation of coronary vascular smooth muscle and coronary vasodilation.

Indications: short-term treatment of hypertension, chronic stable angina.

Dose (adult):

Oral: 20-40 mg 3 times/day, allow 3 days between dose increases.

Oral (sustained release): 30-60 mg twice daily.

IV: 5 mg/hr increased by 2.5 mg/hr every 15 minutes (max of 15 mg/hr).

Clearance: hepatic metabolism; renal elimination.

Contraindications: severe hypotension, second or third degree heart block, sinus bradycardia, advanced heart block, ventricular tachycardia, cardiogenic shock, atrial fibrillation.

Adverse effects: caution when administering in patients with impaired renal or hepatic function or in combination with a beta blocker in CHF patients.

Nifedipine (Procardia)

Actions: blockade of slow calcium channels of vascular smooth muscle and myocardium during depolarization, producing a relaxation of coronary vascular smooth muscle and coronary vasodilation; increases in myocardial perfusion.

Indications: hypertension, angina, hypertrophic cardiomyopathy.

Dose (adult): 10 mg PO 3 times/day as capsules (usual range: 10-30 mg) or 30 mg once daily as sustained release (usual range: 30-60 mg), max dose 120-180 mg/day; 10-20 mg SL.

Dose (ped): hypertensive emergencies: 0.25-0.5 mg/kg/dose PO every 4-6 hrs prn (max dose: 10 mg/dose or 3 mg/kg/24 hr); hypertrophic cardiomyopathy: 0.5-0.9 mg/kg/24 hr PO in 3-4 divided doses.

Clearance: hepatic metabolism.

Contraindications: sick-sinus syndrome, 2nd or 3rd degree AV block, hypotension.

Adverse effects: may cause reflex tachycardia, gastrointestinal tract upset, mild negative inotropic effects, peripheral edema, lightheadedness, nausea.

Comments: sensitive to light; nifedipine should not be used for acute reduction of blood pressure or the control of essential hypertension; avoid within the first week or two after myocardial infarction and in the setting of acute coronary syndrome (when infarction may be imminent).

Nitroglycerin

Actions: vasodilation through nitric oxide-induced relaxation of vascular smooth muscle; venous dilation greater than arterial dilation (decrease of preload > decrease of afterload), coronary artery dilation, decreased systemic vascular resistance, decreased pulmonary vascular resistance.

Indications: myocardial ischemia, hypertension, congestive heart failure, pulmonary hypertension, esophageal spasm, controlled hypotension.

Preparation (ped): weight (kg) x 6 = mg of drug in 100 mL; 1 mL/hr = 1 mcg/kg/min.

Dose (adult):

> **Buccal:** 1 mg every 3-5 hr while awake (3 times/day), titrate as needed.
>
> **Oral:** 2.5-9 mg 2-4 times/day (up to 26 mg 4 times/day).
>
> **IV:** 5 mcg/min, increase 5 mcg/minute every 3-5 minutes to 20 mcg/minute; if no response at 20 mcg/minute increase by 10 mcg/minute every 3-5 minutes, up to 200 mcg/min.
>
> **Ointment:** 1-2 inches every 8 hrs (up to 4-5 inches every 4 hrs).
>
> **Patch/transdermal:** 0.2-0.4 mg/hr initially and titrate to doses of 0.4-0.8 mg/hr; us a 'patch-on' period of 12-14 hrs per day and a 'patch-off' period of 10-12 hrs per day to minimize tolerance.
>
> **Sublingual:** 0.2-0.6 mg every 5 minutes for maximum of 3 doses in 15 minutes; may also use prophylactically 5-10 minutes prior to activities that provoke an attack.
>
> **Translingual:** 1-2 sprays into mouth under tongue every 3.5 minutes for maximum of 3 doses in 15 minutes, may also be used 5-10 minutes prior to activities that provoke an attack.

Dose (ped): continuous infusion: 0.25-0.5 mcg/kg/min, may increase by 0.5-1 mcg/kg/min every 3-5 minutes prn (usual dose: 1-5 mcg/kg/min; max dose: 20 mcg/kg/min).

Clearance: hepatic metabolism, renal elimination.

Contraindications: severe anemia, glaucoma, hypotension, uncontrolled hypokalemia, pericardial tamponade, constrictive pericarditis.

Adverse effects: reflex tachycardia, hypotension, headache, flushing, GI upset, blurred vision, methemoglobinemia.

Comment: tolerance and dependence with chronic use; may be absorbed by plastic in IV tubing; concomitant use with sildenafil (Viagra) may precipitate acute hypotension, myocardial infarction; use with caution in severe renal impairment, increased ICP, hepatic failure.

Nitroprusside (Nipride)

Actions: venous and arterial smooth muscle relaxation (by generation of nitric oxide); arterial dilation greater than venous; increases cardiac output; decreases peripheral resistance; alters V/Q promoting shunting.

Indications: hypertensive crisis, congestive heart failure, reduce afterload in acute mitral or aortic valve regurgitation, controlled hypotension.

Dose (infusion): start at 0.3-0.5 mcg/kg/min and titrate upward every 3-5 minutes to desired effect (up to 10 mcg/kg/min).

Preparation (adult): mix 50 mg/250 cc D_5W.

Preparation (ped): weight (kg) x 6 = mg of drug in 100 mL; 1 mL/hr = 1 mcg/kg/min.

Clearance: RBC and tissue metabolism; renal elimination.

Contraindications: decreased cerebral perfusion, increased ICP, arteriovenous shunt or coarctation of the aorta, hypovolemia, congenital optic atrophy or tobacco amblyopia, hypothyroidism, vitamin B12 deficiency.

Toxicity: nitroprusside is nonenzymatically converted to cyanide, which is converted to thiocyanate; cyanide may produce metabolic acidosis and methemoglobinemia; thiocyanate may produce psychosis and seizures; thiocyanate levels should be <50 mg/L; treatment is with sodium nitrite, sodium thiosulfate, hydroxocobalamin or methylene blue

Adverse effects: hypotension, reflex tachycardia, nausea, abdominal cramps, headaches, restlessness, cyanide and thiocyanate toxicity, CO_2 retention.

Comments: may reverse hypoxic pulmonary vasoconstriction exacerbating intrapulmonary shunting; degraded by light (tubing/container must be covered with aluminum foil).

Norepinephrine (Levophed)

Actions: alpha$_1$, alpha$_2$, beta$_1$ adrenergic receptor agonist causing increased contractility, heart rate, and vasoconstriction; clinically alpha effects are greater than beta effects..

Indications: septic shock, cardiogenic shock with hypotension and decreased SVR, refractory hypotension.

Preparations: norepinephrine bitartrate 2 mg = norepinephrine base 1 mg.

Standard conc.: 4 mg/250 cc D$_5$W; 15 cc/hr = 4 mcg/min.

Dose (adult): 4 mcg/min and titrate to effect (usual range 8-12 mcg/min).

Dose (ped): 0.05-0.1 mcg/kg/min, titrate to effect (max: 2 mcg/kg/min).

Clearance: MAO/COMT metabolism.

Adverse effects: hypertension, arrhythmias, myocardial ischemia, increased uterine contractility, CNS stimulation, vomiting, constricted microcirculation, organ ischemia, ischemic necrosis and sloughing of superficial tissues will result if extravasation occurs (treat with phentolamine 5-10 mg in 10-15 mL saline solution infiltrated into area).

Comments: note the dosage units for adults are in mcg/min compared to mcg/kg/min for children.

Octreotide (Sandostatin)

Actions: somatostatin analogue that suppresses release of serotonin, gastrin, vasoactive intestinal peptide, insulin, glucagon, secretin, motilin.

Indications: control of symptoms in patients with metastatic carcinoid and vasoactive intestinal peptide-secreting tumors; upper gastrointestinal tract bleeding, acute variceal hemorrhage; unlabeled uses include: AIDS-associated secretory diarrhea, cryptosporidiosis, Crushing's syndrome, insulinomas, small bowel fistulas, postgastrectomy dumping syndrome, chemotherapy-induced diarrhea, graft-versus-host disease induced diarrhea, Zollinger-Ellison syndrome.

Dose (adult):
  SC: initial 50 mcg 1-2 times/day and titrate dose based on response.
  Diarrhea: initial 50-100 mcg IV every 8 hrs, increase by 100 mcg/dose at 48 hr intervals; max dose: 500 mcg/dose every 8 hrs.
  Carcinoid: 100-600 mcg/day in 2-4 divided doses
  VIPomas: 200-300 mcg/day in 2-4 divided doses.
  Esophageal variceal bleeding: bolus 25-50 mcg followed by continuous infusion IV of 25-50 mcg/hr.

Dose (ped): 1-10 mcg/kg every 12 hrs beginning at low end of range and increasing by 0.3 mcg/kg/dose at every 3 days; max dose: 1500 mcg/24 hr.

Clearance: hepatic and renal.

Adverse effects: may cause nausea, decreased GI motility, transient hyperglycemia, cholelithiasis, abdominal discomfort, headache, pain at injection site; growth hormone suppression with long term use.

Comments: cyclosporine levels may be reduced.

Omeprazole (Prilosec)

Actions: potent proton pump inhibitor; suppresses gastric acid secretion by inhibiting the parietal cell H+/K+ ATP pump.

Indications: gastric acid hypersecretion conditions; gastritis; gastroesophageal reflux (GERD); erosive gastritis; peptic ulcer disease;

prevention of acid aspiration pneumonitis during surgery.

Dose (adult):

Duodenal ulcer: 20 mg/day PO for 4-8 weeks.

GERD or severe erosive esophagitis: 20 mg/day for 4-8 weeks; maintenance therapy for erosive esophagitis: 20 mg/day.

Gastric ulcer: 40 mg/day PO for 4-8 weeks.

Pathological hypersecretory conditions: 60 mg PO once daily to start; doses up to 120 mg 3 times/day have been administered; administer daily doses >80 mg in divided doses.

Dose (ped): 0.6-0.7 mg/kg/dose PO once daily; increase to 0.6-0.7 mg/kg/dose PO every 12 hrs if needed (effective range: 0.3-3.3 mg/kg/day).

Clearance: extensive hepatic metabolism; 80% renal elimination.

Adverse effects: headache, diarrhea, nausea, vomiting.

Comments: induces some cytochrome P450 enzymes; increases half-life of diazepam, phenytoin, warfarin; may decrease absorption of itraconazole, ketoconazole, iron salts, ampicillin.; administer all doses before meals.

Ondansetron (Zofran)

Actions: serotonin receptor selective antagonist, blocking serotonin, both peripherally on vagal nerve terminals and centrally in the chemoreceptor trigger zone.

Indications: prevention and treatment of chemotherapy-induced and postoperative nausea and vomiting.

Dose (chemotherapy-oral dose): >12 yrs and adults: 8 mg every 8 hrs prn; children 4-11 yrs: 4 mg every 8 hrs prn.

Dose (chemotherapy-IV): children and adults: moderately emetogenic drugs: 0.15 mg/kg/dose at 30 min before, 4 and 8 hrs after emetogenic drugs; highly emetogenic drugs: 0.45 mg/kg/dose (max: 32 mg/dose) 30 min before emetogenic drugs then 0.15 mg/kg/dose every 4 hrs prn.

Dose (PONV): adult: 4 mg IV/IM (or 8 mg PO 1 hr prior to surgery) for prophylaxis or treatment; ped: <30 kg: 1 mg IV every 8 hrs prn, >30 kg: 2 mg IV every 8 hrs prn; alternate ped dosing: 0.05-0.075 mg/kg IV.

Adverse effects: headache, dizziness, musculoskeletal pain, drowsiness, sedation, shivers, reversible transaminase elevation, increased bilirubin, bronchospasm, tachycardia, hypokalemia, lightheadedness, diarrhea.

Comments: all IV doses should be given over >30 seconds; use caution in severe hepatic impairment (max dose: 8 mg).

Oxytocin (Pitocin)

Actions: produces rhythmic uterine smooth muscle contractions by increasing sodium permeability; cause vasodilation of smooth muscle (renal, coronary, and cerebral); stimulates breast milk flow during nursing.

Indications: postpartum hemorrhage, uterine atony, augment labor.

Dose (induction of labor): adult: 0.001-0.002 units/minute IV, increase by 0.001-0.002 units every 15-30 minutes until contraction pattern has been established; max dose of 20 milliunits/min.

Dose (postpartum bleeding): adult: 10-40 units IV (mix 10-40 units in 1000 mL IVF) at a rate to control uterine atony; 10 units IM.

Clearance: tissue metabolism, renal elimination.

Adverse effects: may cause uterine tetany and rupture, fetal distress, anaphylaxis; IV bolus can cause hypotension, tachycardia, dysrhythmia.

Pentobarbital (Nembutal)

Actions: short-acting barbiturate with sedative, hypnotic, and anticonvulsant properties; binds to barbiturate site on GABA receptor complex increasing chloride ion channel openings and exerting increased GABA effect.

Indications: preoperative sedation, insomnia, high-dose barbiturate coma.

Dose (adult):

Hypnotic: 100-200 mg PO at bedtime or 20 mg PO 3-4 times/day; 150-200 mg IM at bedtime; 100 mg IV, may repeat every 2-3 minutes up to a 200-500 mg total dose; 120-200 mg PR at bedtime.

Preoperative sedation: 150-200 mg IM.

Dose (ped):

Sedative: 2-6 mg/kg/day PO divided in 3 doses, max: 100 mg/day.

Hypnotic: 2-6 mg/kg IM, max: 100 mg/day.

Rectal: 2 months-1 yr: 30 mg; 1-4 yrs: 30-60 mg; 5-12 yrs: 60 mg; 12-14 yrs: 60-120 mg.

Preoperative/preprocedure sedation(>6 months): 2-6 mg/kg PO/IM/PR, max: 100 mg/dose; 1-3 mg/kg IV to a max of 100 mg.

Conscious sedation (5-12 yrs): 2 mg/kg IV 5-10 min before procedure.

Dose (pentobarbital coma): 5-15 mg/kg load given slowly over 1-2 hrs, maintenance infusion: 1 mg/kg/hr, may increase to 2-3 mg/kg/hr, maintain burst suppression on EEG.

Clearance: hepatic metabolism.

Contraindications: severe liver impairment, latent porphyria.

Adverse effects: hypotension, somnolence, pain at injection site, confusion, lightheadedness, respiratory depression, dependence.

Comments: do not administer IV at a rate greater than 50 mg/minute.

Phenobarbital (Luminal, Solfoton)

Actions: suppresses discharge and spread from epileptic foci.

Indications: management of generalized tonic-clonic and partial seizures; neonatal seizures; febrile seizures; sedation; sleep disorders; anxiety.

Dose (adult):

Sedation: 30-120 mg/day PO/IM in 2-3 divided doses.

Hypnotic: 100-320 mg IM/IV/SC at bedtime.

Hyperbilirubinemia: 90-180 mg/day PO in 2-3 divided doses.

Preoperative sedation: 100-200 mg IM 60-90 min before procedure.

Dose (ped):

Sedation: 2 mg/kg PO 3 times/day.

Hypnotic: 3-5 mg/kg IV/IM/SC at bedtime.

Hyperbilirubinemia: (<12 yrs) 3-12 mg/kg/day PO in 2-3 divided doses.

Preop sedation: 1-3 mg/kg IV/IM/PO 60-90 min before procedure.

Dose (anticonvulsant: status epilepticus):

Adult and children >12 yrs: 15-20 mg/kg IV initially followed by 120-240 mg/dose at 20 minute intervals until seizures are controlled or a total dose of 1-2 gm; maintenance: 1-3 mg/kg/day IV/PO in divided doses or 50-100 mg 2-3 times/day.

Infant and children <12 yrs: 10-20 mg/kg IV in a single or divided dose, may give additional 5 mg/kg every 15-30 minutes until seizure is controlled or a total dose of 40 mg/kg is reached; maintenance: infants: 5-8 mg/kg/day IV/PO in 1-2 divided doses, children 1-5 yrs: 6-8 mg/kg/day in 1-2 divided doses, children 5-12 yrs: 4-6 mg/kg/day in 1-2 divided doses.

Neonates: 15-20 mg/kg IV in single or divided dose; maintenance: 2-4

mg/kg/day in 1-2 divided doses, increase by 5 mg/kg/day if needed.
Clearance: hepatic metabolism, 25-50% renal elimination unchanged.
Therapeutic level: 15-40 mg/L.
Contraindications: preexisting CNS depression, severe uncontrolled pain, porphyria, severe respiratory disease with dyspnea or obstruction.
Adverse effects: hypotension, drowsiness, cognitive impairment, ataxia, hepatitis, skin rash, respiratory depression, apnea, megaloblastic anemia.
Comments: multiple drug interactions through induction of hepatic enzyme systems; use caution in hepatic or renal disease; paradoxical reaction in children may cause hyperactivity, irritability, insomnia.

Phenoxybenzamine (Dibenzyline)

Actions: long-lasting noncompetitive alpha-adrenergic blockade of postganglionic synapses in exocrine glands and smooth muscle; relaxes urethra and increases opening of the bladder.
Indications: symptomatic management of pheochromocytoma; treatment of hypertensive crisis caused by sympathomimetic amines.
Dose (adult): 10 mg PO twice daily, increase by 10 mg every other day until optimum dose is achieved; usual range: 20-40 mg 2-3 times/day.
Dose (ped): 0.2 mg/kg PO (maximum: 10 mg) once daily, increase by 0.2 mg/kg increments; maintenance dose: 0.4-1.2 mg/kg/day every 6-8 hrs.
Clearance: hepatic metabolism, renal/biliary excretion.
Adverse effects: may cause orthostatic hypotension (may be refractory to norepinephrine), reflex tachycardia, nasal congestion, syncope, miosis.
Comments: use with caution in renal impairment, cerebral or coronary arteriosclerosis.

Phentolamine (Regitine)

Actions: competitively blocks alpha-adrenergic receptors to produce brief antagonism of circulating epinephrine and norepinephrine to reduce hypertension; has positive inotropic and chronotropic effect on the heart.
Indications: diagnosis of pheochromocytoma, treatment of hypertension associated with pheochromocytoma, treatment of dermal necrosis after extravasation of drugs with alpha-adrenergic effects.
Dose (treatment of drug extravasation):
    Adult: 5-10 mg diluted in 10 mL NS infiltrated into area of extravasation within 12 hrs.
    Ped: 0.1-0.2 mg/kg diluted in 10 mL NS infiltrated into area of extravasation within 12 hrs.
Dose (diagnosis of pheochromocytoma):
    Children: 0.05-0.1 mg/kg/dose IV/IM, maximum single dose: 5 mg.
    Adult: 5 mg IV/IM.
Dose (surgery for pheochromocytoma: hypertension):
    Adult: 5 mg IV/IM given 1-2 hrs before procedure, repeat prn q2-3 hrs.
    Children: 0.05-0.1 mg/kg/dose IV/IM given 1-2 hrs before procedure, repeat prn every 2-4 hr until hypertension is controlled; max dose: 5 mg.
Dose (hypertension crisis): adult: 5-20 mg IV.
Adverse effects: may cause hypotension, reflex tachycardia, cerebrovascular spasm, arrhythmias, stimulation of gastrointestinal tract, hypoglycemia.
Comments: use with caution in renal impairment, coronary or cerebral arteriosclerosis.

Phenylephrine (Neo-Synephrine)

Actions: alpha adrenergic agonist (direct) producing vasoconstriction.

Indications: hypotension; SVT; symptomatic relief of nasal and nasopharyngeal congestion; mydriatic; treatment of wide-angle glaucoma.

Dose (adult): bolus: 50-200 mcg IV; infusion: 20-180 mcg/min (usual range: 40-80 mcg/min).

Dose (ped): bolus: 0.5-10 mcg/kg IV; infusion: 0.1-0.5 mcg/kg/min.

Clearance: hepatic metabolism; renal elimination.

Contraindications: pheochromocytoma, severe hypertension, bradycardia, ventricular tachyarrhythmias, narrow-angle glaucoma.

Adverse effects: hypertension, reflex bradycardia, microcirculatory constriction, uterine contraction, uterine vasoconstriction.

Phenytoin (Dilantin)

Actions: anticonvulsant effect: stabilizes neuronal membranes and inhibits depolarization; antiarrhythmic effect: blocks calcium uptake during depolarization, prolongs effective refractory period, suppresses ventricular pacemaker automaticity, shortens action potential in the heart.

Indications: seizure management, ventricular arrhythmias, digoxin-induced arrhythmias, refractory ventricular tachycardia, used for epidermolysis and trigeminal neuralgia.

Dose (status epilepticus):

   Adult: load 15-20 mg/kg IV (max: 1500 mg); maintenance dose: 300 mg/day or 5-6 mg/kg/day in 3 divided doses or 1-2 divided doses if using extended release.

   Infants/children: load 15-20 mg/kg IV; maintenance dose (2-3 divided doses): 6 months-3 yrs: 8-10 mg/kg/day, 4-6 yrs: 7.5-9 mg/kg/day, 7-9 yrs 7-8 mg/kg/day, 10-16 yrs 6-7 mg/kg/day.

   Neonates: load 15-20 mg/kg IV; maintenance of 5-8 mg/kg/day in 2 divided doses (may give every 8 hrs if needed).

Dose (anticonvulsant): children/adult: load 15-20 mg PO/IV (administer oral dose in 3 divided doses given every 2-3 hrs to decrease GI effects), followed by maintenance dose: 300 mg/day or 5-6 mg/kg/day in 3 divided doses.

Dose (antiarrhythmic): 1.5 mg/kg IV every 5 minutes until arrhythmia is suppressed or maximum dose: 10-15 mg/kg.

Clearance: hepatic metabolism; renal elimination.

Contraindications: heart block, sinus bradycardia.

Therapeutic levels: seizure threshold: 10-20 mg/L (free and bound phenytoin), 1-2 mg/L (free only phenytoin).

Adverse effects: may cause nystagmus, diplopia, ataxia, drowsiness, gingival hyperplasia, gastrointestinal upset, hyperglycemia, hirsutism, SLE-like and Stevens-Johnson syndromes; IV form may cause hypotension, arrhythmias, bradycardia, cardiovascular collapse, CNS depression, respiratory arrest, venous irritation and pain.

Comments: induces hepatic microsomal enzymes; crosses the placenta; significant interpatient variation in dose needed to achieve therapeutic concentration; use caution in renal and hepatic impairment.

Phosphorus (NeurtraPhos, K-Phos)

Actions: electrolyte replacement.

Indications: hypophosphatemia, constipation, colonoscopy preparation.

Dose (acute hypophosphatemia): 5-10 mg/kg/dose IV over 6 hrs.

Dose (maintenance replacement): adults: 1.5-2 gm IV over 24 hrs or 3-4.5

gms/day PO in 3-4 divided doses; ped: 15-45 mg/kg IV over 24 hrs or 30-90 mg/kg/day PO in 3-4 divided doses.
Clearance: kidneys reabsorb 80% of dose.
Adverse effects: may cause tetany, hyperphosphatemia, hyperkalemia, hypocalcemia; IV administration may cause hypotension, renal failure.
Comments: use caution in cardiac and renal impairment patients; recommended infusion rate: <3.1 mg/kg/hr of phosphate.

Physostigmine (Antilirium)
Actions: inhibition of cholinesterase, prolongs central and peripheral cholinergic effects.
Indications: postoperative delirium, tricyclic antidepressant overdose, reversal of CNS effects of anticholinergic drugs, reversal agent for nondepolarizing blockade.
Dose (nondepolarizing blockade reversal): 0.01-0.03 mg/kg IV.
Dose (anticholinergic overdose): adults: 0.5-2 mg IV/IM every 15 minutes until response or adverse occurs (repeat 1-4 mg every 30-60 minutes as life-threatening signs recur); ped: 0.01-0.03 mg/kg/dose IV, repeat every 5-10 minutes to a max total dose of 2 mg or until response or adverse effects occur.
Clearance: metabolized by plasma esterases.
Contraindications: asthma, gangrene, severe cardiovascular disease, mechanical obstruction of GI or GU tract.
Adverse effects: may cause bradycardia, tremor, convulsions, hallucinations, psychiatric or CNS depression, mild ganglionic blockade, cholinergic crisis.
Comments: physostigmine antidote: atropine; crosses blood-brain barrier.

Potassium (KCL)
Actions: electrolyte replacement.
Indications: hypokalemia, digoxin toxicity.
Dose (hypokalemia): adult: 10-20 mEq KCL IV over 30-60 minutes (usual infusion: 10 mEq/hr; max dose 150 mEq/day); ped: 0.5-1 mEq/kg/dose KCL IV given as infusion of 0.5 mEq/kg/hr (max: 1 mEq/kg/hr).
Clearance: renal.
Adverse effects: may cause irritation, pain, phlebitis at infusion site; rapid or central IV infusion may cause cardiac arrhythmias.
Comments: central venous line is preferable for administration.

Prednisolone (Pred Forte)
Actions: decreases inflammation by suppression of migration of polymorphonuclear leukocytes and reversal of increased capillary permeability; suppresses the immune system.
Indications: treatment of a variety disorders, anti-inflammatory, immune suppression, allergic states.
Dose (adult): 5-60 mg/day IV/IM/PO (as sodium phosphate salt).
Dose (ped): 0.1-2 mg/kg/day IV/IM/PO (as sodium phosphate salt) in divided doses 1-4 times/day.
Clearance: renal elimination.
Adverse effects: insomnia, nervousness, indigestion, hirsutism, hyperglycemia, diarrhea, HPA axis suppression.

Procainamide (Pronestyl)
Actions: decreases myocardial excitability and conduction velocity and may depress myocardial contractility, by increasing the electrical stimulation

threshold of the ventricle/ HIS-Purkinje system and direct cardiac effects.

Indications: atrial and ventricular arrhythmias.

Dose (ACLS):

> **Adult: load:** 20-30 mg/min until (1) arrhythmia suppressed, (2) hypotension ensues, (3) the QRS complex widened by 50%, or (4) a total of 1 gm or 17 mg/kg has been given; in refractory VF/VT may give 100 mg IV push every 5 minutes.
>
> **Ped:** load 15 mg/kg IV/IO over 30-60 minutes.

Dose (antiarrhythmic):

> **Adult:** load 50-100 mg IV, repeated every 5 minutes until patient controlled (max dose: 1000 mg); maintenance: 1-6 mg/min infusion.
>
> **Ped:** load 2-6 mg/kg/dose IV over 5 minutes (max dose: 100 mg/dose), repeat dose every 5-10 minutes prn up to total maximum of 15 mg/kg; maintenance dose: 20-80 mcg/kg/min by continuous infusion.

Standard concentration (adult): 2 gm/500 cc D_5W: 30 cc/hr = 2 mg/min.

Therapeutic level: 4-10 mcg/mL.

Clearance: hepatic metabolism to active metabolite; renal elimination.

Contraindications: myasthenia gravis, complete heart block, SLE, Torsades de pointes.

Adverse effects: hypotension, heart block, myocardial depression, ventricular dysrhythmias, lupus, fever, agranulocytosis, GI irritation, lupus-like syndrome, positive Coombs' test, confusion.

Comments: use caution in asymptomatic PVCs, digitalis intoxication, CHF, renal or hepatic impairment;

Prochlorperazine (Compazine)

Actions: blocks dopamine (D_1 and D_2) receptors with neuroleptic and antiemetic effects; antimuscarinic and antihistaminic effects; depresses the reticular activating system.

Indications: management of nausea/vomiting; acute/chronic psychosis.

Dose (antiemetic):

> **Adult:** 2.5-10 mg IV (max: 40 mg/day); 5-10 mg IM every 3-4 hrs prn (max: 40 mg/day); 25 mg PR every 12 hrs prn.
>
> **Ped:** (>10 kg or > 2 yrs): 0.1-0.15 mg/kg/dose IM 3-4 times/day prn.

Clearance: hepatic metabolism; renal and biliary

Adverse effects: extrapyramidal reactions (reversed by diphenhydramine), orthostatic hypotension, altered temperature regulation, neuroleptic malignant syndrome, leukopenia, cholestatic jaundice.

Comments: do not use IV in children; avoid use in patients with severe cardiac or hepatic disease.

Promethazine (Phenergan)

Actions: antagonist of H_1, D_2, muscarinic receptors; antiemetic; sedation.

Indications: allergies, anaphylaxis, nausea and vomiting, sedation, antihistamine, motion sickness.

Dose (antiemetic): adult: 12.5-50 mg IV/IM every 4-6 hrs prn; ped: 0.25-1 mg/kg/dose IV/IM/PR every 4-6 hrs prn.

Clearance: hepatic metabolism; renal elimination.

Adverse effects: may cause mild hypotension, mild anticholinergic effects, extrapyramidal effects; intraarterial injection can cause gangrene

Comments: crosses placenta; may interfere with blood grouping, use only in the management of prolonged vomiting of known etiology.

Propofol (Diprivan)

Actions: increases activity of inhibitory GABA synapses; decreases cerebral metabolic rate for oxygen, cerebral blood flow, and ICP; decreases systemic vascular resistance and blood pressure.

Indications: induction/maintenance of anesthesia, sedation, antiemetic.

Dose (induction): adult (<55 yrs): 2-2.5 mg/kg/ IV; adult (>55 yrs): 1-1.5 mg/kg IV; ped: 2-3.5 mg/kg IV.

Dose (maintenance): adult (<55 yrs): 6-12 mg/kg/hr IV (0.1-0.2 mg/kg/minute); adult (>55 yrs): 3-6 mg/kg/hr IV (0.05-0.1 mg/kg/minute); ped: 100-300 mcg/kg/minute.

Dose (sedation): 20-300 mcg/kg/min continuous infusion, titrate to effect.

Dose (intermittent bolus): 25-50 mg IV increments as needed.

Dose (antiemetic): 10-15 mg IV prn.

Clearance: hepatic metabolism.

Adverse effects: may cause pain during administration (pain is reduced by prior administration of opioids or lidocaine), hypotension, respiratory depression, allergic reactions, CNS depression.

Comments: use slower rate of induction in the elderly; do not administer with blood or blood products.

Propranolol (Inderal)

Actions: nonspecific beta-adrenergic blockade; competitive blockade.

Indications: hypertension, dysrhythmias, myocardial ischemia/infarction, thyrotoxicosis, hypertrophic cardiomyopathy, migraine headache, tetralogy of Fallot cyanotic spells, pheochromocytoma.

Dose (tachyarrhythmias): adults: 1 mg/dose IV repeated every 5 minutes up to a total of 5 mg; peds: 0.01-0.1 mg/kg slow IV.

Dose (tetralogy spell): ped: 0.15-0.25 mg/kg/day slow IV, may repeat prn.

Dose (thyrotoxicosis): adult: 1-3 mg slow IV.

Dose (hypertension): adult: test dose of 0.25-0.5 mg IV, then titrate with 0.5 mg increments every 3-5 minutes.

Clearance: hepatic metabolism; renal elimination.

Adverse effects: may cause bradycardia, AV block, hypoglycemia, bronchospasm, CHF, and drowsiness with low doses.

Comments: abrupt withdrawal can precipitate rebound angina.

Prostaglandin E₁ (Alprostadil)

Actions: vascular smooth muscle and uterine smooth muscle relaxation.

Indications: pulmonary vasodilator, maintenance of patent ductus arteriosus.

Preparation: 500 mcg (1 vial) in 99 cc D_5W (5 mcg/cc); alternate preparation: weight (kg) x 60 = mcg of drug in 20 mL; 1 mL/hr = 0.05 mcg/kg/min.

Dose (neonate): start at 0.05 mcg/kg/min IV (0.01 cc/kg/min); titrate to effect or maximum of 0.6 mcg/kg/min (usual dose range: 0.1-0.4 mcg/kg/min); maintenance: if increases in PaO_2 is noted, decrease to lowest effective dose.

Clearance: pulmonary metabolism; renal elimination.

Adverse effects: hypotension, apnea, flushing, bradycardia, inhibits platelet aggregation; in premature newborns produces apnea..

Comments: rapidly metabolized.

Protamine Sulfate

Actions: antagonist of the anticoagulant effect of heparin.

Indications: reversal of the effects of heparin.

Dose: dose is based on the amount of heparin infused and the time since the last dose or end of infusion (see table):

Time Elapsed	Protamine Dose (mg) to Neutralize 100 units Heparin
Few minutes	1-1.5
30-60 minutes	0.5-0.75
60-120 minutes	0.375-0.5
>2 hours	0.25-0.375

Dose (based on ACT): 1.3 mg/kg of protamine for each 100 units of heparin present as calculated from the ACT.

Adverse effects: hypotension (rapid injection secondary to histamine release), pulmonary hypertension and allergic reactions (seen in patients receiving procaine containing insulin preparations and in some patients allergic to fish), myocardial depression,

Comments: transient reversal of heparin may be followed by rebound heparinization; can cause anticoagulation if given in excess relative to amount of circulating heparin; administer slow IV, not to exceed 50 mg/10 min.

Quinidine Gluconate (Quinaglute)

Actions: class 1A antiarrhythmic agent; decreases myocardial excitability and conduction velocity, and myocardial contractility by decreasing sodium influx during depolarization and potassium efflux in repolarization.

Indications: atrial and ventricular arrhythmias.

Dose (adult): load: 200-400 mg/dose IV given at a rate <10 mg/min (may require 500-750 mg), stop infusion if arrhythmia is gone or toxicity occurs (25%-50% QRS widening, HR >120, or loss of P waves); maintenance: quinidine-gluconate sustained release tablets 324-972 mg PO every 8-12 hr.

Dose (ped): load: 2-10 mg/kg/dose IV given at a rate <10 mg/min every 3-6 hrs as needed; maintenance: 15-60 mg/kg/day PO (quinidine sulfate) in 4-5 divided doses or 6 mg/kg PO every 4-6 hrs.

Therapeutic levels: 3-6 mg/L; toxic levels >8 mg/L.

Clearance: hepatic metabolism; renal elimination.

Adverse effects: may cause GI symptoms, hypotension, tinnitus, TTP, rash, heart block, blood dyscrasias, increased ventricular response in atrial tachyarrhythmias, QT prolongation, CHF, mild anticholinergic effects; may potentiate action of oral anticoagulants, increase in digoxin levels.

Comments: adjust levels in renal failure; test dose is commonly given to assess for idiosyncratic reaction to quinidine; 257 mg quinidine gluconate = 200 mg quinidine sulfate.

Ranitidine (Zantac)

Actions: competitive inhibition of histamine at H_2 receptors of the gastric parietal cells; inhibits gastric acid secretion, gastric volume, hydrogen ion.

Indications: duodenal and gastric ulcers; esophageal reflux; reduction of gastric volume; increasing gastric pH; prevention of acid aspiration

pneumonitis during surgery; prevention of stress ulcers.
Dose (adult): 50-100 mg/dose IV every 6-8 hrs; continuous infusion: 6.25 mg/hr (150 mg over 24 hrs) titrated to gastric pH >4.0 for prophylaxis or >7.0 for treatment; max daily dose: 400 mg/day.
Dose (ped): 2-4 mg/kg/day IV divided every 6-8 hrs; continuous infusion: 1 mg/kg/dose for one dose followed by infusion of 0.1-0.125 mg/kg/hr (or 2.4-3 mg/kg/day); max dose: 400 mg/day.
Dose (neonate): 2 mg/kg/day IV divided every 6-8 hrs; continuous infusion: 1.5 mg/kg/dose load followed by 0.04 mg/kg/hr (or 1 mg/kg/day).
Clearance: renal elimination (70% unchanged).
Adverse effects: may cause headache, GI disturbance, malaise, insomnia, sedation, arthralgia, hepatoxicity.
Comments: adjust dose in renal failure.

Ritodrine (Yutopar)

Actions: beta$_2$ adrenergic agonist; decreases uterine contractility.
Indications: tocolysis (inhibition of preterm labor)
Dose (adult): continuous infusion IV: 0.1-0.35 mg/min.
Clearance: renal.
Contraindications: eclampsia, pulmonary hypertension, hyperthyroidism.
Adverse effects: dose related increases in maternal and fetal heart rate and blood pressure due to beta$_1$ stimulation; may cause pulmonary edema, insulin resistance, potentiation of dysrhythmias and hypotension.
Comments: concomitant use of corticosteriods may lead to pulmonary edema.

Scopolamine (Hyoscine)

Actions: peripheral and central cholinergic (muscarinic) antagonism; increases cardiac output, dries secretions, antagonizes histamine and serotonin.
Indications: antisialagogue, sedative, antiemetic, motion sickness, cycloplegia and mydriasis.
Dose (adult): 0.3-0.65 mg IV/IM; may repeat every 6-8 hrs; alternate dosing: antiemetic effect: 0.2-1 mg; inhibition of salivation: 0.2-0.6 mg; amnestic effect: 0.3-0.65 mg; sedation/tranquilization: 0.6 mg.
Dose (ped): 6 mcg/kg/dose IV/IM; may repeat q6-8 hrs; max: 0.3 mg/dose.
Clearance: hepatic metabolism; renal elimination.
Adverse effects: may cause excitement, delirium, transient tachycardia, hyperthermia, urinary retention, blurred vision, photophobia.
Comments: crosses the placenta and blood-brain barrier; excessive CNS depression can be reversed by physostigmine.

Terbutaline (Brethine)

Actions: selective beta2 adrenergic agonist that relaxes bronchial smooth muscle and peripheral vessels..
Indications: bronchospasm; tocolysis.
Dose (adult): bronchospasm: 0.25 mg SC; repeat in 15-30 min prn, max: 0.5 mg within 4 hr period, 2.5-5 mg/dose PO every 6 hrs 3 times/day.
Dose (ped): 3.5-10 mcg/kg/dose SC every 15-20 min; max: 0.4 mg/dose.
Clearance: hepatic metabolism; renal elimination.
Adverse effects: may cause dysrhythmias, pulmonary edema, hypertension, hypokalemia, nervousness, tremor, headache, nausea, tachycardia, CNS excitement, palpitations.
Comments: paradoxical bronchoconstriction may occur.

Trimethaphan (Arfonad)

Actions: blocks nicotinic receptors at autonomic ganglia (ganglionic blocker); direct-acting vasodilator.

Indications: hypertension; controlled hypertension.

Standard concentration (adult): 500 mg in 500 mL of 5% D_5W.

Dose (adult): 0.5-2 mg/min IV continuous infusion, titrate to effect.

Dose (ped): 50-150 mcg/kg/min IV continuous infusion, titrate to effect.

Clearance: primarily pseudocholinesterase metabolism; renal elimination.

Adverse effects: may cause prolonged hypotension, bradycardia in the elderly, tachycardia in the young, histamine release, urinary retention, mydriasis, tachyphylaxis, respiratory depression, ileus dilation.

Comments: mild decrease in cardiac contractility (useful in patients with dissecting aortic aneurysms); potentiates the effects of succinylcholine.

Tromethamine (THAM)

Actions: organic proton acceptor (buffer); advantage of THAM is that it alkalinizes without increasing pCO_2 and sodium.

Indications: metabolic acidosis.

Dose: dose depends on buffer base deficit; when deficit is known: mL tromethanime (0.3 M solution) = body weight (kg) x base deficit (mEq/L) x 1.1; when base deficit is not known: 3-6 mL/kg/dose IV (1-2 mEq/kg/L).

Dose (metabolic acidosis with cardiac arrest): 3.5-6 mL/kg into large peripheral vein up to 500-10000 mL if needed in adults; max dose: 40 mL/kg/day; continuous infusion: infuse slowly at a rate of 3-15 mL/kg/hr.

Dose (ped): alternate dosing: 1.66-3.33 mL/kg/day; typical initial dose: 3-16 mL/kg/hr IV; max: 40 mL/kg/day IV

Clearance: rapidly excreted by kidneys.

Contraindications: anuria, uremia, chronic respiratory acidosis (neonates).

Adverse effects: apnea, hypoglycemia, hypokalemia, alkalosis, transient hypocalcemia, venospasm, tissue necrosis from infiltration

Comments: use caution in renal impairment; 1 mEq THAM = 3.3 mL = 120 mg tromethamine; avoid infusion via umbilical catheters.

Vasopressin (Pitressin, ADH)

Actions: synthetic analogue of arginine vasopressin; antidiuretic (increases urine osmolality and decreases urine volume); produces contraction of the smooth muscle; vasoconstriction of splanchnic, coronary, muscular, and cutaneous vasculature.

Indications: diabetes insipidus; GI bleeding; pulseless VT/VF; shock refractory to fluid and vasopressor therapy.

Standard conc. 200 units vasopressin in 250 cc D_5W (0.8 units/mL).

Dose (GI hemorrhage): adult: initial: 0.2-0.4 units/min then titrate; ped: initial: 0.1-0.3 units/minute, then titrate dose as needed (0.002-0.008 units/kg/minute), continue at same dosage if bleeding stops for 12 hrs, then taper off over 24-48 hrs.

Dose (diabetes insipidus): adult: 5-10 units IM/SC 2-4 times /day as needed; ped: 2.5-5 units IM/SC 2-4 times/day.

Dose (refractory shock): adult: 0.04 units/min infusion.

Dose (cardiac arrest): adult: 40 units IV/IO/ET.

Clearance: hepatic and renal metabolism; renal elimination.

Contraindications: chronic nephritis with nitrogen retention.

Adverse effects: may cause oliguria; water intoxication; pulmonary edema; hypertension, arrhythmias, myocardial ischemia, abdominal cramps, anaphylaxis, contraction of gallbladder, urinary bladder, or uterus; vertigo or nausea; tremor.

Comments: patients with coronary artery disease are often treated with concurrent nitroglycerin; do not abruptly discontinue IV infusion.

Verapamil (Calan)

Actions: blockade of calcium channels in heart; prolongation of PR interval with negative inotropy and chronotropy; systemic and coronary vasodilation.

Indications: supraventricular tachycardia, atrial fibrillation or flutter, Wolff-Parkinson-White syndrome.

Dose (adult): 2.5 -10 mg (75-150 mcg/kg) IV over 2 minutes. If no response in 30 minutes, repeat 5-10 mg.

Dose (ped): 0.1-0.3 mg/kg IV, repeat once if no response in 30 minutes.

Adverse effects: may cause severe bradycardia, AV block, excessive hypotension, congestive heart failure. May increase ventricular response to atrial fibrillation or flutter in patients with accessory tracts.

Vitamin K (Phytonadione)

Indications: hypoprothrombinemia caused by vitamin K deficiency or anticoagulant-induced (overdose); hemorrhagic disease of newborn.

Dose (vitamin K deficiency):
    Adult: 10 mg IV/IM as single dose; 5-25 mg/day PO.
    Ped: 1-22 mg/dose IV/IM as a single dose.

Dose (oral anticoagulant overdose):
    Adult and ped: 2.5-10 mg/dose IV/IM/PO/SC; may be repeated 12-48 hr after PO dose or 6-8 hr after parenteral dose.
    Infant: 1-2 mg/dose IM/IV/SC every 4-8 hrs.

Clearance: hepatic metabolism.

Adverse effects: may cause flushing, dizziness, hypotension, anaphylaxis.

Comments: IV administration should be reserved for emergency situations.

Warfarin (Coumadin)

Actions: interferes with hepatic synthesis of vitamin K dependent coagulation factors (II, VII, IX, X), prothrombin, protein C, protein S; inhibits thrombosis formation or progression; no direct effect on established thrombus.

Indications: anticoagulation.

Dose (adult): 5-15 mg/day PO for 2-5 days, then adjust dose according to results of prothrombin time; usual maintenance dose ranges 2-10 mg/day.

Dose (ped): 0.05-0.34 mg/kg/day PO.

Therapeutic range: prothrombin time should be 1.5-2.5 times the control or INR should be 2-3 times based upon indication.

Contraindications: severe liver or kidney disease; open wounds; uncontrolled bleeding; GI ulcers; neurosurgical procedures; malignant hypertension; pregnancy.

Clearance: hepatic metabolism; renal elimination.

Adverse effects: fever, skin lesions, skin necrosis, anorexia, nausea, vomiting, diarrhea, hemorrhage, and hemoptysis.

Comments: the antidote is vitamin K and fresh frozen plasma.

Drip Rates

cc/hr = (mcg/kg/min x 60 x wt(kg))/mcg/cc

mcg/kg/min = [(cc/hr) x (mcg/cc)]/60 x wt(kg)

Rule of 6: Intravenous infusion solution preparation

Simplified equation: 0.6 x body weight (kg) = amount (mg) of drug to be added to IV fluid to total volume of 100 mL. When infused at 1 mL/hr, then it will deliver the drug at a rate of 0.1 mcg/kg/minute.

Complex equation: 6 x desired dose (mcg/kg/min) x body weight (kg) divided by desired rate (mL/hr) is the mg added to make 100 mL of solution.

Cardiovascular Physiology

Cardiopulmonary/Hemodynamic Parameters		
Parameter	Formula	Normal Range
RA, CVP		0-10 mmHg
LA or LVEDP		4-12 mmHg
RV		15-30/0-10 mmHg
PAS/ PAD		15-30/5-15 mmHg
MPAP	PAD + (PAS-PAD/3)	10-20 mmHg
PCWP		4-15 mmHg
MAP	DBP + (SBP-DBP/3) or	75-110 mmHg
SVR	(MAP-CVP x 79.9)/CO	900-1500 dynes/sec/cm5
PVR	(MPAP-PCWP x 79.9)/CO	50-150 dynes/sec/cm5
CaO_2	(Hgbx1.34)SaO_2+(PaO_2x 0.0031)	16-22 mL O_2/dL blood
CvO_2	(Hgbx1.34)SvO_2+(PaO_2x 0.0031)	12-77 mL O_2/dL blood
C(a-v)O_2	(Hemoglobin x 1.34)(SaO_2 - SvO_2)	3.5-5.5 mL O_2/dL blood
SV	CO x 1000/HR	60-100 mL
CO	SV x HR=VO_2/C(a-v)O_2x10	4-8 liters/min
CI	CO/body surface area	2.5-4.0 L/min/m2
DO_2	CaO_2 x CO x 10	700-1400 mL/min
PAO_2	FIO_2 x (PB-PH_2O)-($PaCO_2$/0.8)	
A-a gradient	[(713)FIO_2-$PaCO_2$ (1.25)]-PaO_2	2-22 mmHg (RA)
Qs/Qt	(CcO_2-CaO_2)/(CcO_2-CvO_2)	0.05 or less
Cr Clearance	(Urine Cr/Serum Cr) x 70	Male=125; Female=105
PaO_2	102-(age/3)	
SvO_2 (mixed)	SaO_2-VO_2/(CO x Hemoglobin)(13.4)	68-77%
VO_2	Hb x 1.34 x CO x 10 x (SaO_2-SvO_2)	
Fick equation (VO_2)	CO x C(a-v)O_2	225-275 mL/min
Body Mass Index	wt (kg)/ht (m)^2	Obese >28;Morbidly >35
V_D/V_T	($PaCO2$-P_ECO_2)/$PaCO_2$	Normal: 33%.

Electrocardiograms			
Interpretation format	**Normal intervals (each small block=0.04 sec)**		
1. Rate	P-R: 0.12-0.20 msec	Q-T (msec)	HR (bpm)
2. Rhythm	QRS: 0.06-0.10 msec	0.33-0.43	60
3. Intervals		0.31-0.41	70
4. Axis		0.29-0.38	80
5. Hypertrophy		0.28-0.36	90
6. Infarction/ischemia		0.27-0.35	100
7. Ectopy			

Lead Changes Due to Injury/Ischemia With Artery/Area of Damage			
EKG lead Changes	**Injury/Infarct Related Artery**	**Area of Damage**	**Associated Complications**
V1-V2	LCA: LAD (septal branch)	Septum, His bundle, bundle branches	Infranodal block and BBBs
V3-V4	LCA: LAD (diagonal branch)	Anterior wall LV	LV dysfunction, CHF, BBBs, complete heart block, PVC
V5-V6 plus 1 and aVL	LCA: circumflex	High lateral wall LV	LV dysfunction, AV nodal block in some
II, III, aVF	RCA: posterior descending branch	Inferior wall LV, posterior wall LV	Hypotension, sensitivity to nitroglycerin and morphine
V4R (II, III, aVF)	RCA: proximal branches	RV, inferior wall LV, posterior wall LV	Hypotension, supranodal and AV-nodal blocks, atrial fib/flutter, PACs
V1-V4 (marked depression)	Either LCA (circumflex) or RCA (posterior descending branch)	Posterior wall LV	LV dysfunction
LCA: left coronary artery; RCA: right coronary artery; LAD: left anterior descending; LV: left ventricle; RV: right ventricle; BBB: bundle branch block			

Electrolyte Abnormalities On Electrocardiography

Hyperkalemia	Peaked T waves, QRS widening, P-R prolongation, loss of P waves, loss of R wave amp, ST depression
Hypokalemia	T wave flattening/inversion, prominent U wave, increased P wave, P-R prolongation, ST depression
Hypercalcemia	Shortening of QT interval, shortened ST segment
Hypocalcemia	Prolongation of QT interval
Hypermagnesemia	Prolonged PR interval, widened QRS
Hypomagnesemia	Increased PR and QT intervals, myocardial irritability, potentiation of digoxin toxicity

Localization of Myocardial Infarctions

Location of MI	Q wave or ST Change	Reciprocal ST Depression
Anterior	V2-V4 (poor R wave prog)	II, III, AVF
Antero-Septal	V1-V3	
Antero-Lateral	I, AVL, V4-V6	
Lateral	I, AVL, V5-V6	V1, V3
Inferior	II, III, AVF	I, AVL
Posterior	Tall R/T waves V1-V3	V1-V3
Subendocardial (Q wave >0.04 sec >25% the height of the R wave)	ST depression in ant leads or inferior leads	

Electrocardiographic Criteria for Cardiac Hypertrophy

LVH Criteria	RVH Criteria	Atrial Hypertrophy
RV5 or RV6 >26 mm SV1 or SV2 + RV5 or RV6 >35 mm R I +S III >25 mm RaVL >13 mm RaVF >20 mm	R>S in V1 or V3 qR in V1 or V3 RAD Wide QRS	RAH: diphasic P with tall initial component LAH: diphasic P with persistent S in V4-V6 wide terminal component

Bundle Branch Block (QRS >0.12 sec)

Left BBB	Right BBB
No septal Q waves in V4-V6, I, AVL RR' or M pattern of QRS in I, aVL, V4-V6 2° ST, T wave change I, aVL, V4-V6	RR' or M pattern of QRS in V1-V3 Deep/round S waves in I, aVL,V4-V6 2° ST, T wave change in V1-V3

Atrioventricular Heart Blocks

1. **First-degree heart block:** PR interval >0.20 sec.
2. **Second degree heart block**
   A. **Mobitz Type I (Wenckebach):** PR interval increases until QRS dropped.
   B. **Mobitz Type II (infra His):** PR interval constant until QRS dropped.
3. **Third degree heart block:** no AV conduction (P has no relation to QRS).

Electrocardiogram Abnormalities

1. **QT interval abnormalities**
   A. **Prolonged QT interval:** hypocalcemia, hypokalemia, hypomagnesemia, acute MI, acute myocarditis, procainamide, quinidine, tricyclics.
   B. **Shortened QT interval:** hypercalcemia, digitalis.
2. **Axis deviation**
   A. **LAD:** LVH, left ant hemiblock, inferior wall MI.
   B. **RAD:** RVH, left post hemiblock, dextrocardia, pulmonary infarct, right bundle branch block, lateral MI.
3. **Cardiac disorders**
   A. **Pericarditis:** diffuse ST elevation concave upward and/or diffuse PR depression and/or diffuse T wave inversion.
   B. **Orthotopic heart transplantation:** the patient's original SA node often remains with the original atria, therefore, two P waves can be seen.
   C. **IHSS:** ventricular hypertrophy, LAD, septal Q waves.
   D. **Myocarditis:** conduction blocks.
   E. **P mitrale:** bifid P wave is associated with left atrial hypertrophy, as seen in mitral stenosis.
4. **Pulmonary disorders**
   A. **COPD:** low voltage, RAD, poor R wave progression.
   B. **Chronic cor pulmonale:** P pulmonale (tall peaked P wave associated with right atrial enlargement) and right ventricular hypertrophy.
   C. **Acute pulmonary embolism:** right ventricular hypertrophy with strain; right bundle branch block; prominent S wave in I, Q wave in III, and inverted T wave in III; may cause non-specific ST changes and atrial dysrhythmias.
5. **Head injuries:** dysrhythmias and electrocardiographic abnormalities in the T wave, U wave, ST segment, and QT interval are common following head injuries but are not necessarily associated with cardiac injury; they likely represent altered autonomic function.
6. **Drugs**
   A. **Digitalis toxicity:** ventricular arrhythmias, conduction abnormalities.
   B. **Quinidine/procainamide:** prolonged QT, flattened T wave, QRS widening.
7. **Hypothermia:** bradycardia, AV junctional, elevated J point (J wave; also called Osborne wave), prolong QT.

EKG Detection of Perioperative Myocardial Ischemia

1. **Single lead EKG sensitivity:** V5 (75%), V4 (61%), V6 (37%), V3 (33%), II (24%), and all others <14%.
2. **Combination leads sensitivity:** leads II and V5 increase sensitivity to 85%, leads V4 and V5 increase sensitivity to 90%, increasing to 96% by combining

II, V4, and V5, and to 100% when five leads were used (V2-V5 and II).

Pacemakers

1. **Preoperative pacemaker evaluation**
   A. Determine the indications for the pacemaker.
   B. Determine type of generator, date placed, and the preset rate.
   C. Define pacemaker function.
   D. The patient should be questioned for history of vertigo, syncope, light headedness, or return of any pre-pacemaker symptoms which may reflect dysfunction of the pacemaker.
   E. Labs: serum electrolytes (hypokalemia can increase the negative cell membrane potential increasing threshold for pacemaker to capture).
   F. Chest x-ray: looking for a dislodged electrode or fracture, and the make and model, if available.
2. **Intraoperative management**
   A. The grounding pad for the electrocautery should be placed as far away from pulse generator as possible.
   B. Monitor heart rate during electrocautery with a stethoscope, pulse oximetry, or arterial line.
   C. A magnet placed over the pulse generator will convert a demand (VVI) pacemaker into an asynchronous (VOO) pacemaker.
3. **Indications for temporary pacemaker:** symptomatic sick sinus syndrome, symptomatic hypertensive carotid sinus syndrome with cardio-inhibitory (not just vasodepressor) response, Mobitz type 2 block, acute MI with RBBB or LBBB, comatose trauma patient with bifascicular block, trifascicular block, symptomatic beta blocker overdose.

Nomenclature for Description of Pacemaker Function				
First letter: chamber paced	Second letter: chamber sensed	Third letter: generator response	Fourth letter: program functions	Fifth letter: antitachycardia functions
V-Ventricle	V-Ventricle	T-Triggered	P-Program[2]	B-Bursts
A-Atrium	A-Atrium	I-Inhibited	M-Multi-program	N-Normal rate competition[4]
D-Dual chamber	D-Dual chamber	D-Dual chamber	C-Communicating[3]	S-Scanning[5]
	O-None (Async)	O-None (Async)	O-None (fixed function)	E-External[6]
		R-Reverse Functions[1]		

1. Pacemaker activated at fast rates only.
2. Rate and/or output only.
3. Telemetry, interrogation (P or M implicit).
4. Paces at normal rate upon sensing tachyarrhythmia (underdrive pacing).
5. Scanning response (such as time extrasystoles).
6. External control (activated by a magnet, radio-frequency, or other means).

Respiratory Physiology

1. **Effects of anesthesia on respiratory function**
   A. FRC is reduced (with general anesthesia in the supine position).
   B. Change in breathing pattern (diaphragmatic breathing)
   C. Reduced alveolar ventilation, depressed CO_2 response curve, reduced hypoxic respiratory drive
   D. Increased shunt (increased (A-a O_2) difference)
   E. Increased dead space (physiological dead space)
   F. Reduced compliance; increased resistance
   G. Increased V/Q abnormality (increased (A-a O_2) difference)
   H. Cilial paralysis, mucosal drying
   I. Depressed airway reflexes
2. **Pulmonary function tests**
   A. **Predicted vital capacity**
      1. Women. (21.78 - [0.101 x age in years]) x height in cm.
      2. Men. (27.63 - [0.112 x age in years]) x height in cm.
   B. **PFTs associated with increased pulmonary morbidity**
      1. FEV_1 < 2 liters.
      2. FEV_1/FVC < 0.5.
      3. Vital capacity < 15 mL/kg.
      4. Maximum breathing capacity < 50% of predicted.
3. **Hemoglobin dissociation curve** (relationship between PaO_2 and SaO_2)
   A. **Factors shifting the curve to the right** (decreasing Hb affinity for O_2).
      1. Increasing hydrogen ion concentration (decreased pH).
      2. Increased 2,3-DPG concentration.
      3. Increased body temperature.
   B. **P_{50}** (oxygen tension at which hemoglobin is 50% saturated)
      1. Normal adult hemoglobin. 26.6 mmHg.
      2. Fetal hemoglobin. 19 mmHg.
      3. Parturient maternal hemoglobin. 30 mmHg.
      4. Sickle hemoglobin. 31 mmHg.
      5. Erythrocytes stored for 28 days at 1-6 °C. 17 mmHg.

PFT Factors Associated With Increased Perioperative Risk			
Factor	Abd Surgery	Thoracotomy	Lob/Pneumonectomy
FVC	< 70%	< 70%	< 50% or < 2 L
FEV_1	< 70%	< 1 L	< 2 L (pneumo); < 1 L (lobe)
FEV_1/FVC	< 50%	< 50%	< 50%
$FEF_{25-75\%}$	< 50%	< 50%	
RV/TLC			> 40%
$PaCO_2$	> 45-50 mmHg	> 45-50 mmHg	> 45-50 mmHg
PaO_2			<50 mmHg
VO_2			< 15 mL/kg/min
Percent values are percent of predicted			

Pulmonary Function Tests				
Test	Normal Adult	Comment	Obstructive Disease	Restrictive Disease
TLC	5-6 L	Distinguishes between restrictive (⇓) and obstructive (⇑)	0/+	-
RV	33% of TLC	Increased in emphysema	+	-
FVC	4-5 L or >80*	Indicates pulmonary reserve	0/-	-
FEV1	75% of FVC or >80*	Large airway flow	0/-	-
FEF25-75%	3-5 L/min or >75*	Small airway flow	-	0
MVV	70-100 L/min	Measure of endurance or fatigue	0/-	-
DLCO	80-100%	Represents functional lung area	-	0/-
0 = normal; - = decreased; + = increased				

TLC: total lung capacity; RV: residual volume; FVC: forced vital capacity; FEV1: forced expiratory volume in the first 1 second; FEF 25-75%: forced expiratory flow from 25-75%; MVV: maximal voluntary ventilation; DLCO: diffusion capacity of carbon monoxide

Pediatric and Adult Respiratory Parameters				
Parameter	Neonate	Infant	5 years	Adult
Resp Rate	40-50	24-30	20	15
TV (mL/kg)	6	6	6	6
Dead space	2 cc/kg			2 cc/kg
FRC (cc/kg)	25	25	35	35
O_2 consumption (cc/kg/min)	5-6			2-3
Alveolar ventilation	130 cc/kg			60 cc/kg
VA/FRC	4.5:1			1.5:1
Closing volume				Increased
Vital Capacity	35 cc/kg			60-70 cc/kg
FRC: functional residual capacity; TV: tidal volume				

Oxygenation and Ventilation

1. Major causes of hypoxemia
   A. Low inspired oxygen concentration (decreased FiO_2).
   B. Hypoventilation.
   C. Shunt (normal shunt about 2%): hypoxemia caused by shunt cannot be overcome by increasing the inspired oxygen concentration.

    D. Ventilation perfusion (V/Q) mismatch: common causes of V/Q mismatch are atelectasis, patient positioning, bronchial intubation, one-lung ventilation, bronchospasm, pneumonia, mucus plugging, acute respiratory distress syndrome (ARDS) and airway obstruction.

    E. Diffusion abnormalities.

    F. Cardiac output - oxygen carrying capacity abnormalities (CO/O_2 capacity): as cardiac output or oxygen carrying capacity decrease, oxygen delivery will decrease resulting in hypoxemia.

2. **Causes of hypercarbia**

    A. Hypoventilation: common causes include muscle paralysis, inadequate mechanical ventilation, inhalational anesthetics, and narcotics.

    B. Increased CO_2 production: including malignant hyperthermia, fever, and thyrotoxicosis.

    C. Iatrogenic: common examples include sodium bicarbonate administration and depletion of the CO_2 absorbent.

3. **Methods to improve oxygenation**

    A. Increase FiO_2.

    B. Increase minute ventilation.

    C. Increase cardiac output (and increase oxygen delivery to tissues).

    D. Increase oxygen carrying capacity (hemoglobin).

    E. Optimize V/Q relationships.

    F. Cardiopulmonary bypass.

    G. Decrease oxygen consumption from pain, shivering, or fever.

Arterial Blood Gases

1. **Golden rules of ABGs**

    A. Decreased $PaCO_2$

        1. pH increases 0.1 unit and serum bicarbonate decreases 2 mEq/l for each acute 10 mmHg decrease in $PaCO_2$.

        2. pH will nearly normalize if hypocarbia is sustained.

        3. Serum bicarbonate will decrease 5-6 mEq/l for each chronic 10 mmHg decrease in $PaCO_2$.

    B. Increased $PaCO_2$

        1. pH decreases 0.05 unit and serum bicarbonate increases 1 mEq/l for each acute 10 mmHg increase in $PaCO_2$.

        2. pH will nearly normalize if hypercarbia is sustained.

        3. Serum bicarbonate will increase 3-4 mEq/l for each chronic 10 mmHg increase in $PaCO_2$.

    C. pH change of 0.15 corresponds to BE change of 10 mEq/l.

2. **Total body bicarbonate deficit** = base deficit (mEq/L) x patient wt (kg) x 0.4.

3. **Bicarbonate deficit** (HCO_3 deficit) = (total body water) x (24 - HCO_3).

4. **Base excess (BE) or deficit**

    A. BE = HCO_3 + 10(pH - 7.40) - 24.

    B. Base excess or deficit is a calculated value that gives an estimation of "acid load."

    C. Negative values of base excess (i.e., deficit) represent metabolic acidosis, and positive values indicated metabolic alkalosis.

5. During apnea, $PaCO_2$ increases 5-6 during the first minute and 3-4 for every minute thereafter.

6. **Henderson-Hasselbach equation**
   A. $pH = 6.1 + \log[(HCO_3)/(0.03 \times PaCO_2)]$
   B. Modified equation. $(H+) = [24 \times pCO_2] / HCO_3$
   C. $pH = pk + \log A^-/HA$
7. **PaO_2 age adjustment:** $PaO_2 = 102 - [\text{age in years}/3]$
8. **Anion gap**
   A. Anion gap = $Na - (Cl + HCO_3)$
   B. Normal anion gap = 8-16 mEq/l

Normal Arterial Blood Gases Values

	Newborn	1-24 mths	7-19 yrs	Adult	Mixed Venous	Venous
pH	7.37	7.40	7.39	7.37-7.44	7.31-7.41	7.31-7.41
PaO_2	15	90	96	80-100	35-40	30-50
$PaCO_2$	33	34	37	35-45	41-51	40-52
O_2 Sat				>98	60-80	60-85
HCO_3	20	20	22	22-26	22-26	22-28

Causes of Metabolic Acidosis

Increased anion gap (S.L.U.M.P.E.D.)	Normal anion gap
Salicylates	Renal causes
Lactate	Renal tubular acidosis
Uremic toxins	Carbonic anhydrase inhibitors
Methanol	Lysine or arginine HCl
Paraldehyde	GI bicarbonate loss
Ethanol/ethylene glycol	Diarrhea
Diabetic ketoacidosis	Pancreatic fistula
	Ureterosigmoidostomy
	Addition of HCl
	Ammonium chloride

Airway Management

Endotracheal Intubation

1. **Airway innervation**
   A. **Nasal mucosa:** sphenopalatine ganglion a branch of the middle division of cranial nerve V (trigeminal Nerve). The ganglion is located on the lateral wall posterior to the middle turbinate.
   B. **Uvula, tonsils, superior pharynx:** innervated by continued branches from the sphenopalatine ganglion.
   C. **Oral pharynx and supraglottic area:** innervated by branches of CN IX (glossopharyngeal nerve). These branches include lingual, pharyngeal, and tonsillar nerves.
   D. **Trachea:** innervated by the recurrent laryngeal nerve.
   E. **Larynx:** sensory and motor is from the Vagus (CN X)
      1. **Sensory:** above the vocal folds innervated by the internal branch of the superior laryngeal nerve; below the vocal folds innervated by the recurrent laryngeal nerve.
      2. **Motor:** all muscles are supplied by the recurrent laryngeal nerve except for the cricothyroid muscle which is supplied by the external branch of the superior laryngeal nerve.

2. **Common indications for endotracheal intubation:** provide patent airway, protection from aspiration, facilitate positive-pressure ventilation, operative position other than supine, operative site near or involving the upper airway, airway maintenance by mask is difficult, disease involving the upper airway, one-lung ventilation, altered level of consciousness, tracheobronchial toilet, severe pulmonary or multisystem injury.

3. **Confirmation of endotracheal Intubation**
   A. Direct visualization of the ET tube passing though the vocal cords.
   B. Carbon dioxide in exhaled gases (documentation of end-tidal CO_2 in at least three consecutive breaths).
   C. Bilateral breath sounds.
   D. Absence of air movement during epigastric auscultation.
   E. Condensation (fogging) of water vapor in the tube during exhalation.
   F. Refilling of reservoir bag during exhalation.
   G. Maintenance of arterial oxygenation.
   H. Chest x-ray: the tip of ET tube should be between the carina and thoracic inlet or approximately at the level of the aortic notch or at the level of T5.

4. **Extubation criteria**

NIF > -20 cm H_2O	Resting min vent < 10 l/min
RR < 30/min	LOC stable or improving
TV > 5 cc/kg	TV/RR > 10
VC > 10 cc/kg	Qs/Qt < 20%
PaO_2 > 65-70 mm (FIO_2 < 40%)	Pmep > +40 cm H_2O
$PaCO_2$ < 50 mm	Vd/Vt < 0.6

5. **Complications of endotracheal intubation**
   A. **Complications occurring during intubation:** aspiration, dental damage (chip tooth), laceration of the lips or gums, laryngeal injury, esophageal intubation, endobronchial intubation, activation of the sympathetic nervous system (high BP and HR), bronchospasm.
   B. **Complications occurring after extubation:** aspiration, laryngospasm,

transient vocal cord incompetence, glottic or subglottic edema, pharyngitis or tracheitis.

6. **Endotracheal tube recommendations**

   A. **Endotracheal tube size** (mm): for children older then 2 years ETT can be estimated by: Age/4 + 4.

   B. **Length of Insertion (cm) of ETT**
      1. Under 1 year: 6 + Wt(kg).
      2. Over 2 years: 12 + Age/2.
      3. Multiply internal diameter (mm) of ETT by 3 to give insertion (cm).
      4. Add 2-3 cm for nasal tube.

   C. **Pediatrics:** generally use uncuffed tubes in patients under 10 years. When a cuff tube is used maintain endotracheal leak at 15-20 cm H_2O.

Endotracheal Tube Sizes and Laryngoscope Blade Size				
Age	Laryngoscope	Endotracheal Tube Size (mm)	Distance at Teeth (cm)	Suction Catheter (F)
Neonate <1000 g	Miller 0	2.5	6.5-7.0	5
Neonate 1000-2000 g		3	7-8	5-6
Neonate 2000-3000 g		3.0-3.5	8-9	6-7
Term Infant	Miller 0-1 Wis-Hipple 1 Robertshaw 0	3.0-3.5	9	7
6 months		3.5-4.0	10	8
1 year	Wis-Hipple 1.5 Robertshaw 1	4.0-4.5	11	8
2 years	Miller 2 Flagg 2	4.5-5.0	12	8
4 years		5.0-5.5	14	10
6 years		5.5	15	10
8 years	Miller2-3 Macintosh 2	6	16	10
10 years		6.5	17	12
12 years	Macintosh 3	7	18	12
Adolescent/ Adult	Macintosh 3 Miller 3	7.0-8.0	20	12

Endotracheal Intubation Under Anesthesia

1. **Preparation for intubation**
   A. **Preoperative evaluation** of the airway will help determine the route (oral or nasal) and method (awake or anesthetized) for tracheal intubation. See preoperative evaluation section for airway exam.
   B. **Equipment:** laryngoscope with working light, endotracheal tubes of appropriate sizes, malleable stylet, oxygen supply, functioning suction catheter, functioning IV, and appropriate anesthetic drugs.
   C. **Cricoid pressure (Sellick's maneuver):** used to minimize the spillage of gastric contents into the pharynx during the period of time from induction of anesthesia (unconsciousness) to successful placement of a cuffed tracheal tube. An assistant's thumb and index finger exert downward pressure on the cricoid cartilage (approximately 5 kg pressure) so as to displace the cartilaginous cricothyroid ring posteriorly and thus compress the esophagus against the underlying cervical vertebrae.
   D. Induction of anesthesia prior to tracheal intubation may include injected and/or inhaled anesthetic drugs.
2. **Orotracheal intubation**
   A. **Head position:** place the head in the "sniffing" position if there is no cervical spine injury. The sniffing position is characterized by flexion of the cervical spine and extension of the head at the atlanto-occipital joint (achieved by placing pads under the occiput to raise the head 8-10 cm). This position serves to align the oral, pharyngeal, and laryngeal axes such that the passage from the lips to the glottic opening is most nearly a straight line. The height of the OR table should be adjusted to bring the patient's head to the level of the anesthesiologist's xiphoid cartilage.
   B. Hold the laryngoscope in the palm of the left hand and introduce the blade into the right side of the patient's mouth. Advance the blade posteriorly and toward the midline, sweeping the tongue to the left. Check that the lower lip is not caught between the lower incisors and the laryngoscope blade. The placement of the blade is dependent on the blade used.
      1. **Macintosh (curve) blade:** the tip of the curved blade is advanced into the valleculum (the space between the base of the tongue and the pharyngeal surface of the epiglottis).
      2. **Miller (straight) blade:** the tip of the straight blade is passed beneath the laryngeal surface of the epiglottis, epiglottis is then lifted to expose the vocal cords.
   C. Regardless of the blade used, lift the laryngoscope upward and forward, in the direction of the long axis of the handle, to bring the larynx into view. Do not use the upper incisors as a fulcrum for leverage because this action may damage the upper incisors and may push the larynx out of sight.
   D. The vocal cords should be visualized prior to endotracheal placement. The glottic opening is recognized by its triangular shape and pale white vocal cords. Posteriorly, the vocal cords terminate in the arytenoid cartilages. The tube should be seen to pass between the cords, anterior to the arytenoids. Insert the tube into the pharynx with the right hand from the right side of the mouth; it should pass without resistance through the vocal cords (about 1-2 cm). The endotracheal tube cuff should lie in the upper trachea but beyond the larynx.
   E. Once the endotracheal tube is in place, inflate the cuff, confirm endotracheal intubation and secure the endotracheal tube. In order to minimize the pressure transmitted to the tracheal mucosa, the cuff should

be inflated with the least amount of air necessary to create a seal during positive pressure ventilation. For patients intubated outside the operating room, obtain a portable chest x-ray following intubation to confirm tube placement and bilateral lung expansion.

3. Nasotracheal intubation

A. A vasoconstrictor should be applied before nasal instrumentation. After anesthesia is induced the mask ventilation is established, the endotracheal tube can be placed.

B. Generously lubricate the nare and endotracheal tube. Soften the endotracheal tube tip by immersing it in hot water. The endotracheal tube should be advanced through the nose directly backward toward the nasopharynx with the Murphy eye orientated anteriorly facing the epiglottis. A loss of resistance marks the entry into the oropharynx.

C. The laryngoscope and Magill forceps can be used to guide the endotracheal tube into the trachea under direct vision (if needed). A fiberoptic bronchoscope can be utilized to direct the tube into the trachea.

4. Rapid sequence induction/intubation

A. **Indications:** patients who are at risk for aspiration (e.g., history of recent meal, gastroesophageal reflux, pregnancy, trauma) and there is reasonable certainty that intubation should not be difficult.

B. **Method**

1. Nonparticulate antacids, H_2-blockers and metoclopramide may be used preoperatively to decrease the acidity and volume of gastric secretions.

2. Equipment similar to that for any intubation but commonly includes several endotracheal tubes with stylet and cuff-inflation syringe in place, laryngoscope blades, functioning suction, and a patent IV.

3. Preoxygenate with 100% oxygen by mask. Four maximal breaths of 100% oxygen over 30 seconds is as effective as breathing 100% oxygen spontaneously for 3-5 minutes.

4. Premedicate as appropriate (fentanyl, atropine, lidocaine, defasiculating agent).

C. Induction is accomplished with any induction agent. Just before administration of the induction agent, cricoid pressure (Sellick's maneuver) should be applied.

D. Muscle relaxant is usually given to help facilitate intubation. Succinylcholine (1-1.5 mg/kg; use 2.0 mg/kg for infants and children) given immediately after the induction agent. Once the induction agent and muscle relaxant are given, there should be no attempt to ventilate the patient by mask.

E. Intubation should be performed as soon as jaw relaxation has occurred. Cricoid pressure should be maintained until confirmation of tracheal placement of the endotracheal tube has ben confirmed. If the first attempt to intubate fails, cricoid pressure should be maintained continuously during all subsequent maneuvers, while mask ventilation with 100% oxygen is administered.

Conscious Intubation

1. Consideration should be given for patients with suspected or previous history of a difficult intubation, acute processes that may comprise the airway, mandibular fractures or other significant facial deformities, morbid obesity, or cancer involving the larynx.

2. Discuss with the patient the indications, reasons, and the plan.

3. **Preparation:** as with all intubations, appropriate equipment, etc, should be readily available. A plan (and a back-up plan) should be formulated.
4. **Preparing the patient:** consider premedicating with drying agent (i.e., glycopyrrolate 0.2 mg IV) 30 minutes before the procedure. If considering a nasal intubation, give 4 drops of 0.25% Norsynephrine to each nare to help minimize bleeding. Other vasoconstrictors include oxymetazoline (Afrin) and cocaine. After standard monitors are placed consider sedation (midazolam, fentanyl, etc.) and titrate to effect.
5. **Topical anesthesia** of the upper airway can be accomplished with various agents (see table) and/or nerve blocks.
6. **Airway nerve blocks**
   A. **Sphenopalatine ganglion** (nasal mucosa)
      1. Cotton pledgets soaked with anesthetic solution (usually 20% benzocaine or 4% lidocaine) are placed in the nasal cavity at a 30 degree cephalad angulation to follow the middle turbinate back to the mucosa overlying the sphenoid bone.
      2. A second set of pledgets is introduced through the nares and passed along the turbinates to the posterior end of the nasal passage.
      3. The pledgets should be left in place for at least 2-3 minutes to allow adequate diffusion of local anesthetic.
   B. **Lesser and pharyngeal palatine nerves**
      1. **Landmarks:** 1 cm medial to the third maxillary molar and 1 cm anterior to the junction of the hard and soft palates (usually 0.5 cm in diameter).
      2. Place a cotton pledget soaked with anesthetic solution on this site and wait 1 minute (provides topical anesthesia).
      3. Using a 25 g spinal needle create a 90 degree bend 3 cm from the tip. Probe the mucosa with the needle to find the a palatine foramen (usually up to 3), angulate the needle 15 degrees medially and advance 3 cm up the canal. After negative aspiration, inject 1-3 cc of 1-2% lidocaine with epinephrine.
   C. **Glossopharyngeal nerve:** insert a 25 g spinal needle into the base of the posterior tonsillar pillar. After negative aspiration, inject 2-3 cc of 1-2% lidocaine with epinephrine. Repeat block on opposite side.
   D. **Superior laryngeal nerve**
      1. Place the patient supine with the neck extended.
      2. Find the thyrohyoid membrane (a soft depression between the hyoid and thyroid bones) and displace the hyoid bone laterally toward the side to be blocked.
      3. Insert a 25 g needle off the greater cornu of the hyoid bone, inferiorly, and advance 2-3 mm. As the needle passes through the thyrohyoid membrane, a slight loss of resistance is felt. Inject 2-3 cc of 1-2 % lidocaine with epinephrine. Repeat block on opposite side.
   E. **Translaryngeal (transtracheal) nerve block**
      1. Landmarks: cricothyroid membrane (located between the thyroid cartilage superiorly and the cricoid cartilage inferiorly).
      2. Insert a 20 g angiocath, bevel up, at the upper edge of cricoid cartilage in the midline. Aspirate for air to confirm placement. Remove the needle, leaving only the angiocatheter. Inject 3-5 cc of 2-4% lidocaine solution at end inspiration. This will usually result in a vigorous cough.
7. **Oral intubations:** after proper preparation of the patient, oral intubation can be accomplished with direct laryngoscopy or indirectly with a rigid stylet fiberoptic laryngoscope (i.e., the Bullard blade).

8. **Nasal intubations**
   A. After proper preparation, nasal intubation can be accomplished blindly or with the assistance of a direct laryngoscopy and Magill.
   B. Blind technique: while listening for breath sounds at the proximal end of the endotracheal tube, advance the tube during inspiration. A cough followed by a deep breath, condensation in the tube from exhaled moisture, and loss of voice suggest tracheal entry.

Fiberoptic-assisted Tracheal Intubation

1. **Indications:** upper airway obstruction, mediastinal mass, subglottic edema, congenital upper airway abnormalities, immobile cervical vertebrae, verify position of a double-lumen endobronchial tube.
2. **Nasal technique:** after the patient's nares and nasopharynx are anesthetized and vasoconstricted, the tracheal tube is passed through the naris into the posterior nasopharynx. The lubricated bronchoscope is then passed through the tracheal tube until the epiglottis and glottic opening are visualized continuing until the carina is identified. Pass the tube over the scope while the view of the carina is maintained.
3. **Oral technique:** an intubating oral airway (or bite block) is inserted after topicalization of the posterior tongue, soft palate, and lateral oropharyngeal areas. The tracheal tube is inserted about 8-10 cm into the airway and the bronchoscope passed through the tube. The posterior tongue, epiglottis, glottis and carina should be visualized in order. The tube is then passed over the scope while keeping the carina in view.

Agents for Awake Intubations			
Medication	**Dose**	**Route**	**Comments**
Cocaine (4-10%)	40-160 mg	Intranasal	Good anesthetic, vasoconstrictor, may cause coronary vasospasm
1% Phenylephrine	1-2 mL	Intranasal	Vasoconstrictor
Cetacaine Spray	2-4 sprays	Oral	Contains benzocaine
2 % Viscous Lidocaine	2-4 mL	Oral	
1% Lidocaine	2-3 mL	Airway blocks	Aspirate before injection
4% Lidocaine	2-3 mL	Transtracheal	Aspirate before injection
Afrin Spray	2-4 sprays	Intranasal	

Transtracheal Ventilation (Cricothyrotomy)

1. **Indications:** can be used as a temporizing measure if mask ventilation and oxygenation become inadequate or is not possible.
2. **Technique:** a catheter (12- or 14-gauge) is connected to a jet-type ventilator, which in turn is connected to an oxygen source capable of delivering gas at a pressure around 50 psi, and inserted into the trachea through the cricothyroid membrane. The gas is delivered intermittently by a hand-held actuator. The duration of ventilation is best assessed by watching the rise and fall of the chest: an I:E ratio of 1:4 seconds is recommended.
3. Oxygenation usually improves rapidly, however, retention of carbon dioxide may limit the duration of the usefulness of the technique.
4. **Complications:** catheter displacement (caused by high pressures created by jet ventilation), pneumomediastinum.

Laryngeal Mask Airway

1. **Indications for LMA**
   A. In place of a face mask or endotracheal tube.
   B. In place of an endotracheal tube, when breathing is being controlled, as long as the inflation pressure is not more than 30 cm H_2O.
   C. To aid in the management of the difficult airway (i.e., the LMA can be used as a guide for fiberoptic intubation).
2. **Contraindications for LMA**
   A. The LMA does not provide an airtight seal of the airway and, thus, does not protect against gastric regurgitation and pulmonary aspiration.
   B. When controlled ventilation is likely to require a high-inflation pressure of more than 30 cm H_2O.
3. **Insertion of the LMA-Classic**
   A. Propofol (2.5-3.0 mg/kg) is the agent of choice for LMA insertion. Propofol relaxes the jaw and pharyngeal muscles better than thiopental.
   B. The leading edge of the deflated cuff should be wrinkle-free and facing away from the aperture. Lubricate only the back side of the cuff with a water soluble lubricant.
   C. The LMA is held like a pencil and is inserted blindly in the midline with concavity forward while pressing on the anterior shaft with the tip of the index finger toward the hard palate and guiding it toward the pharynx.
   D. When the upper esophageal sphincter is reached, a characteristic resistance is felt. The cuff is then inflated with air (the cuff should be inflated without holding the tube to enable the expanding cuff to find its correct position in the pharynx).
   E. When correctly placed, the black vertical line on the posterior aspect of the tube should always face directly backward, toward the head of the patient.
   F. The LMA should be left in place until the patient can open his mouth on command. During emergence, the patient should not be stimulated (i.e., suctioned), and the cuff should not be deflated until the patient can open his mouth on command.
   G. A bite block (or folded gauze) is inserted in the mouth to protect the LMA.
4. **LMA-Fastrach**
   A. **To insert the LMA-Fastrach**
      1. Deflate the cuff of the mask and use a water soluble lubricant on the

posterior surface. Rub the lubricant over the anterior hard palate.
   2. Swing the mask into place in a circular movement maintaining contact against the palate and posterior pharynx. Don't use handle as lever.
   3. Inflate the mask, without holding the tube or handle, to a pressure of approximately 60 cm H_2O.

B. **To insert endotracheal tube and remove the LMA-Fastrach**
   1. Hold the LMA-Fastrach handle while gently inserting the lubricated ET tube into the metal shaft. The use of a standard, curved, PVC ET tube is not recommended.
   2. Advance tube, inflate the ET tube cuff and confirm intubation.
   3. Remove the connector and ease the LMA-Fastrach out by gently swinging the handle caudally. Use the stabilizing rod to keep the ETT in place while removing the LMA-Fastrach until the tube can be grasped at the level of the incisors.
   4. Remove the stabilizing rod and gently unthread the inflation line and pilot balloon of the ET tube. Replace the ET tube connector

5. **LMA as a conduit for tracheal intubation**
   A. The LMA may be used to provide a conduit to facilitate fiberoptic, gum bougie-guided or blind oral tracheal intubation.
   B. Problems include inadequate ET tube length, limitation on ET tube size, and inability to remove the LMA without risking extubation.

6. **Complications of the LMA**
   A. Possibility of regurgitation and pulmonary aspiration.
   B. Oral and pharyngeal mucosa injury during insertion of the LMA.
   C. Laryngospasm and coughing (may occur in lightly anesthetized patient).
   D. Negative pressure pulmonary edema after improper placement in spontaneously breathing patient.
   E. The failure to function properly in the presence of local pharyngeal or laryngeal disease.
   F. The need for neck extension in the patient with cervical spine disorder.

Laryngeal Mask Airway (LMA) Sizes			
Size	Patient	Cuff Vol (ml)	ETT Size (ID)
1	Infant up to 6.5 kg	4	3.5
1.5	5-10 kg	7	4
2	Infants/Children up to 20 kg	10	4.5
2.5	Children between 20 - 30 kg	15	5
3	Children/small adults over 30 kg	20	6.0*
4	Adults 50-70 kg	30	6.0*
5	Adults 70-100 kg	30	7.0*
6	Adults greater then 100 kg	40	7.0*
ETT= endotracheal tube; * = cuffed tube; ID = inner diameter			

Esophageal Tracheal Combitube

1. **Uses:** emergency airway control in the difficult airway. Available only in one adult size (age >15 years and height >5 feet).
2. **Insertion**
   A. With the head in the neutral position, insert the ETC, with gentle pressure, up to the black marks (teeth should be between black marks).
   B. Inflate the first pilot balloon (blue cuff) with 100 cc. As the cuff is inflated, the combitube will pop out 1 cm.
   C. Inflate the second pilot balloon (white cuff) with 10-15 cc.
3. **Placement**
   A. Ventilate via longer (blue) lumen.
   B. If breath sounds are present, the ETC is in the esophagus; ventilate.
   C. If no breath sounds are heard, change ventilation to shorter lumen #2 (clear) and recheck for breath sounds. If breath sounds are present, the ETC is in the trachea; continue to ventilate.
   D. If no breath sounds or breath sounds faint, attempt to improve seal by adding up to 60 cc to balloon number 1.
   E. If unable to ventilate, deflate both cuffs, pull back 3 cm and reinflate cuffs. Ventilate via blue lumen and check for breath sounds. If still no breath sounds, deflate cuffs, remove ETC and start algorithm over.
4. **Contraindications**
   A. Height less than 5 feet (only one size currently available).
   B. Intact gag reflex intact (will not tolerate cuff).
   C. Presence of esophageal disease (potential for bleeding or rupture).
   D. Ingestion of caustic substances (potential for rupture).
   E. Upper airway obstruction (foreign body, glottic edema, epiglottis).
5. **Concerns**
   A. Potential for nasopharyngeal, oropharyngeal or tracheal mucosal damage or edema (particularly if left in for greater than 2-8 hours).
   B. Inability to suction tracheal secretions when in esophageal position.
   C. Only one size available; single use makes it expensive.

Bullard Laryngoscope

1. The Bullard laryngoscope, functioning as an indirect fiberoptic laryngoscope, provides direct visualization of the vocal cords. It is available in both adult and pediatric sizes.
2. The advantage of this laryngoscope is that it can be introduced into the oropharynx with minimal mouth opening (oral opening of 0.64 cm required) and the patient can remain in anatomical position.
3. Preloading the intubating stylet involves lubricating the stylet and positioning the endotracheal tube so that the distal end of the stylet projects through the Murphy's eye of the endotracheal tube.
4. The blade is then inserted into the mouth, with the handle in the horizontal plane, and rotated into the vertical plane allowing it to slide around the midline of the tongue and into the posterior pharynx. Gentle traction is applied against the posterior surface of the tongue to obtain visualization of the glottic aperture.
5. With the stylet pointed directly at the glottic opening, the endotracheal tube is advanced under direct vision into the trachea.

Mechanical Ventilation

1. **Types of mechanical ventilators**
   A. **Time cycled:** the tidal volume is delivered and inspiration ends after a preset time interval.
   B. **Volume cycled:** the tidal volume is delivered and inspiration ends after a preset time interval.
   C. **Pressure cycled:** the tidal volume is delivered and inspiration ends when a preset volume is delivered.
2. **Modes of mechanical ventilation**
   A. **Intermittent positive-pressure ventilatory modes (IPPV).**
      1. **Controlled mechanical ventilation (CMV):** mechanical breaths are delivered at a preset rate and tidal volume regardless of the pt effort.
      2. **Assist-control ventilation (AC):** A preset minute ventilation is delivered regardless of the patient's effort. Ventilator senses patient-initiated spontaneous breath and delivers a preset tidal volume as well.
      3. **Intermittent mandatory ventilation (IMV):** the ventilator provides tidal volume breaths at a preset fixed rate. In between ventilator-delivered breaths, the patient is able to breathe spontaneously at any rate, tidal volume, or pattern.
      4. **Synchronized intermittent mandatory ventilation (SIMV):** similar to IMV, ventilatory breaths timed to coincide with spontaneous effort.
      5. **Continuous positive airway pressure (CPAP):** a preset level of positive airway pressure is maintained throughout the respiratory cycle. The patient must be spontaneously breathing.
      6. **Inspiratory pressure support ventilation (IPS):** a preset pressure is obtained when the patient initiates an inspiratory effort.
   B. **Pressure-controlled ventilation**
      1. Maximum airway pressure is set on the ventilator, and tidal volume becomes the dependent variable.
      2. The duration of inspiration is determined by setting either the inspiratory time or the I:E ratio. Tidal volume is the product of inspiratory flow and inspiratory time.
      3. The primary advantage of pressure-controlled ventilation is reduction in peak airway pressure and potential improvement of gas exchange.
   C. **High-frequency ventilation**
      1. **High-frequency positive pressure ventilation (HFPPV):** similar to conventional ventilation, however, tidal volumes are very small, and cycling frequencies are very fast (60-300).
      2. **High-frequency jet ventilation (HFJV):** a small diameter injecting catheter positioned in the central airway pulses gas along the luminal axis under high pressure at a rapid cycling rate.
   D. **Pressure-controlled inverse ratio ventilation (PC-IRV):** set by choosing a prolonged inspiratory time such that the time spend during inspiration exceeds expiratory time.
3. **Positive end-expiratory pressure (PEEP)**
   A. **Function of PEEP:** increases oxygenation by maximizing the ventilation-perfusion relationship in the lung. PEEP does this by maximizing the FRC (functional residual capacity), keeping lung volumes greater than closing capacity, therefore maintaining airways open and functional.

B. **Adverse effects of PEEP:** decreased cardiac output, hypotension, worsening hypoxia, barotrauma, increased ICP, decreased urine output.

4. **Ventilator Settings**
   A. **FIO_2:** normally start with 40% otherwise use 90-100% until first ABG available (1% decrease in FIO_2 = decrease PaO_2 by 7).
   B. **PEEP:** initially none; start with 5 cm H_2O and increase in 3-5 cm H_2O increments if PaO_2 less than 60 mmHg with FIO_2 > 50%; over 10 cm H_2O normally requires pulmonary artery catheter.
   C. **Rate:** start at 10-14 (for infants start at 25-30).
   D. **Tidal volume:** 10-15 ml/kg (infants 8-12 ml/kg).
   E. **Mode:** IMV, SIMV, CPAP, A/C, PSV.

Oxygen Therapy

A. **Nasal cannulas:** FIO_2 increases by 3-4%/liter of O_2 given (up to 40%); high flow rates may cause dry mucous membranes, gastric distension, headaches.

B. **Face masks**
   A. **Simple mask:** insufficient flow rates may cause CO_2 retention.
   B. **Venturi mask (air entrainment mask):** useful in COPD; if back pressure develops on jet, less room air enters and FIO_2 can elevate unpredictably.
   C. **Partial rebreathing mask:** simple mask with a valveless reservoir bag and exhalation ports; collapsed reservoir bag indicates air leak or inadequate flow of oxygen.
   D. **Nonrebreathing mask:** simple mask with reservoir bag and unidirectional valve; requires tight seal and high flow rate to deliver maximum FIO_2.
   E. **Tracheostomy mask:** provides humidity and controlled oxygen; FIO_2 should be analyzed for each individual patient.
   F. **Aerosol face tent:** delivers oxygen form variable oxygen nebulizer over mouth and nose.

C. **Oxygen tents**
   A. Insufficient flow rates may cause CO_2 retention; can be used to provide humidified air.
   B. **Disadvantages:** development of oxygen gradient; sparks in or near tent may be hazardous; claustrophobia in older children; requires close monitoring of patient and apparatus.

Oxygen Delivery Systems		
	FIO₂ Delivered (%)	Flow Rate (L/min)
Nasal cannula	22-40	0.25-6
Simple mask	35-50	6-10
Partial rebreather	60-95	>6
Nonrebreather	Almost 100	10-15
Venturi mask	24-50 (mask specific)	Variable
Tracheostomy mask	Unpredictable	Variable
Oxygen tent	up to 50	>10

Laboratory Values

Normal Cerebral Spinal Fluid Parameters	
Test	Normal Value
Glucose	40-70 mg/dL
Total Protein	20-45 mg/dL
CSF Pressure	50-180 mm H_2O
Leukocytes	Total<4 per mm3
Lymphocytes	60-70%
Monocytes	30-50%
Neutrophils	1-3%

Normal Renal Parameters	
Test	Normal Value
Cr Clearance Males Females	125 mL/min 105 mL/min
Ur Creat	1.0-1.6 g/d
Ur Protein	<0.15 g/d
Ur K	25-100 meq/d
Ur Na	100-260 meq/d

Normal Serum Chemistries	
Test	Normal Value
Acid Phosphatase	0-5.5 U/L
Albumin	3.5-5.5 g/dL
Alkaline Phosphatase	30-120 U/L
Aminotransferases AST (SGOT) ALT (SGPT)	0-35 U/L 0-35 U/L
Ammonia	80-110 mcg/dL
Amylase	60-80 U/L

Test	Normal Value
Bilirubin Total Direct Indirect	0.3-1.0 mg/dL 0.1-0.3 mg/dL 0.2-0.7 mg/dL
Calcium	8.6-10.5 mg/dL
CO_2	22-30 mEq/L
Chloride	98-106 mEq/L
Total Cholesterol <29 years 30-39 years 40-49 years >50 years	<200 mg/dL <225 mg/dL <245 mg/dL <265 mg/dL
HDL	30-90 mg/dL
LDL	50-190 mg/dL
CPK	25-145 U/L
Creatinine	0.4-1.5 mg/dL
Ferritin	15-200 ng/mL
Glucose	70-140 mg/dL
Iron	80-180 mcg/dL
Iron-Binding	250-450 mcg/dL
Iron-Sat	20-45
LDH	25-100 U/L
Lipase	49-220 U/L
Magnesium	1.6-2.6 mg/dL
Osmolality	285-295
Phosphorus	2.5-4.5 mg/dL
Protein	5.5-8.0 mEq/L
Sodium	136-145 mEq/L
Triglycerides	<60 mg/dL
Urea Nitrogen	10-20 mg/dL
Uric Acid Males Females	 2.5-8.0 mg/dL 1.5-6.0 mg/dL

Complete Blood Count			
	1 month	6-12 years	Adult
Male			
WBC	5.0-19.5	5.0-13.5	4.5-11.0
RBC	3.0-5.4	4.0-5.2	4.6-6.2
Hemoglobin	14.0-18.0	11.5-15.5	14.0-18.0
Hematocrit	31-55	35-45	42-52
RDW			11.5-14.5
Female			
WBC	5.0-19.5	5.0-13.5	4.5-11.0
RBC	3.0-5.4	4.0-5.2	4.2-5.4
Hemoglobin	14.0-18.0	11.5-15.5	12.0-16.0
Hct	31-55	35-45	37-47
RDW			11.5-14.5

Fluid and Electrolyte Management

1. **Functional fluid compartments**
   A. **Total body water (TBW):** 60% (adult males) and 50% (adult females) of ideal body weight (IBW).
   B. **Intracellular fluid (ICF):** comprises approximately 35% of IBW or 60% of TBW. Principal potassium containing space.
   C. **Extracellular fluid (ECF):** accounts for 25% of IBW or 40% of TBW and is subdivided into interstitial fluid (ISF) and blood volume (BV; about 8% of TBW). Principal sodium containing space.
2. **Daily electrolyte requirements**
   A. **Na:** 2-3 mEq/kg/24 hours
   B. **K:** 1-2 mEq/kg/24 hours
   C. **Cl:** 2-3 mEq/kg/24 hours
3. **Perioperative fluid replacement**
   A. **Normal maintenance requirements** (hourly rate based on weight)
      1. **First 10 kg:** 4 mL/kg/hr or 100 mL/kg/day
      2. **Second 10 kg:** add 2 mL/kg/hr or 50 mL/kg/day
      3. **>20 kg:** add 1 mL/kg/hr or 20 mL/kg/day
   B. **Fluid deficit:** primarily NPO deficit caused by patient fasting.
      1. **NPO deficit** = hourly maintenance rate x number of hours NPO
      2. Replace the first half preop and the remaining over the next 2-3 hours.
   C. **Intraoperative fluid loss:** primarily third-space (redistribution) and evaporative losses; amount based on degree of tissue trauma.
      1. Minimal (e.g., herniorrhaphy): 0-2 mL/kg/hr
      2. Moderate (e.g., cholecystectomy): 2-4 mL/kg/hr
      3. Severe (e.g., bowel resection): 4-8 mL/kg/hr
   D. **Blood loss** (see blood therapy section)
      1. Replace each ml of blood loss with 3 ml of cyrstalloid, 1 ml colloid solution or 1 ml PRBC.
      2. Transfusion of red blood cells as necessary to maintain hematocrit.
4. **Calculated osmolality** = 2 Na + glucose/18 + BUN/2.8 + ethanol/4.6 + isopropanol/6 + methanol/3.2 + ethylene glycol/6.2 (norm 280-295).
5. **Calcium disturbances**
   A. Normal plasma concentration is 8.5-10.5 mg/dL with 50% free ionized 40% protein bound.
   B. Normal free ionized concentration is 4.5-5 mg/dL.
   C. Corrected calcium = measured calcium / [0.6 + (total protein / 8.5)].
   D. For each 1 gm/dL change in albumin there is a corresponding 0.8 mg/dL change in total calcium (free ionized calcium is not affected).
   E. Ionized calcium increases 0.16 mg/dL for each decrease of 0.1 unit in plasma pH.
6. **Glucose:** for each 100 mg/dL glucose above normal there is a corresponding fall in sodium by 1.6 mEq/l.

Fluids							
Fluid	Glu	Na	Cl	K	Ca	HCO_3	Kcal/L
D_5W	50						170
NS		154	154				
D5 1/4NS	50	38.5	38.5				170
LR		130	110	4	3	27	<10

Blood Therapy Management

Transfusions

1. **Blood loss management**
   A. Estimated blood volume (EBV)
      1. 95-100 mL/kg for premature infant
      2. 85-90 mL/kg for full-term infant
      3. 80 mL/kg for infants up to 12 months
      4. 70-75 mL/kg for adult men
      5. 65-70 mL/kg for adult women
   B. **Max allowable blood loss**=[EBV x (Hct - target Hct)]/ Hct
   C. Replace every 1 mL blood loss with 3 mL crystalloid or 1 cc PRBC
   D. **PRBC transfusion guidelines**
      1. one unit PRC increases Hct about 3% and Hb about 1 g/dL in adults
      2. 3 mL/kg PRC increases Hb about 1 g/dL
      3. 10 mL/kg PRBC increases Hct about 10%
   E. **Fluid replacement equivalents**
      1. **Crystalloid:** 3 cc/1 cc estimated blood loss (EBL)
      2. **Colloid:** 1 cc/cc EBL
      3. **Whole blood:** 1 cc/cc EBL
      4. **Packed red blood cells (pRBC):** ½ cc/cc EBL
2. **Compatibility testing**
   A. **Type specific:** ABO-Rh typing only; 99.80% compatible.
   B. **Type and screen:** ABO-Rh and screen; 99.94% compatible.
   C. **Type and crossmatch:** ABO-Rh, screen, and crossmatch; 99.95% compatible. Crossmatching confirms ABO-Rh typing, detects antibodies to the other blood group systems, and detects antibodies in low titers.
   D. **Screening donor blood:** hematocrit is determined, if normal, the blood is typed, screened for antibodies, and tested for hepatitis B, hepatitis C, syphilis, HIV-1, HIV-2, and human T-cell lymphotropic viurses I and II. ALT is also measured as a surrogate marker of nonspecific liver infection.
3. **Blood component therapy**
   A. **Whole blood:** 40% hematocrit; used primarily in hemorrhagic shock.
   B. **Packed red blood cells (PRBC):** volume 250-300 mL with a hematocrit of 70-80%; increases adult hemoglobin approximately 1 g/dL.
   C. **Platelets**
      1. One unit of platelets will increases platelet count 5000-10,000/mm^3; usual dose is 1 unit of platelets per 10 kg body weight; single-donor platelets obtained by apheresis are equivalent to 6 platelet concentrate; platelets are stored at room temp; ABO compatibility is not mandatory.
      2. A normal platelet count is 150,000-440,000/mm^3. Thrombocytopenia is defined as <150,000/mm^3. Intraoperative bleeding increases with counts of 40,000-70,000/mm^3, and spontaneous bleeding can occur at counts <20,000/mm^3. During surgery platelet transfusions are probably not required unless count is less then 50,000/mm^3.
   D. **Fresh frozen plasma (FFP):** 250 cc/bag; contains all coagulation factors except platelets; 10-15 mL/kg will increase plasma coagulation factors to 30% of normal; fibrinogen levels increase by 1 mg per mL of plasma transfused; acute reversal of warfarin requires 5-8 mL/kg of FFP. ABO

compatibility is mandatory.

- E. **Cryoprecipitate:** 10-20 mL/bag; contains 100 units factor VIII-C, 100 units factor vWF, 60 units factor XIII, and 250 mg fibrinogen; indications include hpyofibrinogenimia, von Willebrand disease, hemophilia A and preparation of fibrin glue; ABO compatibility not mandatory.
- F. **Albumisol:** 5% and 25% (heat treated at 60 degrees C for 10 hrs).

4. **Complications of transfusions**
  A. **Immune complications**
    1. **Hemolytic reactions**
      A. **Acute hemolytic reactions**
        1. Occurs when ABO-incompatible blood is transfused resulting in acute intravascular hemolysis; severity of a reaction often depends on how much incompatible blood has been given.
        2. **Symptoms** include fever, chills, chest pain, anxiety, back pain, dyspnea; in anesthetized patients, the reaction is manifested by rise in temperature, unexplained tachycardia, hypotension, hemoglobinuria, and diffuse oozing from surgical site. Free hemoglobin in the plasma or urine is presumptive evidence of a hemolytic reaction.
        3. Risk of fatal hemolytic transfusion reaction: 1:600,000 units.
      B. **Delayed hemolytic reactions**
        1. Occurs because of incompatibility of minor antigens (e.g., Kidd, Kelly, Duffy, etc) are characterized by extravascular hemolysis.
        2. The hemolytic reaction is typically delayed 2-21 days after transfusion, and symptoms are generally mild, consisting of malaise, jaundice, and fever. Treatment is supportive.
    2. **Nonhemolytic reactions**
      A. **Febrile reactions**
        1. Most common nonhemolytic reaction (0.5-1.0% of RBC transfusions and up to 30% of platelet transfusions); due to recipient antibodies against donor antigens present on leukocytes and platelets; treatment includes stopping or slowing infusion and antipyretics.
      B. **Urticarial reactions**
        1. Characterized by erythema, hives, and itching without fever.
        2. Occur in 1% of transfusions and are thought to be due to sensitization of the patient to transfused plasma proteins.
        3. Treated with antihistaminic drugs.
      C. **Anaphylactic reactions**
        1. Anaphylactic reactions are rare; about 1:500,000.
        2. Patients with IgA deficiency may be at increased risk of the presence of anti-IgA antibodies that react with transfused IgA.
      D. **Transfusion related acute lung injury (TRALI)**
        1. Due to transfusion of antileukocytic or anti-HLA antibodies that interact with and cause the patient's white cells to aggregate in the pulmonary circulation.
        2. Risk is 1:6000.
        3. Treatment is supportive, mimicking the treatment of ARDS.
      E. **Graft-vs-host disease**
        1. Most commonly seen in immune-compromised patients.
        2. Cellular blood products contain lymphocytes capable of mounting an immune response against the compromised host.

F. **Posttransfusion purpura**
   1. Due to the development of platelet alloantibodies; the platelet count typically drops precipitously 1 week after transfusion.

G. **Immune suppression**
   1. Transfusion of leukocyte-containing blood products appears to be immunosuppressive (can improve allograft survival following renal transplants).
   2. Blood transfusions may increase the incidence of serious infections following surgery or trauma.
   3. Blood transfusions may worsen tumor recurrence and mortality rate following resections of many cancer.

B. **Infectious complications**
   1. **Viral infections**
      A. **Hepatitis:** risk of HBV: 1:137,000; HCV: Hepatitis C: 1:1,000,000.
      B. **HIV/AIDS:** risk of HIV: 1:1,900,000
      C. **Other viral infections**
         1. **Cytomegalovirus and Epstein-Barr virus** are common and usually cause asymptomatic or mild systemic illness.
         2. **HTLV -I and HTLV-II:** 1:641,000
   2. **Parasitic infections:** very rare; include malaria, toxoplasmosis, and Chagas' disease.
   3. **Bacterial infections**
      A. Gram-positive and gram-negative can contaminate blood; rare.
      B. Specific bacterial diseases transmitted by blood include syphilis, brucellosis, salmonellosis, yersiniosis, various rickettsioses.

C. **Massive transfusions**
   1. **Massive transfusion** is defined as the replacement of a patient's total blood volume in less than 24 hours, or as the acute administration of more than half the patient's estimated blood volume per hour.
   2. **The use of universal donor blood** (group O, Rh negative blood)
      A. Group O, Rh negative blood should be reserved for patients close to exsanguination. If time permits, cross-matched or uncross-matched type specific blood should be administered.
      B. Group O, Rh negative blood should not be given as whole blood. The serum contains high anti-A and anti-B titters which may cause hemolysis of recipient red cells.
      C. If more than 4 units of group O, Rh negative whole blood is administered, type-specific blood should not be given subsequently since the potentially high anti-A and anti-B titters could cause hemolysis of the donor blood.
      D. Patients administered up to 10 units of group O, Rh negative packed red blood cells may be switched to type-specific blood, since there is an insignificant risk of hemolysis from the small volume of plasma administered with packed red blood cells.

D. **Other complications**
   1. **Metabolic abnormalities**
      A. Decreased pH secondary to increased hydrogen ion production.
      B. Increase potassium: due to cell lysis; increases with length of storage.
      C. Decrease in 2,3 DPG: consumed by RBCs; P_{50} decreases to 18 mmHg after 1 week and 15 mmHg after 3 weeks.
      D. Citrate toxicity: citrate metabolism to bicarbonate may contribute to metabolic alkalosis; binding of calcium by citrate could result in

hypocalcemia (rare reflecting mobilization of calcium stores in bone and the livers ability to metabolize citrate to bicarbonate.
2. **Microaggregates:** microaggregates consisting of platelets and leukocytes form during storage of whole blood. Micropore filters may decrease help remove these particles.
3. **Hypothermia:** the use of blood warmers (except for platelets) greatly decreases the likelihood of transfusion-related hypothermia.
4. **Coagulopathy disorders**
   A. Usually occurs only after massive transfusion (greater than 10 units).
   B. **Dilutional thrombocytopenia:** common cause of abnormal bleeding in massive transfusion, responds quickly to platelet transfusions.
   C. **Low Factors V and VIII:** factors V and VII are very labile in stored blood and may decrease to levels as low as 15-20% normal, however, this is usually enough for hemostasis.
   D. **Disseminated Intravascular Coagulation:** a hypercoagulable state caused by activation of the clotting system leading to deposition of fibrin in microvasculature which causes a secondary activation of fibrinolysis. resulting in consumption of factors and platelets.

Treatment of Hemolytic Transfusion Reactions

1. Stop the transfusion
2. Check for error in patient identity or donor unit.
3. Send donor unit and newly obtained blood sample to blood bank for recross match.
4. Treat hypotension with fluids and vasopressors as necessary.
5. If transfusion is required, use type O-negative PRBC and type AB FFP.
6. Maintain the urine output at a minimum of 75 to 100 mL/hr by generously administering IV fluids; consider mannitol, 12.5 to 50 grams, or furosemide, 20-40 mg.
7. Monitor for signs of DIC clinically and with appropriate lab studies.
8. Send patient blood sample for direct antiglobulin (Coombs) test, free hemoglobin, haptoglobin; send urine for hemoglobin.

Coagulation Tests

1. Partial thromboplastin time (PTT)
   A. Partial thromboplastin is performed by adding particulate matter to a blood sample to activate the intrinsic coagulation system.
   B. PTT measures the clotting ability of all factors in the intrinsic and common pathways except factor XIII.
   C. PTT is abnormal if there are decreased amounts of coagulation factors, patients on heparin, or if there is a circulating anticoagulant present.
   D. Normal values are between 25 and 37 seconds.
2. **Activated partial thromboplastin time (aPTT)**
   A. An activator is added to the test tube before addition of partial thromboplastin added.
   B. Maximal activation of the contact factors (XII and XI) eliminates the lengthy natural contact activation phase and results in more consistent and reproducible results.

    C. Normal aPTT is 25-35 seconds.

3. Prothrombin time (PT)

    A. Performed by measuring the time needed to form a clot when calcium and a tissue extract are added to plasma.

    B. PT evaluates the activity of fibrinogen, prothrombin and factors V, VII and X; evaluates the intrinsic coagulation system.

    C. Normal PT is 10-12 seconds (depending on control).

4. International normalized ratio (INR)

    A. INR is a means of standardizing PT values; it is the ratio of patient's PT to the control PT value.

    B. INR is calculated as $(Pt_{patient}/Pt_{normal})^{ISI}$ (ISI is the international sensitivity index assigned to the test system).

5. Sonoclot: the Sonoclot is a test of whole blood that utilizes a warmed cuvette and a suspended piston apparatus, This piston vibrates up and down very rapidly in the blood sample and Sonoclot detects any impedance to this vibration. As a result, the test follows the changes in viscosity over time.

6. Activated clotting time (ACT): the ACT provides a global measurement of hemostatic function and is measured after whole blood is exposed to a specific activator of coagulation. The time for in vitro clot formation after whole blood is exposed to diatomaceous earth (Celite) is defined as the ACT. Normal is 90 to 120 seconds. The linear increase in ACT seen with increasing doses of heparin provides a convenient method to monitor anticoagulant effect of heparin. Although the ACT test is simple, it lacks sensitivity to clotting abnormalities.

7. D-dimer and fibrin split products

    A. Fibrin split products: reflects the degradation of fibrinogen and fibrin.

    B. D-dimer: reflects the degradation of cross-linked fibrin; more specific for primary fibrinolysis and DIC

8. Thromboelastrogram (TEG)

    A. A method of testing for global assessment of coagulation. This technique uses a small sample of blood placed in a slowly rotating cuvette at 37°C. A piston is suspended in the cuvette, and as the coagulation proceeds, the tension on the piston is measured. A tracing is generated and several parameters are measured (see below).

    B. Thromboelastrogram parameters

        1. r (reaction time): start of recording until 1 mm deflection (represents initial fibrin formation).

        2. k (clot formation time): measured from r until there is a 20 mm deflection in the tracing.

        3. a (angle): slope of the increase from r time to k time.

        4. MA: maximum amplitude in millimeters, a measure of the maximum clot strength (dependent on fibrinogen, level, platelet numbers, and function).

        5. A^{60}: deflection measure at 60 minutes after MA (represents clot lysis and retraction).

Sickle Cell Anemia

1. Sickle cell anemia is a hereditary hemolytic anemia resulting from the formation of an abnormal hemoglobin (Hb S); sickle hemoglobin has less affinity for oxygen and decreased solubility.

2. Sickle cell trait (HbAS) is a heterozygous state. Only 1% of the red cells in venous circulation of the heterozygote are sickled. These patients are usually asymptomatic. Vigorous physical activity at high altitude, air travel in unpressurized planes, and anesthesia are potentially hazardous.
3. Sickle cell disease (HbSS): homozygous state: 70-98% HbS.
4. Clinical features
   A. Signs and symptoms include anemia (HgB levels 6.5 to 10 gm/dL), obstructive or hemolytic jaundice, joint and bone pain, abdominal and chest pains, lymphadenopathy, chronic leg ulcers, hematuria, epistaxis, priapism, finger clubbing, and skeletal deformities.
   B. The disease is characterized by periodic exaggeration of symptoms or sickle cell crisis. There are four main types of crises.
   C. Vaso-occlusive crises: caused by sickled cells blocking the microvasculature; characterized by sudden onset of pain frequently with no clear-cut precipitating event.
   D. Hemolytic crises: seen in patients with sickle cell disease plus G6PD deficiency, has hematologic features of sudden hemolysis.
   E. Sequestration crises: sequestration of red blood cells in the liver and spleen causing massive, sudden enlargement, and an acute fall in peripheral hematocrit, this can progress to circulatory collapse.
   F. Aplastic crises: characterized by transient episodes of bone marrow depression commonly occurring after viral infection.
5. Anesthetic management
   A. The practice of transfusing these patients to an end point of having 70% hemoglobin A and less than 30% hemoglobin S cells before major surgery remains controversial.
   B. To lessen the risk of intraoperative sickling patients should be kept well oxygenated and well hydrated. Avoid acidosis and hypothermia.

Factor Deficiencies

1. **Factor VIII deficiency (hemophilia A)**
   A. The half life of factor VIII in plasma is 8-12 hours.
   B. Treatment consists of lyophilized factor VIII, cryoprecipitate, or desmopressin. Infusion of 1 unit of factor VIII per kg will increase the factor VIII activity level by 2%. Obtain activity levels of 20-40% before surgery.
   C. Bleeding episodes related to the level of factor VIII activity (normal 100%).
2. **Factor IX deficiency (hemophilia B; Christmas disease)**
   A. The half life of factor IX in plasma is 24 hours.
   B. Therapy consists of factor IX concentrates of FFP. For surgical hemostasis, activity levels of 50% to 80% are necessary.
   C. Infusion of 1 unit of factor IX per kg of body weight will increase the factor IX activity level by 1%.

Spinal and Epidural Anesthesia

General Information

1. **Contraindications to peridural anesthesia**
   A. **Absolute contraindications:** lack of patient consent, localized infection at injection site, allergy to local anesthetics, increased intracranial pressure, coagulopathy or other bleeding diathesis, severe hypovolemia, severe aortic or mitral stenosis.
   B. **Relative contraindications:** localized infection peripheral to regional site, demyelinating CNS disease, patients taking platelet inhibiting drugs.
   C. **Controversial:** prior back surgery at site of injection, inability to communicate with patient, complicated surgery.

2. **Anatomy**
   A. **Spinal canal:** extends from the foramen magnum to the sacral hiatus.
   B. **Spinal cord:** spinal cord extends the length of the vertebral canal during fetal life, ends at L3 at birth, and moves progressively cephalad to reach the adult position of L1-L2 by 2 years of age.
   C. **Subarachnoid space:** subarachnoid space lies between the pia mater and the arachnoid and extends from S2 to the cerebral ventricles.
   D. **Epidural space** contains nerve roots, fat, lymphatic and blood vessels, and areolar tissue.
   E. **Course of anatomy:** skin, subcutaneous tissue, supraspinous ligament, interspinous ligament, ligamentum flavum, epidural space, and dura.

3. **Physiological changes with spinal and epidural anesthesia**
   A. **Neural blockade**
      1. **Sequence of neural blockade**
         A. Sympathetic block with peripheral vasodilation and skin temperature elevation.
         B. Loss of pain and temperature sensation.
         C. Loss of proprioception.
         D. Loss of touch and pressure sensation.
         E. Motor paralysis.
      2. The above sequence of neural blockade occurs because smaller C fibers are blocked more easily than the larger sensory fiber, which in turn are blocked more easily than motor fibers. As a result, the level of autonomic blockade for a spinal anesthetic extends above the level of the sensory blockade by 2-3 segments, while the motor blockade is 2-3 segments below the sensory blockade. During epidural anesthesia there is not a zone of differential nervous system blockade, and the zone of differential motor blockade averages 4 segments below the sensory level.
      3. With epidural anesthesia, the local anesthetics act directly on the spinal nerve roots located in the lateral part of the space. To a lesser extent, diffusion of local anesthetic solutions from the epidural space into the subarachnoid space produces spinal cord effects. As a result, the onset of the block is slower than with spinal anesthesia, and the intensity of the sensory and motor block is less.
   B. **Cardiovascular**
      1. **Hypotension:** the degree of hypotension is directly proportional to the degree of sympathetic blockade.

    2. **Blockade above T4** interrupts cardiac sympathetic fibers, leading to bradycardia, decreased cardiac output, and further decrease in BP.
- C. **Respiratory:** with ascending height of the block into the thoracic area, there is a progressive, ascending intercostal muscle paralysis. The diaphragmatic ventilation is mediated by the phrenic nerve, and typically will remain unaffected even during high cervical blockade.
- D. **Visceral effects**
  1. **Bladder:** sacral blockade results in an atonic bladder.
  2. **Intestine:** with sympathectomy, vagal tone dominates and results in a small, contracted gut with active peristalsis.

4. **Complications**
   - A. **Hypotension:** prehydrating with 500-1000 cc of crystalloid before performing the block will help decrease the incidence of hypotension.
   - B. **Paresthesia or nerve injury:** during placement of the needle or injection of anesthetic, direct trauma to a spinal nerve or intraneural injection may occur.
   - C. **Blood tap or vascular injury:** needle may puncture an epidural vein during needle insertion.
   - D. **Nausea and vomiting:** usually the result of hypotension or unopposed vagal stimulation.
   - E. **Total spinal:** may see apnea with from direct blockade of C3-C5.
   - F. **Backache:** overall the incidence of backache following spinal anesthesia is no different from that following general anesthesia.
   - G. **Postdural puncture headache:** seen 6-48 hours after dural puncture.
   - H. **Urinary retention:** urinary retention may outlast the blockade.
   - I. **Infection:** meningitis, arachnoiditis, and epidural abscess.

Levels and Effects of Blockade		
Cutaneous Level	**Segmental Level**	**Effects**
Fifth Digit	C8	All cardioaccelerator fibers (T1-T4) blocked
Inner Aspect of Arm and Forearm	T1-T2	Some degree of cardioaccelerator blockade
Apex of Axilla	T3	
Nipple	T4-T5	Possible cardioaccelerator blockade
Tip of Xiphoid	T7	Splanchnic (T5-L1) may be blocked
Umbilicus	T10	SNS blockade limited to legs
Inguinal Ligament	T12	No SNS blockade
Lateral Foot	S1	

Spinal Anesthesia

1. **Factors influencing spinal anesthetic**
   A. **Primary factors:** baricity of anesthetic solution, position of the patient, drug dosage, site of injection.
   B. **Other factors:** age, CSF volume, curvature of spine, drug volume, intra-abdominal pressure, needle direction, patient height, pregnancy.
2. **Vasoconstrictors**
   A. Enhances the quality and duration of spinal anesthesia by decreasing the uptake and clearance of local anesthetic from CSF.
   B. Agents: epinephrine (0.1-0.2 mg) and phenylephine (1-2 mg)

Local Anesthetics: Dosages for Spinal Anesthesia						
Drug	Preparation	T10 Level (mg)	T6 Level (mg)	T4 Level (mg)	Duration Plain (min)	Duration w/epi (min)
Procaine	10%	75	125	200	30-45	60-75
Lidocaine	5.0% in 7.5% glucose	25-50	50-75	75-100	45-60	60-90
Tetracaine*	1% in 10% glucose	6-8	8-14	12-20	60-90	120-180
Bupivacaine	0.75% in 8.25% dextrose	6-10	8-14	12-20	90-120	120-150
Ropivacaine	0.2-1%	8-12	12-16	16-18	90	140

*For hypobaric spinal: tetracaine diluted with sterile water to 0.3% solution
**Preparation concentration of tetracaine is 1%; tetracaine is diluted with 5.0% glucose for hyperbaric solution and normal saline for isobaric solution

Epidural Anesthesia

1. **Factors influencing epidural anesthesia**
   A. Local anesthetic selected.
   B. Mass of drug injected (dose, volume, and concentration).
   C. Addition of vasoconstrictors to reduce systemic absorption.
   D. Site injection.
   E. Patients over 40 years of age.
   F. Pregnancy (hormonal and/or mechanical factors).
2. **Epidural insertion sites:** cervical interspaces through T4 are best accessed by a median approach, while a paramedian approach for T4-T9 and a median approach for T9-L5.
3. **Complications of epidural anesthesia** (in addition to those listed above)
   A. **Dural puncture:** unintentional dural puncture occurs in 1% of epidural injections performed.
   B. **Catheter complications**
      1. Inability to insert the catheter.
      2. Catheter can be inserted into an epidural vein.
      3. Catheters can break off or become knotted within the epidural space.

    4. Unintentional subarachnoid injection.
    5. Intravascular injection: may result in local anesthetic overdose where large amounts of local anesthetic are used.
    6. Direct spinal cord injury:
    7. Bloody tap: may result from perforation of an epidural vein.

4. Clinical pharmacology of epidural agents

A. Dosing

    1. **Adults:** 1-2 mL of local anesthetic per segment to be blocked.

    2. **Time to two-segment regression**

        1. The time it takes for a sensory level to decrease by two dermatone levels.

        2. When a two-segment regression has occurred, one can reinject one-third to half the initial activation dose.

B. Hydrophilic opioids (morphine, hydromorphone)

    1. **Properties:** slow onset, long duration, high CSF solubility, extensive CSF spread.

    2. **Advantages:** prolonged single-dose analgesia, thoracic analgesia with lumbar administration, minimal dose compared to IV administration.

    3. **Disadvantages:** delayed onset of analgesia, unpredictable duration, higher incidence of side effects, delayed respiratory depression.

C. Lipophilic opioids (fentanyl, sufentanil)

    1. **Properties:** rapid onset, short duration, low CSF solubility, minimal CSF spread.

    2. **Advantages:** rapid analgesia, decreased side effects, ideal for continuous infusion or PCEA.

    3. **Disadvantages:** systemic absorption, brief single-dose analgesia, limited thoracic analgesia with lumbar administration.

D. Additives

    1. **Epinephrine** may be added to a maximum concentration of 1:200.000.

    2. **Bicarbonate**, 1 cc for each 10 mL of local anesthetic, can be added to speed up onset.

E. Side effects of neuraxial opioids (see table).

Epidural Catheter Insertion Sites	
Procedure	**Insertion Site**
Mastectomy	T1
Thoracotomy	T4
Upper Abdominal Surgery	T7-T8
Lower Abdominal	T10
Lower Extremity Above Knee	L1-L2
Lower Extremity Below Knee	L3-L4
Perineal	L4-L5

Local Anesthetics: Dosages for Epidural Anesthesia					
Drug	Usual Conc %	Usual Vol (mL)	Total Dose (mg)	Onset (min)	Duration (min)
Chloroprocaine	2-3	15-30	300-900	5-15	30-90
Lidocaine	1-2	15-30	150-500	5-15	60-120
Mepivacaine	1-2	15-30	150-300	5-15	60-180
Prilocaine	2-3	15-30	150-600	5-15	60-180
Bupivacaine	0.25-0.75	15-30	37.5-225	5-15	120-240
Etidocaine	1.0-1.5	15-30	150-300	5-15	120-240
Ropivacaine	0.2-1.0	15-30	75-200	10-20	120-240

Neuraxial Opioids: Side Effects and Treatment		
Problem	Treatment Options	Notes
Pruritus	Nalbuphine 5-10 mg IV/IM Diphenhydramine 25-50 mg IV Naloxone 40-80 mcg IV	May be severe after intrathecal morphine
Nausea/ Vomiting	Metoclopramide 5-10 mg IV Nalbuphine 5-10 mg IV/IM Naloxone 40-80 mcg IV	
Respiratory Depression	Naloxone 0.1 mg IV prn	Watch for synergism with other sedatives
Urinary Retention	Urinary Catheter	
Blood Pressure Changes	Fluid hydration Ephedrine Phenylephrine	Most likely after meperidine (local anesthetic effects)

Complications of Neuraxial Blocks

1. **Backache:** usually benign, mild and self-limited; can treat with tylenol, ASA, NSAIDs, warm or cold packs; may be a clinical sign of a more serious complications, such as epidural hematoma or abscess.
2. **Postdural puncture headache (PDPH)**
    A. Characteristics of a postdural puncture headache: postural component (made worse by upright position), frontal or occipital location, tinnitus, diplopia, young females, use of a large-gauge needle.
    B. **Mechanism:** usually due to a continued leak of CSF through the hole in the dura mater, resulting in low CSF pressure, which causes traction on meningeal vessels and nerves.
    C. **Incidence:** the overall incidence is approximately 5-10%.

D. Treatment of a postdural puncture headache
1. Oral Analgesics.
2. Bed rest.
3. Hydration (IV fluids, PO fluids, caffeine containing beverages).
4. Caffeine infusion (500 mg caffeine and sodium benzoate in 1 liter of isotonic crystalloid given over 1-2 hours).
5. Epidural blood patch (placement of 10-20 cc of autologous blood in the epidural space). The success rate is approximately 95% (90% respond after initial patch; 90% of initial non-responders after second patch)..

3. Urinary retention
A. Local anesthetic block of S2-S4 root fibers decreases urinary bladder tone and inhibits the voiding reflex.
B. Neuraxial opioids can interfere with normal voiding.

4. Maternal fever: commonly seen in epidural analgesia for labor resulting from epidural induced shivering or inhibition of sweating and hyperventilation.

5. Transient neurologic symptoms (TNS)
A. Characterized by back pain radiating to the legs without sensory or motor deficits, occurring after the resolution of the block; usually resolves spontaneously within several days; pathogenesis unclear.

6. High or total spinal anesthesia
A. Can result in hypotension, bradycardia, and respiratory insufficiency.
B. Treatment consists of supporting airway, ventilation, and circulation.

7. Subdural injection (during attempted epidural anesthesia)
A. Similar presentation as high spinal but with slower onset.
B. Treatment is supportive.

8. Systemic toxicity
A. Extreme high levels of local anesthetics affects the CNS (seizure and unconsciousness) and the cardiovascular system (hypotension, arrhythmias, cardiovascular collapse).

9. Cauda equina syndrome
A. Characterized by bowel and bladder dysfunction together with evidence of multiple nerve root injury.

10. Meningitis and arachnoiditis

11. Epidural abscess
A. Reported incidence: 1:6500 to 1:500,000 epidurals.
B. Four classic clinical stages
1. Back or vertebral pain that is intensified by percussion over spine.
2. Nerve root or radicular pain develops.
3. Motor and/or sensory deficits or sphincter dysfunction.
4. Paraplegia or paralysis.
C. If suspected: remove catheter (if placed), blood cultures, MRI or CT scan.

12. Spinal or epidural hematoma
A. Incidence of clinically significant hematoma: 1:150,000 for epidurals and 1:220,000 for spinals.
B. Majority occur in patients with abnormal coagulation.

Neuraxial Blockade and Anticoagulant Therapy

1. **Neuraxial blockade should be performed with caution** in the anticoagulated patients because of the increased risk of hematoma formation.
2. **Oral Anticoagulants**
    A. Chronic warfarin therapy: warfarin should be stopped and a normal PT and INR documented prior to the block.
    B. Perioperative thromboembolic prophylaxis: if the initial dose was given more then 24 hours prior to the block, or if more then one dose given, the PT and INR should be checked.
    C. Epidural catheters should be removed within 36 hours after starting warfarin. PT and INR should be checked daily. An INR greater then 3 is an indication to withhold or reduce the dose of warfarin if catheter present. Neurological testing and sensory and motor function should be checked.
3. **Unfractionated heparin**
    A. subcutaneous (mini-dose) heparin prophylaxis: No contraindications to neuraxial block.
    B. IV heparin: IV heparin should be stopped 6 hours prior to block and not restarted for at least 1 hour after. For indwelling catheters, IV heparin should be stopped 2-4 hours before removal of the catheter and not restarted until 1 hour after removal.
4. **Low molecular weight heparin (LMWH)**
    A. Neuraxial blockade should occur at least 12 hours after the last dose. For patients receiving higher doses (enoxaparin 1 mg/kg twice daily) will require longer delays (24 hours).
    B. If a bloody needle or catheter placement occurs, LMWH should be delayed until 24 hours postoperatively.
    C. Postoperative LMWH thromboprophylaxis: epidural catheters should be removed 2 hours prior to first LMWH dose. If catheter already present, the catheter should be removed at least 10 hours after a dose of LMWH and subsequent dosing should not occur for 2 more hours.
5. **Antiplatelet drugs:** aspirin and NSAIDs do not appear to increase risk of hematoma formation. This assumes a normal patient with a normal coagulation profile and not receiving other medications that might affect clotting mechanisms. Blockade should be used with caution.
6. **Fibrinolytic and thrombolytic drugs:** neuraxial block is best avoided in patients receiving these drugs. The length of time neuraxial blockade should be avoided after discontinuing these drugs is unclear

Peripheral Nerve Blocks

General information

1. **Preoperative:** similar to patients receiving general or regional anesthesia, coagulation status should be determined.
2. **Contraindications:** absolute contraindications include lack of patient consent or when nerve blockade would hinder the proposed surgery; relative contraindications include coagulopathy, infection at the skin site, presence of neurologic disease.
3. **Complications** common to all regional nerve blocks: complications to local anesthetics (intravascular injection, overdose, allergic reaction), nerve damage (needle trauma, intraneural injection), and hematomas.
4. **Nerve localization:** paresthesia
   A. Placing a needle in direct contact with a nerve or within the substance of the nerve will stimulate that nerve causing paresthesias.
   B. Injection into a perineural location often results in a brief accentuation of the paresthesia; in contrast, an intraneural injection produces an intense, searing pain that signals the need to immediately terminate the injection.
   C. Correct needle placement can be determined by elicitation of paresthesia, perivascular sheath technique, transarterial placement, and a nerve stimulator.
5. **Nerve block needles**
   A. **Blunt-bevel needle:** designed to minimize trauma upon direct contact with nerves. The angle of the bevel is increased 20-30 degrees, and the sharpness is decreased.
   B. **Insulated needle:** a nonconductor is bonded to the needle except for the last millimeter before the bevel.
   C. **The beaded needle:** a regional needle designed for use with a nerve stimulator.

Peripheral Nerve Blocks

1. **Cervical plexus block**
   A. **Technique:** with the patient's head turned to the opposite side, a line connecting the tip of the mastoid process of the temporal bone and the anterior tubercle of the transverse process of the sixth cervical vertebra (Chassaignac's tubercle, the most prominent of the processes) identifies the approximate plane in which the cervical transverse processes lie. Using a 22 g needle, penetrate the skin over each point, directing the needle in a slightly caudal direction to contact each transverse process. Confirm the position by 'walking' the needle off the tip of the transverse process. Ensure that neither blood nor CSF can be aspirated. Inject 3-5 mL of local anesthetic
   B. **Complications:** blockade of the phrenic nerve, Horner syndrome (ptosis, miosis, enophthalmos, anhydrosis), hoarseness (recurrent laryngeal nerve block), accidental subarachnoid or epidural injection.

2. Brachial plexus blocks

    A. Interscalene block

        1. Technique: the needle is inserted in the interscalene groove at the level of the cricoid cartilage and advanced perpendicular to the skin until a paresthesia is elicited or a transverse spinous process is contacted, at which point 30-40 cc of local anesthetic is injected.

        2. Indications: any procedure on the upper extremity, including the shoulder. This technique has a high rate of failure to achieve full block of the ulnar nerve (10-20%) for hand surgery.

        3. Special contraindications: contralateral phrenic paresis, severe asthma.

        4. Side effects: Horner's syndrome, phrenic paresis.

        5. Complications: proximity of the vertebral artery makes intraarterial injection possible with rapid progression to grand mal seizure after small amounts are injected. The neural foramina can be reached, and massive epidural, subarachnoid, or subdural injection can occur. Stellate ganglion block results in Horner's sign (myosis, ptosis, anhidrosis). Other complications include recurrent laryngeal nerve block (30-50%) leading to hoarseness, phrenic nerve block, pneumothorax, infection, bleeding, and nerve injury.

    B. Supraclavicular block

        1. Indications: procedures on the upper arm, elbow, lower arm and hand.

        2. Special contraindications: hemorrhagic diathesis, contralateral phrenic paresis.

        3. Side effects: Horner's syndrome, phrenic paresis.

        4. Complications: pneumothorax (1-6%) and hemothorax are the most common. Phrenic nerve block and Horner's syndrome may occur.

    C. Axillary block

        1. Indications: procedures on the lower arm and hand.

        2. Anatomy: it should be noted that in the axilla, the musculocutaneous nerve has already left its sheath and lies within the coracobrachialis.

        3. Special contraindications: lymphangitis (presumed infected axillary nodes).

        4. Complications: puncture of the axillary artery, intravenous/intra-arterial injection (systemic toxic reaction), postoperative neuropathies (more common when multiple sites of paresthesia are elicited).

3. Intercostal nerve block

    A. Technique: optimally performed with patient prone or sitting, a 22 g needle is inserted perpendicular to the skin in the posterior axillary line over the lower edge of the rib, the needle then is 'walked' off the rib inferiorly until it slips off the rib, after negative aspiration for blood 5 mL of local anesthetic is injected.

    B. Complications: the principle risks are pneumothorax and accidental intravascular injection of local anesthetic solutions.

4. Nerve blocks of the lower extremity

    A. Sciatic nerve block

        1. Technique: the patient is placed in the Sim's position (the lateral decubitus position with the leg to be blocked uppermost and flexed at the hip and knee) a line is drawn from the posterior iliac spine and the greater trochanter of the femur, the needle is inserted about 5 cm caudad from the midpoint of this line, and about 25 mL of 1.5% lidocaine or 0.5% bupivacaine or ropivacaine is injected after elicitation of a paresthesia.

B. **Femoral nerve block**
1. **Indications:** surgery of the foot and lower leg.
2. **Technique:** insert short-beveled 22 g block needle in a 30-degree cephalad direction just lateral to the femoral artery and just below the inguinal ligament, fell for 2 'pops' as the needle passes first through the fascia lata and then the fascia iliaca, a nerve stimulator can be used looking for quadricep contractions with a stimulating current of 0.3 mA, inject 15 mL of bupivacaine 0.5%.

C. **3 in 1 block** (femoral, obturator, and lateral cutaneous nerves)
1. Technique: identical to femoral nerve block but a greater volume of local anesthetic used (inject 30 mL)

D. **Ankle block** (requires 5 separate nerve blocks)
1. **Posterior tibial nerve:** insert needle behind the posterior tibial artery and advanced until a paresthesia to the sole of the foot is elicited, inject 5 mL of local anesthetic.
2. **Sural nerve:** inject 5 mL of local anesthetic in the groove between the lateral malleolus and calcaneus.
3. **Saphenous nerve:** inject 5 mL of local anesthetic anterior to the medial malleolus.
4. **Deep peroneal nerve:** inject 5 mL of local anesthetic lateral to the anterior tibial artery at the distal end of the tibia at the level of the skin cease.
5. **Superficial peroneal nerve:** infiltrate a ridge of local anesthetic (10 mL) from the anterior tibia to lateral malleolus.

5. **Intravenous regional neural anesthesia** (Bier Block)
A. **Indications:** forearm and hand surgery of short duration; < 90 minutes.
B. **Technique:** place a small gauge IV as distally as possible, place a double tourniquet around the upper arm, exsanguinate the arm by elevating and wrapping it tightly, with the proximal tourniquet inflated inject 40-50 mL of 0.5% lidocaine (ropivacaine 1.2-1.8 mg/kg can also be used), when the patient feels discomfort from the proximal tourniquet inflate the distal cuff then deflate the proximal cuff.
C. **Complications:** local anesthetic toxicity (the tourniquet should be left inflated for at least 20-30 minutes).

6. **Common pediatric blocks**
A. **Ilioinguinal and iliohypogastric nerve blocks**
1. Effective for orchiopexy and hernia repair.
2. Bupivacaine 0.25-0.5% with ½00,000 epi up to a dose of 2 mg/kg is injected just medial to the anterior superior iliac spine in a fan like method. A second injection can be done lateral to the pubic tubercle

B. **Penile nerve block**
1. The penile nerve (a branch of the pudendal nerve) is blocked at the base of the penis with a 25-26 g needle with 1-4 mL of bupivacaine 0.25% without epi at the 10:30 and 1:30 positions. Provides 6 hours.

Pediatric Anesthesia

Pediatric Vital Signs and Weight

1. **Vital signs** (see table)
    A. Typical systemic blood pressure in children 1-10 years of age = 90 mmHg + (child's age in years x 2) mmHg.
    B. Lower limits of systemic blood pressure in children 1-10 years of age = 70 mmHg + (child's age in years x 2) mmHg.
2. **Age and approximate weight**
    A. 28 weeks = 1 kg +/- 100 g/wk from 22-30 weeks
    B. <1 year: ½ age (months) plus 4 kg
    C. 1 year to puberty: 2 times age in years plus 10 kg

Pediatric Vital Signs					
Age	RR	HR (Awake)	HR (Asleep)	SBP	DBP
Preterm	60	120-180	100-180	45-60	20-45
Neonate	40-60	100-180	80-160	55-80	20-60
Infant	30-60	100-160	75-160	87-105	53-66
Toddler	24-40	80-110	60-90	90-105	53-66
Preschooler	22-34	70-110	60-90	95-105	55-70
School Age	18-30	65-110	60-90	97-112	57-71
Adolescent	12-20	60-90	50-90	112-128	66-80

Pediatric Physiology and Pharmacology

1. **Physiologic differences** (as compared to the adult)
    A. **Cardiac:** cardiac output of neonates and infants is dependent on heart rate, since stroke volume is relatively fixed by a noncompliant and poorly developed left ventricle. The sympathetic nervous system and baroreceptor reflexes are not fully mature. The hallmark of hypovolemia is hypotension without tachycardia.
    B. **Respiratory:** increased respiratory rate; tidal volume and dead space per kg are constant; lower functional residual capacity; lower lung compliance; greater chest wall compliance; small alveoli are associated with low lung compliance; hypoxic and hypercapnic ventilatory drives are not well developed in neonates and infants; neonates are obligate nose breathers.
    C. **Temperature:** infants have poor central thermoregulation, thin insulating fat, increased body surface area to mass ratio, and high minute ventilation; heat production in neonates is nonshivering thermogenesis by metabolism of brown fat.
    D. **Renal:** normal renal function by 6-12 months of age; premature neonates may posses decreased creatinine clearance, impaired sodium retention,

glucose excretion, and bicarbonate reabsorption.

E. Metabolic: hypoglycemia is defined as <30 mg/dL in the neonate, and <40 mg/dL in older children.

F. Gastrointestinal: gastric emptying is prolonged, and the lower esophageal sphincter is incompetent, thus the high incidence of gastric reflux.

G. Central nervous system: the CNS is the least mature major organ system at birth predisposing the newborn to intraventricular hemorrhages, seizures, respiratory depression, and retinopathy.

2. **Pharmacologic differences** (as compared to the adult)

   A. Pediatric drug dosing is based upon a per-kilogram recommendation.

   B. Inhalational anesthetics: higher alveolar ventilation, relatively low functional residual capacity (i.e., a higher ratio of minute ventilation to functional residual capacity) contribute to a rapid rise in alveolar anesthetic concentration. The blood/gas coefficients of isoflurane and halothane are lower in neonates than adults. The minimum alveolar concentration is higher in infants than in neonates or adults. The blood pressure of neonates and infants tends to be more sensitive to volatile anesthetics.

   C. Nonvolatile anesthetics: an immature blood-brain barrier and decreased ability to metabolize drugs could increase the sensitivity of neonates to effects on IV anesthetics. Dose of thiopental is similar in peds and adults.

   D. Muscle relaxants: infants require higher doses of succinylcholine per kilogram than do adults because of their larger volume of distribution. Children are more susceptible to cardiac dysrhythmias, myoglobinemia, hyperkalemia, and MH after succinylcholine than adults. Profound bradycardia and sinus arrest may develop in pediatric patients (especially those <6 months of age) following the first dose of succinylcholine without atropine pretreatment. Nondepolarizing agents for infants and children have similar mg/kg requirements.

Pediatric Preoperative Evaluation (see preoperative section)

1. **History**

   A. Maternal health; gestational age and weight; events during labor and delivery (Apgar scores, etc); neonatal hospitalizations; congenital anomalies; medical, surgical and anesthetic history; allergies; medications.

2. **Physical exam**

   A. Airway exam (see preoperative evaluation section).

   B. Vital signs, height and weight.

   C. General appearance should be noted.

3. **Laboratory testing**

   A. Except as noted below, no routine lab testing should be performed.

   1. Tests should be specific for the patient's coexisting condition and planned surgery.

   2. Infants less then 6 months: preoperative hematocrit.

   3. Preterm infant: glucose, calcium, and coagulation studies.

   4. African-American or mixed race ancestry: sickle cell/anemia screening unless status is known.

   5. In children receiving therapeutic drugs: levels should be checked.

   6. Tonsillectomy and adenoidectomy or adenoidectomy: hematocrit (can be done during IV insertion).

4. **Premedications** (see premedication table)

A. Premedications should be considered for all patients. Parental presence in the operating room during induction is a technique increasing in number.

B. The most common premedication is midazolam 0.3-0.5 mg/kg PO 20-45 minutes prior to surgery. See premedication table for complete list.

C. Generally, infants less then 9 months of age require no premedication. Children 9 months to 5 years of age cling to their parents and may require sedation. Older children respond well to information and reassurance.

D. If anticholinergics are consider (generally for children under 1 year of age) they can be administered IV at the time of induction.

5. **Common coexisting and preexisting diseases**

   A. The child with a URI

   1. A URI within 2-4 weeks of general anesthesia and endotracheal intubation can place the child at an increased risk of perioperative pulmonary complications (wheezing, hypoxemia, atelectasis, laryngospasm).

   2. Attempts should be made to differentiate between an infectious cause of rhinorrhea and an allergic or vasomotor cause.

   3. Factors favoring postponing surgery include purulent nasal discharge, upper airway stridor, croup, lower respiratory symptoms (wheezing), severe cough, high fever, and a family history of reactive airway disease.

   4. Factors favoring performing surgery include clear 'allergic ' reactions, economic hardship on family, few and short 'URI-free' periods, and scheduled surgery may itself decrease frequency of URI's.

   B. Prematurity

   1. Prematurity is defined as birth before 37 weeks gestation or weight less than 2500 grams; premature infants are at increased risk for retinopathy of prematurity and apnea of prematurity.

   2. **Apnea of prematurity**

      A. Premature infants less than 50-60 weeks postconceptional age (gestational age plus chronological age) are prone to postoperative episodes of obstructive and central apnea for up to 24 hours.

      B. Risk factors include low gestational age at birth, necrotizing enterocolitis, neurologic problems, anemia (<30%), hypothermia, and sepsis.

      C. Elective or outpatient procedures should be deferred until the preterm infant reaches the age of at least 50 weeks postconception. If surgery planned, infants less than 50 weeks should be monitored with pulse oximetry for at least 12-24 hours; infants between 50-60 weeks postconception should be closely monitored in the recovery room for at least 2 hours.

      D. Regional anesthesia may be associated with a lower incidence.

   3. Retinopathy of prematurity: increased risk in infants with birth weights less than 1,700 grams; avoid hyperoxia.

   C. Intellectual impairment: children with severe developmental delay often have several coexisting disease, most often seizure disorders, gastroesophageal reflux, and chronic lung disease.

   D. Seizure disorders: anticonvulsant regimen and levels should be documented; anticonvulsants should not be withheld the day of surgery.

   E. Trisomy 21 (Down's Syndrome): increased risk of difficult airways, postoperative airway obstruction/croup, sleep apnea and subluxation of the atlanto-occipital joint; routine screening cervical spine radiographs in the asymptomatic child are not indicated.

Pediatric Airway Management

1. **Airway differences** (compared to an adult): large head; tongue larger in relation to the oral cavity; narrow nasal passages; epiglottis is narrow, shorter, U-shaped and protruding; hyoid bone not calcified in the infant; the larynx is higher in the infant neck (C3-4) then in the adult (C5-6) and is angulated and anterior appearing; short trachea and neck; cricoid cartilage (ring) narrowest point of airway in children younger than 8-10 years of age (glottis in adults), obligate nasal breathers (infants less than 6 months)

2. **Pediatric endotracheal tube recommendations** (see airway section)
   A. Uncuffed endotracheal tubes generally used for patients under 10 yrs, however, cuffed tubes have been used safely even in neonates.
   B. Endotracheal (cuffed) tube leak: 15-20 cm H_2O.
   C. Endotracheal tube size (mm): for children older then 2 years ETT can be estimated by: Age/4 + 4.
   D. Length of Insertion (cm) of ETT (oral)
      1. Under 1 year: 6 + Wt(kg).
      2. Over 2 years: 12 + Age/2.
      3. Multiply internal diameter (mm) of ETT by 3 to give insertion (cm).
      4. Add 2-3 cm for nasal tube.

3. **Equipment**
   A. **Reservoir bag:** newborn 0.5 L; 1-3 years 1.0 L; 3-5 years 2.0 L; greater than 5 years 3.0 L.
   B. **Arterial catheters:** neonates/infants 24g; less than 5 years old 22g; greater than 5 years old 20 g.
   C. **Central venous catheters** (heparin-coated)
      1. Depth of catheter (cm) from right internal jugular = pt height (cm)/10
      2. Catheter size recommendations
         A. Premature   3 Fr, 5 cm, single lumen
         B. < 1 year   4 Fr, 8 cm, single lumen
         C. 1-2 year   4 Fr, 8 cm, single lumen
         D. 3-8 year   4 Fr, 13 cm, single lumen
         E. > 8 year   5 Fr, 12 cm, single lumen

4. **Postanesthetic airway complications**
   A. **Laryngospasm**
      1. Laryngospasm, a involuntary spasm of laryngeal musculature caused by stimulation of the superior laryngeal nerve, is best avoided by extubating the patient either awake or while deeply anesthetized.
      2. Recent URI or exposure to secondhand smoke predisposes the patient to laryngospasm. Extubating during stage 2 increases risk.
      3. Treatment includes gentle positive pressure ventilation, forward jaw thrust, intravenous lidocaine (1-1.5 mg/kg) or paralysis.
      4. Postoperative pharyngeal secretions increase risk of laryngospasm, therefore, patients should recover in the lateral position so that oral secretions pool and drain away from the vocal cords.
   B. **Postintubation croup**
      1. Croup is due to glottic or tracheal edema.
      2. Uncuffed endotracheal tubes (in pts <8-10 yrs of age) or cuff tubes with low balloon pressure (10-25 cm H_2O) decrease the incidence of croup.
      3. Postoperative croup is associated with early childhood (1-4 yrs age), repeated intubation attempts, large endotracheal tubes, prolonged surgery, head/neck procedures, and excessive movements of the tube.

4. Treatment includes inhalation of nebulized racemic epinephrine (0.25-0.5 mL of a 2.25% solution in 2.5 mL NS). Intravenous dexamethasone (0.25-0.5 mg/kg) may help prevent edema formation.

Endotracheal Tube Sizes and Laryngoscope Blade Size

Age	Laryngoscope	Endotracheal Tube Size (mm)	Distance at Teeth (cm)	Suction Catheter (F)
Neonate <1000 g	Miller 0	2.5	6.5-7.0	5
Neonate 1000-2000 g		3	7-8	5-6
Neonate 2000-3000 g		3.0-3.5	8-9	6-7
Term Infant	Miller 0-1 Wis-Hipple 1 Robertshaw 0	3.0-3.5	9-10	7-8
6 months		3.5-4.0	10	8
1 year	Wis-Hipple 1.5 Robertshaw 1	4.0-4.5	11	8
2 years	Miller 2 Flagg 2	4.5-5.0	12	8
4 years		5.0-5.5	14	10
6 years		5.5	15	10
8 years	Miller 2-3 Macintosh 2	6	16	10
10 years		6.5	17	12
12 years	Macintosh 3	7	18	12
Adolescent/ Adult	Macintosh 3 Miller 3	7.0-8.0	20	12

Tube Selection for Single Lung Ventilation In Children

Age (yrs)	ETT (ID)	BB (Fr)	Univent	DLT (Fr)
0.5-1	3.5-4.0	5		
1-2	4.0-4.5	5		
2-4	4.5-5.0	5		
4-6	5.0-5.5	5		
6-8	5.5-6.0	6	3.5	
8-10	6.0 cuff	6	3.5	26
10-12	6.5 cuff	6	4.5	26-28

12-14	6.5-7.0 cuff	6	4.5	32
14-16	7.0 cuff	7	6.0	35
16-18	7.0-8.0 cuff	7	7.0	35
ETT: endotracheal tube; BB: bronchial blocker; DLT: double lumen tube				

Neuraxial Blockade in the Pediatric Patient

1. **Pharmacology**
   A. Protein binding of local anesthetics is decreased in neonates because of decreased of albumin.
   B. Increased volume of distribution may decrease free local anesthetic concentrations.
2. **Spinal anesthesia**
   A. Hypobaric solutions are most commonly used.
      1. Bupivacaine 0.75% in 8.25% dextrose, 0.3 mg/kg in infants and children.
      2. Tetracaine 1% with equal volume 10% dextrose, 0.8-1.0 mg/kg in infants and 0.25-0.5 mg/kg in children.
      3. Duration may be prolonged with the addition of epinephrine 10 mcg/kg (up to 0.2 mg).
   B. Complications
      1. Anesthetic level recedes faster in children than adults.
      2. Hypotension is rare in children under 10 years.
      3. Contraindicated in children with CNS anatomic defects and a history of grade III-IV intraventricular hemorrhage.
3. **Caudal and lumbar epidural anesthesia**
   A. Dural sac in the neonate ends at S3.
   B. Caudal epidural provides excellent postoperative analgesia for circumcision, hypospadias repair, orchiopexy, herniorrhaphy and some orthopedic procedures.
   C. Caudal catheters
      1. Infants: 22g catheter placed (40-50 mm) through 20g Tuohy needle.
      2. Children: 20g cath placed (90-100 mm) through 17-18g Tuohy needle.
   D. **Epidural catheters:** older children use 20g cath with 18g Tuohy needle.
   E. Drugs
      1. **Bupivacaine**, 0.125% to 0.25% with or without epi: 0.5-1.0 mL/kg.
      2. **Ropivacaine**, 0.2% with or without epinephrine: 1 mL/kg.
      3. **Lidocaine**, 1%, 0.5 mL/kg
      4. Opioids
         A. Morphine: 25-70 mcg/kg.
         B. Hydromorphone: 6 mcg/kg
         C. Fentanyl
      5. Continuous infusion
         A. Infants and children less than 7 years: load with 0.04 cc/kg/segment of 0.1% bupivacaine (+/- fentanyl 2-3 mcg/cc).
         B. Children older than 7 years load with 0.02 cc/kg/segment of 0.1% bupivacaine (with or without fentanyl 2-3 mcg/cc).
         C. Infusions of 0.1% bupivacaine (with or without fentanyl 2-3 mcg/cc) at 0.1 cc/kg/hr. May be increased up to 0.3 cc/kg/hr.
         D. Fentanyl should not be used in infants under 1 year.

F. **Complications** (similar to adults)
   1. Unintentional dural puncture.
   2. Catheter complications: inability to thread the epidural catheter, epidural catheter inserted into epidural vein, catheter breaks off or becomes knotted, cannulation of the subdural space.
   3. Unintentional subarachnoid injection.
   4. Intravascular injection of local anesthetic.
   5. Local anesthetic overdose.
   6. Direct spinal cord injury.
   7. Blood tap.
   8. Postdural puncture headache.
   9. Epidural abscess or hematoma.

Anesthesia for Common Pediatric Conditions

1. **Acute airway obstruction** (see table)
   A. **Causes:** laryngotracheobronchitis (croup), epiglottis, and foreign-body aspiration.
   B. **Pathophysiology:** inspiratory stridor is the hallmark of upper airway , supraglottic, and glottic obstruction (croup); wheezing generally indicates intrathoracic airway obstruction (foreign-body aspiration).
   C. **Contributing factors**
      1. **Croup (including postintubation or traumatic croup):** traumatic or repeated intubations, tight fitting ETT, coughing/straining on the ETT, change in patient's position during surgery, intubation greater than one hour, head and neck surgery.
   D. **Treatment**
      1. Total obstruction can occur, adequate preparation for a possible tracheostomy should be made prior to induction of anesthesia.
      2. **Epiglottis:** a slow, gentle, inhalational induction followed by intubation to secure the airway (use ETT 0.5 smaller then usual), only then followed by paralysis, is the preferred approach.
      3. **Acute laryngotracheobronchitis (croup):** aerosolized racemic epinephrine and humidified oxygen; the use of steroids (Decadron 0.3-0.5 mg/kg) is controversial; the need for intubation only becomes necessary when airway obstruction becomes severe or prolonged enough to lead to respiratory muscle exhaustion and failure.
      4. **Foreign-body:** an inhalational induction to induce a state of deep anesthesia, provide IV access, and perform gentle, upper airway endoscopy, removing the foreign object if possible, or securing the airway and bypassing it if not.

2. **Hypertrophic pyloric stenosis**
   A. **Manifestations:** persistent vomiting depletes sodium, potassium, chloride, and hydrogen ions, causing hyponatremic, hypokalemic, hypochloremic metabolic alkalosis. Initially, the kidney compensate for the alkalosis by excreting sodium bicarbonate in the urine. Later, as hyponatremia and dehydration worsen, the kidneys must conserve sodium at the expense of hydrogen ion excretion (resulting in paradoxic aciduria). Neonates may be at increased risk for respiratory depression and hypoventilation postoperatively because of persistent metabolic or CSF alkalosis.
   B. **Management:** electrolyte abnormalities must be corrected prior to surgery;

continuous nasogastric suction; increase risk of aspiration; tracheal intubation may be accomplished awake or after the induction of anesthesia; caudal anesthetic (1.25 mg/kg of 0.25% bupivacaine with epi) is useful for decreasing anesthetic requirements and postoperative pain management.

3. Inguinal hernia repair

A. Manifestations: in infants often associated with prematurity, a history of RDS, and congenital heart disease; the preterm infant with inguinal hernia is at increased risk for postoperative apnea and pulmonary complications.

B. Management: caudal anesthesia (0.25% bupivacaine or ropivacaine 0.75 mg/kg) to decrease intraoperative anesthetic requirements and provide postoperative analgesia.

C. Complications: as an intraperitoneal procedure there may be traction on the spermatic cord which can be a stimulus to laryngospasm.

4. Tonsillectomy and adenoidectomy

A. Manifestations: lymphoid hyperplasia can lead to upper airway obstruction, obligate nasal breathing, and pulmonary hypertension; evidence of airway obstruction, snoring, and apnea should be noted.

B. Management: anesthesia induction can be either inhalational or IV and maintenance provided by nearly any means; strict attention to airway patency, hemostasis, and observation until the child is awake and in control of airway and secretions; postoperative vomiting is common.

C. Postoperative bleeding: may be evidenced by restlessness, pallor, tachycardia, or hypotension; if reoperation is necessary to control bleeding, intravascular volume must first be restored; rapid-sequence induction with cricoid pressure after gastric suctioning because of the risk of aspiration (blood in the stomach is common).

5. Myringotomy and insertion of tympanostomy tubes

A. Manifestations: because of the chronic and recurring nature of this illness, it is not uncommon for these patients to have symptoms of an URI on the day of surgery.

B. Management: typically very short procedure; inhalational induction common with oxygen, nitrous oxide and volatile agent; intravenous access is usually not necessary.

6. Ventricular shunts

A. Manifestations: shunts may be required for either internal or external hydrocephalus; all patients should be evaluated for intracranial hypertension (crying, irritability, sudden personality or behavior change, sleepiness, vomiting, and lethargy).

B. Management: induction of anesthesia should consider possible elevated ICP (respiration patterns, induction agents); hyperventilation is effective for acute rises in ICP (only hyperventilate suspected of elevated ICP)

Airway Obstruction in Children			
	Foreign-Body	**Croup**	**Epiglottis**
Etiology	Aspiration	Viral	Bacterial
Age	6 mos - 5 yrs	6 mos -4 yrs	1 yr - adult
Onset	Usually acute	Days (gradual)	Hours
Signs and Symptoms	Cough, voice change, drooling, dysphagia are possible	Low-grade fever, croupy or seal-bark cough, inspiratory stridor, rhinorrhea	Low-pitched inspiratory stridor, pharyngitis, drooling, fever, lethargic to restless, tachypnea, sitting, muffled cough
Obstruction	Supra/subglottic	Subglottic	Supraglottic
Season	None	Winter	None

Anesthesia for Neonatal Emergencies

1. **Congenital diaphragmatic hernia**
   A. **Manifestations:** three types (left or right posterolateral foramen of Bochdalek or anterior foramen of Morgagni) with left most common; a reduction in alveoli and bronchioli (pulmonary hypoplasia) is accompanied by marked elevation in pulmonary vascular resistance; hallmarks include hypoxia, scaphoid abdomen, bowel in the thorax.
   B. **Management:** gastric distention should be minimized by placement of a nasogastric tube and avoidance of high levels of positive-pressure ventilation; sudden fall in lung compliance, blood pressure or oxygenation may signal a contralateral pneumothorax; hyperventilation is recommended to decrease PVR and minimize right-to-left shunting; after hernia reduction, attempts to expand the hypoplastic lung are not recommended.

2. **Tracheoesophageal fistula (TEF)**
   A. **Manifestations:** most common is combination of upper esophagus that ends in a blind pouch and a lower esophagus that connects to the trachea; breathing results in gastric distention; coughing, cyanosis and choking occur with the first feeding; diagnosis made upon failure to pass a catheter into the stomach. Aspiration pneumonia and the coexistence of other congenital anomalies are common
   B. **Management:** awake tracheal intubation after suction of the esophageal pouch (open gastrostomy tube to air if present); correct endotracheal tube position is the tip of the tube distal to the fistula and above the carina; gastrostomy tube is placed after intubation; frequent ETT suction.

3. **Omphalocele and gastroschisis**
   A. **Gastroschisis:** defect in abdominal wall lateral to umbilicus; no hernial sac; no associated congenital anomalies.
   B. **Omphalocele:** defect in abdominal wall at the base of the umbilicus; hernial sac present; associated with congenital anomalies (trisomy 21, cardiac anomalies, diaphragmatic hernia, bladder anomalies).
   C. **Management:** decompress stomach before induction; intubate awake or asleep; avoid nitrous oxide; insure adequate muscle relaxation; replace third-space fluid loses aggressively; the neonate commonly remains

intubated after the procedure and is weaned from the ventilator over the next 1-2 days.

4. **Necrotizing enterocolitis**
   A. **Manifestations:** acquired intestinal tract necrosis that appears in the absence of functional or anatomic lesions. Predominantly in premature. Systemic signs include temperature instability, lethargy, respiratory and circulatory instability, oliguria, and bleeding diathesis.
   B. **Management:** risk of aspiration; avoid nitrous oxide; the major challenge is maintaining an adequate circulating blood volume and preventing aspiration; third-space fluid replacement may exceed 100-200 mL/kg/hr.

5. **Myelodysplasia**
   A. **Manifestations:** failure of neural tube closure can result in abnormalities ranging from spina bifida to myelomeningocele (abnormality involving vertebral bodies, the spinal cord and the brain stem). Ninety percent of myelomeningocele patients have Arnold-Chiari malformation (downward displacement of the brain stem and the cerebellar tonsils through the cervical spinal canal with medullary kinking, blocking normal circulation of the CSF and leads to progressive hydrocephalus.
   B. **Management:** patients come to the OR in the prone position; using sterile towels the patient is placed supine for intubation; anesthesia can be induced with inhalational or IV agents; succinylcholine is not contraindicated; anesthetic technique should allow for rapid extubation following surgery; spinal anesthesia (0.5-0.7 mg/kg of hyperbaric tetracaine with epinephrine) can be used in conjunction.

Cardiac Anesthesia

Pediatric Cardiovascular Physiology

1. **Fetal circulation**
   A. Acidosis, sepsis, hypothermia, hypoxia, and hypercarbia may cause reopening of the fetal shunts and persistence of the fetal circulation.
   B. Diagnosis of persistent pulmonary hypertension of the newborn can be confirmed by measurement of the PaO_2 in blood obtained simultaneously from preductal (right radial) and postductal (umbilical, posterior tibial, dorsalis pedis) arteries. A difference of 20 mmHg verifies the diagnosis.
2. **Closure of the ductus arteriosus**
   A. In the fetus, patency of the ductus arteriosus is maintained by high levels of prostaglandin (PGI_2 and PGE_1).
   B. Functional closure occurs by contraction of the smooth muscle of the ductal wall and usually occurs 10-15 hours after birth. An increase in PO_2 and a decrease in prostaglandins at birth contribute to functional closure.
   C. Permanent anatomic closure of the duct occurs in 4 to 6 weeks.
3. **Closure of the foramen ovale**
   A. Increase in left atrial over right atrial pressure functionally closes the foramen ovale.
   B. Anatomic closure of the foramen ovale occurs between 3 months and 1 year of age, although 20%-30% of adults and 50% of children less than 5 years of age have a probe-patent foramen ovale.
4. **Closure of the ductus venosus**
   A. Decrease in umbilical venous blood flow causes passive closure of the ductus venosus.
   B. The ductus venosus is functionally closed by 1 week of life and anatomically closed by 3 weeks.
5. **Differences between neonatal and adult cardiac physiology**
   A. Infants: there is a parasympathetic nervous system dominance that reflects the relative immaturity of the sympathetic nervous system.
   B. Neonatal hearts have more inelastic membrane masses than elastic contractile mass, thus, infant hearts have less myocardial reserve, a greater sensitivity to drugs causing myocardial depression, and a greater sensitivity to volume overload.
   C. Noncompliant ventricles make stroke volume less responsive to increases in preload or demand. Increases in cardiac output are predominantly dependent on increases in heart rate.
   D. The right and left ventricles are equal in muscle mass at birth. A left to right muscle mass ratio of 2:1 is not achieved until the age of 4-5 months.

Premedication for Adult Cardiac Surgery

1. Traditional premedications have included morphine 0.1-0.15 mg/kg IM, scopolamine 0.3-0.4 mg IM (0.2 mg for patients older than 70 yrs), diazepam 0.15 mg/kg or lorazepam 0.06 mg/kg PO approximately 1-2 hours prior to surgery. Same day admission patients often receive IV fentanyl and a benzodiazepine (i.e., versed) to provide anxiolysis and pain relief instead of

IM predications.

2. The dose of premedication should be reduced in patients with critical aortic or mitral stenosis, those undergoing cardiac transplantation, patients with CHF, and patients with renal or hepatic dysfunction.

3. Patients on heparin should not receive any IM medications. A common predication for heparinized patients includes diazepam 0.15 mg/kg PO (or lorazepam 0.04 mg/kg) and morphine 1-10 mg IV or a combination of fentanyl and versed IV.

4. Other orders and medications

   A. Current cardiac medications should be continued; diuretics are usually held except in patients with CHF or afternoon cases.

   B. Nasal cannula oxygen (2-4 lpm) should be ordered along with the premedication (oxygen should be given to all sedated patients).

Cardiopulmonary Bypass

1. **Prebypass period**

   A. This period is characterized by variable levels of stimulation. Stimulating periods include sternal splitting and retraction, pericardial incision, and aortic root dissection and cannulation.

   B. **Baseline laboratory data:** ABG, Hct, and ACT, should be obtained.

   C. During sternal splitting, the lungs should be deflated.

   D. Aortic root dissection and cannulation: this period can be very stimulating and should be treated aggressively with short-acting agents to minimize the risk of aortic tear or dissection (systolic <100 mmHg).

   E. **Heparinization**

      1. Heparin 300 IU/kg (400 IU/kg if receiving IV heparin): administration is through a centrally placed catheter; aspirate blood both before and after injection; vasodilation may occur with heparin bolus.

      2. Check an ACT 5 minutes after heparin administration to monitor the degree of anticoagulation. ACT should be greater than 400 seconds prior to initiating cardiopulmonary bypass. If needed, an additional 200-300 IU/kg is administered. If this fails, antithrombin III (500-1000 IU) or FFP may be necessary to correct a probable antithrombin III deficiency.

      3. **Heparin induced thrombocytopenia (HIT):** may develop life-threatening thrombotic complications when exposed to heparin. Alternative drugs to heparin include Danaparoid (Orgaran), Lepirudin (Refludan), and Ancrod. One technique for management includes:

         A. All forms of heparin are removed preoperatively.

         B. Dipyridamole 75 mg PO the night before and on-call to OR.

         C. A heparin free PA catheter is used.

         D. Prostaglandin E_1 (PGE_1) is begun before heparinization. The dose is increased as tolerated to 2-4 mcg per minute.

         E. A bypass dose of porcine heparin is administered before aortic cannulation to minimize the likelihood of a repeat dose.

         F. The PGE_1 infusion is discontinued approximately 15 minutes after all of the heparin has been reversed with protamine.

         G. Aspirin is administered early in the postoperative period.

   F. **Checklist prior to initiating cardiopulmonary bypass**

      1. Ensure adequate heparinization (ACT of 400-450 seconds).

2. Turn nitrous oxide off, place on 100% oxygen.
3. Pulmonary artery catheter should be pulled back 3-5 cm.
4. Turn transesophageal echo off.
5. Check anesthetic depth and muscle paralysis (bolus as needed).
6. Exam the face (color), eyes (pupils), and EEG (if used).
7. Record pre-CBP UOP and fluid administration.

2. Bypass period

A. Checklist/monitoring during cardiopulmonary bypass

1. Once adequate flows and venous drainage are established, IV fluids, and positive-pressure ventilation are discontinued.
2. The perfusionist should follow the ACT (to ensure adequate heparinization), ABGs (uncorrected), hematocrit, potassium, calcium.
3. Administer additional anesthetic drugs (muscle relaxants, etc).
4. **Watch for the following**
   A. **Hypotension**: venous cannula problems (kink, malposition, clamp, air lock), inadequate venous return (bleeding hypovolemia, IVC obstruction), pump problems (poor occlusion, low flows), arterial cannula problem (misdirected, kinked, partially clamped, dissection), vasodilation (anesthetics, hemodilution, idiopathic, allergic), transducer or monitoring malfunction (stopcocks the wrong way).
   B. **Hypertension**: pump problems (increased flow), arterial cannula misdirected), vasoconstriction (light anesthesia, response to temperature changes), transducer or monitor malfunction.
   C. **Changes in patients' facial appearance**: suffusion (inadequate SVC drainage), unilateral blanching (innominate artery cannulation), obstruction of jugular venous drainage by caval cannula, head position, neck compression.
   D. **Low venous return:** aortic dissection, bleeding, pooling of blood, allergic reaction, obstruction of venous tubing, lack of venous return.

B. Checklist prior to discontinuing cardiopulmonary bypass

1. Labs: Hct (22-25% ideal), ABGs, potassium, glucose, and calcium.
2. Ventilate lungs with 100% oxygen (consider suctioning first).
3. Core temperature should be normothermic (37°C).
4. Stable rhythm (preferably sinus rhythm) with adequate heart rate (80-100 beats/min); place pacing wires if necessary.
5. Venting of arterial air (verify by TEE if available).
6. All monitors on and recalibrated.
7. If necessary, drug therapy (vasopressors, etc.) should be started.

C. Discontinuation from cardiopulmonary bypass

1. Pressure maintenance: transfuse from CPB reservoir to maintain left atrial pressure or PA occlusion pressure. Optimal filling is determined by blood pressure, cardiac output, and direct observation of the heart.
   A. Maintenance of hemodynamics (see table)
      1. Low cardiac output (despite adequate filling pressure and rhythm) may indicate the need for a positive inotrope. Consider dopamine, dobutamine, amrinone and epinephrine.
      2. High cardiac output but low BP consider a vasoconstrictor.
      3. RV dysfunction: noted by CVP rising out of proportion to left atrial pressure. Treat know causes of elevated PVR (light anesthesia, hypercarbia, hypoxemia, and acidemia). Consider vasodilator therapy (nitroglycerin, nitroprusside) or inotropic

support.
   4. Hypertension: treated to prevent bleeding at the suture lines
      and cannulation sites.
   2. Look at the heart to evaluate overall function (TEE if available).
   3. Return of CPB reservoir blood to patient.
3. **Post cardiopulmonary bypass period**
   A. **Hemodynamic stability is the primary goal.**
   B. **Protamine:** once hemodynamic stability is achieved and the aortic and
      vena caval cannula have been removed, protamine can be given.
      1. Initially 25-50 mg is given over 5 minutes, and the hemodynamic
         response is observed.
      2. Monitor PA pressures while administering.
      3. In general, 1 mg of protamine is given for each 1 mg of heparin given.
      4. After protamine administration, check ACT and compare to baseline.
         Additional protamine can be given if needed.
      5. During transfusion of heparinized pump blood, additional protamine (25-
         50 mg) should be given.
      6. Correct coagulation and other lab adjustments as needed.
   C. Prepare the patient for transfer to ICU.

Post-Cardiopulmonary Bypass Hemodynamics					
	Hypo-volemic	LV Failure	RV Failure	High SVR	Low SVR
Blood Pressure	Low	Low	Low	High	Low
CVP	Low	Normal or high	High	Normal or high	Normal or low
PAP	Low	High	Normal or high	Normal or high	Normal or low
PCWP	Low	High	Normal or low	Normal or high	Normal or low
CO	Low	Low	Low	Low	High
SVR	Normal or high	High	Normal or high	High	Low
Treatment	Volume; vasopressor	Inotrope; reduce afterload; IABP; LVAD	Pulmonary vasodilator; RVAD	Narcotics; vasodilator	Increase hct; vaso-pressors

LV=Left ventricle; RV=Right ventricle; SVR=Systemic vascular resistance; CVP=Central venous pressure; PAP=Pulmonary artery pressure; PCWP=Pulmonary capillary wedge pressure; CO=Cardiac output

Acid-Base Management During Cardiopulmonary Bypass

1. **pH-stat:** requires temperature correction for interpretation of blood gases during CPB. Temperature correction can be accomplished by setting the blood gas analyzer to measure the patient's temperature.
2. **Alpha-stat:** requires no temperature correction for interpreting blood gases. The sample is warmed to 37 degrees C and then measured in the blood gas analyzer as any other sample.

Post-Cardiopulmonary Bypass Bleeding

1. **Differential diagnosis:** uncorrected surgical defects, circulating anticoagulants (residual heparin, heparin rebound, protamine anticoagulation), and platelet defects (thrombocytopenia).
2. **Treatment**
   A. **Circulating anticoagulants:** adequate heparinization should be confirmed with ACT, and additional protamine given if needed.
   B. **Platelet abnormalities:** given after other coagulation deficiencies have been corrected and no surgically correctable lesion exists.
   C. Deficiencies of circulating procoagulants should be corrected by infusing FFP, cryoprecipitate, or fresh donor blood.
3. **Prevention of post-CPB bleeding** (pharmacological factors)
   A. **Desmopressin**
      1. Synthetic product that increases plasma levels of Factor VIII and Von Willebrand factor and decreases bleeding times.
      2. Dosing. 0.3 mcg/kg IV given over 20-30 min.
      3. Side effects. Decreased free water clearance from ADH activity, hypotension, thrombosis, decreased serum sodium, hyponatremic seizures.
   B. **Aprotinin:** inhibitor of several proteases and factor XIIa activation of complement (see drug section).
   C. **Antifibrinolytic agents**
      1. **Epsilon aminocaproic acid (Amicar)**
         A. Synthetic antifibrinolytic: inhibits proteolytic activity of plasmin and conversion of plasminogen to plasmin by plasminogen activator.
         B. Loading dose 100-150 mg/kg IV followed by constant infusion of 10-15 mg/kg/h.
      2. **Tranexamic acid**
         A. Similar mechanism as Amicar but is about 10 times more potent.
         B. Loading dose 10 mg/kg IV followed by infusion of 1 mg/kg/hr.
      3. **Complications of antifibrinolytics**
         A. Bleeding into kidneys or ureters may thrombose and obstruct the upper urinary tract.
         B. Contraindicated in DIC.
         C. Hypotension may occur with rapid administration.
         D. May be associated with thrombosis and subsequent stroke, myocardial infarction or deep vein thrombosis.

Automatic Implantable Cardioverter Defibrillator (AICD)

1. Common indications for AICD implantation
A. Patients with a history of near-sudden death who have not responded to drug therapy and are not candidates for arrhythmia surgery.

B. Patients who have had unsuccessful arrhythmia surgery.

C. Post cardiac arrest patients who have not had an MI and who have no inducible arrhythmia during electrophysiologic testing.

D. Patients undergoing endocardial resection for recurrent VT.

2. Contraindications
A. Uncontrolled congestive heart failure.

B. Frequent recurrences of VT that would rapidly deplete the battery.

3. Intraoperative testing
A. The purpose is to establish the defibrillation threshold (i.e., the minimum energy required to defibrillate the heart to a stable rhythm). Internal paddles should be readily available in the operative field during the entire procedure, and external patches should also be placed preoperatively.

B. If all the tests are successful, an AICD is connected to the leads and ventricular fibrillation is again induced to test the newly implanted unit.

4. Anesthetic considerations
A. Preoperative assessment
1. The indication for the AICD should be noted.

2. Many patients will be taking antidysrhythmic agents at the time of surgery. In theory, the device and defibrillation thresholds should be tested while the patient is on the drug regimen that is planned postoperatively.

3. Antidysrhythmic agent of concern is amiodarone, which is negative inotropic agent and vasodilator. Amiodarone may cause refractory bradycardia or may precipitate a profound and prolonged hypotensive state postoperatively.

B. Intraoperatively monitoring: standard monitors and an arterial line are the minimum required monitors. Central venous access may be considered for administration of vasoactive drugs. PA catheter is generally not needed.

C. Anesthetic technique: general anesthesia with nitrous oxide, narcotic, and muscle relaxant anesthetic is most common.

D. Other considerations
1. Cardioversion is commonly associated with transient hypertension and tachycardia, probably caused by sympathetic outflow.

2. Multiple intraoperative inductions of VT or VF may cause hypotension.

3. External defibrillator must be available.

4. The AICD is occasionally inactivated after being placed to avoid the cautery from trigger the AICD to discharge. The AICD is reactivated postoperatively.

5. Complications
A. Pacemaker interaction
1. Both temporary and permanent pacemakers may interact with a AICD by interfering with dysrhythmia detection.

2. The AICD can be deactivated when using temporary pacing, especially, A-V sequential pacing.

B. Mechanical. lead fractures, lead insulation breaks, and lead migration.

C. Rate miscounting leading to unnecessary shocks.

D. Infection.

Vascular Anesthesia

Carotid Artery Surgery (carotid endarterectomy; CEA)

1. **General considerations**
   A. **Indications:** TIAs associated with ipsilateral severe carotid stenosis (>70% occlusion), severe ipsilateral stenosis in a patient with a minor (incomplete) stroke, and 30-70% occlusion in a patient with ipsilateral symptoms (usually an ulcerated plaque), emboli arising from a carotid lesion, large ulcerated plaque.
   B. **Operative mortality is 1-4%** (primarily due to cardiac complications).
   C. **Perioperative morbidity is 4-10%:** stroke is the most common and expected major complication during and after carotid endarterectomy. Hypertension occurs in about 70% of patients undergoing carotid endarterectomy and is associated with an increase in the risk of stroke.
   D. **Complications:** hematoma with tracheal compression, supraglottic edema, cranial nerve injury (cranial nerves VII, IX, X, and XII), myocardial infarction, intraparenchymal hemorrhage, carotid occlusion, intracerebral hemorrhage, embolism.

2. **Preoperative anesthetic evaluation**
   A. Most patients undergoing CEA are elderly and hypertensive, with generalized arteriosclerosis. Preoperative evaluation should include a through cardiac and neurologic evaluation.
   B. **The anesthetic goal** is to maintain adequate cerebral perfusion without stressing the heart. In addition, the patient should be sufficiently responsive immediately after surgery to obey commands and thereby facilitate neurologic evaluation.

3. **Anesthetic management**
   A. **Anesthetic technique** (general or regional anesthesia can be used)
      1. **Regional anesthesia**
         A. Regional anesthesia can be achieved by performing a superficial and deep cervical plexus block, which effectively blocks the C2-C4 nerves. The principal advantage of this technique is that the patient remains awake and can be examined intraoperatively. The need for a temporary shunt can be assessed and any new neurologic deficits diagnosed during surgery.
         B. Disadvantages of regional anesthesia include patient discomfort and loss of cooperation, confusion, panic, or seizures. The awkwardness of these possibilities discourages the majority from using the technique.
      2. **General anesthesia:** commonly thiopental or propofol followed by nitrous oxide plus a volatile and/or opioids for maintenance.
   B. **Monitoring**
      1. Intraarterial blood pressure monitoring is mandatory.
      2. Additional hemodynamic monitoring should be based primarily on the patients underlying cardiac function. Carotid endarterectomy is not usually associated with significant blood loss or fluid shifts.
      3. Cerebral monitoring: electroencephalogram and somatosensory evoked potentials (SSEP) have been used to determine the need for a shunt.
   C. Despite technique mean arterial blood pressure should be maintained at or slightly above the patient's usual range. During carotid occlusion blood

pressure should be maintained at or up to 20% higher than the patient's highest recorded resting blood pressure while awake.

D. Surgical manipulation of the carotid sinus can cause abrupt bradycardia and hypotension. This may be prevented by infiltration of the sinus with local anesthetic. If infiltration has not been performed, then clamp application may cause hypertension and tachycardia since the sinus is now sensing a low pressure.

E. **Ventilation** should be adjusted to maintain normocapnia. Hypocapnia can produces cerebral vasoconstriction. Hypercapnia can induce intracerebral steal phenomenon.

F. **Heparin (5000-10,000 units IV)** is usually given prior to occlusion of the carotid artery. Protamine, 50-75 mg, can be given for reversal prior to skin closure.

G. Postoperative considerations

1. Postoperative hypertension may be related to surgical denervation of the ipsilateral carotid baroreceptor. Hypertension can stress and rupture the surgical anastomosis resulting in the development of a wound hematoma, which can rapidly compromise the airway.

2. Transient postoperative hoarseness and ipsilateral deviation of the tongue may occur. They are due to surgical retraction of the recurrent laryngeal and hypoglossal nerves, respectively.

Surgery of the Aorta

1. **Ascending aorta**
   A. Surgery routinely uses median sternotomy and CPB.
   B. Anesthesia is similar to that for cardiac operations involving CPB.
   C. The left radial artery should be used to monitor arterial blood pressure, because clamping of the innominate artery maybe necessary during the procedure.

2. **Aortic arch:** usually performed through a median sternotomy with deep hypothermic circulatory arrest. See section on DHCA.

3. **Descending thoracic aorta**
   A. Generally performed through a left thoracotomy without CPB.
   B. **Monitoring**
      1. Arterial blood pressure should be monitored from the right radial artery, since clamping of the left subclavian may be necessary.
      2. Pulmonary artery catheter is helpful for following cardiac function and intraoperative fluid management.
   C. **Cross clamping of the aorta**
      1. Cross clamping results in a sudden increase in left ventricular afterload which may precipitate acute left ventricular failure or myocardial ischemia in patients with underlying ventricular dysfunction or coronary disease. A nitroprusside infusion is usually required to prevent excessive increases in blood pressure.
      2. **Release hypotension:** following the release of the aortic cross clamp, the abrupt decrease in afterload combined with bleeding and the release of vasodilating acid metabolites from the ischemic lower body can precipitate severe systemic hypotension. Decreasing anesthetic depth, volume loading, and partial or slow release of the cross-clamp may help decrease the severity of hypotension.

D. Complications
   A. Paraplegia: the incidence of transient postoperative deficits (11%) and postoperative paraplegia (6%).
   B. The classic deficit is that of an anterior spinal artery syndrome with loss of motor function and pinprick sensation but preservation of vibration and proprioception.
   C. Artery of Adamkiewicz: this artery has a variable origin from the aorta, arising between T5 and T8 in 15% , between T9 and T12 in 60%, and between L1 and L2 in 25% of patients.
   D. Measures used to help protect the spinal cord include: use of a temporary heparin coated shunt or partial cardiopulmonary bypass; mild hypothermia; mannitol (related to its ability to lower cerebrospinal pressure by decreasing its production); and drainage of cerebrospinal fluid.
   E. Renal failure: infusion of mannitol (0.5 g/kg) prior to cross-clamping may decrease the incidence of renal failure. Low dose dopamine has not been shown to be as effective but may be used as an adjunct for persistently low urine output.

4. Abdominal aorta
   A. Either an anterior transperitoneal or an anterolateral retroperitoneal approach is commonly used.
   B. Monitoring includes arterial line, central venous line or pulmonary artery catheter and EKG monitoring with ST segment analysis.
   C. The aorta cross-clamp is usually applied to the supraceliac, suprarenal, or infrarenal aorta. In general, the farther distally the clamp is applied, the less the effect on left ventricular afterload. Heparinization is necessary prior to cross-clamp.
   D. Release of the aortic clamp frequently produces hypotension. The same techniques to prevent release hypotension as discussed above should be used. Cross-clamp placed at the level of the infrarenal aorta in patients with good ventricular function frequently have minimal hemodynamic changes when the clamp is removed.
   E. Fluid requirements are typically increased (up to 10-12 mL/kg/hr) because of the large incision and extensive retroperitoneal surgical dissection. Fluid requirements should be guided by central venous or pulmonary artery pressure monitoring.
   F. Renal prophylaxis with mannitol or low dose dopamine should be considered, especially in patients with preexisting renal disease. Clamping of the infrarenal aorta has been shown to significantly decrease renal blood flow, which may contribute to postoperative renal failure.
   G. Epidurals are commonly placed both for intraoperative and postoperative use. The combined technique of epidural and general anesthesia decreases the general anesthetic requirement.

Thoracic Anesthesia

General Considerations

1. The principal goal is to identify patients at risk for both pulmonary and cardiac complications and to start appropriate perioperative therapy.
2. Pulmonary function tests: helpful in identifying patients at increased risk of developing pulmonary complications and in evaluating responses to preoperative pulmonary therapy.
3. Cessation of smoking for at least 4-8 weeks before surgery is associated with decreased incidence of postoperative respiratory complications.
4. Patients undergoing resection of pulmonary tissue are at increased risk of cardiac dysrhythmias because the decrease in available pulmonary vascular bed can cause postoperative right atrial and ventricular enlargement. Consider prophylactic digitalis or beta blockers.

Evaluation of Lung Resectability

1. Initial evaluation includes PFTs, room air arterial blood gas (ABG) and carbon monoxide diffusion capacity (DLCO).
2. If FEV_1 < 50%, FVC <2L, RV/TLC > 50%, maximum breathing capacity (MBC) < 50% pred, or $PaCO_2$ > 40 mmHg, then resection is often contraindicated unless split function PFTs can document that a disproportionate amount of effective ventilation is coming from lung that is not going to be resected.
3. Low FEV_1 or low FVC suggest limited mechanical reserve. An FEV_1 of less than 800 mL is incompatible with life for most adult humans. Mortality is inversely proportional to FEV_1 (patients with high FEV_1 will do well while patients with low FEV_1 can be expected to require post-operative ventilation for a protracted period of time, and may become impossible to liberate from mechanical ventilation).
4. An FVC 3x TV is necessary for an effective cough. Mortality is also inversely proportional to FVC.
5. An RV/TLC of >50% suggests that the patient has near-terminal COPD with airway closing volumes that are approaching TLC. Surgery can be expected to significantly reduce their remaining reserve and may make them impossible to liberate from the ventilator.
6. **Intraoperative management**
   A. General anesthesia in combination with a thoracic epidural is preferred.
   B. Nitrous oxide can be used (limit use during one-lung anesthesia).

One-Lung Anesthesia

1. **Indications for one-lung anesthesia**
   A. Patient related: confine infection or bleeding to one lung, separate ventilation to each lung (bronchopulmonary fistula, tracheobronchial disruption, large lung cyst or bulla), severe hypoxemia due to unilateral lung disease.
   B. Procedure related: repair of thoracic aortic aneurysm, lung resection

(pneumonectomy, lobectomy, segmental resection), thoracoscopy, esophageal surgery, single lung transplantation, anterior approach to the thoracic spine, bronchoalveolar lavage.

2. **Physiology of one-lung anesthesia**
   A. One-lung anesthesia results in a large ventilation-perfusion mismatch, secondary to a large right-to-left intrapulmonary shunt (20-30%).
   B. Factors known to inhibit hypoxic pulmonary vasoconstriction include: (1) very high or very low pulmonary artery pressures; (2) hypocapnia; (3) vasodilators; (4) high or low mixed venous oxygen; (5) pulmonary infection; (6) volatile anesthetics.
   C. Factors that decrease blood flow to the ventilated lung: high mean airway pressure (high PEEP, hyperventilation, or high peak inspiratory pressures); vasoconstrictors; low FIO_2; intrinsic PEEP (inadequate expiratory times).
   D. Carbon dioxide elimination is usually not affected by one-lung anesthesia provided minute ventilation is unchanged.

3. **Double-lumen endotracheal tubes (DLT)**
   A. There are both right and left-sided DLTs ranging in size from 28-41. Left-sided Robertshaw types are the most common and are designed with a bronchial lumen that has its own cuff and extends distal to the carina. The choice or size of DLT is usually based on the patients height (37 Fr most common for women and 39 Fr most common for men):

Patient height	Tube size	Depth of insertion
136-164 cm	37 Fr	27 cm
165-179 cm	39 Fr	29 cm
180-194 cm	41 Fr	31 cm

   B. **Bronchial blockers:** inflatable devices that re passed alongside or through a single-lumen endotracheal tube to selectively occlude a bronchial orifice. An inflatable catheter (Fogarty embolectomy catheter) can be used as a bronchial blocker in conjunction with a regular endotracheal tube (inside or alongside); a guidewire in the catheter is used to facilitate placement.
   C. **Univent tube:** endotracheal tube with a built-in side channel for a retractable bronchial blocker. After the endotracheal tube is placed the bronchial blocker is advanced, positioned and inflated under direct visualization via a flexible bronchoscope. Once the balloon is inflated, the blocked lung can be vented to the atmosphere and allowed to collapse.
   D. **Complications of DLT:** hypoxemia due to tube malplacement or occlusion; traumatic laryngitis; tracheobronchial rupture resulting from overinflation of the bronchial cuff; inadvertent suturing of the tube to a bronchus during surgery.
   E. **Algorithm for checking placement of a left-sided double-lumen tube**
      1. Inflate the tracheal cuff with 5-10 mL of air.
      2. Check for bilateral breath sounds. Unilateral breath sounds indicate that the tube is too far down (tracheal opening is endobronchial).
      3. Inflate the bronchial cuff with 1-2 mL of air.
      4. Clamp the tracheal lumen.
      5. Check for unilateral left breath sounds.
         A. Persistence of right-sided breath sounds indicates that the bronchial opening is in the trachea (tube should be advanced)
         B. Unilateral right-sided breath sounds indicate incorrect entry of the tube in the right bronchus.
         C. Absence of breath sounds over the entire right lung and the left upper lobe indicates the tube is too far down the left bronchus..
      6. Unclamp the tracheal lumen and clamp the bronchial lumen.

   7. Check for unilateral right breath sounds. Absence or diminution of breath sounds indicates that the tube is not far enough down and the bronchial cuff is occluding the distal tracheal.

   8. When the bronchial lumen is clamped and the vent opened, breath sounds and chest rise should be minimal on the involved side and normal on the other. There should be no leak at the vent port. The reverse is true when the tracheal lumen is clamped and the vent opened. It should be noted that auscultation is the least sensitive method to confirm proper placement.

   9. Use the fiberoptic bronchoscope to verify position. Re-check the position of the tube once you position the patient in the lateral decubitus position. Check the airway pressures during one lung ventilation.

4. **Intraoperative ventilatory management:** higher inspired oxygen concentration usually required, tidal volume 10-12 mg/kg at a rate to maintain the $PaCO_2$ near 35 mmHg; frequent arterial gases should be done to assess oxygenation.

5. **Management of hypoxia during one-lung anesthesia**
   A. Confirm tube placement. Increase oxygen to 100%.
   B. Change tidal volume (8-15 cc/kg) and ventilatory rate.
   C. Periodic inflation of the collapsed lung with 100% oxygen.
   D. Continuous insufflation of oxygen into the collapsed lung.
   E. Adding 5 cm H_2O of continuous positive airway pressure (CPAP) to the collapsed lung.
   F. Adding 5 cm H_2O of positive end expiratory pressure (PEEP) to the ventilated lung.
   G. Adding additional CPAP, followed by additional PEEP.
   H. Early ligation of the ipsilateral pulmonary artery (in a pneumonectomy).

Obstetrical Anesthesia

Fundamentals of Obstetrical Anesthesia

1. Stages of labor
   - A. **First stage:** this stage begins with the onset of regular contractions and ends with full cervical dilation. Pain during the first stage is caused by uterine contractions and cervical dilatation. Pain is carried by the visceral afferent fibers (T10 to L1). Pain at the end of the first stage signals the beginning of fetal descent.
   - B. **Second stage:** this stage begins with full cervical dilation and ends with delivery of the infant. Pain in the second stage of labor is due to stretching of the birth canal, vulva, and perineum and is conveyed by the afferent fibers of the posterior roots of the S2 to S4 nerves.
   - C. **Third stage:** begins with the delivery of the infant and ends with the delivery of the placenta.
2. Physiological changes in pregnancy
   - A. **Hematological changes:** increased plasma volume (40-50%), increased total blood volume (25-40%), dilutional anemia (hematocrit 31.9-36.5%).
   - B. **Cardiovascular changes:** increased cardiac output (30-50%), decreased systemic vascular resistance (35%), increased heart rate (15-20 bpm).
   - C. **Pulmonary changes:** increased minute ventilation (50%), decreased functional residual capacity (20%), airway edema (can make for difficult intubation), decreased $PaCO_2$ and PaO_2 (about 10 mmHg each).
   - D. **Gastrointestinal changes:** prolonged gastric emptying, decreased lower esophageal sphincter tone.
   - E. **Altered drug responses:** decreased requirements for inhaled anesthetics (MAC), decreased local anesthetic requirements.
   - F. **Aortocaval compression syndrome**
     1. Caused by impaired venous return when the gravid uterus compresses the inferior vena cava, decreasing venous return to the heart.
     2. **Symptoms:** hypotension, tachycardia, pallor, sweating, nausea, vomiting, and changes in cerebration.
     3. Aortocaval compression is prevented by uterine displacement (lateral position) to increase venous return.
3. Fetal heart monitoring
   - A. **Beat-to-beat variability:** fetal heart rate varies 5-20 bpm with a normal heart rate range of 120-160 bpm; variability is associated with fetal well-being; fetal distress due to arterial hypoxemia, acidosis, or CNS damage is associated with minimal to absent variability of FHR (drug induced loss of variability does not appear deleterious).
   - B. **Early decelerations:** slowing of the FHR that begins with the onset of the uterine contraction; caused by head compression (vagal stimulation); not indicative of fetal distress and do not require intervention.
   - C. **Late decelerations:** characterized by slowing of the FHR that begins 10-30 seconds after the onset of the uterine contraction; reflects hypoxia caused by uteroplacental insufficiency; associated with fetal distress.
   - D. **Variable decelerations:** deceleration patterns are variable in magnitude, duration, and time of onset; caused by umbilical cord compression; unless prolonged beyond 30-60 seconds, associated with fetal bradycardia (<70 bpm), or occur in a pattern that persists for more than 30 minutes, they are

usually benign.

E. **Fetal blood sampling:** a pH higher than 7.25 is usually associated with a vigorous neonate, whereas a pH less than 7.20 suggests that the fetus is acidotic and depressed; a pH in the range of 7.20 to 7.25 requires close monitoring and repeat scalp monitoring.

4. **Medications used during labor**
   A. **Vasopressors:** hypotension can result from regional anesthesia, aorto-caval compression, or peripartum hemorrhage. Ephedrine provides both cardiac stimulation and increased uterine blood flow. Ephedrine is the drug of choice for the treatment of maternal hypotension. Phenylephrine, being a pure alpha-adrenergic agent, increases maternal blood pressure at the expense of uteroplacental blood flow.
   B. **Oxytocin (Pitocin)**
      1. **Indications:** oxytocin stimulates uterine contractions a, used to induce or augment labor, to control postpartum bleeding and uterine atony.
      2. Oxytocin stimulates frequency/force of contractions of uterine smooth muscle and may cause hypotension, dysrhythmias, and tachycardia.
   C. **Tocolytics**
      1. **Indications:** used to delay or stop premature labor, to slow or arrest labor while initiating other therapeutic measures.
      2. **Contraindications:** chorioamnionitis, fetal distress, preeclampsia or eclampsia (PIH) and severe hemorrhage.
      3. **Terbutaline and ritodrine**
         A. **Selective beta-2 agonist:** beta-2 stimulation also produces bronchodilation and vasodilation and may result in tachycardia; may cause dysrhythmias, pulmonary edema, hypertension, hypokalemia, or CNS excitement.
         B. **Terbutaline dose:** 10 mcg/min IV infusion; titrate to a maximum dose of 80 mcg/min.
         C. **Ritodrine dose:** IV infusion of 0.1-0.35 mg/min.
      4. **Magnesium sulfate** is used most commonly in PIH, but it is also used as a tocolytic (see section on magnesium sulfate).

Anesthesia for Labor and Delivery

1. **Common parenteral pain medications:** meperidine (25-50 mg IV; 50-100 mg IM), morphine (2-5 mg IV), fentanyl (25-50 mcg IV), butorphanol (2mg) and nalbuphine (10 mg) are frequently used to relieve pain and anxiety.
2. **Lumbar epidural blockade**
   A. Epidurals are placed usually after the patient is in active labor (5-6 cm dilated in a primipara, 3-4 cm in a multipara).
   B. Contraindications include patient refusal, coagulation disorder (e.g., in abruption or preeclampsia), infection at the site of catheter placement, and hypovolemia.
   C. **Technique**
      1. A 30 mL dose of a nonparticulate antacid should be given.
      2. Place epidural in usual manner after maternal informed consent, hydration, and placement of appropriate monitors.
      3. Test dose: use 3 mL of lidocaine 1.5% with epi to rule out accidental IV or subarachnoid injection (maybe inconclusive because of heart rate variability in the laboring patient).

D. Initial epidural block (options)
    1. Bupivacaine 0.125-0.25%, lidocaine 1%, or chloroprocaine 2% (8-15 mL).
    2. Sufentanil 10-15 mcg or 100-200 mcg fentanyl in 10 mL of saline.
    3. Bupivacaine 0.0625% + fentanyl 50 mcg or sufentanil 10 mcg.
E. Subsequent analgesia (options)
    1. Intermittent: rebolus as needed to maintain maternal comfort.
    2. Continuous infusions options (rate = 8-15 mL/hr)
        A. Bupivacaine 0.04-0.125% + fentanyl 1-2 mcg/mL or sufentanil 0.1-0.3 mcg/mL.
        B. Bupivacaine 0.125% without opiate.
    3. Patient controlled epidural analgesia (using above mixtures baseline infusion 4-6 mL/hr with controlled bolus of 3-4 mL q20-30 minutes).
F. Blood pressure should be monitored every few minutes for 20-30 minutes and every 10-15 minutes thereafter until block wears off.
G. Patients should be maintained in the lateral position and turned side-to-side every hour to avoid a one-sided block.
H. Sensory level, adequacy of anesthesia and motor block should be checked regularly. Watch for intravascular or subarachnoid migration.
I. Adjust infusion rate and concentration as needed to control pain.
3. Intrathecal opioids for labor
    A. Can be used for multiparas in very active labor (6-9 cm) or primiparas who are fully dilated with significant pain. They can also be used for patients in early labor, 2-4 cm dilated, prior to active phase.
    B. Fentanyl 10-25 mcg in 1 cc preservative free saline provides about 30-120 minutes of analgesia.
    C. Meperidine 10-20 mg provides about 2 hours of analgesia.
    D. Sufentanil 10 mcg in 1 cc preservative free saline provides about 60-180 minutes of analgesia.
4. Spinal anesthesia for labor (saddle block)
    A. Commonly used if a forceps delivery is required or in the postpartum period, for repair of traumatic lacerations of the vagina or rectum or for removal of retained placenta.
    B. Bupivacaine 1.25-2.5 mg (with sufentanil 10 mcg or fentanyl 25 mcg) or hyperbaric 5% lidocaine 20-40 mg injected intrathecally.
5. Combined spinal-epidural for labor
    A. Combined spinal/epidural may be useful for patients presenting in early labor because the spinal can be given to help with early labor pain, while the epidural can be activated after the patient is in active labor.
    B. Spinal: 25 mcg fentanyl or 10 mcg Sufentanil in 1 cc PF saline.
    C. An epidural is initiated as noted above after the pain returns.
6. Paracervical block: local anesthetic is injected in the submucosa of the fornix of the vagina lateral to the cervix; only effective during the first stage of labor; high incidence of fetal bradycardia.
7. Pudendal block: 10 mL of local anesthetic is placed transvaginally behind each sacrospinous ligament provides complete analgesia for episiotomy and its repair and is sufficient for low forceps deliveries.
8. General anesthesia: rarely used and requires intubation.

Anesthesia for Cesarean Section

1. **Anesthetic management**
   A. All patients should have a wedge under the right hip for left uterine displacement (15 degrees) and should receive Bicitra 30 cc PO (metoclopramide 10 mg IV is optional).
   B. Maternal informed consent, hydration (based on clinical setting), and placement of appropriate monitors.
   C. Pre-op labs: hematocrit, hemoglobin, clot to blood bank; patients with PIH check PT/PTT, platelet, and bleeding time prior to block (if used).
   D. If systolic blood pressure falls by 30% or below 90 mmHg, ensure left uterine displacement and increase IV infusion rate. If blood pressure is still not restored, administer 5-15 mg ephedrine IV, repeat prn.
   E. If the block (epidural or spinal) becomes "patchy" prior to delivery of the baby, should be treated with ketamine, 10-20 mg IV, or 40-50% nitrous; after delivery, fentanyl 0.5-1.0 mcg/kg IV and/or versed 0.25-1.0 mg.
   F. If anesthesia remains inadequate with spinal or epidural block, proceed to general anesthesia with endotracheal intubation.
   G. After placenta delivered, oxytocin 20-40 units should be added to IV fluids (if uterine bleeding does not decrease may give Methergine 0.2 mg IM).

2. **Epidural anesthesia**
   A. Place catheter in usual manner and give test dose.
   B. **Local anesthetic options** (15-30 mL total dose in 5 mL increments)
      1. Lidocaine 1.5-2%
      2. Bupivacaine 0.5%
      3. Chloroprocaine 3%
   C. **Additives**
      1. Epinephrine may be added to a maximum conc. of 1:200,000.
      2. Sodium bicarbonate, 1 cc for each 10 cc of local anesthetic, can be added to speed up onset.
   D. **Opioid options**
      1. Fentanyl 50-100 mcg or sufentanil 10-20 mcg.
      2. Duramorph 3-5 mg given after the umbilical cord is clamped, provides 18-24 hours of postoperative pain relief.

3. **Spinal anesthesia**
   A. **Local anesthetic options**
      1. Lidocaine 5% (60-75 mg)
      2. Bupivacaine 0.75% (8-15 mg)
      3. Tetracaine 1% (7-10 mg)
   B. **Additives**
      1. Epinephrine 0.2 mg
   C. **Opioid options**
      1. Fentanyl 10-25 mcg or sufentanil 10 mcg.
      2. Duramorph 0.10-0.25 mg provides 18-24 hours of postoperative pain relief.

4. **General anesthesia**
   A. Generally reserved for emergency cesarean sections when regional anesthesia is refused or contraindicated, when substantial hemorrhage is anticipated, or when uterine relaxation is required.
   B. General anesthesia allows for rapid induction, control of airway, and decreased incidence of hypotension. Aspiration and failed intubation remain a major cause of morbidity and mortality.

C. **Technique**
1. Patients should be premedicated with Bicitra, 30 cc, consider metoclopramide 10 mg, cimetidine, 300 mg, or ranitidine, 50 mg.
2. Position the patient with left uterine displacement. Standard monitors, fetal heart rate monitor.
3. Preoxygenate with 100% oxygen for 3 minutes or 5-6 deep breaths.
4. Rapid-sequence induction with cricoid pressure is performed with thiopental 4-5 mg/kg or propofol 2 mg/kg (ketamine 1 mg/kg for asthmatics and hemodynamically unstable patients) and succinylcholine 1.5 mg/kg.
5. Anesthesia is maintained with a 50% mixture of nitrous and oxygen, combined with a volatile agent (enflurane 0.5-0.75% or isoflurane 0.75%). Use muscle relaxant as necessary. Hyperventilation should be avoided because of adverse effects on uterine blood flow.
6. After the umbilical cord is clamped, a muscle relaxant may be administered (usually one dose of atracurium, 0.5 mg/kg, or vecuronium, 0.05 mg/kg), fentanyl 100-150 mcg, versed 1-2 mg, and nitrous 70%/oxygen 30%, consider discontinuing or using low doses of inhalation agent.
7. Oxytocin (10-40 units/l) is added to the IV infusion after delivery of the placenta to stimulate uterine contraction.
8. Prior to extubation an orogastric tube should be passed to empty the stomach. Extubate when the patient is awake.

Pregnancy Induced Hypertension (PIH)

1. **Incidence:** 5-15% of all pregnancies and is major cause of obstetric and perinatal morbidity and mortality. The cause is unknown and symptoms usually abates within 48 hours following delivery.
2. PIH is a syndrome manifesting after the 20th week of gestation characterized by hypertension (greater then 140/90 mmHg or a greater then 30/15 mmHg increase from baseline), proteinuria (> 500 mg/day), generalized edema, and complaints of headache. Severe PIH is defined as BP > 160/110, pulmonary edema, proteinuria >5 gm/day, oliguria, central nervous system manifestations, hepatic tenderness, or HEELP syndrome.
3. **Eclampsia** occurs when PIH progresses to seizures and is associated with a maternal mortality of about 10%.
4. **Predisposing factors:** multiple gestation, major uterine anomalies, chronic hypertension, chronic renal disease, diabetes, polyhydramnios, molar pregnancy, fetal hydrops. PIH chiefly affects primigravidas (especially those with vascular disorders).
5. **Pathophysiology:** remains unclear, may be related to abnormal prostaglandin metabolism and endothelial dysfunction that lead to vascular hyperreactivity. Patients with PIH have elevated levels of thromboxane A_2 (potent vasoconstrictor and promoter of platelet aggregation) production and decreased prostacylin (potent vasodilator and inhibitor of platelet aggregation) production.
6. **Manifestations**
   A. **Hematologic:** decrease in intravascular volume (primarily plasma), disseminated intravascular coagulation characterized initially by reduction in platelets; later by rise in fibrin degradation products, fall in fibrinogen level, increased PT/PTT.

    B. Cerebral: hyperreflexia, CNS irritability increase, coma, increased intracranial pressure, altered consciousness.

    C. Respiratory: upper airway and laryngeal edema.

    D. Cardiac: arteriolar constriction and increase of peripheral resistance leading to increased BP.

    E. Ophthalmic: retinal arteriolar spasm, blurred vision, retinal edema and possible retina detachment.

    F. Renal: reduction in renal blood flow and GFR, elevated plasma uric acid (increased levels correlate with severity of disease), deposition of fibrin in glomeruli.

    G. Hepatic: elevated LFTs, hepatocellular damage or edema secondary to vasospasm, epigastric or right upper quadrant abdominal pain.

7. **General management**
   A. **Definitive therapy** includes delivery of fetus and the placenta with symptoms usually resolving within 48 hours.
   B. **Antihypertensive drugs:** hydralazine is the agent of choice because it increases both uteroplacental and renal blood flow. Labetalol can also be used. Continuous infusions of nitroprusside can be used in treating hypertensive crisis or acute increases in blood pressure.
   C. **Fluid management:** fluids are generally not restricted. Intravascular depletion should be corrected with crystalloids.
   D. **Magnesium therapy:** magnesium sulfate is a mild vasodilator and central nervous system depressant. Give 2-4 gram loading dose (slow IV over 5-15 minutes), followed by continuous infusion of 1-3 gm/hour. Therapeutic maternal blood levels of 4-6 mEq/l should be maintained

8. **Anesthetic management**
   A. All patients should have a bleeding time, platelet count, coagulation profile, CBC, Mg level, fibrinogen, fibrin split products, electrolytes, uric acid level, and LFTs prior to anesthesia.
   B. **Before placing block** prehydrate as guided by clinical exam, urine output, oxygenation, and central venous pressure monitoring (if used).
   C. Patients should have blood pressure under control (DBP<110) before starting epidural. Epidural anesthesia is the preferred method of analgesia for vaginal delivery and cesarean section in most patients including those with eclampsia. Spinal can be used. General anesthetics are reserved for fetal distress, coagulopathies or hypovolemia.
   D. **Exaggerated edema** of the upper airway structures may require the use of smaller tracheal tubes than anticipated.
   E. **Indications for invasive monitoring**
      1. Unresponsive or refractory hypertension: increased systemic vascular resistance or increased cardiac output.
      2. Pulmonary edema: cardiogenic or left ventricular failure, increased systemic vascular resistance, or noncardiogenic volume overload.
      3. Persistent arterial desaturation.
      4. Oliguria unresponsive to modest fluid loading: low preload, severe increased systemic vascular resistance with low cardiac output, selective renal artery vasoconstriction.

9. **HELLP syndrome**
   A. **HELLP syndrome:** hemolysis, elevated liver enzymes, low platelets.
   B. **Incidence:** 4-12% of severe PIH patients.
   C. **Reported perinatal mortality:** 7.7-60%; maternal mortality 3.5-24.2%.
   D. **Diagnostic criteria:** platelet count less than 100,000/mm³, hemolysis by peripheral smear and increased bilirubin greater than 1.2 mg/dL, SGOT

greater than 70 U/L and LDH greater than 600 U/L.

E. High incidence of maternal complications including abruptio placenta, coagulopathy (DIC, prolonged PT and PTT), acute renal failure, ruptured hepatic hematoma.

Peripartum Hemorrhage

1. **Placenta previa**: abnormal implantation of the placenta in the lower uterine segment; incidence is 0.1-1.0% (higher in subsequent pregnancies); presents with painless vaginal bleeding typically around the 32nd week of gestation; potential for massive blood loss; risk factors include prior uterine scar, prior placenta previa, advanced maternal age, and multiparity.

2. **Abruptio placentae:** premature separation of a normally implanted placenta after 20 weeks of gestation; incidence is 0.2-2.4%; may present with painful vaginal bleeding, hemorrhagic shock, fetal distress, irritable uterus; potential for massive blood loss (blood loss may be concealed), disseminated intravascular coagulation (DIC), acute renal failure; risk factors: hypertension, uterine abnormalities, history of cocaine abuse.

3. **Uterine rupture:** incidence: 0.008-0.1% ; majority are spontaneous without explanation; risk factors: previous uterine surgery, prolonged intrauterine manipulation, rapid spontaneous delivery, excessive oxytocin stimulation; may present with sudden onset of breakthrough pain (although most patients with uterine rupture have no pain) with or without vaginal bleeding, abnormalities in fetal heart rate, irritable uterus; potential for massive blood loss.

4. **Vasa previa:** a condition in which the umbilical card of the fetus passes in front of the presenting part making them vulnerable to trauma during vaginal examination or during artificial rupture of membranes; bleeding here is from the fetal circulation only.

5. **Retained placenta:** incidence is about 1% of all vaginal deliveries and usually requires manual exploration of the uterus; if no epidural or spinal was used analgesia can be provided with IV opioids, nitrous oxide, or small doses of ketamine; if uterine relaxation is required, and bleeding is minimal, nitroglycerin, 50-100 mcg boluses, can be given (occasionally general anesthesia is required for relaxation).

6. **Uterine atony:** occurs in 2-5% of patients; treated with IV oxytocin to cause uterine contractions; if this fails, methergine 0.2 mg IM should be given. If these measures fail, then emergency hysterectomy or internal iliac artery ligation may be necessary.

7. **Laceration** of the vagina, cervix or perineum are common.

8. **Uterine inversion** is very rare and is a true obstetrical emergency; general anesthesia is generally required to allow immediate uterine relaxation; these patients can exsanguinate rapidly.

Anesthesia for Nonobstetric Surgery During Pregnancy

1. Approximately 1-2% of pregnant patients require surgery during their pregnancy. Maternal morbidity and mortality is unchanged from that of nonpregnant women, but fetal mortality ranges from 5-35%.

2. **Avoidance of teratogenic drugs:** the critical period of organogenesis is between 15 and 56 days; there is no clear evidence that anesthetics

administered during pregnancy are teratogenic.

3. **Avoidance of intrauterine fetal hypoxia and acidosis:** minimized by avoiding maternal hypotension (with left uterine displacement), arterial hypoxemia, and excessive changes in $PaCO_2$.

4. **Prevention of premature labor:** the underlying pathology necessitating the surgery, and not the anesthetic technique, determines the onset of premature labor.

5. **Anesthetic management:** regional anesthesia should be used when possible to minimize fetal exposure; fetal heart rate and uterine activity should be monitored with a doppler and tocodynamometer after the 16th week of gestation; if general anesthesia is chosen it is recommended to use low concentrations of volatile drugs and FIO_2 greater than 50%.

Neuroanesthesia

Neurophysiology and Neuropharmacology

1. Cerebrospinal fluid (CSF)
   A. **Produced at a rate of 0.3 cc/min** primarily by the choroid plexuses of the cerebral (mainly lateral) ventricles. CSF is reabsorbed at a rate of 0.3-0.4 cc/min into the venous system by the villi in the arachnoid membrane.
   B. CSF production is decreased by carbonic anhydrase inhibitors (acetazolamide), corticosteroids, spironolactone, loop diuretics (furosemide), isoflurane, and vasoconstrictors.
   C. **Cerebral spinal fluid volume:** 100-150 mL normal.
2. Cerebral blood flow
   A. **Cerebral blood flow rates** averages 50 mL/100 gm/min and represents 15-20% of cardiac output and consumes 20% of the oxygen. CBF rates below 20-25 mL/100 gm/min are associated with cerebral impairment.
   B. **Cerebral blood flow regulation and determinants**
      1. **$PaCO_2$:** for every 1 mmHg change in $PaCO_2$ there is a corresponding change in CBF by 1-2 mL/100 g/min. Cerebral blood flow is directly proportionate to $PaCO_2$ between tensions of 20 and 80 mmHg.
      2. **PaO_2:** no significant increase in CBF until below 50 mmHg.
      3. **Temperature:** cerebral blood flow changes 5-7% per degree Celsius. Hypothermia decreases both $CMRO_2$ and CBF. Cerebral metabolic rate decreases 7% for every 1 degree Celsius reduction in temperature.
      4. **Cerebral perfusion pressure (CPP):** CPP = MAP-ICP (or cerebral venous pressure, whichever is greater). Normal CPP is 80-100 mmHg. CPP less than 50 mmHg often show slowing on the EEG.
      5. **Cerebral perfusion pressure autoregulation:** chronic hypertension shifts the autoregulation curve to the right; autoregulation is impaired in presence of intracranial tumors or volatile anesthetics.
      6. **Hematocrit:** CBF increases with decreasing viscosity (hematocrit). Optimal cerebral oxygen delivery occurs at Hct between 30-34%.
      7. Regionally, CBF and metabolism are tightly coupled. An increase in cortical activity will lead to a corresponding increase in CBF.
      8. Sympathetic tone does not appreciably affect CBF.
3. Intracranial pressure (ICP)
   A. **Normal ICP is 5-10 mmHg.**
   B. **Intracranial hypertension** is defined as a sustained increase in ICP above 15 mmHg. When intracranial pressure exceeds 30 mmHg, cerebral blood flow progressively decreases and a vicious cycle is established: ischemia causes brain edema, which in turn increases intracranial pressure, resulting in more ischemia.
   C. Periodic increases in arterial blood pressure with reflex slowing of the heart rate (Cushing response) are often observed and can be correlated with abrupt increases in intracranial pressure lasting 1-15 minutes.
   D. **Cerebral perfusion pressure (CPP)** = MAP - ICP (or CVP).
   E. **Increased intracranial pressure**
      1. **Symptoms:** nausea/vomiting, mental status changes (drowsiness progressing to coma), personality changes, visual changes, neck stiffness, focal deficits, hypertension, bradycardia, absent brain stem reflexes, decerebrate posturing, fixed and dilated pupils, respiratory

rhythm changes (irregular rhythm or apnea).
2. **Signs:** headache, papilledema, posturing, bulging fontanelles in infants, seizures, altered patterns of breathing, cushing's reflex (hypertension and bradycardia).
3. **Radiologic signs**
   A. **X-ray:** suture separation, erosion of clinoid process, copper-beaten skull.
   B. **CT/MRI scans:** midline shift, cerebral edema, mass lesions, abnormal ventricular size, obliteration of basal cistern.
4. **Cushing reflex**
   A. **Cushing reflex:** periodic increases in arterial blood pressure with reflex slowing of the heart is the Cushing response and often observed and correlated with abrupt increases in intracranial pressure (plateau or A waves) lasting 1-15 minutes.
   B. **Cushing triad:** hypertension, bradycardia, respiratory disturbances (late and unreliable sign that usually just proceeds brain herniation).
   C. Continued profound sympathetic nervous system (SNS) discharge during Cushing's reflex may hide a state of hypovolemia. If the Cushing source is taken away by surgical intervention and/or the SNS response is ablated by anesthesia, one may encounter profound and resistant hypotension.
5. **Compensatory mechanisms for increased ICP:** displacement of CSF from the cranial to the spinal compartment, increase in CSF absorption, decrease in CSF production, decrease in total cerebral blood volume.
6. **Treatment of elevated ICP.**
   A. **Reduce cerebral blood volume**
      1. Hyperventilation ($PaCO_2$ 20-25 mmHg). Excessive hyperventilation ($PaCO_2$ <20) may cause cerebral ischemia.
      2. Prevent straining or coughing on the endotracheal tube.
      3. Elevation of the head to encourage venous drainage.
   B. **Reduce cerebrospinal fluid volume**
      1. Ventriculostomy or lumbar subarachnoid catheter.
      2. Decrease CSF production with acetazolamide.
      3. Recent studies suggest that administration of hypertonic saline and mannitol reduce the production of CSF and may contribute to the immediate effect of ICP reduction.
      4. Reduce brain volume by decreasing brain water with osmotic diuretics (20% mannitol 0.25 - 1.0 g/kg); mannitol is thought to reduce cerebral swelling by osmotic dehydration, loop diuretics (furosemide 0.5 mg/kg), and steroids (Decadron).
      5. Barbiturates are potent cerebral vasoconstrictors that decrease cerebral blood volume while decreasing cerebral metabolic rate.

4. **Methods of cerebral protection**
   A. **Barbiturates, etomidate, propofol, and isoflurane** may offer protection against focal ischemia and incomplete global ischemia by producing complete electrical silence of the brain and eliminated the metabolic cost of electrical activity; unfortunately, they have no effect on basal energy requirements.
   B. **Hypothermia**
      1. $CMRO_2$ is decreased by 7% for every 1 degree Celsius reduction.
      2. Hypothermia decreases both basal and electrical metabolic require-

ments throughout the brain; metabolic requirement continue to decrease even after complete electrical silence; most effective method for protecting the brain during focal and global ischemia.

C. **Calcium channel blockers** (nimodipine and nicardipine) may be beneficial in reducing neurologic injury following hemorrhagic and ischemic strokes.

D. **Maintenance of optimal cerebral perfusion pressure** is critical (maintaining normal arterial blood pressure, intracranial pressure, oxygen carrying capacity, arterial oxygen tension and hematocrit maintained 30-34%). Hyperglycemia aggravates neurologic injuries and should be avoided.

5. **Pharmacology in neurosurgical patients**
   A. **Inhalational anesthetics**
      1. Volatile agents administered during normocapnia in concentrations higher then 0.6 MAC produce cerebral vasodilation, decreased cerebral vascular resistance, and resulting dose-dependent increases in CBF despite concomitant decreases in $CMRO_2$.
      2. Enflurane increases CSF formation and retard absorption. Halothane impedes CSF absorption but only minimally retards formation.
   B. Most intravenous agents cause coupled reduction in CBF and $CMRO_2$ in a dose-dependent manner. Ketamine is the only intravenous anesthetic that dilates the cerebral vasculature and increases CBF.
   C. All muscle relaxants, except succinylcholine, have no direct effect on CBF and $CMRO_2$. Succinylcholine causes a transient increase in CBF and $CMRO_2$.
   D. Opioids in the absence of hypoventilation decrease CBF and possible ICP.

Anesthesia for Craniotomy

1. **Preoperative preparation**
   A. Evidence of increased ICP should be sought (nausea, vomiting, hypertension, bradycardia, personality change, altered LOC, altered patterns of breathing, papilledema, seizures).
   B. Physical examination should include a neurologic assessment documenting mental status and any existing sensory or motor deficits.
   C. CT and MRI scans should be reviewed for evidence of brain edema, a midline shift greater than 0.5 cm, and ventricular size.

2. **Premedication**
   A. Premedication is best avoided when increased ICP is suspected.
   B. Corticosteroids and anticonvulsant therapy should be continued up until the time of surgery.

3. **Monitoring**
   A. In addition to standard ASA monitors, direct intraarterial pressure monitoring and bladder catheterization are indicated for most patients undergoing craniotomy.
   B. Central venous catheter is useful for guiding fluid management, possible treatment of venous air embolism, and to give vasopressors.

4. **Induction and maintenance of anesthesia**
   A. Induction must be accomplished without increasing ICP or compromising CBF. Hypertension, hypotension, hypoxia, hypercarbia, and coughing should be avoided.
   B. Thiopental, propofol, etomidate may be used for IV induction and are

       unlikely to adversely increase ICP.

   C. Nondepolarizing agents are the muscle relaxants of choice. The hemodynamic response to laryngoscopy can be blunted by pretreatment with lidocaine, labetalol, opioids, and/or esmolol.

   D. Anesthesia is usually maintained with a combination of a opioid, low-dose volatile agent, and muscle relaxant. Anesthetic requirements are decreased after craniotomy and dural opening, since the brain parenchyma is devoid of sensation.

5. Emergence should occur slow and controlled. Straining, coughing and hypertension should be avoided.

Neurotrauma

1. Head trauma

   A. Glasgow Coma Scale (GCS) correlates with the severity of injury and outcome. Total score possible = 3-15.

      1. Best motor response: 6-obeys commands; 5-localizes pain; 4-withdrawals; 3-flexion: decorticate rigidity; 2-extension: decerebrate rigidity; 1-no motor response.

      2. Best verbal response: 5-oriented, conversant; 4-disoriented, conversant; 3-inappropriate words; 2-incomprehensible sounds; 1-no verbalization/response.

      3. Eye opening: 4-spontaneous; 3-to verbal stimulation; 2-to pain; 1-no response.

   B. Cushing triad: hypertension, bradycardia, respiratory disturbances (late and unreliable sign that usually just proceeds brain herniation).

   C. Preoperative

      1. All patients are regarded as having a full stomach and treated as such.

      2. Hypotension in the setting of head trauma is nearly always related to other associated injuries. Correction of hypotension and control of any bleeding take precedence over radiographic studies and definitive neurological treatment because systolic arterial blood pressures of less than 80 mmHg correlate with a poor outcome.

      3. Dysrhythmias and electrocardiographic abnormalities in the T wave, U wave, ST segment, and QT interval are common following head injuries but are not necessarily associated with cardiac injury.

   D. Intraoperative

      1. Management is similar to other mass lesions with elevated ICP

      2. CPP should be maintained between 70 and 110 mmHg.

      3. Dextrose containing solutions may exacerbate ischemic brain damage and should be avoided in the absence of documented hypoglycemia.

2. Spinal cord injury

   A. Lesions involving phrenic nerve (C3-C5) usually result in apnea requiring intubation and mechanical ventilatory support. Lesions below C5-C6 may cause up to 70% reduction in vital capacity and FEV_1 with impaired ventilation and oxygenation. Lesions involving T1-T4 (cardiac accelerator nerves) may lead to bradycardia, bradydysrhythmias, atrioventricular block and cardiac arrest. T7 or higher is the critical level for significant alveolar ventilation impairment.

   B. Spinal shock is seen in high spinal cord injuries lasting from a few hours to several weeks; characterized by loss of sympathetic tone in capacitance and resistance vessels below the level of the lesion; flaccid paralysis; total

absence of visceral and somatic sensation below level of injury; paralytic ileus; loss of spinal cord reflexes below level of injury.
C. Autonomic hyperreflexia is associated with lesions above T5, not a problem during acute management (appears following resolution of spinal shock and return of spinal cord reflexes).
D. Methylprednisolone: 30 mg/kg IV loading dose, followed by 5.4 mg/kg/hr for 23 hours may improve the functional recovery if treatment is begun within 8 hrs following injury.
E. Succinylcholine: safe for use during the first 24-48 hours.

Trauma Anesthesia

Initial Survey and Resuscitation

1. **Five rules of trauma**
   A. The stomach is always full.
   B. The cervical spine is always unstable.
   C. Altered mental status is caused by head injury.
   D. Partial airway obstruction may progress rapidly to complete airway obstruction.
   E. The patient is always hypovolemic.
2. **Airway and breathing**
   A. All patients should have initial stabilization of the cervical spine before any airway manipulation. Assume a cervical spine injury in any patient with multi-system trauma, especially with an altered LOC or a blunt injury above the clavicle. Maintain the cervical spine in a neutral position with inline stabilization when establishing an airway.
   B. The airway should be assessed for patency. All secretions, blood, vomitus, and foreign bodies should be removed. Measures to establish a patent airway should protect the cervical spine. The chin lift or jaw thrust maneuvers are recommended to achieve this task.
   C. All patients should receive supplemental oxygen (face mask, bag-valve mask, endotracheal tube).
   D. Patients who arrive intubated, should have placement confirmed (i.e., bilateral breath sounds with good chest rise, direct laryngoscopy, or capnography).
3. **Circulation**
   A. Hypotension following injury must be considered to be hypovolemic in origin until proven otherwise. Volume resuscitation begins immediately with the establishment of intravenous access.
   B. A minimum of two large-caliber intravenous catheters should be established. Blood and fluid warmers should be used.

Trauma Intubations and Anesthetic Management

1. **Indications for airway intervention**
   A. **Airway obstruction.**
      1. Hypoxia and hypercarbia (shock or cardiac arrest).
      2. Controlled hyperventilation (obvious intracranial injury or GCS of < 9).
      3. Protection against pulmonary aspiration (drug overdose).
      4. Airway injury (inhalation injuries).
      5. Sedation for diagnostic procedures (patients who are intoxicated or suffering from possible head injury that are unable to lie still for necessary diagnostic studies).
      6. Prophylactic intubation (patients with impending respiratory failure).
      7. Airway or midface injuries (possible airway compromise)
      8. Large flail segment.
   B. **Preparation**
      1. All multiple trauma patients should be assumed to have a cervical spine

injury and a full stomach. Portable cervical spine x-rays will miss 5% to 15% of injuries. Complete evaluation of the cervical spine may require a CT scan or multiple radiographs and clinical exam. Cervical spine injury is unlikely in alert patients without neck pain or tenderness.

2. Patients who arrive ventilated with an esophageal obturator airway (EOA) should have a more definitive airway placed before the EOA is removed. After the trachea has been intubated, the stomach should be suctioned prior to the removal of the EOA.

3. In alert patients with potential spinal cord injuries, document any movement of extremities before and after intubation.

4. The airway should be examined to detect potentially difficult intubation.

5. Airway equipment (laryngoscope, endotracheal tubes, suction) should be set-up prior to the patients arrival.

C. Endotracheal trauma intubation

1. Preoxygenation
A. All patients should be preoxygenated to minimize hypoxia.
B. Administration of 100% oxygen to an individual with normal spontaneous ventilation for 3 minutes or 4-6 vital capacity breaths will generally result in 95-98% nitrogen washout.

2. Orotracheal intubation, facilitated by the use of muscle relaxants and general anesthesia, is the technique of choice for intubating the trachea of trauma patients.

3. Nasotracheal intubation
A. Contraindications to nasotracheal intubation include: apnea; upper airway foreign body, abscess, or tumor; nasal obstruction; central facial fractures; acute epiglottitis (blind technique); basal skull fractures; coagulopathy; and cardiac or other prosthesis.
B. Not commonly used in trauma patients.

4. Cricothyroidotomy: the need for cricothyroidotomy due to severe maxillofacial trauma or an inability to perform oral-tracheal intubation occurs in less than 1% of all trauma patients requiring intubation on admission. It may be used as a primary airway, with injuries to the pharynx for example, or after failure of orotracheal intubation. It may be a full surgical approach or via a percutaneous needle cricothyroidotomy with high flow oxygen.

5. If there is difficulty or delay in intubating the trachea in any trauma patient with respiratory comprise, a tracheotomy or cricothyroidotomy should be performed immediately.

2. Intraoperative management
A. Two functioning large bore IVs should be placed before induction. Blood should be available before incision is made, if possible.

B. Induction
1. All trauma patients should be assumed to have full stomachs.
2. When general anesthesia is planned, rapid sequence induction with cricoid pressure is the method of choice.
3. Reduced doses of induction agent or no induction agent may be appropriate in severely injured, obtunded patients. Ketamine 0.25-0.5 mg/kg IV is the induction agent of choice in hypovolemia.

C. Maintenance
1. Narcotic based anesthetic is recommended for stable patients. For unstable patients, scopolamine/oxygen/pancuronium can be used until hemodynamically stable then small incremental doses. Prophylactic use of scopolamine (0.1-0.2 mg IVP) or midazolam (1-3 mg IVP) may

be considered.

2. Avoid using nitrous oxide.
3. The patient should be kept warm (blanket warmer, fluid warmer, and a bear hugger on the upper body or lower body). Hypothermia worsens acid-base disorders, coagulopathies, and myocardial function.

Burns

1. **Preoperative evaluation**
   A. First-degree burns are limited to the epithelium, second-degree burns extend into the dermis, and third-degree burns are full thickness.
   B. The size of the burn should be estimated as a percentage of the total body surface area (%TBSA).
   C. Indications for early intubation include hypoxemia not correctable with oxygen, upper airway edema, or the presence of copious secretions.
2. **Perioperative management**
   A. **Cardiovascular system**
      1. Burn patients require aggressive fluid resuscitation during the first 24-48 hours.
      2. Fluid replacement protocols
         A. Parkland formula: 4.0 cc of Ringer's lactate/kg /%TBSA/24 hours.
         B. Half the calculated fluid deficit is administered during the first 8 hours after the burn injury, and the remainder is given over the next 16 hours. Daily maintenance fluid requirements should be given concurrently.
         C. Early cardiovascular effects include decreased cardiac output, decreased arterial blood pressure, and increased capillary permeability.
   B. **Respiratory system**
      1. Thermal injury of the face and upper airway are common. Inhalational injury should be suspected in the presence of facial or intraoral burns, singed nasal hairs, a brassy cough, carbonaceous sputum, and wheezing. Before airway edema occurs, endotracheal intubation should be performed.
      2. Carbon monoxide poisoning is defined as greater than 20% carboxyhemoglobin in the blood. Tissue hypoxia ensues.
      3. Manifestations of carbon monoxide poisoning include irritability, headache, nausea/vomiting, visual disturbances, seizures, coma, or death.
      4. Pulse oximetry overestimates the oxyhemoglobin saturation in the presence of carboxyhemoglobin because the absorption spectrum is similar. The classic cherry red color of the skin is a sign of high concentrations of carbon monoxide.
   C. **Anesthetic considerations**
      1. Succinylcholine is contraindicated 24 hours to 2 years after major burns because it can produce profound hyperkalemia and cardiac arrest.
      2. Nondepolarizing muscle relaxants are used when muscle relaxation is required. Burn patients require higher than normal doses of nondepolarizing muscle relaxants.
      3. Burn patients may have increased narcotic requirements because of tolerance and increases in the apparent volume of distribution.

Cardiac Tamponade

1. **Manifestations**
   A. **Dyspnea, orthopnea, tachycardia:** Beck's triad consists of hypotension, distant heart sounds, distention of jugular veins.
   B. **Paradoxical pulse** (>10 mmHg decline in BP during inspiration).
   C. The principle hemodynamic feature is a decrease in cardiac output from a reduced stroke volume with an increase in central venous pressure. Equalization of diastolic pressures occur throughout the heart. Impairment of both diastolic filling and atrial emptying abolishes the 'y' descent; the 'x' descent is normal.
   D. **EKG:** ST segment changes, electrical alternans.
   E. **CXR:** silhouette normal or slightly enlarged.
   F. **Transesophageal echo** is the best diagnostic tool.
2. **Anesthetic considerations**
   A. **Maintain filling pressures** (to maximize stroke volume): support myocardial contractility with inotropic support if necessary. Avoid bradycardia.
   B. **Avoid positive pressure ventilation** because increased intrathoracic pressure will impede venous return and exacerbate underfilling of the cardiac chambers.
   C. **Pre-induction monitors:** standard monitors plus arterial line and central venous line (and pulmonary artery catheter if needed).
   D. Hemodynamically unstable patients should be managed with pericardiocentesis (under local anesthesia) prior to induction (the removal of even a small amount of fluid can improve cardiac performance).
   E. **Induction:** ketamine is the drug of choice, however, ketamine depresses myocardial contractility and may precipitate hemodynamic deterioration when used in the presence of hypovolemia and maximal sympathetic outflow.

Ophthalmologic Anesthesia

1. **Physiology of intraocular pressure**
   A. Normal intraocular pressure is maintained between 10 and 20 mmHg.
   B. Intraocular pressure is controlled primarily by regulation of the outflow resistance at the trabecular meshwork. Acute changes in choroidal blood volume can produce rapid increases in intraocular pressure. Hypercapnia can lead to choroidal congestion and increased intraocular pressure. The increases in venous pressure associated with coughing, straining, or vomiting can raise IOP to 30 to 50 mmHg. Similar increases can be seen at intubation. Intraocular pressure can also be increased by extrinsic compression of the globe. The force of the eyelid in a normal blink may cause an increase of 10 mmHg; a forceful lid squeeze can increase IOP to over 50 mmHg; a poorly placed anesthesia mask could increase IOP to the point of zero blood flow.

2. **Oculocardiac reflex**
   A. External pressure on the globe or surgical traction (stretch) of extraocular muscles (particularly the medial rectus muscle) can elicit the reflex producing cardiac dysrhythmias ranging from bradycardia and ventricular ectopy to sinus arrest or ventricular fibrillation. Hypercarbia or hypoxemia may increase the incidence and severity of this reflex.
   B. The reflex is trigeminovagal reflex arc. The afferent limb is from orbital contents to the ciliary ganglion to the ophthalmic division of the trigeminal nerve to the sensory nucleus of the trigeminal nerve near the fourth ventricle. The efferent limb is via the vagus nerve. The reflex fatigues with repeated traction on the extraocular muscles.
   C. **Prevention**
      1. Retrobulbar block is not uniformly effective in preventing the reflex (retrobulbar block may elicit the oculocardiac reflex).
      2. Anticholinergic medication can be effective, however caution must be used in the elderly.
      3. Deepen anesthesia.
      4. Factors associated with increased susceptibility include anxiety, hypoxia, hypercarbia, and light anesthesia.
   D. **Treatment**
      1. Request the surgeon to stop manipulation.
      2. Assess adequate ventilation, oxygenation, and depth of anesthesia.
      3. If severe or persistent bradycardia, give atropine (7-10 mcg/kg).
      4. In recurrent episodes, infiltration of the rectus muscles with local anesthetics.

3. **Intraocular gas expansion**
   A. A gas bubble may be injected into the posterior chamber during vitreous surgery to flatten a detached retina.
   B. The air bubble is absorbed within 5 days by gradual diffusion.
   C. Sulfur hexafluoride, an inert gas that is less soluble in blood than nitrogen, provides a longer duration (up to 10 days) than an air bubble.
   D. Nitrous oxide should be discontinued at least 15 minutes prior to the injection of air or sulfur hexafluoride. Nitrous oxide should be avoided until the bubble is absorbed (5 days for air and 10 days for sulfur hexafluoride).

4. **Anesthetic drugs**
    A. Most anesthetic drugs either lower or have no effect on intraocular pressure. An exception is ketamine, and possibly etomidate.
    B. Ketamine effects are controversial, but is generally felt to moderately increase intraocular pressure. Ketamine increases choroidal blood flow, increases nystagmus, and increases extraocular muscle tone via blepharospasm.
    C. Etomidate, which is associated with a high incidence of myoclonus (10-60%), may increase intraocular pressure.
    D. Succinylcholine can cause a 5-10 mmHg increase in intraocular pressure for 5-10 minutes. Succinylcholine can potentially increase intraocular pressure by dilating choroidal blood vessels and increases in extraocular muscle tone. Pretreatment with a defasiculating dose of a nondepolarizing muscle relaxant does not reliably eliminate the effect of succinylcholine on intraocular pressure. Nondepolarizing muscle relaxants do not increase intraocular pressure.

5. **Systemic effects of ophthalmic drugs**
    A. **Anticholinesterases** (echothiophate, phospholine iodide): systemic absorption leads to inhibition of plasma cholinesterase which may lead to prolongation of the duration of action of succinylcholine. Takes 3 weeks for pseudocholinesterase levels to return to 50% of normal. The metabolism of mivacurium and ester-type local anesthetics may also be affected.
    B. **Cholinergics** (pilocarpine, acetylcholine): used to induce miosis; toxicity may manifest in bradycardia or acute bronchospasm.
    C. **Anticholinergics** (atropine, scopolamine): used to cause mydriasis; systemic absorption may lead to tachycardia, dry skin, fever, and agitation.
    D. **Beta-blockers** (timolol maleate): systemic absorption may cause beta-blockade (bradycardia, bronchospasm, or exacerbation of congestive heart failure). Betaxolol seems to be oculo-specific with minimal side effects.
    E. **Carbonic anhydrase inhibitors** (acetazolamide, Diamox): used to decrease aqueous production; induces an alkaline diuresis. Side effects include diuresis and hypokalemic metabolic acidosis.

6. **Retrobulbar blockade**
    A. **Technique:** local anesthetic is injected behind the eye into the cone formed by the extraocular muscles. Lidocaine and bupivacaine are the most commonly used local anesthetics. Hyaluronidase, a hydrolyzer of connective tissue polysaccharides, is commonly added to enhance the spread of local anesthetic.
    B. **Complications:** retrobulbar hemorrhage, globe perforation, optic nerve atrophy, convulsions, oculocardiac reflex, loss of consciousness, and respiratory arrest.
    C. **Post-retrobulbar apnea syndrome:** due to injection of local anesthetic into the optic nerve sheath with spread into the cerebrospinal fluid. Apnea typically occurs within 20 minutes and may last 15-60 minutes. Ventilation must be constantly monitored in patients with retrobulbar blocks.
    D. Facial nerve block prevents squinting of the eyelid. Major complications include subcutaneous hemorrhage.

7. **Open eye injury**
    A. Considerations include the possibility of recent food ingestion and the need to avoid even small increases in IOP if the injured eye is salvageable.
    B. Rapid tracheal intubation facilitated by succinylcholine (or other muscle relaxant) must be balanced against possible increases in IOP.

Anesthesia for Select Cases

Transurethral Resection of the Prostate

1. **Complications**
   A. Intravascular absorption of irrigating fluid: the amount of solution absorbed depends on the hydrostatic pressure of the irrigating fluid, the duration of time sinuses are exposed to irrigating fluid (10 to 30 mL of irrigating fluid is absorbed per minute), and the number and sizes of the venous sinuses opened during resection. Absorption of the irrigating fluid can result in fluid overload, serum hypoosmolality, hyponatremia, hyperglycemia, hyperammonemia, hemolysis.
   B. Autotransfusion secondary to lithotomy position: hypothermia may occur. Bacteremia has an incidence of 10% in patients with sterile urine and an incidence of 50% in patients with infected urine.
   C. Blood loss: related to vascularity of the prostate gland, technique, weight of the prostate resected, length of the operation; blood loss ranges from 2-4 mL/min during resection.
   D. Perforation of bladder or urethra.
   E. Transient blindness: attributed to absorption of glycine and its metabolic byproduct, ammonia, acting as an inhibitory neurotransmitter in the retina.
   F. CNS toxicity: result of oxidative biotransformation of glycine to ammonia.
   G. CNS symptoms: apprehension, irritability, confusion, headache, seizures, transient blindness, and coma, have all been attributed to hyponatremia and hyposmolarity.
2. **Intraoperative management:** regional or general anesthesia can be used; it is important to monitor these patients carefully for signs and symptoms of excessive intravascular absorption of irrigating solution.
3. **Management of TURP (water-intoxication) syndrome**
   A. Obtain serum sodium and arterial blood gas, provide supplemental oxygen, support blood pressure, terminate procedure as soon as possible, consider invasive monitors.
   B. Serum sodium >120 mEq/L: fluid restriction; brisk diuresis with loop diuretics.
   C. Serum sodium <120 mEq/L: loop diuretics; consider hypertonic saline (e.g., 3% or 5% saline) infused at a rate which does not exceed 100 mL/hr. Allow sodium to rise by 0.5-2.0 mEq/L/hr; stop hypertonic saline and loop diuretics once sodium is 120-130 mEq/L.

Extracorporeal Shock Wave Lithotripsy

1. **Side effects**
   A. Immersion into the water bath causes peripheral venous compression, resulting in an increase in central blood volume and central venous pressure (about 8-11 mmHg). Some experience hypotension owing to vasodilation from the warm water. In patients with cardiac disease, immersion should be achieved slowly.
   B. During immersion or emersion, cardiac dysrhythmias may occur reflecting changes in right atrial pressure. Shock waves are triggered from the EKG

to occur 20 msec after the R wave to minimize the risk of dysrhythmias.
  C. Immersion lithotripsy increases the work of breathing.
2. **Anesthetic Management**
  A. Regional or general anesthesia can be used. Regional anesthesia has the advantage that the patient is awake and cooperative. Regional anesthetic requires a T6 sensory level.
  B. Monitors, epidural catheter insertion site, vascular access sites should be protected with water impermeable dressings.
  C. Maintenance of adequate urine output with IV fluids to help facilitate passage of disintegrated stones. Monitoring of body temperate is useful to detect changes owing to water immersion.

Electroconvulsive Therapy

1. **Side effects**
  A. Increased cerebral blood flow, increased intragastric pressure, apnea.
  B. Cardiovascular response: initial parasympathetic outflow may result in bradycardia, followed by a sympathetic outflow, which produces hypertension, tachycardia and cardiac dysrhythmias, lasting 5-10 minutes.
2. **Anesthetic Management**
  A. Methohexital 0.5-1.0 mg/kg (or thiopental, propofol or etomidate) and succinylcholine 0.25-0.5 mg/kg (or mivacurium or rapacuronium).
  B. Place blood pressure cuff on the opposite arm of the IV and inflate prior to giving of succinylcholine to allow for motor expression of the seizure.
  C. Induced seizures should last longer than 25 seconds and should be terminated if they last longer than 3 minutes.
  D. Administration of an anticholinergic before induction may prevent initial bradycardia; hypertension and tachycardia can be treated with labetalol.

Laparoscopic Surgery

1. **Contraindications** (relative and absolute): increased intracranial pressure, patients with ventriculoperitoneal or peritoneojugular shunts, hypovolemia, CHF, previous abdominal surgery with significant adhesions, morbid obesity, pregnancy, and coagulopathy.
2. **Pulmonary effects:** laparoscopy creates a pneumoperitoneum with pressurized CO_2 (pressures up to 30 cm H_2O). The resulting increase in intra-abdominal pressure displaces the diaphragm cephalad, causing a decrease in lung compliance and an increase in peak inspiratory pressure. Atelectasis, diminished functional residual capacity, ventilation/perfusion mismatch, and pulmonary shunting contribute to a decrease in arterial oxygenation. The high solubility of CO_2 increases systemic absorption which can lead to increased arterial CO_2 levels.
3. **Cardiac effects:** moderate insufflation can increase effective cardiac filling because blood tends to be forced out of the abdomen and into the chest. Higher insufflation pressures (greater than 25 cm H_2O), however, tends to collapse the major abdominal veins which compromises venous return and leads to a drop in preload and cardiac output in some patients. Hypercarbia may stimulate the sympathetic nervous system and thus increase blood pressure, heart rate, and risk of dysrhythmias.

4. **Management of anesthesia**
    A. **Patient position:** Trendelenburg is often associated with a decrease in FRC, VC, TLV, and pulmonary compliance.
    B. **Anesthetic technique:** general anesthesia with endotracheal intubation.
5. **Complications:** hemorrhage, peritonitis, subcutaneous emphysemas pneumomediastinum, pneumothorax, and venous air embolism. Vagal stimulation during trocar insertion, peritoneal insufflation, or manipulation of viscera can result in bradycardia and sinus arrest.

Liposuction

1. **Potential liposuction perioperative complications**
    A. Pulmonary embolism (thrombus or fat).
    B. Massive fluid dislocation (internal burn).
    C. 60-70% wetting solution absorption.
    D. Organ or vessel perforation with wand.
    E. Lidocaine toxicity.
    F. Hypothermia from several liters of infiltrate.
2. **Anesthetic considerations**
    A. **Fluid balance:** up to 70% of the fluid remains trapped subdermally and is absorbed gradually. Suction extraction of subcutaneous tissue causes a burn-like trauma.
    B. Temperature control.
    C. **Lidocaine megadosing:** for tumescent infiltration with highly diluted lidocaine and epinephrine doses up to 35 mg/kg are considered safe. Deaths attributed to lidocaine toxicity appear to be caused by terminal asystole subsequent to progressive local anesthetic depression of intra-cardiac conduction and ventricular contractility.

Myasthenia Gravis and Myasthenic Syndrome

1. Myasthenia gravis is characterized by weakness and easy fatigability of skeletal muscle. The weakness is thought to be due to autoimmune destruction or inactivation of postsynaptic acetylcholine receptors at the neuromuscular junction. Muscle strength characteristically improves with rest but deteriorates rapidly with repeated effort.
2. **Osserman classification**
    A. Type I: Involvement of extraocular muscles only.
    B. Type IIa: Mild skeletal muscle weakness, spares muscles of respiration.
    C. Type IIb: More severe skeletal muscle weakness with bulbar involvement.
    D. Type III: Acute onset, rapid deterioration, severe bulbar and skeletal muscle involvement.
    E. Type IV: Late, severe involvement of bulbar and skeletal muscle.
3. **Treatment of myasthenia gravis**
    A. Treatment consists of anticholinesterase drugs, immunosuppressants, glucocorticoids, plasmapheresis, and thymectomy.
    B. Anticholinesterase drugs (usually pyridostigmine) inhibit the breakdown of acetylcholine by tissue cholinesterase, increasing the amount of acetylcholine at the neuromuscular junction.
    C. Cholinergic crisis is characterized by increased weakness and excessive

muscarinic effect, including salivation, diarrhea, miosis, and bradycardia.
   D. Edrophonium test: used to differentiate a cholinergic crisis form a myasthenic crisis. Increased weakness after up to 10 mg of intravenous edrophonium is indicative of cholinergic crisis, whereas increasing strength implies myasthenic crisis.
4. **Pre-op predictors for post-op ventilation** (after transsternal thymectomy).
   A. Duration of disease greater than 6 years.
   B. Presence of COPD or other lung disease unrelated to myasthenia.
   C. Pyridostigmine dose greater than 750 mg/day.
   D. Preoperative FVC less than 2.9 liters.
5. **Anesthetic concerns** muscle relaxants should be avoided. The response to succinylcholine is unpredictable. Patients may manifest a relative resistance, a prolonged effect, or an unusual response (phase II block).
6. **Myasthenic syndrome**, also called **Eaton-Lambert syndrome**, is a paraneoplastic syndrome characterized by proximal muscle weakness, which typically affects the lower extremities. Myasthenic syndrome is usually associated with small-cell carcinoma of the lung. In contrast to myasthenia gravis, the muscle weakness improves with repeated effort and is unaffected by anticholinesterase drugs.
7. Patients with the myasthenic syndrome are very sensitive to both depolarizing and nondepolarizing muscle relaxants.

Anesthesia for Organ Harvest

1. **The donor**
   A. Brain death should be pronounced prior to going to the OR.
   B. **Clinical criteria for brain death**
      1. Cerebral unresponsiveness, irreversible coma.
      2. Brain stem unresponsiveness.
      3. Fixed and dilated pupils, doll's eyes, negative caloric test, absent corneal reflex.
      4. Absent gag and cough reflex, apnea (no respiratory efforts with $PaCO_2$ greater than 60 mmHg).
      5. No posturing (spinal reflexes may be present).
   C. Ancillary tests
      1. Isoelectric electroencephalogram.
      2. Absent CBF by intracranial angiography or nuclear brain scan.
      3. Body temperature less than 95 degrees F.
      4. Absence of drug intoxication or neuromuscular blocking agents.
      5. Corrected metabolic abnormalities.
2. **Donor management**
   A. **Overall goals** are restoration and maintenance of hemodynamic and vascular stability. Hemodynamics should be maintained as follows:
      1. Systolic blood pressure greater than 100 mmHg.
      2. Central venous pressure 10-12 mmHg.
      3. Urine output greater than 100 cc/hour.
      4. P_aO_2 greater than 100 mmHg.
   B. **Physiologic changes associated with brain death**
      1. **Cardiovascular instability** is a common feature, secondary to loss of neurologic control of the myocardium and vascular tree. Fluid resuscitation should be used to keep systolic blood pressure greater

than 100 mmHg and mean arterial pressure greater than 70 mmHg.

2. **Central diabetes insipidus** may occur from hypothalamic failure resulting in extreme salt and water wasting from the kidneys. Massive loss of fluid and electrolytes that may occur. Aqueous pitressin should be administered in doses of 10 units intravenously every 4 hours to bring urine output down to 150-200 cc per hour.

3. **Loss of thermoregulatory control:** after brain death, body temperature drifts downward to core temperature.

4. **Neurogenic pulmonary edema** may be present.

5. **Coagulopathy:** the release of tissue fibrinolytic agent from a necrotic brain may initiates coagulopathy.

6. **Hypoxia:** pulmonary insufficiency secondary to trauma and/or shock should be treated with mechanical ventilation, positive end-expiratory pressure (PEEP), and inspired oxygen fraction sufficient to maintain adequate peripheral oxygen delivery.

7. **Overall hypovolemia** is the most important variable affecting donor organ perfusion. Ringer's lactate should be infused to establish a central venous pressure of 10-12 mmHg. Hematocrit should be maintained about 30%.

8. **Anesthesia** is not needed in the brain dead patient. However, significant hemodynamic responses to surgical stimuli commonly occur in the brain-dead donor during organ harvesting. These responses may reflect some residual lower medullary function (visceral and somatic reflexes). Movement secondary to spinal reflex action should be controlled. Patients are routinely declared dead prior to going to the operating room.

Induced Hypotension

1. **Indications:** to reduce intraoperative blood loss and to produce a relatively bloodless surgical site, to help manage patients who refuse blood transfusions, when reduction in MAP decreases the risk of vessel rupture.

2. **Contraindications:** vascular insufficiency (to brain, heart, or kidney), cardiac instability, uncontrolled hypertension, hypovolemia, polycythemia, allergy to hypotensive agents, increased ICP (controversial), lack of experience or understanding of technique.

3. **Anesthetic considerations**
   A. MAP of 50-60 mmHg in young, healthy patients and MAP of 60-70 mmHg in suitable older patients.
   B. Ventilation should be controlled and aimed at maintaining normocarbia.
   C. Maintain normovolemia, careful volume replacement is essential.
   D. Continuous invasive arterial pressure monitoring is indicated. Consider CVP and PAP.

4. **Anesthetic technique**
   A. Inhalational: has been used as a sole agent; however, not recommended because of the inability to quickly reverse. Commonly used in conjunction with direct vasodilator.
   B. Vasodilator agents: continuous infusions allow easy titration and control of BP, commonly used agents include sodium nitroprusside, nitroglycerin, and trimethaphan.
   C. Beta-adrenergic blockers: decrease MAP by their negative inotropic properties. Labetalol and esmolol are most commonly used. Because of

their low hypotensive potency there are commonly used in conjunction with other agents.

5. **Complications:** cerebral ischemia, thrombosis, or edema; acute renal failure; myocardial infarction, congestive heart failure, or arrest; reactive hemorrhage with hematoma formation.

Acute Pain Management

Patient-controlled Analgesia (PCA)

1. The success of PCA depends on patient selection. Patients who are too old, too confused, too young, or unable to control the button and those who don't want the treatment are poor candidates. Teaching improves success.
2. Pediatric PCA: children as young as 6 to 7 years of age can independently use the PCA pump to provide good postoperative pain relief.

Patient-Controlled Analgesia: Adult			
Opioid	Bolus Dose	Lockout (min)	Basal Rate
Morphine	1-3 mg	10-20	0-1 mg/hr
Meperidine	10-15 mg	5-15	0-20 mg/hr
Fentanyl	15-25 mcg	10-20	0-50 mcg/hr
Sufentanil	2.5-5 mcg	10-20	0-10 mcg/hr
Hydromorphone	0.2-0.5 mg	10-20	0-0.5 mg/hr

Note: the above doses are suggested for an average size healthy adult; adjustments must be made according to the condition of the patient and prior opioid use.

Patient-Controlled Analgesia: Pediatric			
Opioid	Bolus Dose	Lockout (min)	Basal Rate
Morphine	20 mcg/kg	10-20	0-15 mcg/kg/hr
Fentanyl	0.25 mcg/kg	10-20	0-0.15 mcg/kg
Hydromorphone	5 mcg/kg	10-20	1-3 mcg/kg/hr

Note: the above doses are suggested for a healthy pediatric patient; adjustments must be made according to the condition of the patient and prior opioid use.

Opioid Analgesics: Continuous Infusions for Infants (<4 months)		
Opioid	Bolus Dose	Infusion
Morphine	0.02-0.05 mg/kg	0.02-0.05 mg/kg/hr
Fentanyl	1.0-2.0 mcg/kg	1-4 mcg/kg/hr

Neuraxial Blockade and Intraspinal Opioids

1. **Benefits of epidural analgesia:** superior pain relief, decreased incidence of pulmonary complications, decreased incidence of cardiovascular complications, earlier return of bowel function.
2. Contraindications: patient refusal, coagulopathy, platelet abnormalities, bacteremia, and the presence of infection or tumor at the site of puncture.
3. **Optimal epidural placement for postop local anesthetic administration**
   A. Thoracotomy: T4-T6.
   B. Upper abdominal/flank: T8.
   C. Lower abdominal: T10-T12.
   D. Lower extremity/pelvic: L2-L4.
4. **Side effects of peridural administered opioids**
   A. **Nausea/vomiting:** opioids in the vomiting center and the chemoreceptor trigger zone in the medulla can cause nausea or vomiting.
   B. **Pruritus:** histamine release may play a small role.
   C. **Respiratory depression**
      1. Patients at risk are the elderly; patients who receive concomitant systemic opiates or sedatives; and patients who have received large doses of spinal opiates.
      2. Early respiratory depression can occur within two hours of spinal opioid administration and is similar to that observed with parenteral administration of an opioid. With hydrophilic agents (i.e., morphine), late respiratory depression commonly peaks at 12 or 13 hours after the initial dose but can occur as late as 24 hours.
   D. **Urinary retention.**
   E. **Delayed gastric emptying.**
5. **Management of opioid related side effects**
   A. **Nausea/vomiting**
      1. Metoclopramide (Reglan): 10-20 mg IV q4 hrs.
      2. Droperidol (Inapsine): 0.625 mg IV q4 hrs; can cause dysphoria, hypotension.
   B. **Pruritus**
      1. Naloxone (Narcan): 10-40 mcg/hr IV continuous infusion; will not significantly reverse analgesia at recommended doses.
      2. Diphenhydramine (Benadryl): 25-50 mg IV q4 hrs; sedative effect.
   C. **Respiratory depression**
      1. Naloxone (Narcan): 40-100 mcg/bolus titrated q2-3 minutes; larger than necessary dosage may result in significant reversal of analgesia, nausea, vomiting, sweating, and/or circulatory stress.
   D. **Urinary retention:** Foley as needed.
6. **Management fo inadequate analgesia provided by epidural infusion**
   A. **Evaluate proper placement of catheter**
      1. Give 5-7 mL of the opioid and local anesthetic solution, if analgesia remains inadequate after 15-30 minutes, give a test dose of local anesthetic (2% lidocaine with epi).
      2. If test dose produces a bilateral sensory block catheter location is confirmed and infusion rate was probably insufficient (increase rate).
      3. If test dose produces a unilateral block it is likely the catheter is placed laterally, withdrawal catheter 1-2 cm.
      4. If test dose produces no response catheter is not in the epidural space. The catheter should be removed and patient switched to PCA.

Epidural Opioids for Postoperative Analgesia

Drug	Bolus Dose	Onset (min)	Peak (min)	Duration (hr)	Infusion Rate
Meperidine	25-100 mg	5-10	12-30	4-6	5-20 mg/hr
Morphine	2-5 mg	20	30-60	12-24	0.3-0.9 mg/hr
Methadone	1-5 mg	10-15	15-20	6-10	0.3-0.5 mg/hr
Hydro-morphone	0.75-1.5 mg	10-15	20-30	6-18	0.1-0.2 mg/hr
Fentanyl	50-100 mcg	5-10	10-20	1-4	25-50 mcg/hr
Sufentanil	20-50 mcg	5-15	20-30	2-6	10-25 mcg/hr

Continuous Epidural Infusion Analgesia

Local Anesthetics
 Bupivacaine 0.0625%-0.125%
 Ropivacaine 0.05%-0.2%

Opioids
 Fentanyl 1-5 mcg/mL
 Hydromorphone 10-30 mcg/mL
 Morphine 0.01-0.1 mg/mL
 Sufentanil 1-3 mcg/mL

Adjunctive Additives
 Clonidine 1 mcg/mL

Infusion Rates
 Usual rate: 4-16 mL/hr

Epidural Infusion Regimens for Pediatrics

Solutions
 <1 year old: 0.1% bupivacaine without fentanyl
 1-7 years of age: 0.1% bupivacaine with 2 mcg/mL fentanyl
 >7 years of age: 0.1% bupivacaine with 10-20 mcg/mL hydromorphone

Rate of infusion
 Start: 0.1 mL/kg per hour
 Break through pain: increase in increments up to 0.3 mL/kg per hour
 Bolusing catheter:
  <6 kg: 1 mL of 1% lidocaine with 1:200,000 epinephrine
  6-15 kg: 2 mL of 1% lidocaine with 1:200,000 epinephrine
  >15 kg: 5 mL of 1% lidocaine with 1:200,000 epinephrine

Intrathecal Opioids			
Opioid	Dose	Onset (min)	Duration (hr)
Morphine	0.15-0.6 mg	15-45	8-24
Fentanyl	10-25 mcg	2-5	1-3
Sufentanil	5-15 mcg	2-5	2-4

Chronic Pain Management

Myofascial Pain

1. Myofascial pain is characterized by pain referred from active trigger points (a hyperirritable locus, which may be palpable as an exquisitely tender, taut band within skeletal muscle). Compression of these points elicits a characteristic and reproducible pattern of referred pain remote from the location of the tender trigger.
2. Treatment includes injecting local anesthetic solution (1-3 mL dose of 0.5% lidocaine or 0.25% bupivacaine with triamcinolone 10-25 mg) into the trigger point. Additionally, physical therapy, moist heat, ultrasound, electrical stimulation, and muscle stretching are helpful.

Occipital Neuralgia

1. Occipital neuralgia results from stretching or entrapment of the occipital nerve that frequently follows neck injury (e.g., whiplash) and presents with aching pain in the suboccipital region that may radiate across the scalp or into the neck.
2. Treatment includes an occipital nerve block with local anesthetic and triamcinolone (generally done in a series of 3 for extended pain relief).

Postherpetic Neuralgia

1. Acute herpes zoster represents a reactivation of the varicella-zoster virus.
2. Presents as a vesicular, dermatomal (T3-L3 most common) rash that is usually associated with severe pain. Pain usually precedes the rash.
3. Treatment includes oral analgesics, antiviral therapy, lidocaine patches, and sympathetic blocks.

Complex Regional Pain Syndrome

1. Definition
   A. A pain syndrome characterized by a previous injury to the affected area, followed by persistent and disproportional pain and accompanied at some point by autonomic changes, not necessarily seen at the time of the physical examination and not following any dermatomal distribution.
   B. **Type 1 (CRPS type 1: reflex sympathetic dystrophy):** usually develops as a consequence of trauma affecting the limbs, with or without an obvious peripheral nerve injury. Characterized by diffuse limb pain associated with a burning or stabbing sensation.
   C. **Type 2 (CRPS type 2: causalgia):** usually develops as a consequence of trauma involving partial injury of a nerve or one of its major branches in the region of the limb innervated by the damaged nerve. Characterized by nerve injury, burning pain, cutaneous hypersensitivity.

D. Pain with CRPS is generally attributed to sympathetic efferent function referred to as sympathetically mediated pain, however, typically there is also a component of pain not influenced by sympathetic activity and is referred to as sympathetically independent pain.

2. Treatment

A. The goal of treatment is functional restoration. Physical therapy plays a central role. Pharmacologic therapy and regional anesthetic blocks are principally adjuncts to physical therapy.

B. Sympathetic blocks (stellate ganglion block; lumbar sympathetic block) is useful to help confirm the diagnosis and facilitate physical therapy. Treatment usually consists of a series of local anesthetic blocks.

C. Drug treatments include neuropathic pain medications (neurontin, TCA's, other anticonvulsants, local anesthetics), NSAIDs, and opioids.

D. Other modalities include intravenous regional sympatholytic blockade, TENS, spinal cord stimulation, and surgical sympathectomy for chronic cases.

Stages of Complex Regional Pain Syndrome Types I and II			
Characteristic	Acute Phase (Stage 1)	Dystrophic Phase (Stage 2)	Atrophic Phase (Stage 3)
Pain	Localized, severe, burning, worsens by light touch	Diffuse, throbbing, increase with motion	Less severe, often involves other extremities
Extremity	Warm	Cold, cyanotic, edema, muscle wasting	severe muscle atrophy, thin, contractures
Skin	Dry, red	Sweaty, brittle nails/hair	Glossy, pale, atrophic
X-Ray	Normal	Osteoporosis	Severe osteoporosis, ankylosis of joints
Duration	1-3 months	3-6 months	Indefinite

Low Back Pain

1. **Low back pain is very common** and can be due to multiple, often coexistent mechanisms. A few common causes include:
   A. Mechanical low back pain is aching in nature that typically gets worse throughout the day and better with rest.
   B. Discogenic pain often is burning and aching in nature, and may be constant.
   C. Radicular pain radiates below the knee and may be coupled with numbness and/or paresthesias.
2. **Lumbosacral radiculopathy**
   A. Pain is usually the result of inflammation of the nerve root or mechanical compression of the dorsal root ganglion (usually associated with a

herniated disc). In addition to pain, numbness, motor loss, depending on which fibers are involved, may be present.

B. After a full evaluation has been done to rule out the presence of infection or space-occupying lesion, administration of epidural corticosteroids (methylprednisolone 80 mg or triamcinolone 50 mg) into the epidural space as close to the affected nerve root as possible can be performed.

3. Lumbosacral arthropathies

A. Degeneration and inflammation of the lumbar facet joints and sacroiliac joints may produce low back pain radiating to the lower extremities that is difficult to distinguish from lumbosacral radiculopathy.

B. Facet joint syndrome

1. Pain from facet joints tend to be localized to the back with radiation to the buttock and posterior thigh (and rarely below the knee joint). Pain also occurs with extension and rotation of the spine. Accounts for about 15% of low back pain.
2. Diagnosis can be make by diagnostic blockade with local anesthetic. Radiological studies are rarely helpful in making the diagnosis.
3. Medial branch rhizotomy can provide long-term analgesia for facet joint disease in the lumbar and cervical spine.

C. Sacroiliac joint syndrome

1. Found to cause localized pain over the joint and referred pain to the lower extremity. Accounts for about 15% of low back pain.
2. The diagnosis can be confirmed by prolong relief following injection of local anesthetic into the sacroiliac joint.

Postanesthesia Care Unit

Postoperative Hemodynamic Complications

1. **Hypotension**
   A. **Causes:** arterial hypoxemia, hypovolemia (most common), decreased myocardial contractility (myocardial ischemia, pulmonary edema), decreased systemic vascular resistance (neuroaxial anesthesia, sepsis), cardiac dysrhythmias, pulmonary embolus, pneumothorax, cardiac tamponade, spurious (large cuff).
   B. **Treatment:** fluid challenge; pharmacologic treatment includes inotropic agents (dopamine, dobutamine, epinephrine) and alpha receptor agonists (phenylephrine, epinephrine). CVP and PA catheter monitoring may be needed to guide therapy.
2. **Hypertension**
   A. **Causes:** enhanced SNS activity (pain, gastric distension, bladder distension), preoperative hypertension, hypervolemia, hypoxemia, spurious (small cuff), increased intracranial pressure, and vasopressors.
   B. **Treatment:** management begins with identification and correction of the initiating cause; various medications can be used to treat hypertension including beta blockers (labetalol 5-10 mg IV, esmolol 10-100 mg IV), calcium channel blockers (nifedipine 5-10 mg SL, verapamil 2.5-5 mg IV), nitroprusside or nitroglycerin; regardless of drug selected it is important to accurately monitor blood pressure.
3. **Cardiac dysrhythmias**
   A. **Causes:** arterial hypoxemia, hypercarbia, hypovolemia, pain, electrolyte and acid-base imbalances, myocardial ischemia, increased ICP, drug toxicity (digitalis), hypothermia, anticholinesterases and malignant hyperthermia.
   B. **Treatment:** supplemental oxygen should be given while the etiology is being investigated; most dysrhythmias do not require treatment.

Postoperative Respiratory and Airway Complications

1. Respiratory problems are the most frequently encountered complications in the PACU, with the majority related to airway obstruction, hypoventilation, or hypoxemia.
2. **Hypoxemia**
   A. **Causes:** right-to-left intrapulmonary shunt (atelectasis), mismatching of ventilation-to-perfusion (decreased functional residual capacity), decreased cardiac output, alveolar hypoventilation, diffusion hypoxia, upper airway obstruction, bronchospasm, aspiration of gastric contents, pulmonary edema, pneumothorax and pulmonary embolism, obesity, advanced age, and posthyperventilation hypoxia.
   B. **Clinical signs of hypoxia** (restlessness, tachycardia, cardiac irritability hypertension, hypotension) are nonspecific; obtunded, bradycardia, hypotension, and cardiac arrest are late signs.
   C. Increased intrapulmonary shunting relative to closing capacity is the most common cause of hypoxemia following general anesthesia.
   D. **Treatment:** oxygen therapy with or without positive airway pressure.

Additional treatment should be directed at the underlying cause.

3. **Hypoventilation**
   A. **Causes:** drug-induced central nervous system depression (residual anesthesia), suboptimal ventilatory muscle mechanics, increased production of carbon dioxide, decreased ventilatory drive, pulmonary, and respiratory muscle insufficiency (preexistent respiratory disease, inadequate reversal of neuromuscular blockade, inadequate analgesia, and bronchospasm).
   B. Hypoventilation in the PACU is most commonly caused by residual depressant effects of anesthetic agents on respiratory drive or persistent neuromuscular blockade.
   C. **Treatment:** should be directed at the underlying cause. Marked hypoventilation may require controlled ventilation until contributory factors are identified and corrected.

4. **Upper airway obstruction** (stridor)
   A. **Causes:** include incomplete anesthetic recovery, laryngospasm, airway edema, wound hematoma, and vocal cord paralysis. Airway obstruction in unconscious patients is most commonly due to the tongue falling back against the posterior pharynx.
   B. **Treatment:** supplemental oxygen while corrective measures are undertaken. Jaw thrust, head-tilt, oral or nasal airways often alleviate the problem.

5. **Laryngospasm and laryngeal edema**
   A. Laryngospasm is a forceful involuntary spasm of the laryngeal musculature caused by sensory stimulation of the superior laryngeal nerve. Triggering stimuli include pharyngeal secretions or extubating in stage 2. The large negative intrathoracic pressures generated by the struggling patient in laryngospasm can cause pulmonary edema.
   B. **Treatment of laryngospasm:** initial treatment includes 100% oxygen, anterior mandibular displacement, and gentle CPAP (may be applied by face mask). If laryngospasm persists and hypoxia develops, succinylcholine (0.25-1.0 mg/kg; 10-20 mg) should be given in order to paralyze the laryngeal muscles and allow controlled ventilation.
   C. **Treatment of glottic edema and subglottic edema:** administer warm, humidified oxygen by mask, inhalation of racemic epinephrine 2.25% (0.5-1 mL in 2 mL NS), repeated every 20 minutes, dexamethasone 0.1-0.5 mg/kg IV maybe considered. Reintubation with a smaller tube may be helpful.

Postoperative Neurologic Complications

1. **Delayed awakening:** the most frequent cause of a delayed awakening is the persistent effect of anesthesia or sedation. Other causes include recurarization, severe hypothermia, hypoglycemia, and neurologic disorders.
2. **Emergence delirium (agitation):** is characterized by excitement, alternating with lethargy, disorientation, and inappropriate behavior. Potential causes include arterial hypoxemia, hypercapnia, pain, unrecognized gastric dilation, urinary retention, and previous administration of atropine. Treatment includes haloperidol, titrated in 1-2 mg IV increments. Benzodiazepines may be added if agitation is severe. Physostigmine (0.5-2.0 mg IV) may reverse anticholinergic delirium.

Postoperative Nausea and Vomiting

1. **Risk factors**
   A. **Patient risk factors:** short fasting status, anxiety, younger age, female, obesity, gastroparesis, pain, history of postoperative nausea/vomiting or motion sickness.
   B. **Surgery-related factors:** gynecological, abdominal, ENT, ophthalmic, and plastic surgery; endocrine effects of surgery; duration of surgery.
   C. **Anesthesia-related factors:** premedicants (morphine and other opioids), anesthetics agents (nitrous oxide, inhalational agents, etomidate, methohexital, ketamine), anticholinesterase reversal agents, gastric distention, longer duration of anesthesia, mask ventilation, intraoperative pain medications, regional anesthesia(lower risk).
   D. **Postoperative factors:** pain, dizziness, movement after surgery, premature oral intake, opioid administration.

Treatment of Postoperative Nausea and Vomiting (PONV)				
Drug	Adult Dose	Peds Dose	Duration	Caution Use In
Droperidol	0.625-1.25 mg IV/IM	50-75 mcg/kg IV/IM	3-4 hr	Parkinson, hypovolemia
Metoclopramide	10 mg IV/IM (max 20 mg)	0.1 mg/kg (max 5 mg)	1-2 hr	GI obstruction, seizures, Parkinson
Trimethobenzamide	200 mg IM/PR	<14 kg: 100 mg >14 kg: 100-200 mg	6-8 hr	Benzocaine allergy, Reye's syndrome
Ondansetron	4-8 mg IV	0.1 mg/kg IV	4-6	Prolong cardiac conduction
Dolasetron	12.5 mg IV	0.35 mg/kg	7 hr	Prolong cardiac conduction
Granisetron	1-3 mg IV	10 mcg/kg IV	24 hr	Liver disease
Propofol	10-20 mg IV			
Dexamethasone	8-10 mg IV	0.15-1 mg/kg		
Betamethasone	12 mg IV			
Promethazine	12.5-25 mg IV/IM	0.25-1 mg/kg IV/IM	4 hr	Seizures, hypovolemia, Parkinson
Prochlorperazine	2.5-10 mg IV/IM	0.1-0.15 mg/kg IV/IM	6-12 hr	Seizures, hypovolemia, Parkinson

Postanesthesia Care Unit Pain Control (see section on acute pain management)

1. **Moderate to severe postoperative pain in the PACU**
   A. Meperidine 25-150 mg (0.25-0.5 mg/kg in children).
   B. Morphine 2-4 mg (0.025-0.05 mg/kg in children).
   C. Fentanyl 12.5-50 mcg IV.
2. **Nonsteroidal anti-inflammatory drugs** are an effective complement to opioids. Ketorolac 30 mg IV followed by 15 mg q6-8 hrs.
3. **Patient-controlled and continuous epidural analgesia** should be started in the PACU.

Miscellaneous Postanesthesia Complications

1. **Renal dysfunction:** oliguria (urine output less then 0.5 mL/kg/hour) most likely reflects decreased renal blood flow due to hypovolemia or decreased cardiac output.
2. **Bleeding abnormalities:** causes include inadequate surgical hemostasis or coagulopathies.
3. **Shivering** (hypothermia)
   A. Shivering can occur secondary to hypothermia or the effects of anesthetic agents (most often volatile anesthetics).
   B. Shivering should be treated with warming measures (Bair Huggar system). Small doses of meperidine (12.5-25 mg) IV.

Postanesthesia Care Unit Discharge Criteria

1. All patients should be evaluated by an anesthesiologist prior to discharge; patients should have been observed for respiratory depression for at least 30 minutes after the last dose of parenteral narcotic.
   A. Patients receiving regional anesthesia should show signs of resolution of both sensory and motor blockade prior to discharge.
   B. Other minimum discharge criteria include stable vital signs, alert and oriented (or to baseline), able to maintain adequate oxygen saturation, free of nausea/vomiting, absence of bleeding, adequate urine output, adequate pain control, stabilization or resolution of any problems, and movement of extremity following regional anesthesia.

Malignant Hyperthermia

1. **Definition** malignant hyperthermia is a fulminant skeletal muscle hypermetabolic syndrome occurring in genetically susceptible patients after exposure to an anesthetic triggering agent. Triggering anesthetics include halothane, enflurane, isoflurane, desflurane, sevoflurane, and succinylcholine.
2. **Etiology**: the gene for malignant hyperthermia is the genetic coding site for the calcium release channel of skeletal muscle sarcoplasmic reticulum. The syndrome is caused by a reduction in the reuptake of calcium by the sarcoplasmic reticulum necessary for termination of muscle contraction, resulting in a sustained muscle contraction.
3. **Clinical findings**
   A. **Signs of onset:** tachycardia, tachypnea, hypercarbia (increased end-tidal CO_2 is the most sensitive clinical sign).
   B. **Early signs:** tachycardia, tachypnea, unstable blood pressure, arrhythmias, cyanosis, mottling, sweating, rapid temperature increase, and cola-colored urine.
   C. **Late (6-24 hours) signs:** pyrexia, skeletal muscle swelling, left heart failure, renal failure, DIC, hepatic failure.
   D. **Muscle rigidity** in the presence of neuromuscular blockade. Masseter spasm after giving succinylcholine is associated with malignant hyperthermia.
   E. The presence of a large difference between mixed venous and arterial carbon dioxide tensions confirms the diagnosis of malignant hyperthermia.
   F. **Laboratory:** respiratory and metabolic acidosis, hypoxemia, increased serum levels of potassium, calcium, myoglobin, CPK, and myoglobinuria.
4. **Incidence and mortality**
   A. **Children:** approx 1:15,000 general anesthetics.
   B. **Adults:** approx 1:40,000 general anesthetics when succinylcholine is used; approx 1:220,000 general anesthetics when agents other than succinylcholine are used.
   C. Familial autosomal dominant transmission with variable penetrance.
   D. **Mortality:** 10% overall; up to 70% without dantrolene therapy. Early therapy reduces mortality for less than 5%.
5. **Anesthesia for malignant hyperthermia susceptible patients**
   A. Malignant hyperthermia may be triggered in susceptible patients who have had previous uneventful responses to triggering agents.
   B. Pretreatment with dantrolene is not recommended. If deemed necessary, may give 2.4 mg/kg IV over 10-30 minutes prior to induction.
   C. The anesthesia machine should be prepared by flushing the circuit with ten liters per minute of oxygen for 20 minutes. Changing the fresh gas hose will hasten the reduction of the concentration of inhalation agents. Fresh carbon dioxide absorbent and fresh delivery tubing are also recommended.
6. **Malignant hyperthermia treatment protocol**
   A. **Stop triggering anesthetic agent immediately,** conclude surgery as soon as possible. Continue with safe agents if surgery cannot be stopped.
   B. **Hyperventilate:** 100% oxygen, high flows, use new circuit and soda lime.
   C. **Administer dantrolene** 2.5 mg/kg IV; repeat every 5-10 minutes until symptoms are controlled or a total dose of up to 10 mg/kg is given.
   D. **Correct metabolic acidosis:** administer sodium bicarbonate, 1-2 mEq/kg IV guided by arterial pH and pCO_2. Follow with ABG.

    E. Hyperkalemia: correct with bicarbonate or with glucose, 25-50 gm IV, and regular insulin, 10-20 u.

    F. Actively cool patient
      1. Iced IV NS (not LR) 15 mL/kg every 10 minutes times three if needed.
      2. Lavage stomach, bladder, rectum, peritoneal and thoracic cavities.
      3. Surface cooling with ice and hypothermia blanket.

    G. Maintain urine output >1-2 mL/kg/hr. If needed, mannitol 0.25 g/kg IV or furosemide 1 mg/kg IV (up to 4 times) and/or hydration.

    H. Labs: PT, PTT, platelets, urine myoglobin, ABG, K, Ca, lactate, CPK.

    I. Consider invasive monitoring: arterial blood pressure and CVP.

    J. Postoperatively: continue dantrolene 1 mg/kg IV q6 hours x 72 hrs to prevent recurrence. Observe in ICU until stable for 24-48 hrs. Calcium channel blockers should not be given when dantrolene is administered because hyperkalemia and myocardial depression may occur.

Allergic Drug Reactions

1. **Anaphylaxis**
   A. **Anaphylaxis is an allergic reaction** which is mediated by an antigen-antibody reaction (type I hypersensitivity reaction). This reaction is initiated by antigen binding to immunoglobulin E (IgE) antibodies on the surface of mast cells and basophils, causing the release of chemical mediators, including, leukotrienes, histamine, prostaglandins, kinins, and platelet-activating factor.
   B. **Clinical manifestations of anaphylaxis**
      1. **Cardiovascular:** hypotension, tachycardia, dysrhythmias.
      2. **Pulmonary:** bronchospasm, cough, dyspnea, pulmonary edema, laryngeal edema, hypoxemia.
      3. **Dermatologic:** urticaria, facial edema, pruritus.
2. **Anaphylactoid reactions**
   A. Anaphylactoid reactions resemble anaphylaxis but are not mediated by IgE and do not require prior sensitization to an antigen.
   B. Although the mechanisms differ, anaphylactic and anaphylactoid reactions can be clinically indistinguishable and equally life-threatening.
3. **Treatment of anaphylactic and anaphylactoid reactions**
   A. **Initial therapy**
      1. Discontinue drug administration and all anesthetic agents.
      2. Administer 100% oxygen.
      3. Intravenous fluids (1-5 liters of LR).
      4. Epinephrine (10-100 mcg IV bolus for hypotension; 0.1-0.5 mg IV for cardiovascular collapse).
   B. **Secondary treatment**
      1. Benadryl 0.5-1 mg/kg or 50-75 mg IV.
      2. Epinephrine 2-4 mcg/min, norepinephrine 2-4 mcg/min.
      3. Aminophylline 5-6 mg/kg IV over 20 minutes.
      4. 1-2 grams methylprednisolone or 0.25-1 gram hydrocortisone.
      5. Sodium bicarbonate 0.5-1 mEq/kg.
      6. Airway evaluation (prior to extubation).

Venous Air Embolism

1. **General information**
   A. Air can be entrained into a vein whenever there is an open vein and a negative intravenous pressure relative to atmospheric pressure. This can occur any time the surgical field is above right atrial level (neurosurgical procedures and operations involving the neck, thorax, abdomen, pelvis, open heart, liver and vena cava laceration repairs, total hip replacement).
   B. Incidence is highest during sitting craniotomies (20-40%).
   C. The physiological consequences of venous air embolism depends on both the total volume of air and the rate of air entry.
   D. Patients with probe-patent foramen ovale (10-25% incidence) have an increased risk of paradoxical air embolism.

2. **Diagnosis**
   A. **During controlled ventilation** of the lungs, sudden attempts by the patient to initiate a spontaneous breath (gasp reflex) may be the first indication of venous air embolism.
   B. **Decreased PaO_2, TcO_2, and increased ETN_2 (most specific)** normally occur before one sees a sudden decrease in $ETCO_2$ and/or an increase in CVP.
   C. **Late signs:** hypotension, tachycardia, cardiac dysrhythmias and cyanosis.
   D. **Consequences depend of the volume and rate of air entry.**
      1. CVP increases 0.4 mL of air/kg/min.
      2. Heart rate increases at 0.42 mL of air/kg/min.
      3. EKG changes occur at 0.6 mL of air/kg/min.
      4. Blood pressure decreases at 0.69 mL of air/kg/min.
      5. A mill wheel murmur is heard at 2.0 mL of air/kg/min.
      6. Embolism of greater than 2.0 mL of air/kg/min is potentially lethal.

3. **Monitoring**
   A. **Transesophageal echocardiography (TEE)** is the most sensitive. Sensitivity = 0.015 mL of air/kg/min.
   B. **Doppler:** sensitivity equals 0.02 mL of air/kg/min.
   C. **End-tidal N_2** monitoring is very specific.
   D. **End-tidal CO_2** and pulmonary artery pressure monitoring are less sensitive but remain important monitors for venous air embolism.

4. **Treatment**
   A. Notify surgeon to flood surgical field with saline or pack and apply bone wax to the skull edges until the entry site identified.
   B. Place the patient in the left lateral decubitus position with a slight head-down tilt in an attempt to dislodge a possible air lock.
   C. Nitrous oxide (if used) should be discontinued and 100% oxygen given.
   D. The central venous catheter should be aspirated in an attempt to retrieve the entrained air.
   E. Support cardiovascular system with volume, inotropes, and/or vasopressors.
   F. Increase venous pressure with bilateral jugular vein compression may slow air entrainment and cause back bleeding.
   G. Consider adding PEEP in effort to increase cerebral venous pressure (however, this may increase risk of paradoxical embolism).

Latex Allergy

1. **Risk factors for latex allergy**
   A. Chronic exposure to latex and a history of atopy increases the risk of sensitization. Patients undergoing frequent procedures with latex items (e.g., repeated urinary bladder catheterization) are at higher risk.
   B. Patients with neural tube defects (meningomyelocele, spina bifida) and those with congenital abnormalities of the genitourinary tract are at higher risk.
2. **Pathophysiology:** most reactions involve a direct IgE-mediated immune response to polypeptides in natural latex. Some cases of contact dermatitis may be due to a type four hypersensitivity reaction to chemicals introduced in the manufacturing process.
3. **Preoperative evaluation**
   A. **History** in patients at risk, particularly those with co-existing atopy and/or multiple allergies, should include history of balloon or glove intolerance and allergies to medical products used in chronic care (e.g., catheters). Elective patients in whom latex allergy is suspected should be referred to an allergist.
   B. Diagnostic tests: routine diagnostic testing in the at-risk population is not recommended (only those with a positive history). Available tests:
      1. Skin-prick test: less sensitive than intradermal test but more sensitive than RAST.
      2. Radioallergosorbent test (RAST): an in-vitro test for IgE antibodies in the patient's serum.
   C. **Pre-operative medications:** routine preoperative H_1 and H_2 blockers and steroids is no longer recommended.
   D. **Scheduling:** since latex is an aeroallergen and present in the operating room air for at least an hour after the use of latex gloves, whenever possible your patient should be scheduled as the first case of the day.
4. **Anesthesia equipment**
   A. Common anesthesia equipment that contain latex include gloves, tourniquets, endotracheal tube, ventilator bellows, intravenous injection ports, blood pressure cuffs, and face masks.
   B. Non-latex supplies that are commonly required include glass syringes, drugs in glass in ampules, IV tubing without latex injection ports, neoprene gloves, ambu bag with silicone valves, and neoprene bellows for the Ohmeda ventilator.
   C. The most important precaution is the use of non-latex gloves.
   D. Miscellaneous equipment: sleeve on the fibreoptic bronchoscope, esophageal stethoscope, and cuff on the LMA airway are all non-latex (silicon).
5. **Preoperative preparation**
   A. Check latex allergy cart for supplies. Call pharmacy and order all drugs that may be needed (dispensed in glass syringe).
   B. Notify O.R. nurses. No latex gloves or latex products should come into contact with the patient. Neoprene (non-latex) gloves need to be obtained.
6. **Anesthesia setup and care**
   A. Set up a regular circuit on the anesthesia machine, and use a neoprene reservoir bag. Use plastic masks (adult or pediatric).
   B. Draw up drugs in glass syringes from glass ampules. In an emergency, the

rubber stoppers can be removed.
- **C.** IV infusion setup with two three way stopcocks and no injection ports. (Alternatively tape all injection ports over and do not use).
- **D.** Use Webril under tourniquet or BP cuff if rubber, angiocaths are safe.
- **E.** Latex allergy should not alter the choice of anesthetic technique. There are no drugs that are specifically contraindicated.

7. **Diagnosis of latex anaphylaxis**
- **A.** Anaphylaxis has been reported even in patients pre-treated with H_1, H_2 blockers and steroids and managed in a latex-free environment.
- **B.** Onset is generally 20 - 60 minutes after exposure to the antigen.
- **C.** Anaphylaxis presents with the clinical triad of hypotension (most common sign), rash, and bronchospasm.
- **D.** Serum mast cell tryptase levels are high during an episode and up to 4 hours after. This test will help confirm the diagnosis of anaphylaxis, but it will not identify latex as the antigen.

8. **Treatment of latex anaphylaxis**
- **A.** Treatment of latex anaphylaxis does not differ from the treatment of other forms of anaphylactic reaction.
- **B. Primary treatment**
  1. Stop administration of latex, administer 100% oxygen.
  2. Restore intravascular volume (2-4 L of crystalloid).
  3. Epinephrine: start with a dose of 10 mcg, or 0.1 mcg/kg and escalate rapidly to higher doses depending on the response.
- **C. Secondary treatment**
  1. Corticosteroids (0.25-1 g hydrocortisone or 1-2 g methyl-prednisolone).
  2. Diphenhydramine 50-75 mg IV.
  3. Aminophylline 5-6 mg/kg over 20 minutes.

Index

Order Form

Current Clinical Strategies books can also be purchased at all medical bookstores

Title	Price
Treatment Guidelines in Medicine, 2004 Edition	$19.95
Psychiatry History Taking, Third Edition	$12.95
Psychiatry, 2003-2004 Edition	$12.95
Pediatric Drug Reference, 2004 Edition	$9.95
Anesthesiology, 2004-2005 Edition	$16.95
Manual of HIV/AIDS Therapy, 2003 Edition	$12.95
Medicine, 2002-2003 Edition	$16.95
Pediatric Treatment Guidelines, 2004 Edition	$19.95
Physician's Drug Manual, 2003 Edition	$9.95
Surgery, 2004 Edition	$12.95
Gynecology and Obstetrics, 2004 Edition	$16.95
Pediatrics, 2004 Edition	$12.95
Family Medicine, 2004 Edition	$26.95
History and Physical Examination in Medicine, Tenth Edition	$14.95
Outpatient and Primary Care Medicine, 2003 Edition	$16.95
Critical Care Medicine, 2003-2004 Edition	$16.95
Handbook of Psychiatric Drugs, 2004 Edition	$12.95
Pediatric History and Physical Examination, Fourth Edition	$12.95
Current Clinical Strategies CD-ROM Collection for Palm, Pocket PC, Windows, and Macintosh	$49.95

Palm, Pocket PC, Windows and Macintosh versions of all books are available on CD-ROM. Add $14.00 to the list price of each title.

Quantity	Title	Amount

Order by Phone: 800-331-8227 or 949-348-8404
Fax: 800-965-9420 or 949-348-8405
Internet Orders: http://www.ccspublishing.com/ccs
E-mail Orders: bookorders@ccspublishing.com
Mail Orders:

Current Clinical Strategies Publishing
27071 Cabot Road, Suite 126
Laguna Hills, California 92653

Credit Card Number: _____

Exp: ____/____

A shipping charge of $4.00 will be added to each order

Signature: _____

Check Enclosed _____

Phone Number: (_____)_____

Name and Address (Print):

_____

_____

_____

_____